The Caribbean Novel since 1945

Caribbean Studies Series
Anton L. Allahar and Shona N. Jackson
Series Editors

The
Caribbean Novel
since 1945:
Cultural Practice,
Form, and
the Nation-State

Michael Niblett

University Press of Mississippi   Jackson

www.upress.state.ms.us

The University Press of Mississippi is a member of the Association of American University Presses.

Copyright © 2012 by University Press of Mississippi
Manufactured in the United States of America

First printing 2012
Insert infinity sign

Library of Congress Cataloging-in-Publication Data
Niblett, Michael.
The caribbean novel since 1945 : cultural practice, form, and the nation-state / Michael Niblett.
    p. cm. — (Caribbean studies series)
Includes bibliographical references and index.
ISBN 978-1-61703-247-9 (cloth : alk. paper) — ISBN 978-1-61703-248-6 (ebook) 1. Caribbean
fiction—History and criticism. 2. Postmodernism in literature. 3. Caribbean Area—Civilization. I.
Title.
PN849.C3N53 2012
809.3'99729—dc23   2011026498

British Library Cataloging-in-Publication Data available

Contents

Acknowledgments

I would like to thank David Dabydeen for all his help and support over the years. He has been a fantastic supervisor, colleague, and friend, generous with his time and a pleasure to know. Many thanks to John Thieme and John Gilmore, who read and commented on large sections of this work. Thanks, likewise, to Neil Lazarus, who commented on an earlier version of parts of the book. I am indebted to the University Press of Mississippi and, in particular, Craig Gill and Walter Biggins. Many thanks to the anonymous reviewer who provided a range of insightful comments on the manuscript, and to Bill Henry for his careful and astute reading of the work. I gratefully acknowledge the support of the Arts and Humanities Research Council, which funded my studies. I owe a debt of thanks to the Centre for Caribbean Studies and the Centre for Translation and Comparative Cultural Studies at the University of Warwick. Many thanks to Lynn Guyver, in particular, and to Kerry Drakeley, Maureen Tustin, and Caroline Parker for all the help they have given me. I am grateful to all the people I've had the chance to hang around with while working on this book. Kerstin Oloff and Sharae Deckard have been great friends, sometime flatmates, and a source of intellectual inspiration. Equally, it has been top quality to know and work with Jim Graham, Claire Westall, Teresa Bailach, and Chris Campbell. Likewise, many thanks to Steve Barrell and Torri Wang for walks, bears, mycology, and TV. Thanks to Mark, Rochelle, and Simon in Leamington, to Emma and John, and warm thanks to Tijana Nikolic. Many thanks to my parents, my family, and Jack and Fen for all that they have done for me.

Parts of chapter 4 previously appeared as "Modernity, Cultural Practice, and the Caribbean Literary Field: Crossing Boundaries in Erna Brodber's *Jane and Louisa Will Soon Come Home*," *Caribbean Review of Gender Studies* 2 (May 2008). Parts of the introduction and chapter 3 previously appeared, in different form, as "The Manioc and the Made-in-France: Reconsidering Creolization and Commodity Fetishism in Caribbean Literature and Theory," in *Breaking Ground: Readings in Caribbean History and Culture*, ed. D. A. Dunkley (Lanham, Md.: Lexington Books, 2011).

The Caribbean Novel since 1945

Introduction

Cultural Practice, Creolization, and the Nation-State

In January 1946, President Élie Lescot of Haiti was toppled in a revolution that, for at least some of its participants, drew its inspiration from surrealism. The visit of the surrealist writer André Breton to Port-au-Prince a month earlier had encouraged the radical student newspaper *La Ruche*—edited by, among others, René Dépestre and Jacques-Stéphen Alexis—to dedicate a special edition to Breton in which, galvanized by his lectures, they called for national insurrection.[1] The authorities promptly seized the newspaper and imprisoned the editorial team, sparking student protests and, on the back of this unrest, a general strike. The rapidity with which the strike took hold is an indication that while the *La Ruche* affair may have acted as something of a catalyst, a desire for change among a broad cross section of the population had been building for some time. During the U.S. occupation of Haiti between 1915 and 1934, a spirit of resistant nationalism had helped to unite Haitians across lines of color and ideology. However, the end of the occupation saw the reemergence of old tensions. When Lescot came to power in 1941, his policies only exacerbated the problem, alienating both the rural peasantry and the black urban elite. A pro-American *mulâtre*, he granted the U.S.-controlled Haitian-American Society for the Development of Agriculture the right to expropriate peasant land for planting rubber trees, while also waging an "antisuperstition" campaign against the vodun religion.[2] By systematically filling his administration with light-skinned individuals, moreover, he defied the convention of at least appearing to reward competence over color and antagonized the black middle classes.[3] The resentment bred by these actions prompted the emergence of a general front opposed to the ruling elite, paving the way for the revolution's success.

The overthrow of Lescot thus seemed to represent a moment of promise for Haiti: it was, as Martin Munro observes, the "first instance of a successful popular revolt against a U.S.-backed regime in postwar New World politics."[4] As such, it chimed with the prevailing "democratic and anti-colonial hopes that the immediate aftermath of the [Second World War] had lit on every continent": "We wanted," wrote René Dépestre, "to demystify a society still shaped profoundly by a colonial heritage that the Haitian Revolution (1791–1804) had not succeeded in effacing from our national life."[5] Such sentiments make it easy to see why surrealism, with its emphasis on the disruption of reified lifeworlds, should appeal to Haiti's radical intellectuals. Yet this is not to say that surrealist literary aesthetics simply provided an imported model for the Haitian writer to imitate (in the way that earlier poetic conventions—Parnassian verse, for example—had done). The emphasis now fell on the development of an indigenous Caribbean aesthetic, with authors seeking inspiration in radical black journals such as *Légitime défense* (1932) and *Tropiques* (1941–45), as well as in the work of writers like Jacques Roumain and Aimé Césaire (who had visited Haiti the year before Breton). To match an insurrectionary politics, an insurrectionary literary style was required.

However, the potential of the 1946 revolution quickly dissipated. Popular protest may have brought Lescot down, but it was a military junta that took control of his removal from office and installed the new president, Dumarsais Estimé, a provincial schoolteacher from the black middle class. In retrospect it is clear that the ousting of Lescot, which for the *La Ruche* group was to put an end to reactionary, racialized politics, ironically set the stage for the political dominance of Haiti's *noiriste* factions, in particular the *authentiques*, who would seek to justify their leadership of the country on the grounds that their race made them the natural representatives of the Haitian people.[6] The ultimate beneficiary of this shift in power was François Duvalier. Backed by the army, he secured the presidency in 1957, inaugurating a repressive dictatorship in which racial mystification was consistently used to obscure exploitative socioeconomic relations.

I begin with these events in Haiti because they introduce many of the issues addressed in this study: national insurrection and decolonization, the struggle for state power, ethnic chauvinism, class conflict, the relationship between rural and urban areas, and neocolonialism and imperialism. Of primary concern, however, is another issue to which the foregoing history draws attention: the relationship between national transformation and literary form. The starting point for this book on the Caribbean novel since 1945 is the postwar conjunction that Dépestre characterized as full of "democratic and anti-colonial hopes."[7] This was a period when the colonial edifice seemed to be crumbling and popular nationalist movements were emerging across the Caribbean to challenge for power. At the same time, fiction from the region was registering significant changes in style and form.[8] We have already seen the overlap between the politics and aesthetics of liberation in Haiti. But one could just as well begin with Jamaica's winning the right to internal self-government in 1944 and the appearance five years later of V. S. Reid's seminal novel *New Day*, which, in retelling the island's history from the Morant Bay rebellion of 1865 to the promulgation of the new constitution, pioneered the use of a modified Jamaican vernacular. Or one could take the granting of *département* status to Martinique, Guadeloupe, and French Guiana in 1946: seemingly holding out the promise of equality, this move was promoted by Césaire, a deputy in France's Constituent Assembly and the author whose *Cahier d'un retour au pays natal* (1939) had earlier given lyrical expression to the revolutionary cry of negritude. Or, at a later date, expectations were again raised by the Cuban Revolution of 1959, which encouraged the return to Havana of "many aspiring writers scattered throughout Europe and the United States who saw in the revolution the affirmation of all their hopes for national renewal."[9]

These examples could be said to bear out Frantz Fanon's observation in *The Wretched of the Earth* that the "crystallization of the national consciousness will both disrupt literary styles and themes, and also create a completely new public."[10] With this in mind, this book will examine the way in which Caribbean fiction has registered and represented the nation-state, understanding the nation in its relationship to the state as, pace Michel-Rolph Trouillot, the "culture and history of a class-divided civil society, as they relate to issues of state power . . . . [The nation] is that part of the historically derived cultural repertoire that is translated in political terms."[11] I emphasize the distinction between nation and state because their conflation in much of the criticism produced in the field of postcolonial studies has led in practice to a lack of consideration of state issues, and of the social dimensions of the anticolonial struggle, in favor of a more narrowly national (and national-cultural) focus, usually framed in relation to problems of identity and representation.[12] While identity and representation remain important areas of concern here, I hope that the attention to nation *and* state in the Caribbean context will allow for a better understanding of conflicts over modalities of social organization, as well as of the complex and variable forms that the relationship between state and nation can take.

However, of equal interest are instances where the representation of the nation runs into difficulty. This might happen because an independent nation-state is absent (as in the cases of the French *départements* or Puerto Rico) or because other forms of community—the diaspora, for example—are posited as the content of experience. But it might also occur because of a disjuncture between state and nation. Most commonly in the region, this has arisen when nationalist projects have failed to meet the needs and desires of the people—a dissipation of potential epitomized by the events in Haiti after 1946. As we will see, the crises suffered by such projects (and later by the nation-state itself under the pressures of neoliberal globalization) are frequently translated into crises of representation. In turn, confronted by societies struggling with new and inherited modes of oppression, Caribbean writers have sought to reshape the novel form in an effort to articulate new possibilities for social regeneration and to project original kinds of collectivities (Fanon's "completely new public").

Integral to such attempts to renarrate social experience have been other forms of cultural practice. Any endeavor to recover the histories repressed under colonialism, and to construct a Caribbean aesthetic able to integrate this past into a critical or emancipatory vision of the present, will entail consideration of such practices, since they have so often served as repositories of memory and vessels for subaltern agency. Hence do we find the Créolistes—Jean Bernabé,

Patrick Chamoiseau, and Raphaël Confiant—in their now widely cited manifesto, *Éloge de la créolité*, arguing that "our writing must accept without reservation our popular beliefs, our magico-religious practices, our marvellous realism, the rituals tied to the 'milan,' to the phenomena of the '*majò*,' to the '*ladja*' duels, to the '*koudmen*.'"[13] Similarly, Wilson Harris identifies cultural vestiges and practices such as limbo, vodun, Carib bush-baby omens, Arawak zemi, and Latin and English inheritances as "epic stratagems available to Caribbean man in the dilemmas of history which surround him."[14] Indeed, he goes on to contend that in fact "the subtle key to a philosophy of history is embedded in the misunderstood arts of the Caribbean," such as limbo, vodun, and so forth.[15] These practices contain within themselves a means to rethink how we might understand the region and the experiences of its peoples. In registering both the specificity of those experiences and the world-historical forces that have shaped the Caribbean, they embody a philosophy of history that is, as Harris puts it, "original to us and yet capable of universal application."[16]

Echoing Harris, but in terms that make explicit the social imperatives at stake in this emphasis on such cultural resources, Earl Lovelace argues that the indigenous traditions of the folk—"indigenous" here used in such a way as to include the process of indigenization[17]—should be seen not merely as "lower class entertainments" but as enabling the establishment of "the philosophical bases of our own civilization."[18] Such traditions, he reiterates, must be returned to as "a source of philosophy or ethics or economics"; and if colonial distortion has circumscribed their meaning, as it has done with the folkloric figure of Anancy, for example (who is seen only as "a scamp, a smart-man"), then it is necessary to revise such bias, to conceive of Anancy "not as a trickster, or 'smart-man,' but as a subtle philosopher tricking the individual into the recognition of the consequences of bad choices and bad faith."[19] Lovelace's perspective highlights the social or class content of these indigenous folk resources: not only do they provide the foundation for an alternative cultural identity to the historyless nonidentity imposed by the oppressor, but they do so in conjunction with a view to the total transformation of society, to its reorganization in relation to the needs of the poor and the powerless. Lovelace, moreover, goes on to emphasize the critical importance of the body to such cultural practices. A locus for the exercise of domination on the one hand, the body has been a key site of resistance on the other. Through activities such as dance and ritual, the body has been able to articulate a sense of agency and personhood otherwise denied in colonial and, often, despite independence, postcolonial contexts. I turn next to this corporeal history.

Among the Caribbean folktales collected and reworked in Raphaël Confiant's *Contes créoles des Amériques*, "La bête-à-sept-têtes" (The Seven-Headed Beast) provides a useful illustration of the historical content embedded in such tales.

When Ma Lôlô discovers one morning that the Beast has not only "devoured all that she had planted in her garden" (dévoré tout ce qu'elle avait planté dans son jardin) but also left in its wake a mountain of excrement, she bursts into such a fit of anger that the monster reappears and, via a magic incantation, forces her to eat its feces.[20] The next day, accompanied by the eldest of her three sons, Ma Lôlô returns to the garden, only for the same fate to befall them both. On the third day, she and the second son are subjected to the Beast's vindictiveness. On the fourth day, however, she arrives with her youngest son, Ti-Pascal, whose powerful talisman causes the Beast's heads to fall off. The monster immediately grows a new set, and a series of beheadings and reheadings ensues before Ti-Pascal finally overcomes his adversary with the help of a potion.

This tale slyly confronts and denounces the system of plantation slavery. The Beast's destruction of Ma Lôlô's garden and the theft of her produce figure the colonial exploitation of land and labor, its power to make her eat excrement suggesting the control exerted by the colonizer over the bodies of the colonized, and in particular the violence inflicted on the female body under slavery.[21] Ti-Pascal's eventual victory, however, represents the hope that a way can be found to overcome a seemingly unstoppable oppressor (although that it is Ti-Pascal who assumes the active role, while his mother remains a passive victim, indicates a problematic gendering of resistance, an issue to which I return later in this study). The tale as Confiant presents it, moreover, retains elements of performativity (songs, chants, calls to the audience) that highlight its oral provenance and draw attention to the fact that it was itself a form of opposition to the attempted regulation of corporeality by the plantation regime.

Thus the story underscores the dual character of the body as a site of both domination and resistance and emphasizes its significance to any analysis of the historical experiences of Caribbean societies. Understood as constitutively shaped by material conditions of existence and discursive practices, and differentiated along lines of sex, gender, class, race, ethnicity, and sexuality (categories that are themselves structured and restructured by the dominant mode of production), the body is central to the reproduction of social life—and, more specifically, to the reorganization of societies under capitalism and the institutionalization of colonial power relations. The economic connection between the development of Europe from the sixteenth century onward and the expropriation of resources from the New World is well established. So too is the way in which, as Marx put it, the "veiled slavery of the wage-labourers in Europe needed the unqualified slavery of the New World as its pedestal."[22] But these connections also produced and necessitated correspondences at the corporeal level.

The reprogramming of populations for life and work in the world of market capitalism entailed a reprogramming of the body. The production of the isolated individual—the monadic subject of capitalist modernity—took place against the backdrop of the increasing rationalization of society, whereby "the traditional or 'natural' [*naturwüchsige*] unities, social forms, human relations, cultural events, even religious systems, are broken up in order to be reconstructed more efficiently in the form of post-natural processes or mechanisms."[23] Across what were emerging as the core economies of Europe, this process of rationalization meant the separation of the workers from the land and their conversion into "free" wage laborers. Unable to immediately adapt themselves to their new condition, however, the workers were subjected to regulation designed to refit them for insertion into the new socioeconomic structures. As Marx summarizes it: "The agricultural folk [were] first forcibly expropriated from the soil, driven from their homes, turned into vagabonds, and then whipped, branded and tortured by grotesquely terroristic laws into accepting the discipline necessary for the system of wage-labour."[24] This remolding of the body into an isolated, productive unit of energy intensified with the expansion of the factory system. Here the division and supervision of labor, and regulation by the clock and bell, became the norm.

But these changes were crosscut, too, by a new sexual division of labor and the reorganization of gender relations. As Silvia Federici points out, the "primitive accumulation" on which the development of capitalist relations was premised included the subjugation of "women's labour and women's reproductive function to the reproduction of the work-force," the "construction of a new patriarchal order, based on the exclusion of women from waged-work and their subordination to men," and the "mechanization of the proletarian body and its transformation, in the case of women, into a machine for the production of new workers."[25] In this view, we must understand gender not as a "purely cultural reality" but as "a specification of class relations," with feminine and masculine identities coded as the carriers of specific work functions.[26]

New modalities of thought also emerged from the reorganization of society. Capitalism's separation of "living and active humanity" from the "natural, inorganic conditions of their metabolic exchange with nature" impacted on the structure of Enlightenment thinking.[27] An opposition was established between nature and culture that was to underpin a notion of progress as requiring nature's subjugation by culture. Culture, or the "human mind, which overcomes superstition," was equated with the consolidation of an abstracted, sovereign subject over and against the profusion of matter.[28] At the level of the individual, this schema relegated the body to the status of messy corporeality and so positioned it as needing constant regulation by the mind. Integrated also into the new sexual division of labor, the schema identified women with a "degraded conception of corporeal reality" and thereby construed them as inferior to men, who were viewed as more closely associated with the mind and rationality.[29]

Such hierarchies became similarly integral to the ideological presentation of class relations. If the proletariat were to be equated with the body, a mass to be disciplined by the factory, workhouse, and prison, then the bourgeoisie were to be equated with the mind. This entailed the production of a corporeality that was likewise highly regulated, only in less oppressive and spectacular ways.[30] Through schooling and socialization, the middle classes were inculcated with manners, habits, and dispositions that emphasized control over the "low" body and its "vulgar" impulses: corporeality was enclosed to ensure the subject "progressed" beyond the blurring of nature and culture to become the rational monad of modernity—a "privatised and largely passive 'consciousness' systematically detached from [the] world."[31] Importantly, this form of bodily regulation enabled an appearance of self-determination by way of its naturalization in the very habits of the individual: under the auspices of an inculcated internal limit as to what constitutes rational behavior, the bourgeois subject became self-regulating.

Pierre Bourdieu's theory of practice provides a particularly rewarding way of thinking about how social structures and relations of power are reproduced in and through the body. Positing a dialectical relationship between material determinants and mental schemata, Bourdieu argues that existence is shaped by the interaction between the body and a structured organization of space and time. The structures constitutive of a particular type of environment (for example, the material conditions of existence characteristic of a class condition) produce habitus, "systems of durable, transposable dispositions, structured structures predisposed to function as structuring structures, that is, as principles which generate and organize practices and representations."[32] Through the habitus, "the structure of which it is the product governs practice, not along the paths of mechanical determinism, but within the constraints and limits initially set on its inventions."[33] However, within these constraints resides the potential for the production of an infinite series of thoughts, perceptions, expressions, and actions, which can also feed back to—and so perpetuate or modify—the underlying structure. As the product of the history inculcated into individuals via practices shaped by objective conditions, the habitus is an incorporated history, an "embodied history, internalized as a second nature and so forgotten as history."[34]

Bourdieu's theory thus draws attention once again to the body as a key site for the contestation of relations of power that would present themselves as inevitable. Moreover, while his analyses apply to social reproduction and class domination in general, much of what they uncover was more obviously visible in the context of slavery, where conditions did not allow for the indirect, impersonal domination that the system of wage labor ultimately secures.[35] Instead the colonizer had to rely on elementary physical violence in conjunction with explicit symbolic domination to inculcate the enslaved with a habitus attuned to the power relations of the plantation regime. Indeed, the institutional containment and regulation of the body in Europe—the reduction of the corporeal to "low" matter in need of subjugation by a rational mind—had its extreme and

bloody underside exposed in the colonies. Here the same ideologies were rearticulated to facilitate the codification of the enslaved as uncivilized physicality
and the colonizer as civilizing consciousness. Thus we have Russell McDougall's
observation that "the great age of global exploration solidified into Empire at
roughly the same time that [the] relocation of the body [in confinement] took
place. The age of imperialism 'completed' the body."[36] In other words, the conquest of the New World's "wilderness" and the taming of the colonized were to
signal both the final triumph of culture over nature and the consolidation of the
bourgeois sovereign subject. Bodily behavior, in fact, became something of an
obsession for colonists in the Caribbean, the "unseemly gestures" and "lascivi-
ous attitudes" of the enslaved and their postemancipation descendants being a
common source of concern.[37] Underlying this concern was the implicit recognition that such movements, and the dances, rituals, and other cultural practices
they were associated with, signaled a historicity—a creative agency—that the
colonized were not supposed to possess. The obsessive regulation of the colonized's corporeality was meant to reduce the body to nothing more than an au-
tomatic component in the system; but the imposition of a habitus adjusted to
the colonial order was never absolute, and in the "unseemly" or undisciplined
gestures of the colonized lay the means to contest this system.

Denied access to other forms of historical inscription, the enslaved turned
to the amanuensis of the flesh to sustain a countermemory. After emancipation, the body would continue in its role as archive and expressive instrument,
reembodying past articulations of resistance and community against new kinds
of constraints. Moreover, it would play a similar role for other peoples who were
brought to the region and subjected to the depredations of the colonial order,
most notably the indentured East Indians. Hence, writes Lovelace:

> When we look at our dances and listen to our songs, when we experience the vi-
> tality and power of the steelband and hear a stickfight chant and watch the leaps
> and dexterity of the bongo dance . . . , we know we have a history of ourselves as
> subjects. It has not been erased, for it is carried in our bodies.[38]

The body as it links to the practices of the subaltern class thus opens on to a
history that has persisted beneath the apparently ahistorical condition imposed
by colonialism. These corporeal practices manifest a habitus coexistent with but
different from that structured by the colonial regime. As such, they contain the
seeds of a potential alternative to the colonial habitus, for they carry a social
content that presupposes new social relations and forms of collectivity. Hence
the importance of cultural practice to the national liberation struggle, in which
embodied local practice or knowledge is transformed into a national culture that
incarnates a national consciousness. For liberation theorists like Fanon and
Amilcar Cabral, moreover, this national consciousness was supposed to give on

to a social consciousness that would demand the total transformation of society in line with the needs of the poor and the powerless. The antecedents of this transformation lie in those subaltern cultural practices and their opposition to the dominant order.

We can trace the importance of such cultural forms to the development of anticolonial nationalisms in the Caribbean more concretely through religious practice. Religion has been central to a number of resistance movements throughout the region. In the Anglophone Caribbean, for instance, resistance by the enslaved, such as Tacky's Rebellion in 1760 and the so-called Baptist War of 1831–32 in Jamaica, drew on religious belief as a source of unity and inspiration. Equally, in the postemancipation period, religion played a key role in events such as the Morant Bay rebellion of 1865. Significantly, the various religious movements involved in these events did not just serve to encourage their communities' actions but were bound up with the very creation and coming to consciousness of those communities. Tacky's Rebellion provides the clearest example here: researchers have argued that it was the first slave rebellion to incorporate people of different tribal origins, something Monica Schuler attributes to the rise of Myal as a Pan-African religion "which addressed itself to the entire slave society, rather than to the microcosms of separate African groups."[39] The role of Myal in the rebellion was thus linked to its rallying of a resistant Pan-African ethnic identity, but one that was at the same time already gesturing toward an Afro-Jamaican identity. In bringing the separate tribal traditions together within the space of Jamaica, Myal—itself an apparently new Caribbean phenomenon modeled on West African secret cult societies—emphasized the common African connection yet also signaled the transformation of these traditions within the new environment, a transformation tied to the claim now made to this environment. Here, then, a creolized religious practice became inseparable from the development of a kind of proto-creole nationalism.

Unsurprisingly, the Haitian Revolution provides the most striking instance of such developments. Again, Afro-Caribbean religious (and bodily) practice played a central role in raising a resistant consciousness: according to Haitian oral tradition, the revolution began "with the dance of the *lwa*, led by a *mambo* (priestess) and the famed Boukman, at a ceremony at Bois Caïman."[40] This consciousness would develop into a national consciousness during the struggle that would see Haiti become the second state in the hemisphere to declare itself independent and the first black republic. To the extent that it institutionalized "blackness" as the index of Haitian citizenship—the Imperial Constitution of 1815, promulgated by Jean-Jacques Dessalines (the first chief of state of the independent Haiti), stated that all Haitians were to be referred to as *noirs* and that "no white man, whatever his nationality, should set foot in Haiti as a master or property owner"[41]—the republic could be said to have defined itself in terms of a racial nationalism. Yet Dessalines's emphasis on Haitians as *noirs* was in fact meant to defuse (unsuccessfully, as it turned out) the antagonism between blacks and mulattoes in the country: *noir* was to be an ideological concept that would identify all Haitian citizens whatever their shade of skin.[42] Moreover, while Africa remained a source of inspiration among many Haitian politicians and intellectuals (albeit one they were ambivalent about), they nevertheless clearly emphasized the national specificity of the Haitian experience. Some even began to conceive this specificity in terms of the creolization of cultural influences: "We quite like the American are transplanted, stripped of traditions," wrote Emile Nau in 1836, "but there is in the fusion of European and African cultures, which constitutes our national character, something that makes us less French than the American is English. This advantage is a real one."[43]

Such thinking was complemented by the impulse among several of the revolution's architects, as well as later intellectuals, to situate and conceptualize Haiti within the modern world order.[44] Despite its isolation by the imperial powers, Haiti was to be not an anomalous enclave but a modern nation-state in which diverse legacies, including, for example, the universalism of French revolutionary rhetoric, were to be indigenized and given radical new meaning as part of an attempt to model an alternative articulation of modernity. Useful here is Michael Dash's gloss on C. L. R. James's understanding of the Haitian Revolution and its aftermath. In James's view, writes Dash, the desire for emancipation was "expressed in the form of the struggle to become [a] modern state . . . and to achieve technological power":

> By focusing on state formation as an alternative revolutionary strategy, James was already shifting attention from resistance as *marronnage* (that is, the creation of isolated communities, united by shared defiance of a dominant force) to the importance of the state—a state that would try to restructure relations shaped by the plantation or colonialism and produce a new self consciousness through the creolizing power of the state.[45]

The revolutionary state, then, was to transform the modern condition into which Haiti had been thrust by the plantation system (for in its agro-industrial organization, the plantation was, as James argued, a "modern system"),[46] producing an indigenized Haitian consciousness coincident with a Haitian nation-state organized around the social needs and demands of the Haitian people.

Chapters 1 and 2 in particular will examine in more detail the elaboration of this and other nationalist projects in the Caribbean. But it is worth making a few general remarks here. The examples cited earlier underscore the significance of cultural practice to anticolonial resistance, as well as to the cultivation of a national consciousness. As Neil Larsen asks in his glossing of Fanon: "Does not the 'national question' become in fact the question of national *culture* itself as precisely that sphere within which a 'national consciousness' makes the concrete transition from purely objective political theory and strategy to the more subjective level of mass, everyday experience?"[47] But they also highlight the question of the form of the nation-state and its coincidence (or otherwise) with the lived experiences and demands of the majority of its inhabitants, a question that, in the Caribbean context, is inseparable from a consideration of indigenization and creolization as processes that have indelibly marked the social fabric. Fundamental to this book is the understanding that these issues will be registered—in however mediated a fashion—in literary form, for there is "no material content, no formal category of artistic creation, however mysteriously transmitted and itself unaware of the process, which did not originate in the empirical reality from which it breaks free."[48] How, then, have those histories of rupture and reconstruction, of excision and regrafting, of creolization and indigenization, found their way into the form of the Caribbean novel? How has the Caribbean novel articulated the particular character of modernity in the region, and how has it offered utopian glimpses of different social formations? And how has the nation—itself having served to mediate social consciousness and cultural practice—been mediated in literary form? These are the key questions that underwrite this book.

In the remainder of this introduction, I make the case for my approach to the foregoing themes. My emphasis on the nation-state in particular requires some discussion, given what is fast becoming the orthodoxy of postnationalism in the academy, not least within the field of postcolonial studies. Indeed, in what was, at least until the mid-1990s, its dominant poststructuralist avatar, the critical thrust of this field—its disavowal of all forms of nationalism, hostility toward totalities, and celebration of liminality, migrancy, and border crossing—has been integral to the elaboration of postnational perspectives. I am thinking, for example, of the work of Homi Bhabha, whose antihistoricist conceptualization of the nation as narration has provided the vocabulary for many of the current dismissals of the nation-state as a relevant unit of analysis. The distrust of nationalisms exhibited by much postcolonialist-poststructuralist criticism can be traced to the setbacks suffered by national liberation movements following the reassertion of imperial dominance in the 1970s and their own failures in delivering on emancipatory promises.[49] More recent arguments for thinking postnationally tend to combine this distrust with what is claimed to be the obsolescence of the nation-state in the age of globalization. However, the undifferentiating disavowal of all nationalisms, in the first instance, and approaches to globalization, in the second, that overstate its impact and overlook the way it is articulated with nation-states (and not necessarily in opposition to them) raises a series of problems that I want to take up here in relation to the Caribbean. These include a failure to theorize fully the workings of power at a global level; a lack of attention to intrastate struggles (including class conflict); a celebration of global flows and cultural hybridity that obscures structural inequalities and downplays the often violent nature of such interactions; and a haziness (arising from the relative lack of consideration given to state issues) about how and where an emancipatory politics might be grounded.

Let me first reemphasize that in attending to the nation-state, I am not seeking to reinstall it as the exclusive object of analysis and identification. Nor do I wish to treat it as a discrete or essential unit or view literary categories as equally essential units coinciding with national borders. Rather, my argument takes as its point of departure a world-systems standpoint, understanding the production of localities, nations, and regions in terms of how they are systemically related at a global level as specific social formations registering differential articulations of capitalist modernity as itself a worldwide, singular, and simultaneous yet everywhere uneven and heterogeneous phenomenon.[50] Such an approach seems, in fact, to be demanded here, given the Caribbean's historic imbrication in international movements of commodities and people, and the way its national territories have so often been marked by regional determinations—not least in the spheres of economics (due to the small size of many of the states) and literature (due to the tendency for writers to migrate around the region). The restructuring of the global economy since the early 1970s under the aegis of what Samir Amin terms the "the logic of unilateral capital" has deepened the massively uneven integration of the Caribbean into the world market, simultaneously driving many of its nation-states into crisis.[51] To be clear, therefore, I am not suggesting that the nation-state in the current conjuncture has not run into difficulties, difficulties that threaten to destroy its historical role as a center for the accumulation of capital. But I do not think that these difficulties mean that we should abandon thinking about it. Indeed, in many ways they make such thinking even more necessary if one is to understand the pressures that weigh on the populations that remain within—and subject to—nation-states.

Moreover, critically analyzing the discourse of globalized flows and endless border crossings might help better to explain the power relations and historical forces that determine contemporary experience. Certain formulations of that discourse, especially those derived from postmodern or postcolonialist-poststructuralist paradigms, have tended to reify—in the very rush to expose all "given" social formations as formal constructs—the fluid vectors and non-totalizable fragments that the deconstruction of totalities is meant to unleash. The touchstone for such theorizations has been the idea of hybridity. Again, Bhabha's work is instructive here: not only does he define postcolonialism as a concept that works against nationalism, but he also deploys hybridity as that which disrupts nationalism's "unisonant discourse."[52] A variety of subsequent theorists, even if they otherwise disagree with Bhabha's position, have continued to employ hybridity in similar fashion.[53] As Shalini Puri argues in her critical commentary on this tendency, hybridity—now often used interchangeably with terms such as creolization, *mestizaje*, and transculturation—has been both abstracted from a series of cultural practices into an "epistemological principle" and yoked squarely to postnationalism.[54]

The way those other terms have been adopted as near synonyms for hybridity indicates the extent to which the hybridization discourse has consumed the theoretical production of the Caribbean, where much of the intellectual work on creolization and the like was first performed. Indeed, as a number of critics have observed, the Caribbean itself has increasingly been abstracted into an emblem of a putative global hybridity, best captured in James Clifford's oft-cited remark "We are all Caribbeans now in our urban archipelagos . . . hybrid and heteroglot."[55] This formulation conveys some sense of how such abstractions can all too easily elide social and structural inequalities ("we" are manifestly not "all Caribbeans" when it comes to the particular political-economic pressures that weigh on different regions, nations, and localities; indeed, Caribbeans are not all the same Caribbeans with regard to how they experience such pressures). But it also points to the way in which the use of the Caribbean in conjunction with discourses such as creolization to name a global reality understood as defined by uncontained cultural flows and postnational fragmentation actually works against the general thrust of those discourses as they were formulated in the Caribbean. Indeed, the conflation of the concepts of creolization, transculturation, and *mestizaje*, which had been invested with specific sociopolitical valences in certain concrete contexts, is achieved by emptying them precisely of this sociopolitical content to leave them as little more than catchwords for cultural dispositions.

Broadly speaking, these concepts have tended in the Caribbean to be articulated *with* nationalist projects, not against them.[56] Of course, different states or movements or thinkers have employed them at different times for different ends, from reactionary attempts to mask class or racial domination to progressive programs aimed at bringing about radical social change. As this implies, a term like "creolization" was not simply a descriptive moniker; it was a way of understanding social relations, its meaning and role thus something to be fought over by competing interests with opposing views on how to organize society. Contrary to how the idea is often seen today, therefore, creolization (or transculturation or *mestizaje*) is not inherently emancipatory; it has the potential to become so, but only when linked—as it was in certain formulations in the Caribbean—to a critique of the existing social order and a historically grounded political project aimed at transforming state institutions, class relations, and economic modalities. Mimi Sheller accurately summarizes what is at stake here when she observes:

> Earlier generations of Caribbean intellectuals invented theoretical terms such as "transculturation" (Ortiz . . .), "creolization" (Brathwaite . . .), and "transversality"

(Glissant . . .) to craft powerful tools for intellectual critique of Western colonialism and imperialism, tools appropriate to a specific context and grounded in Caribbean realities.[57]

However, she continues:

The explosive, politically engaged, and conflictual mode of conceptualising creolization in the nationalist period of the 1970s has been met with a later usage, from a different (metropolitan) location, in which creolization refers to *any* encounter and mixing of dislocated cultures. This dislocation has enabled non-Caribbean metropolitan theorists to pirate the terminology of creolization for their own projects of de-centring and "global" mobility.[58]

Lost in this "pirating" are the political meanings and subaltern agency associated with those earlier conceptualizations, which were bound up with a broader insistence on struggling for the realization of the social demands of the poor and the powerless.

Before looking more closely at the theoretical coinages cited by Sheller, I take as a point of comparison an influential formulation of Caribbeanness from the 1990s, one that accords well with Sheller's account of the general thrust of later projects of decentering and global mobility. This is Antonio Benítez-Rojo's *The Repeating Island: The Caribbean and the Postmodern Perspective*. Of course, this study is not written by a "non-Caribbean" theorist, and it remains very much concerned with the historical, geographic, social, and cultural specificities of the region. Nevertheless, in conceptualizing the Caribbean as "a meta-archipelago" that has "neither a boundary nor a center" and thus "flows outward past the limits of its own sea" to anywhere from Bombay and the Gambia to Canton and Bristol, Benítez-Rojo's arguments do chime somewhat problematically with those dehistoricizing appropriations of the region as an abstract sign of hybridity.[59] He argues that the, as he sees it, polyrhythmic, fractal, and chaotic quality of Caribbean cultural practices embodies the possibility of social transformation through an ability to sublimate violence: "Within this chaos of differences and repetitions, of combinations and permutations, there are regular dynamics that co-exist, and which, once broached within an aesthetic experience, lead the performer to re-create a world without violence."[60] Missing here is a consideration of the material contestation of the dominant order that would have also to take place if this desire to "re-create" the world is to become the progressive project it is clearly meant to be. In a move that corresponds to Bhabha's privileging of the agonistic over the antagonistic, social conflict is evacuated, so that those polyrhythmic cultural practices now appear inherently emancipatory. Even then the lack of attention to social determinants raises the further problem as to where such emancipatory potential could be grounded. Benítez-Rojo's arguments begin from an analysis of the socioeconomic organization of the Caribbean under the plantation system, which he views as central to the creolization process on account of its role in the violent bringing together of cultures. But in moving to talk about the transformative potential of the resulting creolized cultural practices, he offers no comparable consideration of the social formations that might materialize this potential: creolization or the polyrhythmic interaction of cultures is reduced to an "aesthetic experience."

This, I suggest, is a far cry from those earlier theories of Caribbean cultural dynamics. Fernando Ortiz's concept of transculturation is instructive here, not least because Benítez-Rojo devotes a chapter to Ortiz in *The Repeating Island* in which he seeks to align Ortiz's work with the critical thrust of his own. Beginning with the claim that Ortiz's *Cuban Counterpoint: Tobacco and Sugar* touches on several of the interests of postmodern criticism but ultimately offers something different, Benítez-Rojo argues that the text suggests that "Caribbeanness should not be looked for in tobacco or in sugar, but rather in the counterpoint of the myth of the Peoples of the Sea and the theorem of the West."[61] I find this reading problematic for a number of reasons. First, Benítez-Rojo displaces Ortiz's emphasis on the materialities of tobacco and sugar. His own counterpoint of the West and the Peoples of the Sea—the latter defined as societies that are born from marine cultural flows and "undeveloped in the epistemological, theoretical, technological, industrial, imperialist, etc., senses"[62]—ultimately fetishizes both. Each is assigned its own kinds of knowledge and reduced to, in the case of the Peoples of the Sea, a geographically nonspecific and socially undifferentiated cultural grouping, and, in the case of the West, an equally undifferentiated quasi-geographical unit. Although Benítez-Rojo speaks of the historical connections between the West and the so-called undeveloped world, his culturalist emphases obscure the unequal power relations and the systemic imbrication of these sites that produce them as "developed" and "undeveloped." Combined with that elision of their internal social differentiation, what we are left with is transculturation as the interaction of cultural substances as they flow around the globe.

It seems to me that Ortiz's ideas are better served in Fernando Coronil's analysis of *Cuban Counterpoint*, which Coronil reads as enabling the demystification of the same kinds of reified categories that Benítez-Rojo seems to reestablish with his talk of the West and the Peoples of the Sea. "By examining how cultures shape each other contrapuntally," contends Coronil,

> Ortiz shows the extent to which their fixed and separate boundaries are the artifice of unequal power relations. A contrapuntal perspective may permit us to see how the Three Worlds schema is underwritten by fetishized geohistorical categories which conceal their genesis in inequality and domination.[63]

Though both Coronil and Benítez-Rojo hold up contrapuntal cultural interaction as centrally important, the different conclusions they come to in their discussions of Ortiz reflect contrasting understandings of what such interaction entails. Benítez-Rojo's approach recalls the difficulties identified by Jonathan Friedman with theories of creolization. Friedman argues that the "mingling of cultures . . . is a metaphor that can only succeed in terms of a previous metaphor, that of culture as matter, in this case, apparently, a fluid."[64] He goes on to observe that this "substantialization of culture also leads to an understanding of the latter in terms of products rather than production," so that "while allusion is made to the 'social organization of meaning,' the social organization as such all but disappears in references to *flows* of meaning."[65] We can see clear parallels here with the way Benítez-Rojo's theorization of cultural counterpoint turns away from the issue of social reproduction and presents culture as a fluid substance. But this is not how cultural interaction qua transculturation is conceived in Ortiz's work, where it is better understood precisely as a social process and as inseparable from indigenization in a particular environment.

Speaking of the different social groups and cultures that arrived in Cuba, Ortiz describes how each was torn from its "native moorings" and had to face the "problem of disadjustment and readjustment, of deculturation and acculturation."[66] But he locates these transculturations *within* the production of social reality: they cannot be divorced from the related disadjustment and readjustment of socioeconomic structures and techniques of production, which in turn reorganize social relations and determine the framework—the relations of power and modalities of domination and resistance—in which cultural practices are reproduced and refashioned. On the influx of peoples from across the Atlantic, whose diverse origins he carefully differentiates rather than subsuming under the sign of the West, he notes that "some of the white men brought with them a feudal economy," while others "were urged on by mercantile and even industrial capitalism":

> And so various types of economy came in, confused with each other and in a state of transition, to set themselves up over other types, different and intermingled too, but primitive and impossible of adaptation to the needs of the white men at that close of the Middle Ages. The mere fact of having crossed the sea had changed their outlook. . . . And all of them, warriors, friars, merchants, peasants, came in search of adventure, severing their links with an old society to graft themselves on another, new in climate, in people, in food, customs, and hazards.[67]

Signal in this description of the transculturation process is the way it invokes the "transmigration" not of cultural substances but of socioeconomic structures and multiple class fractions, all of which are readapted and transformed within the new environment. Turning next to the arrival of enslaved Africans, Ortiz is again careful to differentiate between the diverse cultures and levels of economic development of these peoples. Again, too, he describes their experiences not simply in terms of a "mingling" of cultures but in relation to their position within the plantation system and the particular organization of labor, land, and property it instantiated. Thus it is within the totality of these readjustments and the related production of new social relations that, as practices are refunctioned and reassembled, culture is remade.

The perspective on cultural interaction that Ortiz's work opens up for us, then, emphasizes culture as practice and the materialities of the social world. The disassembly, intermixture, and reassembly of cultural forms are not independent of—nor in themselves determining of (as they often seem to become in more culturalist readings)—social reality but folded into its very production. This helps us understand the apparent contradiction that Coronil highlights in *Cuban Counterpoint* between Ortiz's declaration that tobacco and sugar are "the two most important figures in the history of Cuba" and his claim that the "real history of Cuba is the history of its intermeshed transculturations."[68] In fact, as Coronil points out, this contradiction is precisely one in appearance only, for in Ortiz's thinking, those transculturations are inseparable from the relations of production that organize Cuban reality: they are a part of the interactions and conflicts between human actors that determine, and are determined by, the socioeconomic structures that produce the commodities of tobacco and sugar, these commodities subsequently appearing as independent entities, and the social organization that determined their production as inevitable. For Coronil, Ortiz's personification of tobacco and sugar helps reveal precisely how the appearance of commodities as "agents in their own right . . . conceals their origins in conflictual relations of production and confirms a commonsense perception of these relations as natural and necessary."[69] By treating tobacco and sugar not as things but as social actors, Coronil suggests, Ortiz "in effect brings them back to the social world which creates them, resocializes them as it were, and in so doing illuminates the society that has given rise to them."[70] Thus tobacco and sugar *are* the "two most important figures in the history of Cuba," but only insofar as these commodities contain and conceal the social relations and collective labor that enable their production.

From this perspective, we can understand transculturation as not just a description of a process but an optic on commodity fetishism that can be used to unmask the human agency and structural determinants this fetishism occults. Once related to the whole network of human relations that organize reality, transculturation becomes a way to map the social totality, restoring a sense of historicity to social formations that otherwise appear immutable. As Coronil puts it, transculturation "breathes life into reified categories, bringing into the open concealed exchanges among peoples and releasing histories buried within fixed identities."[71] Rather than stopping where it identifies the heterogeneous

forces at work in society—as many later theories of hybridity do—transculturation moves to enable a totalizing perspective. By so doing—and without being
in itself inherently emancipating—it highlights the possibility of reorganizing a
hegemonic social order grasped now as the product of specific social relations.

Various other Caribbean theories of cultural interaction, while they need to be
differentiated from transculturation, nevertheless share with it certain features
that not only distinguish them from those later, problematic appropriations of
ideas like creolization but also enable us to establish an alternative genealogy
for such theories that should revise how they are understood more generally. As
in Ortiz's work, these formulations display an emphasis on the materialities of
the social world, on conflictual relations of production, and on a dereifying totalizing perspective. For example, meditating on cultural identity and Indian labor,
George Lamming argues that "the concept of labour and the relations experienced in the process of labour is the foundation of all culture, and this is crucial
to what I mean by the Indian presence as a creative Caribbean reality":

> For it is through work that men and women make nature a part of their history.
> The way we see, the way we hear, our nurtured sense of touch and smell, the whole
> complex of feelings which we call sensibility, is influenced by the particular fea-
> tures of the landscape which has been humanized by our work; there can be no
> history of Trinidad and Guyana that is not also a history of the humanization of
> those landscapes by Indian and other forces of labour.[72]

A process of creolization is implied here (indeed, Lamming later uses both that
term and "transculturation"), but it is understood in the context of indigenization through the reproduction of the social world and a material (bodily) interaction with the environment. According to this view, then, it is a case not of Indian
cultural legacies flowing into the Caribbean melting pot but of the imbrication
of the Indian community in a Caribbean social reality via the community's contribution to the very act of materially reproducing that reality. Similarly, when
Walter Rodney refers to creolization in his discussion of the relationship between people of African and Indian descent in late-nineteenth-century Guyana,
he does so in relation to their "work environment and their responses to capital
at the point of production."[73] Moreover, he locates any progressive potential that
creolization might contain firmly within the context of a wider social struggle:
its significance lies in the possibility of its helping to bring people together to
strengthen a class-based alliance geared toward restructuring socioeconomic relations.[74]

In fact, creolization would increasingly be used as a way to articulate a class-
based critique of the bourgeois nationalisms of the 1960s and 1970s in the Anglophone Caribbean. This theorization of creolization was used against other
claims to creoleness, which had been deployed to cement class domination (fur-

ther giving the lie to celebrations of creolization as necessarily progressive). In Jamaica, for instance, lighter-skinned middle-class people of mixed African and European descent had sought to idealize such a mixture as a means to facilitate national integration; yet by doing so, they set themselves up—as the group that most closely reflected this mix racially—as the "natural" representatives of the nation over and above lower- and middle-class blacks.[75] In *The Development of Creole Society in Jamaica* (1971), Kamau Brathwaite attacked this idealization of creoleness as inspired by colonialist conceptions of society:

> The educated middle class, most finished product of unfinished creolization; in-fluential, possessed of a shadow power; rootless (eschewing the folk) or Euro-ori-entated with a local gloss; Creo- or Afro-Saxons. For them society is "plural" in so far as it appears to remain divided into its old colonial alignments. They are "West Indian" in that they are (or can be) critical of the colonial power. But they are dependent upon it.[76]

Brathwaite was writing in the context of increasing popular disillusionment with postindependence realities, in particular the failures of elites to push through anything more than constitutional reform. Among a broad section of "the working class, the radical or revolutionary intelligentsia, and the very volatile urban youth" developed a renewed sense of cultural nationalism and a desire for wide-ranging social change.[77] Brathwaite's alternative view of creoleness to that upheld by the middle class accords with these sentiments, its foundation the traditions and practices of what he calls the "folk." Having discussed the development of creole society in eighteenth- and nineteenth-century Jamaica, he muses about whether "the process of creolization will be resumed in such a way that the 'little' tradition of the (ex-)slaves will be able to . . . provide a basis for creative reconstruction."[78] Here again creolization means more than just the mixing of cultures. Instead it represents a conflictual, class-differentiated process that is to be supported only insofar as it is connected to the possibility of political reconstruction—of the reorganization of the state and the renewal of national consciousness in line with those folk traditions and the alternative social consciousness they embody.

Turning now to the Francophone Caribbean, we can observe similar features in Édouard Glissant's theorization of creolization. Although Glissant is responding to a different sociopolitical context—that of departmentalization—the thrust of his thinking is inextricable from a challenge to the existing organization of the state and to the role of the elite (in this case as little more than a cipher through which France maintains its grip on the *départements*). Indeed, in the seminal *Le discours antillais*, Glissant insists that when a population lacks control over the socioeconomic "structurations" of its own reality, cultural practice will become reified and hollow.[79] Thus once more it is made clear that if creolization is to aid in the construction of an emancipated cultural identity, it can only do so as part of a wider project with the aim of fundamentally reorganizing the social world and state institutions.

Despite its increasingly routine citation in evocations of creolization as the global flow of cultural forms, Glissant's work—and indeed that of the other thinkers we have just examined—retains a sense of the grounds on which a new order is to be erected. Rather than jumping from the identification of creolization to the assumption that the dominant order is thereby overturned, there is an emphasis on where and how the potentially progressive thrust of certain creolized practices might be materialized. Often that site is the nation-state. Now, it may be that other forms of identification will be equally important (Glissant's simultaneous emphasis on the significance of the region is instructive here). Moreover, the struggle cannot be prosecuted successfully on the national terrain alone: what is confronted—whether in the guise of colonialism, imperialism, or neoliberal globalization—is an international system, so that any attempt to overthrow that system must ultimately be global in scope. Nevertheless the works of Ortiz, Lamming, Rodney, Brathwaite, and Glissant share an assumption regarding the need to secure a new and different sociopolitical dispensation, and the nation-state continues to offer a means of doing so, even if only as a transitional ground in the struggle to realize a form of collectivity yet to come.

For this reason, despite claims that it is increasingly obsolescent in a postnational, globalized world, the nation-state remains central to the concerns of this book. In fact, as suggested earlier, those charges of obsolescence seem to have been overstated. While the drive toward the transnationalization of capital has intensified over the last forty years, and the autocentricity of the nation-state has weakened, the tension between nation-statism and internationalization is not new, nor are those apparently contradictory tendencies necessarily mutually exclusive. Capitalist expansion has historically been bound up with the formation of nation-states, and even in the contemporary period, private capital, including multinational corporations, continues to rely on the state for, among other things, the "guaranteeing of supplies of skilled labour power," the "orderly regulation of commercial relations with other capitals and the provision of a stable currency," and "the taking of measures to protect firms against the sudden dangers presented by the collapse of large suppliers and customers."[80] Moreover, certain states—primarily core capitalist ones—remain capable of regulating capital to some extent through national policies such as pay scales and minimum wages. But that some states are better able to do so than others only highlights that, while the world might be more closely integrated, the articulation of economic and political power continues to be, as Puri puts it, "highly unequal along axes of both class and nation."[81]

Puri's reference to class also points up the internal impact on nation-states of globally uneven development, in particular the way in which different class fractions are differentially integrated into the world system. In peripheral countries especially, the benefits that might accrue to elites who work with or enable the penetration of transnational capital frequently come at the cost of the security of the masses, for whom—broadly speaking—neoliberal policies of deregulation and privatization mean the driving down of wages and the reduction of social and distributive policies. Moreover, imported global products that carry associations of First World power and luxury may well be appropriated by local elites as a means to reinforce their own power and status.[82] A number of theories of globalization present the assimilation of such products into local meanings as evidence of the way that hybridization undermines claims that globalization will result in homogenization. This may well be the case, but such hybridization does not equally undermine either intrastate class domination or, more generally, the baleful impact of the capitalist law of value, an effect that the more enthusiastic celebrations of hybridity as an emancipatory force tend to overlook.[83]

One way of approaching such matters would be via the concept of cultural imperialism, but cultural imperialism understood not as the straightforward imposition of Western culture and products on the non-West, but as the penetration of what Leslie Sklair has called the transnational "culture-ideology of consumption."[84] This better captures the world-systemic quality of the social and cultural logic of late capitalism—its multiple sites and drivers that expose the fallacy of reducing it to the export of Western goods. Thinking in these terms helps avoid overemphasizing cultural products at the expense of the modalities of social reproduction. It spotlights the way this culture-ideology is inextricable from a process whereby the material instance of generalized commodity production rips through the social fabric, destroying or restructuring lifeways and writing itself on cultural practice, not least at the level of the body.

The issues at stake here, and their implications for Caribbean societies, are perhaps best summarized by Lovelace in his essay "In the Dance." Highlighting the undeniable failures of various national projects in the Caribbean while emphasizing the importance of what they once stood for, he suggests:

> Perhaps what has changed is that where once we were colonised by governments, we are now dominated by multinational outfits. National development is a term increasingly out of use. What we have is development by any who have the means to do so. We deceive ourselves if we believe that colonialism is dead, that there are no more struggles, no larger themes to relate to, that we are individuals in the global village waiting to be inspired. . . . In a sense, what we face today is a struggle between the promise of National Independence and being diffused into an impotent individualism by the propaganda of the post-colonial world.[85]

Crucial here is that without denying the changed global context and the multinational pressures that undermine the already questionable autocentricity of the nation-state, Lovelace underscores the significance of the promise of national independence as the potential grounds on which to combat contemporary domination. Moreover, he is speaking not only of domination exercised by international actors but also of inequalities within the nation-state and of the need to fulfill the social goals that national independence was supposed to achieve but did not.

Tellingly, Lovelace uses dance—bodily movement—as an analogy for these issues. He describes the attainment of national independence as having been like getting to the entrance of a dance, finding there is some kind of restriction ("maybe it is the dress code, or your colour, or your class, or you don't know the people"), focusing all your energies on getting in by fixing yourself up right, but then finding that once you get in, "you feel you must behave in a certain way, you feel you must restrict your behaviour to what you believe that they would expect of you."[86] By contrast, what is required once you are in the dance is to dance on your own terms. "Your job," says Lovelace, addressing a "child of Independence," "is to dance. You have the self-confidence and we hope, the moves; and if you don't have them, you have to get them, you have to learn them. The dance is yours. You have to take over the fete."[87] The need for a dance that is different in (bodily) form to the restricted version practiced previously figures the need for a new form of politics while also pointing to cultural practice as that which contains the resources to shape this politics insofar as it embodies a social content.

Nevertheless, for this content to become something grasped by all at the level of everyday experience, it must still be mediated. As indicated earlier, for writers like Fanon and Cabral during the era of national liberation—and, it would seem, for Lovelace, given his emphasis on national independence—it was precisely the nation that was to play this mediating role. As Neil Lazarus observes, discussing Cabral's formulation of the relationship between "converted" intellectuals and "the people," in the "modern era (and not only in the 'Third World'), the nation has been one of the privileged sites—perhaps *the* privileged site—for the forging of this articulation between universalist intellectualism and popular consciousness."[88] He goes on to quote Achin Vanaik to the effect that "the nation-state for the first time invests ordinary people (through the principle of equal citizenship rights) with an authority and importance that is historically unique. To date the zenith of popular individual empowerment is political citizenship, whose frame of operation is the nation-state or multinational state."[89]

The failings of various national independence movements, in the Caribbean as elsewhere, have led to a questioning of the role of the nation-state in this regard. Nevertheless, while the world political system continues to be organized as a hierarchically structured system of nation-states, this unit will remain an indispensable political space through which to pursue the struggle against imperialism as it is experienced by the mass of the people in their daily lives.[90] This experience, moreover, will continue to be felt most sharply at the level of the body, which remains a privileged medium for the exercise of both domination and resistance.

This book comprises five chapters that treat a selection of Caribbean novels from 1945 to the present in more or less chronological fashion. Chapter 1 considers evocations of the nation-state in narratives from the 1940s and 1950s, setting them in the context of the growing social and political unrest of the time and the upsurge in anticolonial and anti-imperial movements struggling for independence or for the thoroughgoing reorganization of societies already nominally independent (Cuba and Haiti, for example). The chapter provides a brief overview of a range of texts with the aim of identifying key themes and tropes while also establishing a theoretical framework for considering the relationship between the nation, cultural practice, and literary form.

Chapter 2 explores the dissipation of many of the hopes and promises generated by national independence as a result of continued imperialist pressures and the failings of native elites. Examining works by Wilson Harris, Earl Lovelace, Marie Chauvet, and Enrique Laguerre, I consider how the difficulties experienced by the body politic are not only registered in these texts via the image of the physical body but also shown to be connected materially to its dispositions and inculcated behaviors. The crisis of political representation, I argue, finds its literary corollary in a crisis of aesthetic representation, figured most notably through the malfunctioning of the topos of the tragic sacrifice.

Chapter 3 continues in this vein, examining the increasingly fraught representations of individuals and communities in the 1970s and 1980s as the shortcomings of various national projects became ever more apparent or, as in the case of the French *départements*, the possibility of even obtaining independence seemed to recede. Through an analysis of novels by Lovelace, Patrick Chamoiseau, and Luis Rafael Sánchez, I explore themes of language, madness, folklorization, and commodity fetishism. I argue that despite the strangulation of cultural and political expression these texts document, they nevertheless imply that new social relations and forms of collectivity can be articulated, though they embed that suggestion less in any explicit avowal than in the challenges and innovations of their aesthetics.

Chapter 4 subsequently considers how such stylistic innovations and the utopian potential they contain are extended, in work by Chamoiseau, Lovelace, and Erna Brodber, among others, into whole aesthetic programs that flesh out projected new modes of collectivity. These writers fashion a new kind of epic form that draws on Caribbean religio-cultural practices centered on possession rites and ego displacement and refracts the potential lineaments of a reconfigured nation-state.

Chapter 5 explores how the utopian imaginings of the texts considered in chapter 4 remain unfulfilled in the contemporary Caribbean as a result of the continuation both of imperialist exploitation (now euphemized as globalization) and of internal problems such as ethnic conflict and parasitic indigenous elites. I begin, however, by reexamining some of the themes broached in chapter 4 in terms of Francophone Indo-Caribbean literature, a hitherto relatively understudied corpus. I then switch to the Anglophone Caribbean to examine work from the 1980s, 1990s, and the first decade of the twenty-first century by a series of women writers, including Oonya Kempadoo, Margaret Cezair-Thompson, Michelle Cliff, and Shani Mootoo, whose novels mediate the crises suffered by the nation-state since the 1970s through the lens of gender relations and issues of sexuality. I also examine the particular problems that confronted Cuba following the collapse of the Soviet Union after 1989. I end by considering the claims of regionalism while continuing to insist on the importance of the nation-state to any effort to combat the imperialist logic of global capital.

1

The Promise of National Independence: Modernity, Allegory, and Sacrifice

I begin this chapter with a brief consideration of Jacques Roumain's seminal novel *Gouverneurs de la rosée* (Masters of the Dew) (1944), a work that could be said to mark a period of transition in Caribbean literature. Roumain's tale of the protagonist Manuel's return to Haiti from Cuba and his attempt to reunite the drought-stricken peasant community of his native village of Fonds Rouge was an international success and represents the high point of Haitian indigenism. Like Césaire's *Cahier d'un retour au pays natal* (1939), Reid's *New Day* (1949), and Carpentier's *El reino de este mundo* (1949), Roumain's novel is one of those texts that seem to lay the ground for the boom in Caribbean literature in the 1950s. Roumain emerged as a significant influence on a younger generation of writers, his work resonating both with the desire to develop an indigenous Caribbean aesthetic and with the upsurge in anticolonial feeling in the middle decades of the twentieth century. Indeed, the growing social and political unrest sweeping the archipelago at the time forms the backdrop to the action in the book. Manuel's radicalism stems from his experience of the class struggle when working as a cane cutter in Cuba, and his vision for Haiti chimes with the contemporary push for independence from colonial and (in the case of Haiti) neocolonial domination:

> We don't know yet what a force we are, what a single force—all the peasants, all the Negroes of plain and hill, all united. Some day, when we get wise to that, we'll rise up from one end of the country to the other. Then we'll call a General Assembly of the Masters of the Dew, a great big *coumbite* of farmers, and we'll clear out poverty and plant a new life.[1]

Yet for all it seems to point forward to the literary and social concerns developed by later writers, *Masters of the Dew* also signals the end of a certain approach to those concerns. As Selwyn R. Cudjoe notes, the text "climaxed a particular era in Caribbean literature."[2] Roumain's novel stands as a masterpiece of the peasant novel, but while narratives about the peasantry would continue to appear, the intensification of social change across the Caribbean in the postwar years, including greater industrialization and rapid urbanization, meant it would become increasingly difficult for authors to reproduce the image of a self-contained, organic community—as represented by Fonds Rouge—without retreating from history. *Masters of the Dew* does in fact gesture toward such changes. After all, Manuel is a migrant worker who has received his political education on the agro-industrial plantations of Cuba. His vision for Haiti, meanwhile, is one of modernization: the religious paradigms of the masses are to be replaced by a sense of collectivity founded on organized labor; as Michael Dash observes, it is clear that "Roumain wished to see in the *coumbite* a modern-day 'Bois-Caïman' ceremony where the transfer from the sacred to the secular is made and masses mobilized using an ancient rite."[3] In articulating this transition from the mythic to the modern, Roumain's novel looks to reconcile the different modalities of social life associated with these terms: the organic unity of the village is to be retained in the context of a new, modernizing national project.

This attempted reconciliation, however, becomes the source of a series of contradictions in the text. One of the most notable is that Dash identifies between, on the one hand, a "revolutionary internationalism," which is translated into history and the class struggle and is represented by Manuel as radicalized laborer, and, on the other, a "cultural nationalism," which is translated into foundational romance—the "rhetoric of blood and territory"—and is represented by Manuel as sacrificial hero whose death heralds the rebirth of the community.[4] If, as Terry Eagleton contends (following Walter Benjamin's theory of tragedy), it is through the sacrificial "death of the hero" that "the community comes to consciousness of its subjection to mythological forces," then Manuel's Christlike death at the hands of Gervilen should awaken the Fonds Rouge villagers to the need to abandon their fatalism and excessive reliance on the supernatural.[5] And to a degree it does: the community reunites to dig the channel that will bring water to the village. Yet it is at this point, too, that the novel consolidates the mythological vision of the organic wholeness of the community, as in the final scene fertility returns to the land, suggesting the restoration of the village to an Edenic originality. The attempt both to expose the historical forces that contribute to Haiti's impoverishment and to maintain the image of an isolated and enclosed rural collectivity can therefore not be sustained. The text ultimately falls back into an ahistorical imaginary, a trajectory emphasized, as Dash points out, by its leaving unresolved the question of Hilarion, the rural policeman who intends to use his position to expropriate the peasants' land.[6]

The novel's inability to bring together its emphasis on history with its celebration of organic communal life stems from the fact that the historical perspective ultimately reveals the village to be not an isolated enclave but part of a wider economic and political system (already partly figured in Hilarion, who identifies himself as a representative of "established law and order" and "the Government").[7] Moreover, the same historical process also portends the transformation or even collapse of communities like Fonds Rouge under the pressure of socioeconomic change (also already alluded to in the novel through references to villagers migrating to the city).

It is worth noting here, too, the novel's problematic representation of gender relations. At the story's end, it is not only the land that is invested with new life but also Manuel's lover Annaise, who is revealed to be pregnant with his child. The conflation of Annaise with the land would seem to repeat the masculinist, colonial trope of the landscape as a female body to be entered and given meaning by the male explorer. Such imagery is especially telling given that one of the key shortcomings of many nationalist projects in the Caribbean was their marginalization of women and failure to overturn the heteropatriarchal relations of power embedded in the colonial state. Despite the fundamental role women played in the independence struggles, there was a tendency, particularly within bourgeois nationalist movements, to confine them to specific roles and identities. As M. Jacqui Alexander observes:

> It was in the creation of the women's wing of these [nationalist] parties and in their organization of "culture" that one begins to detect a gendered call to patriotic duty. Women were to fiercely defend the nation by protecting their honour, by guarding the nuclear, conjugal family . . . [and] by guarding "culture" defined as the transmission of a fixed set of proper values to the children of the nation. . . . She was expected to represent and uphold a respectable femininity and, in so doing, displace the figure of the white madonna. Patriotic duty for men, on the other hand, consisted in rendering public service to the country.[8]

Masters of the Dew repeats this codification of women as helpmates and protectors of the family, in contrast to men as active participants in reshaping the public sphere: whereas Manuel gives birth to a renewed community, Annaise is confined to the task of reproductive labor. Insofar as the production of gender identities must be understood as imbricated in class relations and the specific division of labor imposed by the dominant mode of production, the failure to challenge conventional gender models bespeaks a failure to fully transform the existing socioeconomic relations. In this regard, the retention of masculinist tropes in Roumain's novel gestures to a potential limitation in the attempted narration of a total break with the inherited structures of colonial capitalist power.

I return to the foregoing issues throughout this chapter as I examine how Caribbean novels from the 1940s and 1950s sought to engage with and articulate the momentous upheavals taking place across the archipelago. The changing circumstances meant that literary form, too, had now to be recast if it was to narrate and interrogate the newly emergent sociopolitical realities.

To begin analyzing these trends, let us first take a closer look at *Masters of the Dew* and the national project adumbrated there. Manuel's desire for a *coumbite* of farmers that will "clear out poverty and plant a new life" clearly entails the reorganization of the state in line with the social needs of the poor and the power-less. Indeed, it looks to the plot system of the peasantry as the potential basis on which to erect this new order. The importance attached to the plot system in this regard derives from its historical role as a site of resistance to the colonial organization of land and production. During the period of slavery, plots, gardens, and provision grounds were cultivated by the enslaved, either in village yards or on the plantation backlands and other marginal areas. Jean Besson describes how planters

> allocated provision grounds to the slaves to produce a cheap and reliable food supply. The slaves, however, used the land to create a domestic economy well beyond the planters' rationale, producing surpluses for sale in public markets. Moreover, the provision grounds complemented the village yards in providing some economic independence and a degree of social and cultural autonomy within the slave plantation system.[9]

After emancipation, many newly free men and women left the estates to pursue "various different individual and collective forms of tenancies, sharecropping and freehold arrangements," establishing a peasantry that formed the core of what Clive Thomas calls a "counter-plantation system."[10] This system was oriented around both the sociocultural practices and the economic requirements of the peasantry, in contrast to the external colonial orientation of the plantation regime. Hence, as Mimi Sheller observes, "peasant landholding as an alternative to sugar monoculture became the key terrain for wresting economic power from planters, and with it political and civil power as well."[11] The self-sufficiency and diversification of output enabled by peasant agriculture provided a potential material basis for independence and for the reorganization of society along lines different from those institutionalized by the colonial state. As such, it is not surprising that the state sought to ensure the peasantry was "marginalized, excluded from the political process and denied social mobility."[12]

In Haiti, attempts to realize the potential of peasant landholding stretch back to the immediate postindependence period, when Dessalines endeavored to divide up and redistribute the land, most notably the private property of the *anciens libres*.[13] In the mid-nineteenth century, the Piquet Rebellion saw the Haitian peasantry fighting for social and agrarian reform: the actions of the Piquets, argues Sheller, suggest a movement "with democratic aims and a clear critique of landowner-merchant domination and unmitigated control of the state."[14] During the U.S. occupation of the island, the struggle of the peasantry to retain control over its land coalesced around the *cacos* rebellion from 1918 to 1920, led by Charlemagne Péralte and Benoît Batraville. Dash contends that *Masters of the Dew* "has its genesis in the thirties and in Roumain's fascination with Charlemagne Péralte and the caco resistance movement."[15] In this view, the novel can be seen as projecting the utopian achievement of the *cacos'* aims through the rejuvenation of the self-sufficient Fonds Rouge community, itself a synecdoche for the nation-state.

Yet we have already noted the problematic romanticization of the village collectivity, which destabilizes its functioning as an image for the nation by creating a tension between an ahistorical vision of Edenic wholeness and the plan for a new national *coumbite* predicated on modernization. For all that it arises from the contradictory ideological tendencies within the text, however, this clash of topoi does register a historical reality, albeit one that is obscured precisely by that tropological encoding. The novel bears the impress of a changing social world in which the socioeconomic structures of an expanding industrial capitalism were increasingly colliding with the means of production and subsistence practiced by the peasantry in rural areas. In fact, the peasantry had always coexisted alongside and been imbricated in not only the plantation system but also the market system of the towns and city. However, the peasants' marginalization and exclusion from the political process by the colonial state occluded this relationship. Consequently the peasantry appeared as a discrete "backward" unit separated from the modernized, more "advanced" sites of production and commerce.[16] Because of the formal conventions the novel deploys, *Masters of the Dew* cannot succeed in fully penetrating this reified order of appearances. Although (as noted earlier) it does gesture to the interconnection of the rural world with a wider socioeconomic system, the text ultimately sets them apart again by parceling out the narrative between the naturalistic recording of history (which tends toward documenting only the visible reality of the separation) and the romanticism of the final portrayal of the village. What I want to suggest, however, is that in the political unconscious of the text (to borrow Fredric Jameson's phrase)[17] we can read not only a recognition of the simultaneity of the peasant mode of existence with developments in the modernizing urban areas, but also the beginnings of an attempt to find a form that could articulate their interconnection.

To illustrate this idea, I turn to a point that Dash makes regarding the frequently lyrical presentation of the landscape in *Masters of the Dew*—what he calls Roumain's "aesthetic of renascence in his contemplation of his native land."

> Roumain's work easily transcends the vision of despair so frequently found in the Caribbean novel of protest and is perhaps the first to present the Haitian and, by analogy, the Caribbean landscape with this sense of elation and wonder. This concept is later explored much more intensely in the theories of "Marvellous Realism" developed by Roumain's literary successor, Jacques-Stéphen Alexis.[18]

What interests me here is Dash's identification of the way Roumain's narration of the landscape seems to be moving toward a kind of proto-marvelous realism. The following passage bears out Dash's point, I believe; but I cite also the narrative segment that precedes it (spoken by Manuel's mother), for together they suggest something of the significance of that point for our purposes:

> "There are too many of these young girls who've lost their respect for the ways of our ancestors. The city has turned their heads. . . . The land is no longer good enough for them. They'd rather go to work as cooks for some rich mulattoes. As if that was the thing to do!"

> Brother, you don't know the spring at Mahotière? Then you're not from around here, brother. Between the legs of the mountain that spring flows. You leave the huts and the fields and by the ease of the slope you reach the ravine. It's a cool ravine because of the steep cliffs and the branches of the *mombin* trees that shade it. Ferns are everywhere in its oozing humidity, and a mat of watercress and mint wades in its cooling current. Under the rocks you catch crayfish. . . . And with rice it's a very good dish, take my word for it.[19]

The evocation of the countryside here certainly conveys a "sense of elation and wonder"; and in the sexualized, anthropomorphic description of the mountain, one can detect what Jameson characterizes as the defining feature of Alejo Carpentier's concept of *lo real maravilloso*, that is, "a certain poetic transfiguration of the object world itself—not so much a fantastic narrative, then, as a metamorphosis in perception."[20] But it is interesting, too, how this lyrical paean immediately follows the comments of Manuel's mother on the migration of village girls to the city to work in its burgeoning service economy. This juxtaposition could be read as emphasizing the novel's tendency toward narrative bifurcation, with a changing historical reality recorded on one side and a romanticized portrait of a wondrous rural world presented on the other. Yet it is also noteworthy how the passage on the countryside is framed: the text is temporarily narrated from the perspective of a local peasant speaking to an outsider, who has the marvels of the landscape opened up to him. If we bear this in mind and set it against the backdrop of that mention of the city, we can read the sense of the marvelous invoked here less as a form of romantic transcendence and more as a recognition of the historical reality of Haiti. That is, it registers the shock of history itself—the outsider's sudden awareness of that other world, the peasant way of life and mode of subsistence (highlighted by the reference to catching crayfish) that coexist alongside the world of the city.

Things will perhaps become clearer if we recall that marvelous realism in its various guises (including magic realism) has frequently been understood as an aesthetic response to just this kind of coexistence of realities and the effects of uneven and combined development. Jameson hypothesizes that "magic realism depends on a content which betrays the overlap or the coexistence of precapitalist with nascent capitalist or technological features," which makes its "organizing category" the concept of "modes of production, and in particular of a mode of production still locked in conflict with traces of the older mode (if not with foreshadowings of the emergence of a future one)."[21] This quality, Jameson argues, accounts for the particular emphasis that Carpentier gives to his conception of the marvelous real: it is "not a realism to be transfigured by the 'supplement' of a magical perspective but a reality which is already in and of itself magical or fantastic."[22] Neil Larsen, in his analysis of the affinity for surrealism in Latin American literature and its role in the development of magical realism, similarly points to the determining influence of uneven development. In surrealism, the technique of montage was deployed to create a sense of shock—by juxtaposing familiar objects in unfamiliar sequences and contexts—designed to defamiliarize the everyday and undermine a routinized bourgeois existence, at least in Europe. But suppose, writes Larsen, that "the familiarized or routinized object world were structured in such a way that the shock effects of montage were themselves the spontaneous, even, in a sense, the routine experiences of everyday life."[23] This is precisely the reality that writers like Carpentier encountered in the Caribbean and continue to encounter: one in which socioeconomic disparities mean that the most modern structures sit alongside those associated with earlier historical moments. Montage proves so pertinent a technique here because "in its juxtaposition of the most disparate elements, it supplies a 'dialectical image' of the possible *unity* of an existence *already* in a condition of disparity. . . . The shock afforded by 'magical realist' montage is thus not limited to the shock of the 'real' as something exceeding the merely dreamed or imagined. . . . It is the shock of recognizing that this 'real' is the result of a unitary, total historical process."[24]

It is, I have tried to suggest, this particular moment of shock that *Masters of the Dew* is starting to register, the text groping toward a form able to articulate the simultaneity of disparate realities. Let me reemphasize that those realities were closely interrelated despite their differences. The peasantry was rarely absolutely disjoined from the colonial economy—although the exact nature of their relationship varied across the region—and in many instances, peasants took up part-time work on the plantations or produced goods to be sold at market. Surpluses, too, were frequently marketed, as they had also been by the enslaved. Taking the example of Jamaica, Sydney Mintz has shown how there arose a historical, functional, and psychological interdependence between small-farm cultivation and the marketing system, so that "changes in either of these institutional segments of Jamaican culture would result in changes in the other." Indeed, he continues, had "it not been for the pattern of subsistence-plot cultivation under slavery, and the perpetuation of subsistence cultivation by the growth of a rural peasantry after emancipation . . . the Jamaican economy would have taken on a very different character."[25] Again, such relationships varied from territory to territory. Nevertheless Mintz's comments reaffirm the general significance of the simultaneous opposition and interconnection between plot and plantation—a claim that Sylvia Wynter similarly makes in her article "Novel and History, Plot and Plantation" (1971), in which she argues that "the history of Caribbean society is that of a dual relation between plantation and plot, the two poles of which originate in a single historical process, [and] the ambivalence between the two has been and is the distinguishing characteristic of the Caribbean response."[26]

Marvelous or magical realism can be viewed as just such a response. Indeed, it is noteworthy that Wynter's argument, while not referencing magical realism directly, draws on the work of Miguel Angel Asturias, who in novels such as *Hombres de maiz* (Men of Maize) (1949) had dramatized the relation between plot and plantation, and whose fiction is regarded as at the forefront of the emergence of magical realism.[27] Carpentier's now famous prologue to *El reino de este mundo* (The Kingdom of This World), in which he outlined his conception of *lo real maravilloso*, appeared in the same year as *Men of Maize*. The novel itself is an excellent example of the attempt, in Michael Denning's words, "to capture the temporal dislocations, the juxtaposition of different modes of life—the mythic and the modern—that had resulted from a history of conquest, enslavement, and colonization."[28] Nowhere is this more the case than in the depiction of the execution of Macandal. Tied to the stake, he begins "howling unknown spells and violently thrusting his torso forward":

> The bonds fell off and the body of the Negro rose in the air, flying overhead, until it plunged into the black waves of the sea of slaves. A single cry filled the square:
> "Macandal saved!"
> Pandemonium followed. . . . And the noise and screaming and uproar were such that very few saw that Macandal, held by ten soldiers, had been thrust head first into the fire.[29]

Here a single event is inscribed within two very different realities that coexist in the same space. This synchronicity of the nonsynchronous (to borrow Ernst Bloch's formulation)[30] is emphasized by the way the narrative presents the incident with no acknowledgment of the disjunction: Macandal does not "appear" to fly away, he just does; nor has he "in fact" been killed, he just is. Both outcomes are recorded as having occurred and sit alongside each other in a contradictory unity.

But if Carpentier's novel registers this historically determined condition of coexistent yet disparate modes of life, his actual theorization of *lo real maravilloso* is problematic, tending to naturalize the condition as an inherent feature of the New World. Those disjunctions and overlaps become the stuff of cultural essences, so that, as the Haitian philosopher Jacques Gourgue puts it in a critique of Carpentier, "the real marvellous would be intrinsically linked to poorly industrialized countries . . . [and so] justify hazy ideas and illogical actions that one would prefer to leave hidden behind the mountain of centuries."[31] Larsen, too, has noted how Carpentier's claims for the *real maravilloso* turn it back into "something exceeding the merely dreamed or imagined," thereby remystifying history rather than exposing its dynamics.[32] It is to those dynamics as they have unfolded in the Caribbean that I now turn to better grasp how writers after Roumain and the Carpentier of *The Kingdom of This World* sought to articulate the complex reality of the region. To do so, we need to take a closer look at the "total" (Larsen) or "single" (Wynter) historical process that shaped the Caribbean's entry into modernity.

The work of Sidney Mintz offers a useful starting point here. Mintz has consistently emphasized what he sees as the Caribbean region's fundamental modernity. Writing about the rise of the plantation system from the sixteenth century onward and the importation of enslaved and indentured labor, he observes:

> The enterprises for which these people were carried across oceans were intimately associated with Europe and its growth. Their development was an instance of precocious modernity, an unanticipated (indeed unnoticed) modernity—unnoticed especially, perhaps, because it was happening to people most of whom were forcibly stolen from the worlds outside the West. No one imagined that such people would become "modern"—since there was no such thing; no one recognised that the raw, outpost societies into which such people were thrust might become the first of their kind.[33]

Underlying this "precocious modernity" was the complex agro-industrial character of the plantation, its unity of field and factory and the application of technical features in operations that predated the Industrial Revolution.[34] Equally important, though, was the impact this economic organization had on the labor force. For Mintz, the particular form of socialization occasioned by conditions on the plantation imposed a modern cast on the human beings shoehorned into its structures. The stripping of kinship and community, the extirpation of familial matrices, the forced transportation and resettlement alongside culturally unlike peoples—all of this constituted a form of brutality that, while taking place within the seemingly precapitalist institution of slavery, in fact reflected the harsh exigencies of modern capitalist industrialization. As the colonized sought to resist these pressures, moreover, they built ways of life that were both unique and paradigmatically modern.[35]

A number of significant premises underpin Mintz's argument. Modernity here is defined centrally by the process of capitalist industrialization. But the emphasis on the "precocious modernity" of the Caribbean underscores that this is not a reiteration of the (Eurocentric) view of modernization as identical to the spread of Westernization. Mintz's reasoning rests on a challenge to the notion of capitalism and modernity as essentially Western phenomena that have their telos in that quasi-geographic area, a telos subsequently exported elsewhere as part of the continuous expansion of capital.[36] Rather, the implication is that capitalism is to be viewed as tendentially a world system from the outset, inaugurating a modern global history that is, however, differentially articulated in different localities.[37] These differential articulations ultimately index the limits and contradictions of capitalism itself—its inability to realize its own universalizing tendencies. Indeed, capitalist modernity, as Neil Lazarus puts it, is "characterised by unevenness: that is, by the dynamics of development and underdevelopment, autocentricity and dependency, the production and entrenchment of localisms (to a point approaching irreducibility) within larger processes of globalization, incorporation, and homogenisation."[38] The historical circumstances of the Caribbean bear out this world-systemic perspective, not only in light of the integrity of the plantation system to the economic development of western Europe but also with regard to the region's precociously modern stamp. This last point serves to emphasize how, far from being outside or lagging behind a modernity supposedly pioneered in the West, the Caribbean was negotiating its own distinctive experience of modernity, one that saw precipitately modern forms emerge in tandem with underdevelopment.

Indeed, if the Caribbean's modernity was precocious, as Mintz claims, then it was also violent and explosive—an "irruption into modernity," in the words of Édouard Glissant.[39] Although Glissant is referring specifically here to the literary sphere, and to the emergence of a national literature with decolonization (a point I return to later), his characterization could just as well apply to the impact of the region's integration into the capitalist world system. Indeed, he talks also of the Caribbean's "lived modernity," defining "lived" as "that which is abruptly imposed."[40] Certainly this reflects the socioeconomic development of the area under colonialism, its subjection to the brutal imposition of externally oriented economic models. However, not only did the demands of the metropolitan core—its appetite for commodities and thirst for primitive accumulation—push the colony toward the precipitate semi-industrialization Mintz identifies, but these same demands also had a countervailing effect, requiring that the colony be locked into a state of underdevelopment as the condition for its being the pedestal for development elsewhere. Nothing illustrates this point better than the seemingly contradictory circumstance of slavery existing within capitalist agro-industrial enterprises, an overlap of realities exacerbated by extremely uneven internal development resulting from the grossly lopsided concentrations of wealth produced by the plantation system.[41] The situation was further complicated, as we have seen, by the emergence of peasantries, or, more properly speaking, "reconstituted peasantries," to use Mintz's well-known description, the phrase signaling that these peasants had "begun other than as peasants—

in slavery, as deserters or runaways, as plantation labourers, or whatever—and becom[e] peasants in some kind of resistant response to an externally imposed regimen."[42] Such peasantries were thus formed as a way to negotiate the pressures of industrialization and capitalist modernity; they were not (in contrast to the situation in the core economies of western Europe) part of a preexisting social formation being gradually rendered residual by the growing dominance of capitalism.

I rehearse these arguments around the precocious, irruptive, and uneven articulation of modernity in the Caribbean because this articulation is inextricable from the particular shape assumed by the region's cultural and literary fields. Now, I use the term "fields" here specifically in the sense of the concept developed by Pierre Bourdieu. For Bourdieu, the field is the structured space of a particular domain (the political, educational, cultural, and so on) in which there exists a series of possible positions occupied by "agents" or "products" (including cultural products like the novel) whose relations structure the shape of that field. These relations are determined by the amount of capital—not only economic but also cultural, social, or other types of symbolic capital—that agents possess. The fields are structurally homologous, but not identical. Each is relatively autonomous and cannot be reduced in crudely deterministic fashion to, say, economics: changes in one field are not directly reflected in another but rather play out in accordance with the laws of functioning of that other field. Thus, in discussing the literary field, Bourdieu argues that the "important fact, for the interpretation of works, is that this autonomous social universe functions somewhat like a prism which *refracts* every external determination: demographic, economic or political events are always retranslated according to the specific logic of the field, and it is by this intermediary that they act on the logic of the development of works."[43] What interests me about this formulation is the way that it allows for a reading of literary form in relation to those external determinants without reducing the relationship to a one-to-one reflection or equivalence. By translating social reality into its own logic, the literary field turns the investigation of that reality into something internal to the literary work. In this view—and both to anticipate my argument and to further clarify my earlier remarks on marvelous realism—the kinds of contradictions and unevenness in the economy I have been discussing will be registered in terms of contradictions and clashes in literary forms and styles.

Although he does not draw on Bourdieu, the Brazilian literary critic Roberto Schwarz's similar emphasis on structural homologies and the likeness of unlike structures—most notably in his analysis of the works of José de Alencar and Machado de Assis—demonstrates brilliantly how this perspective might be applied to a situation of imperialist underdevelopment. Schwarz too posits society, in its relation to the literary object, as "an internal force, encapsulated within a formal device that reconfigures itself autonomously."[44] Situating Brazilian culture within the world-historical context of capitalist modernity, he shows how the economic and ideological contradictions that arise out of Brazil's global dependency affect its literature. Specifically, he is concerned with what happens when an imported form confronts a local content, highlighting the incongruities and conflicts "that occurred as a result of the transplantation of the novel and of European culture to our country."[45] Commenting on Alencar's novel *Senhora*, he writes:

> The roots of our artistic problem, one of formal unity, lay in the unusual nature of our ideological grounding and ultimately, at the bottom of this, in our dependent-independent position in the concert of nations—even if these things were not specifically addressed in Alencar's book. It is a literary expression of the difficulties we had in trying to integrate both localist and European tonalities, controlled by the ideologies of favour and liberalism respectively. Not that the novel could actually eradicate this opposition; but it had to discover some arrangement by which these elements, instead of producing an incongruent form, would become part of a regulated system, with its own logic and its own—our own—problems, dealt with on their own appropriate level.[46]

For Schwarz, it is the greatness of Machado to have produced such a system, turning what in Alencar was a literary defect into a constructive principle. The process, Schwarz argues, is "a complex variant of the so-called dialectic of form and content: our literary material only achieves sufficient density when it takes in, at the level of content, the unsuitability of the European form, without which we cannot be complete."[47]

What makes Schwarz's analysis so arresting is the more general applicability of his conclusions to literary production in other contexts of uneven development and dependency. Indeed, in elaborating an argument similar to Schwarz's, Glissant extends its compass to the national literatures of decolonizing countries. His theorization of their "irruption into modernity" echoes the Brazilian in its insistence on the need for disjunctions between form and content, and between formal models, to be dramatized and critiqued. The liberation and decolonization movements, Glissant argues, have "allowed peoples who yesterday inhabited the hidden side of the earth . . . to assert themselves in the face of a total world culture."[48] The context in which this self-assertion takes place—a context that is itself the product of imperialism and combined and uneven development, the context of a "total world culture"—is, however, an overdetermined one. The emerging national literatures confront a series of literary and cultural forms—both imported genres and indigenous styles—all at the same time. They must articulate and affirm the community while simultaneously critiquing the imposed models through which this has been done elsewhere. "The main difficulty facing national literatures today, as they are defined here," writes

Glissant, "is that they must combine mythification and demystification, this primal innocence with a learned craftiness."

> The fact is that these literatures do not have the time to develop harmoniously from the collective lyricism of Homer to the mordant scrutiny of Beckett. They must include all at once struggle, aggressiveness, belonging, lucidity, distrust of self, absolute love, contours of the landscape, emptiness of the cities, victories, and confrontations.

"This," he concludes, "is what I call our irruption into modernity."[49] Glissant's argument thus emphasizes how, in the Caribbean, that history of precipitous development combined with underdevelopment is registered homologically in the literary field, where it is translated into the coexistence of literary forms from different historical moments—the juxtaposition of elements of ancient epic, for example, alongside the kinds of narrative techniques associated with European high modernist works.

The Caribbean literary field is thus very different from its western European counterpart, which has tended to impose the strict categorization of forms and their assignment to a particular moment in an extended literary evolution.[50] But it is the distinctive shape of the Caribbean field that, in translating the irruptive and uneven character of modernity in the region, enables the disparate realities that result from this unevenness to be articulated as a unity, and so helps to create a dialectical image of a utopian future emancipated from the ravages of underdevelopment. This dialectical image, in other words, by revealing the unity of that condition of disparity, would expose its historicity and so point toward the possibility of its transformation. In later chapters I examine some fully fledged examples of this kind of emancipatory vision. Here, however, I continue to focus on early literary attempts to understand and articulate a divided historical experience.

Integral to the development of a narrative able to capture the overdetermined history of the Caribbean was not only the systematic inscription of formal incongruities but also the increasing incorporation of indigenous cultural forms and practices. The latter—including, for example, oral discourses and storytelling rituals, musical traditions, and religious practices such as vodun, Santeria, Shango, and Myal—were either noncanonical or considered inappropriate as literary subject matter, at least from the perspective of the traditional European literary field, which in addition to its hierarchical categorization of genres also maintained the separation of the aesthetic sphere from other fields of cultural and social life.[51] In the Caribbean, those other forms and practices had historically provided a means of expression when other outlets such as writing had been restricted or forbidden (most notably during the time of slavery). In being called on to function alongside consecrated literary conventions, they brought that embodied subaltern history into juxtaposition with elite articulations. We have already seen this to some extent in Carpentier's *The Kingdom of This World*, with its *real maravilloso* running together of the official history of Macandal's death alongside the mythic account of his escape, an account preserved, we are told, through the "tales" and "simple little songs" of the enslaved.[52]

Equally pertinent, however, is Jacques-Stéphen Alexis's own theory of *réalisme merveilleux*. Analyzing Haitian art, Alexis argues that it is "greatly differentiated from the Western art which has enriched us":

> Order, beauty, logic and controlled sensitiveness, we have received all that, but we intend to surpass it. Haitian art, in effect, presents the real, with its accompaniment of the strange and fantastic, of dreams and half light, of the mysterious and marvellous. . . . This art does not shrink from deformity, from shocks, from violent contrast, . . . and, astonishing result, it achieves a new balance, more contrasted, a composition equally harmonious in its contradictions, a wholly internal grace, born of singularity and antithesis.[53]

Here, then, the marvelous real is again associated with the simultaneity of contrasting features as elements of Western art are juxtaposed with what Alexis goes on to clarify as elements connected to African and Afro-Caribbean religio-cultural practices and worldviews: "the myth, the symbol; the stylised, the heraldic, even the hieratic."[54] This marvelous tendency will be present across the Caribbean, moreover, because of the "cultural confluence" of the region.[55] Yet—and it is here that Alexis seems further away than Carpentier from retreating into cultural essences—this condition is not a natural attribute of the New World but the result of historical and socioeconomic forces. Indeed, he explicitly associates "the possible dynamic integration of the Marvellous in realism" with the overlap of "modern life with its stern rates of production, with its concentration of great masses of men into industrial armies," with a life lived "in contact with Nature."[56] "The under-developed populations of the world," he writes, "know a blend of mechanical civilization and 'natural' life, so to speak."[57] By establishing this link to historical phenomena, Alexis makes of the marvelous real an aesthetic practice that responds to the concrete particularities of Haitian and, more generally, Caribbean experience. As such, not only does it provide a means to elucidate—rather than mystify—the determinants of this experience (Alexis argues that Haitians "express their whole consciousness of reality by the use of the Marvellous" in stories, songs, and so forth),[58] but also it becomes serviceable as an optic through which we can see different configurations of that condition of coexistent yet nonsynchronous realities.[59]

In light of Alexis's theorization of the marvelous real, we can return to what might be considered a discrepancy in my earlier discussion of modernity, as well as begin to identify the historical reasons for the emergence of conceptions of the Caribbean marvelous in the 1940s and 1950s. I noted that Glissant speaks of the "irruption into modernity" of the decolonizing countries, thus locating that irruption—and the related emergence of national literatures" that juxtapose radically different formal models—in the period of national liberation. Yet I also argued that the Caribbean enters modernity with its integration into the capitalist world system, a moment for which the year 1492 might stand as a convenient if imperfect marker. This difference in periodization can be explained by Glissant's emphasizing the point at which the decolonizing countries become visible on the world stage (recall that he refers to them as having until then inhabited "the hidden side of the earth"). While I think it preferable to conceive of the Caribbean's modernity in terms of the *longue durée* of the world system, Glissant's accent on the irruptive difference in the region's relationship to modernity signaled by the decolonization period makes sense inasmuch as it captures that moment when various territories did seek to stake a claim to modernity on their own terms.

We can also perceive a deeper historical connection between these social changes and the literary transformations taking place. Since the unrest of the 1930s, the colonial authorities had been seeking to recalibrate the relationship between center and periphery, promoting development to alleviate tensions in the region. With regards to the Anglophone Caribbean, notes Clive Thomas, "More and more people, including the Colonial Office, began to believe that a country could only break out of the 'vicious circles of poverty' or 'the disequilibrium traps of underdevelopment and dependence' if it diversified and became differentiated through developing a broad-based manufacturing sector."[60] Of course, this expansion in manufacturing as envisaged by the Colonial Office was geared toward satisfying the imperialist demands of the metropole. In fact, as Thomas observes, "Britain's policies encouraged increasing domination of the region's economy by transnational corporations (TNCs) and reinforced the 'centre/periphery' legacy of the Second World War."[61] At the same time, however, many of the emerging national independence movements were increasingly emphasizing large-scale industrialization as a way to secure an end to dependency. The model for these industrialization strategies was Puerto Rico's Operation Bootstrap, which was based on attracting foreign investment into the country to encourage rapid development. In the French Antilles, the situation was slightly different, though in some respects the consequences were analogous: departmentalization in 1946 led to greater assimilation into the metropole and with it an influx of subsidies and imported goods that provided the semblance of development; yet beneath this modernized superstructure, autonomous economic bases were being eroded.

While it is perhaps problematic to speak of that mid-twentieth-century period as witnessing an "irruption into modernity," therefore, it is certainly the case that in the Caribbean something of an irruption into *modernization* was occurring. The resulting social changes included a substantial increase in rural-to-urban migration as large numbers of peasants left the land to find work in the city.[62] Dozens of Caribbean novels deal with this migratory movement and its impact. Indeed, we have already seen how it forms the backdrop to *Masters of the Dew*. And we have seen, too, how that novel seems at times to verge on tipping into a kind of proto-marvelous realism—the result, it was suggested, of the text registering in its political unconscious the "shock" of history, the coexistence of the rural peasant world and the modernizing city. Now, though, this coexistence was becoming not only increasingly visible but also increasingly intimate, with the peasantry actually appearing within the cityscape. Hence—and thus to historicize properly my earlier commentary on marvelous realism—that shock could move firmly into the consciousness of texts: as Denning argues, marvelous or magical realism, emerging out of "the clash of peasant and proletarian worlds," is "perhaps best seen as a second stage in the proletarian avant-garde. If the first moment was dominated by a paradoxically ahistorical modernism that tried to document the lived experience of the radically new factory and tenement, the magical realism of 1949 is the return of the repressed history, lived and witnessed by the exiles and migrants."[63] The paradoxically ahistorical modernism Denning refers to could be said to apply to many of the 1930s barracks-yard novels from the Anglophone Caribbean, including, for example, C. L. R. James's *Minty Alley* (1936), with its detailed observations on working-class life but lack of the wider spatial and temporal compass that would set those details in context. With *Masters of the Dew*, we witnessed a tendency to lapse into a similar kind of ahistoricism, albeit in relation to the rural world. It is only with later novels like Alexis's *L'espace d'un cillement* (In the Flicker of an Eyelid) (1959) that we see the more systematic integration of the shock of history and the co-existence of nonsynchronous worlds.

Indeed, Alexis's novel is particularly interesting in this respect, since the highly structured allegorical framework that underpins *In the Flicker of an Eyelid* organizes history in such a way as to come close to providing the dialectical image of a projected future I spoke of earlier. The novel thematizes the "return of the repressed history," in Denning's phrase, and mediates it formally through the use of a marvelous real style. Martin Munro contends that in this text "the magical realism of Alexis's previous two fictional works gives way to a profoundly realistic engagement with urban living."[64] However, I would argue that, bearing out my reading of Alexis's marvelous real as a phenomenon deriving from, and expressive of, a condition of uneven and combined development, *In the Flicker of an Eyelid* does deploy this narrative modality in articulating the Port-au-Prince cityscape. True, the marvelous real is more obviously present in Alexis's earlier *Les arbres musiciens* (1957), in which the isolated mountain area inhabited by the character Gonaïbo, who lives in a sort of mythic existence in harmony with nature, is penetrated by the U.S. occupiers. As they clear the land for new sugar plantations, Gonaïbo suffers, as Munro puts it, the "irruption of the American 'real' (the machinery, the pollution) into his own reality."[65] Yet rather than seeing this only as the clash of "real" and "mythic" cultural dispositions, we might also understand it in terms of the collision of a precapitalist mode of production with a capitalist one. In this view, it becomes easier to establish continuities with *In the Flicker of an Eyelid*, for a similar sense of irruption is present here, only now it is felt in relation to the teeming social and economic worlds that overlap and coexist within the city.

The Sensation Bar—the location for much of the novel's action and the workplace of its heroine La Niña, a prostitute—serves as a microcosm of this condition. It is packed with proletarian workers, migrants, U.S. marines, merchants, and bourgeois mulattoes. Just outside the bar, meanwhile, the "peasants are trading their bits of nothing for dirt."[66] It is this dizzying accumulation of realities that invests the text with its marvelous quality. But, as suggested earlier, that quality is there too in the narrative style, which reflects Alexis's emphasis on heightening the senses as a key to the marvelous and its enabling of a "whole consciousness of reality." Take, for example, the following passage, in which the novel's hero, El Caucho, is watching La Niña:

> Why did those feet, little live animals with an existence nearly separate from the rest of the body, produce a vibration in his head, a shock, a recoil? Why do the roses of her eyes have that vibrancy . . . ? It's as if, at some earlier time, he had had a dream, quickly forgotten, and this reality suddenly revived the old dream, gave substance to a vague image, lost and then lost again, an image that had never materialized despite the retinal persistence. Those feet are two living animals—the roses of her eyes are two flower sorceresses. (25)

Here the marvelous transmutation in El Caucho's perception of La Niña's physical features not only sharpens his awareness of her presence but also begins to awaken his memory. El Caucho and La Niña in fact knew each other as children in Oriente in Cuba. Both, however, have repressed this memory, just as they have repressed much of their past to be able to cope with the present.

The recovery of this personal history becomes a central theme in the novel, especially with respect to La Niña, who has been desensitized by her life as a prostitute. As her doctor explains to her when she asks why she cannot remember her past, this shutting down of the senses has been necessary for her survival: "You don't want to remember," he tells her. "You prefer to bury the past because it's more convenient. . . . You're probably right to do it that way. With your character and type of work, it's probably far better for you not to have any memories" (117–18). Accordingly, it is the gradual restoration of La Niña's senses—her return to her body, as it were—that signals the recovery of her memories and of her sense of selfhood. This restoration is inextricable from

El Caucho, whose love helps to resensitize her body, and who undergoes a similar experience, with both of them confronting their repressed past as they consummate their relationship: "Bodies joined, Rafaël and Eglantina [El Caucho's and La Niña's real names, also now recovered] are living a moment of fullness, vibrant and gentle—they are stirring up their beginnings, their childish love; they see everything again. The nearby sea and trade winds blow all around and create the aria of this romance from their past" (217). As their newly heightened senses thereby bring the past into the present, El Caucho and La Niña accede to a "whole consciousness of reality," to an apprehension of their lives from their shared origins in rural Oriente to their time in Port-au-Prince.

However, this theme of the recovery and sharpening of the senses is also present in the text on a formal level. The book is organized into six "mansions," each representing one of the five senses plus the "sixth sense." These in turn are connected to another framing device, that of the Christian Passion. The action in the novel takes place during Holy Week, the days of which correspond to the mansions. Events can thus be seen as leading up to the "resurrection" of the protagonists. Again, this is especially the case for La Niña, whose suffering on a number of occasions is portrayed in terms of martyrdom and the crucifixion. But it is not the Christian tradition alone that is being evoked by the use of Holy Week as a backdrop: the novel also depicts the vodun celebrations occurring at the same time, thus emphasizing the creolized condition of Haitian society. In fact, the whole allegorical structure of the novel as it relates to the individual lives of both protagonists can be rearticulated on another level, that of the collectivity. La Niña quite clearly stands as a figure for Haiti, her sexual exploitation at the hands of U.S. marines representing the country's penetration and abuse by the United States, and her subsequent "resurrection" imaging its liberation. (La Niña's martyrdom and "crucifixion" recall Manuel's role as a sacrificial victim but also raise a series of issues around gender, to which I return in a moment.) El Caucho, meanwhile, could be said to figure the pan-Caribbean, given his peripatetic wanderings across the region. As such, his contribution to La Niña's renewal is suggestive of the importance of regional solidarity to the struggle of individual nations for freedom (indeed, El Caucho explicitly advocates Caribbean federation [73]).

But the novel's allegorical significance goes further than this. El Caucho, again like Manuel, also personifies the contemporary social transformations occurring across the region; he too has been radicalized by the struggle against colonialism and capitalism and wishes to see the reorganization of society for the benefit of the poor and powerless. Moreover, the return of El Caucho's and La Niña's repressed personal histories could be said to figure the return of a repressed social history, irrupting into visibility on the back of economic and demographic changes. Indeed, the protagonists' recovery of their past in Oriente, a past associated with a rural existence, suggests the emerging recognition of the symbiosis of the rural peasant world and the city. But whereas in Roumain the rural world was ultimately idealized and resituated as an organic whole outside history, in Alexis's text there is a sense that, while it is vital that the rural world and its connection to the urban core be acknowledged, it is also undergoing irrevocable historical change. This change brings loss, but also new socioeconomic dynamics, including greater urbanization, which give rise to the possibility that as the old order collapses, society can be reorganized in the way that El Caucho envisions.

Thus, if *Masters of the Dew* gestured to the potential of this period but could not project its historical fulfillment because of its inseparability from the breakdown of the very community it wished to consecrate, *In the Flicker of an Eyelid* looks forward to the new social relations and forms of collectivity that might materialize this promise. Both novels share the theme of sacrifice and renewal, but in Alexis's text, the different type of community that this process will inaugurate is, precisely, still to come. Hence the significance of allegory as a structural principle in the novel: because the truly liberated nation-state remains an abstract potential, its literary projection reflects this quality in an abstract formal mode.

In this respect, it is interesting that Alexis introduces a second sacrificial motif at the end of the text, one that displaces the expected narrative closure that seems set to follow the martyrdom-resurrection cycle of the six mansions and its culmination in the consummation of El Caucho and La Niña's love. In a final coda, we see La Niña leave El Caucho and set off to secure her autonomy so that she might return to him as a fully independent person, capable of delivering herself from historylessness. In this she is heeding the words of her doctor: "to have a right to your memories, you mustn't depend on anyone else; you have to be able to live by your own means" (119). This too clearly has an allegorical resonance: the need to secure a nation-state free from the ties of dependency. But it might also be read as a form of self-critique, complicating the novel's use of a series of masculinist tropes that recall those in *Masters of the Dew*. The manner in which La Niña is "reborn" and her body resensitized through her heterosexual relationship with El Caucho, her symbolic conflation with Haiti as a land under threat of penetration, and the difference between La Niña as emblematic of a country seeking liberation and El Caucho as personifying the forces that will effect this liberation (she as passive and he as active, in other words)—all these themes suggest the persistence of heteropatriarchal social relations. Thus La Niña's desire to leave El Caucho, sacrificing the relationship to affirm her independence, can be read as signaling the need to root out such power relations just as much as those of economic dependency.

That La Niña's departure suspends narrative resolution indicates that genuine and thoroughgoing liberation lies in the future. More is required than the restoration of identity symbolized by La Niña's reclamation of selfhood; the achievement of national independence alone is insufficient without the full-scale reorganization of society. Only against the backdrop of this kind of revolution could the text figure the long-term success of El Caucho and La Niña's relationship. Such an interpretation is supported by Alexis's own comments on the novel: in one interview, note Coates and Danticat, he spoke of La Niña and El Caucho

> meeting once more, in Cuba, in the fourth volume that was supposed to follow *In the Flicker*. After years of facing the difficulties of everyday life and their differences in character, "their love will be a little more possible." Replying to the question why that love would be more viable in Cuba, Alexis replied categorically that "Cuba [meaning revolutionary Cuba] is the Caribbean future."[67]

In *In the Flicker of an Eyelid*, however, both that future and its potential literary figuration remain beyond the horizon.

A raft of other Caribbean novels engage with this period of promise in which new freedoms and new forms of liberated statehood were on the cusp of emerging. I now consider several Anglophone and Francophone texts from the 1950s. Broadly speaking, the transformations taking place then and in the preceding couple of decades affected territories across the region and were registered in the corresponding literatures. Think, for instance, of Dora Alonso's *Tierra adentro* (1944), with its focus on the problems of the peasantry in rural Cuba; or the Dominican Andrés Francisco Requena's *Los enemigos de la tierra* (1942), which chronicles the migration of a peasant to the city to work in the sugar mills; or, in Puerto Rico, Pedro Juvenal Rosa's *Las masas mandan* (1936) or Enrique Laguerre's cycles of novels from the 1940s and 1950s; or Cola Debrot's *Mijn zuster de negerin* (1935), with its return to a rural plantation in Curaçao and evocation of the collapse of the old order. However, my concern here ultimately is with tracing the mutations in certain topoi, so I concentrate on the Anglophone and Francophone traditions, not only because such topoi are most prominent there, but also to avoid obscuring the specificities of different national trajectories during this period within too broad a framework (the distinctive situations of Cuba [the revolution] and the Dominican Republic [the Trujillo dictatorship] serve in particular as warnings against overgeneralization).

First, though, I want to address an issue raised in the foregoing analysis of Alexis: national allegory. It is impossible to introduce this term without at least making reference to the controversy surrounding Jameson's essay "Third-World Literature in the Era of Multinational Capitalism" (1986), in which he (in)famously argued that "all third-world texts are necessarily . . . allegorical, and in a very specific way: they are to be read as what I will call *national allegories*."[68] I do not wish to dwell on the debates sparked by this essay, except to say that I find

some of the rereadings of it that seek to offer a qualified defense more suggestive than many of the blanket condemnations that followed in the wake of Aijaz
Ahmad's now equally famous rejoinder.[69] Neil Larsen, for instance, argues that
while it is potentially erroneous to reduce a priori every instance of "third world
literature" to national allegory, it

> seems to me correct to regard this allegorising process as a *structural tendency* in
> the narrative forms of "peripheral" modernities—a tendency that may, in many in-
> stances, never amount to *more* than an abstract possibility. If it can be allowed that
> the third world nation exists, on one plane at least, only as an abstract possibility
> . . . then it follows that attempts to represent the nation, to portray it in a narrative
> or symbolic medium, will reflect this abstraction within the formal medium itself.[70]

Larsen's hypothesis reinforces my reading of *In the Flicker of an Eyelid* as using
allegory to represent a nation that is yet to come. But the question remains as
to why the personal relationship between El Caucho and La Niña appears so
overdetermined as to make the national reading unavoidable. The novel's situating of the action within the context of imperialism ensures that invocations of
autonomy and self-determination resonate against this backdrop. It is for this
reason that those resonances sound in terms of national freedom: it is the nation-state that mediates between individuals or collectivities and the pressures
exerted by imperialism, the effects of which are registered in terms precisely
of the internal organization of the nation-state and the position assigned to it
in the world system. Consequently any struggle for meaningful independence
must pass through nationalism, even if this is not in itself an end point (indeed, in Alexis's novel, regionalism is just as important).[71] Thus, as Neil Lazarus
observes in his own "qualified defence" of Jameson's essay, if the Third World
is taken to name a political desire—that of anti-imperialism and popular self-
determination—rather than a particular place, it "seems plausible to propose
that literature which rises to the challenge of 'third-worldness' will of necessity allegorise the nation."[72] Assuredly, Alexis's novel is saturated with this Third
World desire, so that even as the accent falls on the love story and individual
autonomy, the national dimensions are inescapable.

But here we might also introduce Imre Szeman's "Who's Afraid of National
Allegory?" which offers an equally insightful take on Jameson's essay. Szeman
points to the emphasis on "cultural revolution" in Jameson's analysis of the dif-
fering relationships between the public and the private in the First and Third
Worlds, and on the need for such a revolution in the context of decolonization
to divest the colonized of the habits and psychic structures implanted by colonialism. Because these are determined by political and economic relationships, they cannot be dealt with only by psychological therapies; but political
and economic transformation alone is similarly not enough. Thus, argues Sze-

man, Jameson's concept of national allegory "points to the ways in which the psychological points to the political and the trauma of subalternity finds itself 'projected outwards' (allegorically) into the 'cultural.' Very crudely, the cultural is what lies 'between' the psychological and the political, unifying 'theory and practice' in such a way that it is *only* there that the 'baleful and crippling' habits that are the residue of colonialism can be addressed and potentially overcome."[73] Of particular interest to me here is the way Szeman's reading draws attention both to the importance of the body to the dynamics of colonization and decolonization and to the weight its literary representation will bear. What his exegesis suggests is that insofar as the cultural mediates the history of colonial power relations—indeed, insofar as colonialism has written itself on social and cultural practice—representations of such practices will on some level speak to the impact of domination. They are thus also likely to demonstrate (recalling Larsen and Lazarus here) a structural tendency to speak to the national as inextricably bound up with the functioning of domination and as the arena through which any social and cultural transformation must pass if thoroughgoing liberation is to be achieved. Allegory as it is used here, then, is (as Jameson stressed in his essay) not of the order of a one-to-one equivalence; rather, it refers to a mode of reading that would be able to locate the multiple determinations in which experience is enmeshed.

As an example of this, I want to look now at Sam Selvon's *A Brighter Sun*, published in 1952. This novel is amenable to a national-allegory reading, with the development of its hero Tiger's consciousness reflecting the development of national consciousness in Trinidad in the 1930s and 1940s. But in line with the foregoing arguments, this allegorization is more complex than the personal simply mirroring the political. The novel references and thematizes many of the historical changes I have already discussed. Tiger leaves his Indian peasant family—workers on a plantation in the sugarcane district of Chaguanas—and travels to the village of Barataria, just outside Port of Spain. Barataria itself experiences rapid semi-urbanization as part of a wider process of modernization (symptomatically, one now sees "a thatched hut, and next to it a small modern bungalow"),[74] while Port of Spain too is developing in uneven fashion: "[Tiger] compared the broken-down hovels staining the Laventille hillside with the houses of the white people. Over there, nastiness and poverty, a tin cup of weak tea and a johnny cake or a roti. Over there, motorcars and—what did white people eat?" (98). The opening of U.S. military bases during the war intensifies this irruption into modernization, leading not only to an influx of hard currency, but also to the building of new infrastructure, including the "Churchill-Roosevelt Highway" on which Tiger himself labors after having abandoned subsistence farming on his own plot. However, Selvon does not just seek to describe the socioeconomic transformations taking place. His novel—like those of Alexis and Roumain—also registers the search for a form capable of articulating the impact of those changes, in particular the increasing overlap and juxtaposition of social worlds.

In "The Folk and Caribbean Literature," Gordon Rohlehr emphasizes how West Indian writers like Selvon and Roger Mais were confronted with the problem of "understanding and expressing the flow between rural 'folk' sensibility and experiences of semi- or total urbanisation."[75] Commenting on Lamming's remarks regarding the preoccupation of West Indian writers with "peasant" societies (in which Lamming labels Selvon's work "essentially peasant"), Rohlehr argues that a "more pliable theory is required, one which can accommodate the interplay between country, town and big city, between peasant, artisan and city-slicker or factory worker, and between the ill-defined classes of the West Indies."[76] In an expanded version of the article, he pointed to Selvon's use in *A Brighter Sun* of a "linguistic continuum paralleling the socio-cultural one" to express that overlap of realities.[77] Something similar is going on, I would argue, at the related level of narrative form. Specifically, I have in mind the newsreel technique deployed at the beginning of a number of chapters, which juxtaposes world-historical events such as the outbreak of World War II with seemingly trivial local occurrences:

> On New Year's Day, 1939, while Trinidadians who had money or hopes of winning money were attending the races in Queen's Park Savannah, Port of Spain, a number of Jewish refugees fleeing Nazi persecution in Europe landed on the island. There was an almost instant increase in the rental of residences and business places, and later more refugees were refused entrance. A development plan costing $14,000,000 was approved by the Secretary of State for the Colonies but nipped in the bud when war was declared. . . . Emergency regulations were introduced, mail and telegrams censored, the churches prayed for peace, and the adjacent territorial waters were proclaimed a prohibited area. A man went about the streets of the city riding a bicycle and balancing a bottle of rum on his head. An East Indian, reputedly mad, walked to the wharf and dipped a key in the sea and went away muttering to himself. A big burly Negro called Mussolini, one-legged and arrogant, chased a small boy who was teasing him and fell down, cursing loudly, much to the amusement of passers-by. (3)

On the one hand, a kind of epic realism seems to be at work here, the text evoking a broad sweep of history to set the events in Trinidad in context. On the other, there is the simultaneous introduction of the modernist technique of montage—indeed, as noted earlier, the narrative appears to replicate the style of the modern technology of the newsreel. But this contrast is then pushed further to the point of dissonance by the running together of international incidents with the random trivia of everyday life, the affairs of government with the stuff of local hearsay.

We might see in this dissonance a version of the phenomenon that Schwarz analyzed in the context of Brazil: the incongruities that result when an imported form runs up against local tonalities—incongruities that for Schwarz could not be divorced from Brazil's dependent position within the capitalist world system. In Selvon's text, the modernist narrative technique of the newsreel montage confronts a local content (the cyclist with the rum, the mad Indian, the one-legged Negro) that seems to deflate and ironize that form. Moreover, this content would appear far better adapted to a different kind of formal mode—say, the oral tale. What Selvon does, then, is to produce something like a second-order montage at the level of form, which takes in, at the level of content, the modernist aesthetic of the newsreel montage in juxtaposition with that local material seemingly garnered from gossip and rumor. In this way, the narrative underscores Trinidad's unevenly developed and dependent status (already invoked explicitly through the references to the colonial development plan) by figuring it, formally, in that deployment of a modernist aesthetic ill adapted to, and destabilized by its encounter with, a local experience of history.

Incidentally, it is worth noting that we began by talking about marvelous realism's affinity for montage, yet with Selvon we are dealing with a narrative form closer to social realism. Neil Larsen's work again provides a way of thinking about this shift. Earlier we noted his emphasis on the difference between montage in its surrealist usage in Europe, where it served to defamiliarize the everyday, and montage in its marvelous realist usage in the Caribbean and Latin America, where its shock effects are in fact the routine experiences of everyday life, the juxtaposition of radically different lifeworlds, a historical reality resulting from uneven development. Consequently an approach that in Europe might have produced a fantastical image here produces something nearer a realistic portrayal of society, and increasingly so as that coexistence of disparate realities becomes ever more visible as a result of socioeconomic and demographic change. Hence the move from a marvelous to a social realism is not the leap it might have seemed, for in this context, far from being antithetical, these narrative modes are allied by the demands of articulating the complexities of the social reality.[78]

If Selvon produces a literary homologue of the condition of dependency and uneven development, then does *A Brighter Sun* in turn furnish a dialectical image that might serve as the projected homologue of the transformation of that condition? Certainly the novel would seem to stage a search for one, while implying that the anticipated independent nation-state will provide the grounds for the realization of such a transformation. As suggested earlier, the emergence of this potential national polity is figured through Tiger and his rising self-awareness, and this connection is established in part by the way he mediates the search for a dialectical image via his own struggle to make sense of the world around him. We have already seen Tiger's growing consciousness of the situation in Trinidad in the scene where he muses on the difference between Laventille and the whites' quarter. This forms part of a longer episode in which he goes to Port of Spain for the first time, his visit a metonym for the clash of worlds produced by rural-to-urban migration. But the trip also figures the way in which the socio-economic and demographic changes taking place represent a moment of great potential. As Tiger looks out across Port of Spain from atop a hill, the narrative conveys the expansion of his consciousness:

> The wind came down from the hills behind St. Anns in thrusts of sweet, wild smells, and again he felt the power in it he would have liked to possess. . . . He felt as limitless as the space between him and the sky. Tiger didn't know the sky didn't exist except as a reflection: to him it was real, a blue bowl covering the world. Clouds were there because there had to be rain for things to grow; he knew which ones portended rainfall—not those white ones flying now, but great grey ones, tumbling into one another, until the whole sky was like slate. How high those clouds is? How high the sky? It must be good to fork up the land in the sky, it so blue! And everything you plant, it must be to come out blue too. There would be books to tell him of all that, of course. He must hurry up and learn to read. . . . Why hadn't they sent him to school, instead of having him work so many years in the canefields? (99)

The shift here from the third person to a discourse clearly mediated through Tiger's thoughts emphasizes his acceding to a more comprehensive grasp of the world around him—to his inscribing himself into that world in terms of his own consciousness of it rather than via an external optic. As such, the passage gestures to a future in which Trinidad is "grasped" indigenously, freed from the influence of the colonial power. Indeed, as Tiger begins to desire to know more about the landscape, he comes to a question that of necessity implicates the structures put in place by the colonial system as a whole: why did he have to work in the fields rather than go to school?

As Tiger matures, he becomes increasingly aware that something is systemically wrong with society and that change will come only through collective action. This is most evident after his attempts to find someone to treat his sick wife Urmilla, when he is turned away by both an Indian and a black doctor before a white European helps him. The next day, when Tiger goes to harangue the first two, a crowd gathers around him:

> "I had to go quite in Port of Spain, in St. Clair, and who you think I get? A wite doctor, man! You don't see how is a shame? I mean, you don't see how wite man must always laugh at we coloured people, because we so stupid? You don't see it is that black people can't get on in this country at all at all?"

The people murmured in agreement. A wrong done to one is a wrong done to all.

"Same ting happen wen my old queen was sick, no doctor won't come, we had was wait till morning." . . .

"But what we going to do about this thing, man?" Tiger cried. "How long this kind of thing going on? Why the people who ruling we don't do something about it? Why weself don't do something about it?" (189)

Tiger's newfound awareness of the problems in society pushes him toward his call for collective action. But crucially this collectivity is defined across ethnic lines: the way he uses "coloured" and "black" here suggests they have become political (rather than racial) labels for "weself." Indeed, when Tiger says "we," he is apparently invoking a shared Trinidadian identity. Moreover, this proto-nationalist sentiment is articulated in class terms: Tiger's ire is directed at the fact he was turned away on account of his poverty by the bourgeois Indian and black doctors—"these damn people," he cries, "who have money and moving in society, who does laugh and spit on we poor people" (188)—thereby implying that the "something" he suggests needs to be done would have to involve the reorganization of society for the benefit of the people.

Tiger's experiences thus do seem to allegorize the emergence of a national consciousness in the manner that my reading of Jameson's theory of national allegory indicated they might: that is, not via the simple mirroring of the political in the personal, but through the way Tiger's personal ordeals necessarily assume a public dimension, since the conditions and problems he confronts in his everyday life are inextricable from the systemic impact of colonialism and imperialism. Thus any attempt to alter the pattern of his existence will implicate, at some level, the colonial organization of the state. It is for this reason that questions regarding the nation and the possible instantiation of a different type of state seem to loom over so many passages in the novel, for it is through the nation-state that any challenge to the colonial order would have to pass for its aims to be realized.

Think, for example, of the plots of land farmed by Tiger and his companions. Tiger acquires his plot after moving away from the plantation, and insofar as his new life broadens his experiences and contributes to raising his consciousness, it is of a piece with the more general sense of potential associated with the changes under way in this period: the erosion of the old order and the rise of new freedoms; modernization and its attendant economic opportunities; and the more widespread articulation of the demands of the people (not least as access to education expanded). The representation of the plots ties them to this potential. The self-sufficiency they embody not only invokes the legacy of peasant land-holdings as a potential material basis for economic autonomy but also functions as a motif for the possible future form of an independent nation-state. Take the conversations between Tiger and Sookdeo, the old Indian with a neighboring plot. Sookdeo's garden is a haphazard mix of crops and weeds that, despite the chaos, is very successful. His planting methods are derived from experience and inherited knowledge and thus gesture to the plot tradition of the peasantry. He also ignores the advice of the "agriculture man" from the government, who comes with "plenty book knowledge" to help the smallholders increase their yield (77). Tiger, however, does follow the agriculturalist's recommendations, with some success, although he is equally keen to learn from Sookdeo's experience. In one sense, this simply exemplifies a wider theme in the novel: Tiger's having to negotiate between knowledge gained through practice and knowledge gained through abstract learning. But on another level, the accommodation Tiger seeks over agricultural methods could be seen as figuring the necessity for a future nation-state to integrate that tradition of resistance and self-sufficiency represented by the peasantry and the plot system with the kinds of modern technologies for which the government adviser stands. In other words, Tiger's approach to his plot could be regarded as emblematic of the search for a modern self-determining collectivity with its foundations in indigenous knowledge and practice.

This line of thought might seem to be stretching the point somewhat. But the interpretation is given credence, I believe, by the subsequent destruction of the plots to make way for the highway the U.S. Army is building. As noted earlier, Tiger quits the land to work for the Americans. Just as their arrival on the island in some ways contributes to the emergence of new freedoms, not least because the Americans pay higher wages, so Tiger's time as part of the road surveying party seems to hold out the promise of acquiring new skills and knowledge. Yet the work ultimately becomes alienating, and although he does learn about technologies such as the theodolite, he does not have the opportunity to grasp them for himself in the way that Fanon, for example, suggested was necessary as part of the process of decolonization and nation building:

> If the building of a bridge does not enrich the awareness of those who work on it, then that bridge ought not to be built. . . . The bridge should not be "parachuted down" from above; it should not be imposed by a *deus ex machina* upon the social scene; on the contrary it should come from the muscles and the brains of the citizens. Certainly, there may well be need of engineers and architects; but the local party leaders should be always present, so that the new techniques can make their way into the cerebral desert of the citizen.[79]

The same point can be made with respect to the road, which is very much imposed from above by the U.S. military. That it also causes the destruction of the plots and, indirectly, the death of Sookdeo, who never recovers from the loss of his garden, freights everything with added symbolic weight. More than ever, the plots look like figures for an emergent self-determining collectivity, for their fate seems to point emblematically to the danger that, even as the old order falls away, the promise of change and of freedom from dependency is already being threatened by U.S. imperialism.

A number of other novels from the Anglophone Caribbean in the 1950s evoke the sense of promise awakened in the preceding decades, while also portending how this potential for transformation might be lost. Ralph de Boissière's *Crown Jewel* (1952), for example, invokes the turbulence of the 1930s and its occasioning of, as James put it with respect to the Haitian Revolution, "one of those rare moments when society is at [the] boiling point and therefore fluid."[80] Set in Trinidad, the novel offers a fictionalized account of the rise of unionism and working-class leaders such as Uriah Butler and Jim Barratt (embodied in the character of Ben Le Maître). Under pressure from popular action for change, the entrenched structures of the ruling order are crumbling, with the greater social mobility this engenders symbolized by the relationship between the middle-class French Creole André de Coudray and the working-class black Elena Henriques. Indeed, their relationship looks forward to the political conjunction of the 1950s in which de Boissière was writing, figuring as it does the alliance between the black and brown middle classes and the working-class masses that formed the backbone of the anticolonial nationalist movements.

George Lamming's *In the Castle of My Skin* (1953), meanwhile, conveys a similar sense of fluidity through the child narrator G.'s inchoate consciousness. Again we see the breakdown of the rigid colonial hierarchy—summarized as "The landlord. The overseer. The villager"—under the pressure of socioeconomic and political change.[81] The novel's Barbadian villagers are left confounded as age-old certainties regarding the land are overthrown, yet there emerges too a new consciousness of oppression, an awareness articulated most clearly by Trumper, who returns to the village from the United States able to buy a piece of land but determined not to, since he recognizes that it would "make the people who sellin' it think they doin' the right thing."[82] The narrative, however, also points to the possible dissipation of this potential for transformation through the machinations of Mr. Slime, whose complicity in the dispossession of the villagers foretells the failings of the rising national bourgeoisie.

Less obviously, it is possible to read another well-known text from this period, V. S. Naipaul's *Miguel Street* (1959), as an allegory of contemporary social change in which the emphasis again falls on the loss of a potential for renewal. In the eyes of the novel's child narrator, Miguel Street is a place of endless possibility, its inhabitants infused with an energy for self-invention. However, as the protagonist grows older, he begins to regard many of these projections as hollow or self-deluding, and indeed, most end tragically. The hardening of the growing boy's naive consciousness thus parallels the congealment of the street's promise, a motif that is connected tangentially to the wider changes occurring in Trinidad. For example, one year after the death of the failed poet B. Wordsworth, the narrator can "find no sign of the poet's house. It hadn't vanished, just like that. It had been pulled down, and a big, two-storied building had taken its place . . . and there was brick and concrete everywhere. . . . It was just as though B. Wordsworth had never existed."[83] The possibility for self-invention embodied by B. Wordsworth is not fulfilled; it is buried and lost, just as the land is concreted over. As with the road in *A Brighter Sun*, then, the literal and figurative petrifaction of the street seems to point to the ossification of the moment when (pace James) society is fluid, and so to foreshadow later disappointments over the potential for national self-invention.

A comparable pattern is evident in a number of Francophone Caribbean novels from the same period (only for Martinique, Guadeloupe, and French Guiana, the anticipation of collective renewal hinged less on prospective independence than on departmentalization, which many regarded as a stepping-stone to greater freedom). In the Martinican Joseph Zobel's *La rue Cases-Nègres* (1950), the phenomenon of rural-to-urban migration is once more of central importance, structuring the journey of the protagonist José from a rural plantation to the town of Petit Bourg to the capital Fort-de-France. Each stage signals a breakdown in tradition, but also the appearance of new possibilities. The death of the storyteller Médouze, for instance, signifies the demise of the customs connected to the plantation; but the knowledge that the old man embodied is preserved by José, only now in conjunction with the skills he learns at school. The novel's depiction of Fort-de-France, meanwhile, shows how entrenched power relations are under pressure from greater social mobility. The socioeconomic forces driving these changes, however, also sow the seeds of future difficulties, notably cultural alienation and the renewal of class domination.

Similarly, Glissant's first novel, *La Lézarde* (The Ripening) (1958), is set against the backdrop of the Martinican elections of 1945, which hold out the potential for the radical political transformation of the island. The key to this transformation (echoing to some extent both Roumain and Selvon) lies in the coming together of the country and the city, and of tradition and modernity. The country-tradition axis is represented by Thaël, a mountain dweller who knows "the old legends, who cares for the mysteries and who speaks like a prophet."[84] He is counterpointed to Mathieu, one of a group of political activists from the city and a historian whose approach to the past is heavily intellectualized. His alliance with Thaël provides a dialectical image of the potential unity of existence, which in turn points to the possibility of effecting liberation from a historical condition of disparity and dependency. The action designed to materially fulfill this possibility in the novel is mediated through the imagery of sacrifice. Mathieu and his group have enlisted Thaël to kill a government official, Garin, whom they view as an obstacle to political change. In carrying out this task, Thaël sacrifices his purity—he "falls" from the Edenic idyll of his mountain home—to help found the new social order. Yet the narrative is freighted with portents that the ultimate aim of this sacrificial act will prove elusive. After carrying out the murder and spending time in the plains, Thaël wishes to return to his rural idyll with his lover Valérie—a retreat from history that recalls the conclusion of *Masters of the Dew*. However, Valérie is savaged by Thaël's dogs, and the narrative ends on the image of her bloody corpse, with Thaël facing up to the prospect of journeying back down to the plains.

Glissant's text thus returns us to the motif of sacrifice with which we began our discussion of Roumain. But if in Roumain's work, Manuel's death coincided with Eagleton's definition of sacrifice as "the performative act which brings a new social order into being," in *The Ripening* this motif is beginning to become associated with the failure to realize a potential for transformation.[85] The conclusion of Glissant's novel also brings the issue of gender relations back into focus. An instructive comparison might be drawn between Valérie's death, wherein she too becomes something of a sacrificial victim, and La Niña's sacrificial status in Alexis's *In the Flicker of an Eyelid*. That novel ends with La Niña postponing her relationship with El Caucho to secure autonomy on her own terms, a gesture that figured, I argued, the need not only to achieve national independence but also to struggle for the total reorganization of society, including the dismantling of patriarchal power relations. By contrast, Valérie's death at the very moment she and Thaël look to begin their life together not only points figuratively to the problems that will beset the attempt to establish a new political order, but might also be read as suggesting, more specifically, that significant among those problems will be the maintenance of patriarchal frameworks and the continuation of the specific violence done to female corporeality. Indeed, it is clear from a number of the other texts cited earlier that more often than not, the rapid social and political changes they depict do not include a radical overhaul of gender relations. One thinks, for example, of the position of Urmilla in Selvon's *A Brighter Sun*, and in particular of the stillbirth of her son as a consequence of Tiger beating her.

The persistence of such patriarchal relations of power must be seen as itself a sign that certain underlying socioeconomic relationships remain in place. Thus the connection implicit in Glissant's novel between the violent subjugation of women's bodies and the trope of tragic sacrifice, itself problematic in gender terms insofar as it frequently taps into a masculinist narrative of heroic male deeds supported by passive female helpmates, further associates this trope with a more general failure to realize a potential for social transformation.

This association is reinforced in other novels from the period. Take, for example, John Hearne's *Voices under the Window* (1955). In terms of symbolism, it is possible to draw a comparison here with de Boissière's *Crown Jewel*. That novel had the romance between André de Coudray and Elena Henriques, which allegorized the alliance between the middle and working classes. Hearne's text has the romance between the middle-class, light-skinned politician Mark Lattimer and Brysie, the black schoolteacher from the countryside, figuring the connection sought by middle-class nationalist leaders to the mass of the population. But in contrast to de Boissière's work, the symbolism of *Voices under the Window* seems to foretell the failure of that alliance (and it is significant here, too, that this symbolism is so closely tied to the image of heteropatriarchal romance). Mark is stabbed by a black working-class rioter during disturbances in the city, the incident assuming a sacrificial air, since it occurs after he has entered the mob to rescue a child. This selfless act is linked to the more general sacrifice he makes in dedicating himself to a progressive nationalist politics. Yet as he lies dying, secluded in a room while the riot continues below, the scene seems to bespeak the gap that is already appearing between the politicians and those they claim to lead, the exhaustion of Mark's mortally wounded body suggestive of the troubles that will surround the attempt to vitalize a national body.

Similarly, Andrew Salkey's *A Quality of Violence* (1959), although it returns to 1900, examines issues around sacrifice and the renewal of the community, with sacrifice again associated not with the success but with the failure of such renewal. Indeed, the sacrificial act becomes entangled in a web of violence that is itself inextricable from attempts by various individuals to exert leadership over the collectivity.

Finally, to conclude this chapter, I want to consider Roger Mais's *The Hills Were Joyful Together* (1953) and *Brother Man* (1954). Both involve tragic narratives, and in the second novel, the theme of sacrifice reappears alongside the figure of a Christlike savior who seeks to raise the consciousness of the community. Both books also exhibit a form that registers and responds to the changing socioeconomic conditions of the period. One of the reasons for the difference between Roumain's novel and those of later writers like Alexis and Selvon, as I suggested earlier, is that Roumain was still able to evoke an integral community that, though divided, was nevertheless a recognizably consistent grouping. As such, it provided a basis for the dynamics of tragic sacrifice, whereby the victim steps outside the group (as Manuel does) to refashion it through the representative deed of self-giving.[86] This, however, presupposes the existence of the group in the first place. As we have seen, for many Caribbean writers of the 1950s, the pertinent issue was precisely the erosion of integral, Fonds Rouge–style peasant communities and the need to come to terms with the heterogeneous realities that make up the cityscape. Mais, too, confronts this dilemma, as Gordon Rohlehr points out:

> Mais's people are more normally the dispossessed of the towns, than peasants attached to the land. Sandwiched between the lane and the gully in their barrack houses, they have no land. What is important is Mais's ability to suggest that they are able to reconstruct a community in spite of the harshness of their experience,

that the fragments of communal experience knit into a single tragedy, character flowing into character, as if the entire group were a single person. This accounts for both the fragmentation of form in *The Hills Were Joyful Together* and for the way Mais contrives to blend the disparate voices and modes into a single weighty philosophising voice. The nature of the society which Mais has to explore inspires a quest for form. The need to suggest the dichotomy of fragmentation and communion, expresses itself in the movement of the novel between anecdote and pseudo-philosophical chorus.[87]

Mais's technique of moving between individual and choral voices thus reflects his response to the need for a form capable of articulating as a unity the disparate and fragmented social worlds of the urban environment while also conveying the way in which the inhabitants of the yard have forged a new community (most evident during the evening of the big fish fry, for example).

This reconstruction of communal experience provides the necessary backdrop for the tragic action in the novel, including the deaths of Rema, Bedosa, Euphemia, and Surjue, the last of whom is shot while trying to escape from prison to get back to the yard to see Rema. The novel concludes with the image of his corpse—"He lay on his back, his arms flung wide, staring up at the silent unequivocal stars"—which in its Christlike, crucified posture seems to betoken a tragic sacrifice at the hands of the colonial order (represented by the prison).[88] Yet this tragedy does not appear to portend the overthrowing of that order. Crucially, Surjue does not make it back to the yard; he is not reunited with the community, and his death does not signal its renewal. The same is true for the other tragedies that occur throughout the text: they do not pave the way for the instantiation of a new social order but suggest that the reconstructed community is already being torn apart by the pressures exerted by the colonial state. As Cudjoe observes, the violence that permeates the novel represents the "turning inward of colonial violence"; it does not offer a route to making that community the basis of a reorganized state and a "reality which is structured in the context of the people's reality and indigenous to the culture."[89]

In *Brother Man*, the theme of tragic sacrifice is far more explicit. The titular Rastafarian assumes the mantle of scapegoat, stepping outside the group—he rises "above and beyond the petty envies, and covetousness, and hates, and desires, and all the gossip that went about them from day to day"—and taking on to himself its hate and frustrations.[90] Toward the end of the novel, he is mauled by a mob as the people vent their anger. Brother Man's behavior can thus be seen as drawing the poison of that inwardly directed violence we witnessed in *The Hills Were Joyful Together*. His beating is meant to stand for the expiation of the community, so that when he rises from his sickbed—three days after the incident, in a further allusion to Christ—it should signal the renewal of the collectivity, raising their consciousnesses in preparation for focusing their actions on the colonial order. Yet the text gives no sense that this will be achieved: although the neighbors come to check on him while he recovers, ashamed of their actions, this appears to represent more a personal, spiritual success for Brother Man; his sacrifice is not shown as having heightened the people's awareness of the causes of their misery or as having aided in the establishment of a collective platform from which to challenge the contours of a reified social order.

There is, perhaps, a counterweight to this pessimistic reading of the novel's conclusion in the form of the relationship between Brother Man and Minette, the homeless girl he has taken in off the street and who eventually becomes his lover. Not only do we see the expansion of Minette's consciousness and the emergence of a more assured self-identity over the course of her time with Brother Man, but also she becomes integral to his own sense of self (witness his need to reveal to her his past experiences) and to his struggles with the community. It is she who cares for and supports him after his mauling by the crowd, and in the final scene, she is intimately associated with his "resurrection" from the sickbed: "And she went before him," begins the novel's concluding line, "carrying herself proudly, shielding the little flame of the candle with her hand."[91] Certainly, then, in terms of this narrative of personal union, Brother Man's sacrifice could be said to give on to an image that might stand as a figure for a potential new form of collectivity. Moreover, the sense of equality and mutual support between the two characters suggests a move away from the violence and asymmetries of patriarchal social relations.

Despite this, however, I would argue that the limitations surrounding Brother Man's sacrifice persist insofar as the personal communion between him and Minette, and the active role she takes in his "resurrection," are precisely personal, private affairs carried out in the domestic space. The actual public act of the tragic sacrifice remains the domain only of Brother Man. Thus, if the novel points to a form of social renewal beyond that mediated by the masculinist trope of the suffering male hero, this is still very much a tentative, marginal proposition. The dominant, public model for rejuvenating the community remains encoded in the motif of the tragic sacrifice, which, as noted earlier, seems incapable now of projecting a general heightening of popular consciousness.

From being integral to the rebirth of the community in *Masters of the Dew*, therefore, the sacrificial topos has become linked to the failure to fulfill the potential for the thoroughgoing transformation of the colonial state. In finishing, I want to suggest that this topos figures a certain type of politics, a certain means of organizing a political movement. In other words, to switch to our earlier Bourdieusian terminology, the trope of tragic sacrifice is the translation into the logic of the literary field of a particular political dispensation, one that is bound up with the emergence of a national consciousness and of the possibility of instituting an independent nation-state. As such, we can see the reworking or transformation of that topos as *refracting* certain transformations in the sociopolitical arena and in the relationships between the elite and the masses, mediating within the literary object itself the problems encountered in the external world. Indeed—and I explore this idea further in the next chapter—it is possible to view the crisis that the trope undergoes, its inability to signify the renewal of the community, as figuring a crisis in the political sphere, an inability to fulfill the demands of the community.

2

"The people living a life every man for himself": Problems in the Postindependence Body (Politic)

In the previous chapter, I touched on the issue of national allegory, arguing that for all the controversy surrounding Fredric Jameson's theorization of this concept in relation to Third World literature, it remained a useful perspective from which to begin to consider the narrative codification of social experience in contexts of imperialist domination. Of particular interest was Jameson's related emphasis on the importance of cultural revolution. Such a revolution is a necessary element in the decolonization process, enabling colonized peoples to divest themselves of the habits and psychic structures implanted by colonialism, the vectors of which penetrate to the level of everyday bodily practice. The struggle against domination will thus be waged in part on the terrain of the corporeal. This helps explain the symbolic weight with which the body is frequently endowed in Caribbean fiction. Indeed, it points to the likelihood that representations of the body, as well as of cultural practice more generally, will display a tendency to speak, at some level, to the national as inextricably bound up with the functioning of that domination, and as the arena in which—in the context of an imperialist world system structured around nation-states—the struggle for liberation must pass. Having earlier examined how Caribbean texts from the 1950s both articulated the promise of an independent nation-state and foreshadowed the potential problems it might encounter, in this chapter I explore the materialization of those problems. Focusing in particular on Wilson Harris's *The Secret Ladder* (1963) and Earl Lovelace's *The Wine of Astonishment* (1982), I consider how the transformations and difficulties experienced by the body politic are not only registered in these works through the image of the physical body but also shown to be connected materially to its dispositions and inculcated behaviors.

The 1960s saw a number of territories in the Anglophone Caribbean achieve independence, capitalizing on the social and political gains made in the preceding decades. Yet it soon became clear that in many instances, the potential of these developments would not be realized. In Jamaica, Trinidad, and Barbados, for example, the backbone of the nationalist movement had been the strategic alliance between proletarian organizations and middle-class political parties. Once the leaders of the independence movements came to power, however, they sought, as Clive Thomas argues, to "*demobilise and de-politicise* the masses to pre-

vent the further entrenchment of mass politics in the society at large." This occurred, continues Thomas,

> because the petty-bourgeoisie (along with the other intermediate strata from
> which the mass movement's leaders were recruited) was essentially a colonial
> creation with limited objectives. . . . Their struggles were not therefore oriented
> towards a revolutionary reversal of power relations in favour of the poor and pow-
> erless. For them, the independence settlement provided a means of excluding the
> masses from effective power.[1]

Indeed, these leaders displayed many of the traits for which the national bourgeoisie of decolonizing countries were condemned by liberation theorists such
as Fanon and Cabral.[2] Lacking the economic power of a "proper" bourgeoisie,
they comprised a comprador class, often serving as local agents for foreign capital. Even where they contested foreign influence, they usually intended only to
substitute it for a native version, using state power to cement their position of
privilege at the expense of the people. The nationalist project thus seemed to go
no further than "constitutionalist decolonization"; political power was seized
and the franchise extended to the majority, but a radical reorganization of the
structural coordinates of the colonial state was not on the agenda.[3] As a result,
by 1970 the "dominant paradigm was influenced not so much by the realization
of political independence as by the perception that what had been achieved had
not gone far enough and needed to be complemented by new struggles aimed at
achieving economic as well as political independence."[4]

I return in more detail to the particular problems attending the national
bourgeoisie in the Caribbean when I consider Lovelace's *The Wine of Astonishment*. Before that I want to focus on Harris's radically utopian vision of social
and cultural transformation in *The Guyana Quartet*, of which *The Secret Ladder*
forms the final book of a tetralogy that includes *Palace of the Peacock* (1960), *The
Far Journey of Oudin* (1961), and *The Whole Armour* (1962). Harris's challenging
and experimental texts have been the focus of much debate. There has been a
tendency, however, for some critics to view his work as sui generis, an approach
exemplified by Andrew Bundy in the introduction to his edited collection of Harris's essays. Commenting on the author's emigration to England in 1959 and the
contemporary boom in Caribbean writing, Bundy remarks that "literary London
published and created an international forum [for] West Indian writers at a time
when there was not a single serious publisher in the Caribbean, yet it would be
misleading to view Harris as part of those movements. Harris's study of the fabric of the imagination sets his writing apart from the concerns of West Indian
Caribbean writers."[5] The claim that Harris was not "part of those movements"
associated with Caribbean writers in London seems something of an overstate-
ment given his involvement in projects such as the Caribbean Artists' Move-

ment.[6] Moreover, in suggesting that Harris's fictional concerns diverge markedly from those of other Caribbean writers, Bundy appears implicitly to want to abstract Harris's work from its concrete social context in favor of emphasizing the author's personal vision. Indeed, his emphasis in the introduction is very much on the mythical—even mystical—qualities of the work.

In this sense, Bundy's perspective shares something with the myth that, as Gregory Shaw observes, has built up around Harris as "a writer who ventured into the South American heartland, experienced a special vision of some sort and returned to tell the world."[7] Shaw goes on to suggest that some critics assume that "the unique experience and vision are sufficient justification for a shockingly experimental style."[8] While it is undoubtedly true that Harris's experiences as a land surveyor in the Guyanese interior have had a profound impact on his fiction, and that his style is highly distinctive, his concerns do not seem—contra Bundy—all that far away from those of a number of his contemporaries and in fact become more understandable when considered in relation to work by those contemporaries. Similarly, while Harris's novels tend toward abstraction, close attention to the historical context in which they appeared provides a deeper understanding of their formal qualities than does the emphasis on their being the product of a special vision.

Indeed, not only can the texts that comprise *The Guyana Quartet* be seen as registering thematically the social issues confronting Guyana in the 1960s, but it is also possible to understand their "shockingly experimental style" as the translation into the logic of the literary field of the particular forces prevalent in the Guyanese political field since the 1950s. As James Millette has argued, the decolonization process in Guyana was different from that occurring in any other British West Indian colony, with the Marxist-Leninist People's Progressive Party (PPP), dominated by the Indo-Guyanese Cheddi Jagan and the Afro-Guyanese Forbes Burnham, articulating "from its very founding a consistently radical political programme":

> On nearly all the major questions of the day, Guyana, in the era of PPP-dominated administrations, had a different point of view. In a very short space of time it distanced itself from those parties whose principal goal was what has been called "constitutional decolonization." In all the other colonies, the objectives of the decolonization movement were understated so as to embrace political, but not ideological or economic decolonization. In Guyana, political decolonization was a stage, even if an important first stage, in the radical transformation of society.[9]

Millette suggests that the radical views of the PPP were ultimately those that "large numbers of people were espousing in the post-independence Caribbean as early as 1965" as the limitations of constitutionalist decolonization became apparent (and, too, as the Cuban Revolution seemed to offer an alternative path).[10]

Harris's formal radicalism could, in this light, be seen as the result of the mediation within the literary object of the more radical social and political project that was the focus of struggle in Guyana. The increasing recognition that meaningful freedom would have to involve a more thoroughgoing decolonization of institutions and habits becomes Harris's attempt to explode the conventions of what he identifies as traditional realism.

This particular mediation of the political in the literary can be discerned in *Palace of the Peacock*. The multiracial boat crew, whose journey upstream into the Guyanese interior the novel recounts, stands as an allegory for Guyana's ethnically diverse populace—although, as Jeremy Poynting has pointed out, the East Indian component is missing (this community is treated separately in *The Far Journey of Oudin*).[11] We might also note that women are absent except in the form of Donne's mistress Mariella and the old Arawak woman, an absence that should alert us to the potentially masculinist nature of the thematization of the nation here, but also to the possibility that Harris is preparing to critique this same masculinism, especially given the representations of patriarchal sexual abuse that feature in the novel.

The divisions between the boat crew and the absence of an East Indian are suggestive of the racial tensions that had come to the fore in Guyana since the mid-twentieth century. In 1953 national elections saw Jagan's PPP win a majority of seats on the legislative council, only to be forced from power 133 days later by the British government. With Cold War anxieties sharpening, both Britain and the United States were wary of what they perceived to be a communist takeover. They set out to eradicate the PPP, Britain instigating a divide-and-rule process through the Robertson Commission of Inquiry, and the United States deploying the CIA to cultivate racial division.[12] By the end of the decade, the PPP had split into two opposing parties: one (the PPP) led by Jagan and drawing the majority of its support from the Indo-Guyanese community, the other (the People's National Congress [PNC]) led by Burnham and backed primarily by the Afro-Guyanese community. This ethnic polarization intensified to the point that between 1962 and 1964 the country suffered a "spate of ethno-political hostilities involving near-genocidal warfare between East Indian and African politicised communities."[13]

Set against this backdrop, the emphasis in *Palace of the Peacock*—indeed, in all the novels of the quartet—on the establishment of a cross-cultural community clearly resonates with a desire to see the resolution of the enmities plaguing the body politic. The final vision of the crew resurrected into a new apprehension of themselves and of their entwined histories—"I felt the faces before me begin to fade and part company from me and from themselves as if our need of one another was now fulfilled, and our distance from each other was the distance of sacrament, the sacrament and embrace we knew in one muse and one undying soul"[14]—appears as a utopian figure for the lineaments of a future independent nation-state. However, the extreme, otherworldly character of this vision—it might usefully be contrasted, for example, with the image of the plots and the allegorical weight they bear in Selvon's *A Brighter Sun*—underscores the extent of the transformations necessary to reconstruct the social world. The novel suggests, moreover, that such a reconstruction of the present also requires a rethinking of the past. Evoking a range of periods from Guyanese history, the narrative demonstrates how eclipsed perspectives must be unearthed so that "the series of subtle and nebulous links which are latent within [the West Indian]" can be brought to fulfillment.[15] "How can one begin to reconcile the broken parts of such an enormous heritage?" asks Harris of the multiple legacies present in the Caribbean.[16] The declaration at the end of *Palace of the Peacock* that the crew "had all come home at last to the compassion of the nameless unflinching folk" is the signal that such reconciliation has been achieved here (110).

This return to the folk, though, should not be construed as a return to a retrograde nativism or an immutable past. Rather, it represents what Glissant terms a "return to the point of entanglement, from which we were forcefully turned away; that is where we must ultimately put to work the forces of creolization, or perish."[17] The point of entanglement for Glissant as much as for Harris is the point of contact between diverse histories and modes of existence. It is a dynamic, conflictual site; Glissant calls it the point "where our problems lay in wait for us,"[18] and Harris views it as simultaneously constituting the problem (the colonial conquest, for example) and containing within itself the seeds of a radically different future to the one that was materialized under imperialism. This unfulfilled potential—a potential Harris elsewhere refers to as a "phenomenal legacy"[19]—is represented by the folk in *Palace of the Peacock* and must be uncovered to rethink history: as a past that did not come to fruition, it must be brought into and concretized in the present so as to transform the future.

The promise Harris locates in this unfinished past is, to reiterate, that of cross-cultural community. The way in which he inscribes cultural heterogeneity and the imbrication of historical legacies into his writing is well documented, and I will not rehearse such arguments here.[20] Instead what interests me is the connection between these concerns and the issue of the state, specifically the groundwork necessary to effect the state's total reorganization. Scholars have tended to consider Harris's work from a perspective that shares much with the approaches predominant in postcolonial studies, including an idealist emphasis on hybridity as inherently subversive and emancipatory—as being able to undo the power relations of colonialism through its exposure of their ambivalence, an ambivalence that is considered to have always already been at work in such power relations, so that their overthrow is really no more than the revelation of what they were all along.[21] Clearly elements of Harris's theoretical and literary production do lend themselves to this sort of poststructuralist-inflected understanding—it would not be hard, for instance, to elaborate a reading of the vision of cross-culturality that climaxes *Palace of the Peacock* as the exposure of the inherent "ambivalence" of the colonizer-colonized dyad. I want to suggest, however, that it is possible to offer a more materially grounded take on Harris's return to the point of entanglement and the image of liberation he proffers.[22]

By portraying the stripping away, over the course of seven days, of the crew's habits and frames of perception—of "every eccentric spar and creed and wishful certainty they had always adored in every past adventure and world" (79)—*Palace of the Peacock* narrates a kind of reverse creation myth. The significance of going back to a moment of genesis in this way, at least in terms of how Harris's novel might be said to register the political struggles in Guyana in the 1950s and 1960s, becomes evident if we consider the process by which the state naturalizes the particular organization of the social world it imposes. Bourdieu contends that if the state

> is able to exert symbolic violence, it is because it incarnates itself simultaneously in objectivity, in the form of specific organizational structures and mechanisms, and in subjectivity, in the form of mental structures and categories of perception and thought. By realizing itself in social structures and in the mental structures adapted to them, the instituted institution makes us forget that it issues out of a long series of acts of *institution* (in the active sense) and hence has all the appearances of the *natural*.
>
> This is why there is no more potent tool for rupture than the reconstruction of genesis: by bringing back into view the conflicts and confrontations of the early beginnings and therefore all the discarded possibilities, it retrieves the possibility that things could (and still could be) otherwise. And, through such a practical Utopia, it questions the "possible" which, among all others, was actualised.[23]

Bourdieu's thinking here is inextricable from his conception of the habitus, and of the way in which bodies and minds are inculcated with practices and dispositions that endow them with principles of vision and division attuned to the structures that organize the social order. The implications of this for relations of domination are clear: "Symbolic violence rests on the adjustment between the structures constitutive of the habitus of the dominated and the structure of the relation of domination to which they apply: the dominated perceive the dominant through the categories that the relation of domination has produced and which are thus identical to the interests of the dominant."[24] Like Bourdieu's "practical Utopia" that, by reconstructing the moment of genesis, denaturalizes these categories, Harris's text stages the utopian rupture of that adjustment between mental and objective structures. When the crewman Vigilance recognizes the "enormous spiritual distance and inner bleeding substance [that] lay between himself and that crust and shell he had once thought he inhabited" (83), the moment suggests the sloughing off of the bodily and perceptual dispositions with which he had been inculcated. As the dominant principles of vision and division disintegrate, the instituted objective structures that govern the organization and apprehension of space and time lose their appearance of immutability. As a result, alternatives become thinkable for the crew: "It was as if something had snapped again, a prison door, a chain, and a rush and flight of appearances jostled each other—past, present and future in one constantly vanishing and reappearing cloud and mist" (44).

With the interrelated breakdown of the bodily habitus and the givenness of the ruling space-time conventions comes a new understanding of the social and cultural relations that bind the crew together. Introducing what will become a recurrent motif for Harris, the novel shows the boundaries that separate the crew into isolated individuals collapsing, so that subjectivities become extended, concertina-like, through other subjectivities: "The monstrous thought came to them that they had been shattered and were reflected again in each other at the bottom of the stream" (80). This recognition of mutuality is inextricable from the attempt to narrate beyond the horizon of reified mental and social structures—beyond the horizon of a particular habitus imbricated in the organization of a particular type of state—to a point of "genesis" wherein other forms are still possible. Thus intimated are the relations between individuals, and between individuals and the world, that would have to be institutionalized to sustain a different form of community.

Despite the undeniably metaphysical tendency in Harris's thought, then, his approach does implicate issues connected to the social and institutional aspects of the decolonization process. Indeed, it is interesting to note the characteristics shared by the concepts that underwrite *Palace of the Peacock* with the political thinking behind certain Caribbean subaltern anticolonial movements. Take, for example, Claudius Henry and the African Reform Church, an organization active in Jamaica in the late 1950s and 1960s. Having worked with Edna Fisher to build up the church, the doctrine of which combined elements of Rastafarian ideas with new rituals, Henry attempted to stage a rebellion against the colonial state in Jamaica.[25] According to Anthony Bogues, Henry's politics were the "politics of dread": drawing on the black redemptive tradition, they displayed its distinctive emphasis on making God into a human (in this instance, the Rastafarian belief in God's incarnation as Haile Selassie). For this reason, contends Bogues, Henry did not "operate a conception of God in history as a form of 'providential design'"; instead "biblical texts served only as codes, as referents and sources for his human agency, not as commands."[26]

While Henry's nationalism was ultimately focused on Africa, we can identify clear affinities between his prophetic redemptive standpoint and Harris's articulation of the redemption of history, his bringing of an unfinished past into the present to serve as an image for a future to be actualized in the now. Both would seem to be influenced by the notion of temporality characteristic of medieval

Christianity, wherein "simultaneity related to the convergence of past and future in an instantaneous present, in a prophetic notion of scriptural eternity."[27] *Palace of the Peacock* offers something like a secularized version of this in its final sequence, in which the past of the folk (in the sense that they represent an unfulfilled historical potential) converges in a present that is at the same time presented as the prophetic ground of the future (though in contrast to Henry, the future Harris envisions is a Caribbean, cross-cultural one rather than an African one).

Further marking the radicalism of Henry's politics was the different temper of their anticolonialism as compared to that which characterized the Creole nationalist movement (represented in Jamaica by Norman Manley's PNP). While the PNP, notes Bogues,

> worked within the parameters of the colonial epistemic project, holding fast to the symbolic order and government rationalities bequeathed to it, Henry and others challenged these orders. In the final analysis, for the Creole nationalist the space of the political was narrow and institutional, [whereas] for Henry and others it was *ontological*. In Henry's ideational framework, the life-world of the African *human* was constructed by history. For displaced African people the question was how to reorder that history and establish a new ground for African humanness.[28]

Again, for Harris the question is how to establish a new ground for Caribbean humanness, but his work evinces a similar emphasis on the political space as ontological and not just institutional.

Furthermore, Bogues shows how Henry's attempt to reground politics was inextricable from a challenge to the habitus associated with the black and brown bourgeoisie and adjusted to the type of "constitutionally decolonized" state that Creole nationalists sought to institute—a habitus that retained the impress of colonial frameworks:

> In the post-independence period the population was to be educated about particular norms of citizenship. A certain kind of citizen was to be created, one who would be Caribbean, who would be Creole, who would accept middle class leadership and values, who would wear respectability like a Sunday-best outfit, . . . comport themselves with proper gestures, respect authority and uphold Christian values. . . . Such a subject could gain access into the new national community, becoming its corner stone.[29]

This genus of disciplined body had its antecedents in the postemancipation period and the idea put forward by sections of the British ruling class that black colonials could be educated to fit them for "civilization." Significantly, given the issues raised in the previous chapter over the persistence of patriarchal power relations, this colonialist effort to police the body involved also the production and regulation of gender identities, a process that was then perpetuated by the bourgeois nationalist movements as part of their bid to secure legitimacy. "Black nationalist masculinity," argues Alexander, "needed to demonstrate that it was now capable of ruling, which is to say, it needed to demonstrate moral rectitude, particularly on questions of paternity." This required "distancing itself from irresponsible Black working-class masculinity that spawned the 'bastard,' the 'illegitimate.' . . . It also required distancing itself from, while simultaneously attempting to control, Black working-class femininity that ostensibly harboured a profligate sexuality: the 'Jezebel' and the whore who was not completely socialized into housewifery, but whose labour would be mobilized to help consolidate popular nationalism."[30]

Ultimately the retention of the colonialist conception of the "respectable" body within the ideological schema of the bourgeois anticolonialists was as limiting in its own way as the failure fully to dismantle the colonial state. What both Henry's and Harris's perspectives share is a concern with overthrowing such habitus to further social change. But to concretize that change requires the concomitant reorganization of the state, and while Harris points toward the lineaments of a radically different form of community, one that draws its coordinates from indigenous Caribbean resources, his approach has limitations that undermine the purchase of the image of a liberated collectivity he invokes.

I will come back to these limitations in a moment. First I want to turn to *The Secret Ladder*, a novel in which issues of state are much more to the fore, and the utopianism of *Palace of the Peacock* is somewhat tempered—a response, I argue, to the worsening conditions in Guyana at the time. As Kerstin Oloff suggests, *The Secret Ladder* can be read as "an attempt to re-ground [*Palace of the Peacock*] in a dialectical fashion," with the later novel (set sometime in the mid-twentieth century) featuring another multiracial boat crew journeying upriver, this time as part of a government expedition led by the land surveyor Russell Fenwick, whose dinghy is named *Palace of the Peacock*.[31] Fenwick has gone to chart the flow of the Canje River as part of a proposed scheme to construct a reservoir that will irrigate East Indian coastal plantations. He is, as Robert Carr notes, "a representative of the new nationalist cadres in the Guyanese civil service," who "takes up the subject position of the new man in the jungle, voiding the leases and invading zones held by legendary but subaltern national renegades—descendents of slaves escaped into the bush, Amerindian tribes fleeing the European invasion of Central America—the better to map the terrain of the future, and investigate the social body with an eye to the transformation of government."[32] In short, the middle-class Fenwick's mission is tied to the wider developmental project of integrating the Guyanese territory into a national whole, of charting the contours of a productive and potentially independent nation-state. His encounter with

Poseidon, the elderly ruler of the descendants of a tribe of runaway slaves who survive as subsistence farmers around the Canje, signals another instance of the collision of the modernizing elements of the city with the means of survival maintained by the peasantry in rural areas.

This encounter should hold out the promise of a new political dispensation in which the multiple strata of an unevenly developed society are brought together, negating the existing form of that society and laying the foundations for an inclusive, emancipatory mode of collectivity. However, for Poseidon and his followers, whose land will be flooded if the new reservoir is built, the encroachment of Fenwick's team on their territory represents a continuation of the colonial expeditions they defied in the past. When they sabotage Fenwick's river gauge, which stands as a marker both of modern scientific knowledge and for the administrative strategy through which the terrain is to be mapped and assimilated into a new national polity, it appears they are rejecting the seemingly progressive potential of the surveyor's project. Yet their sense that what they are confronting is in fact still bounded by colonialist imperatives demonstrates an astute reading of the situation—a key issue in a novel where the motifs of reading and gauging are central (the book itself is split into three sections, "The Day Readers," "The Night Readers," and "The Reading"). Indeed, Fenwick's use of the river gauge reveals the persistence of such colonial paradigms, and behind them the exploitative demands of the capitalist mode of production and certain precepts of Enlightenment thinking.

As Fenwick gauges the river's height, "staring up curiously as if he saw an introspective ladder of climbing numbers," he becomes a kind of disembodied scientific eye, his mind abstracted from the natural environment he is there to record and classify.[33] Indeed, the more he attempts to quantify the material world, the more he loses touch with its actuality, hence the transformation in the scientific optics he deploys from the "actual feet and decimals placed on a strip of vulgar wood" into that introspective ladder without clear referent (357). Such disembodied matrices come to influence his whole approach to the landscape. "The truth is you poring over them chart and tide-map . . . too hard" (366), Jordan, the cook, tells him. And although Fenwick knows that to conceptualize the topography in this way can be misleading, he appears unable to do things differently.

It is possible to view Fenwick's behavior in terms of Adorno and Horkheimer's conception of the dialectic of Enlightenment. As I pointed out in the introduction, the material and ideological demands of capitalism entailed the separation of human beings from nature, what Marx described as the dissolution of the worker's "relation to the earth—land and soil—as natural condition of production—to which he relates as to his own inorganic body."[34] This separation also came to structure the new modalities of Enlightenment thought whereby an opposition was established between culture and nature, with progress defined by the ability of the human mind (itself identified with culture) to hold sway over a disenchanted nature. In this framework, nature becomes "the chaotic matter of mere classification and the all-powerful self becomes mere possession—abstract identity."[35] The result of this new relationship between the isolated individual of capitalist modernity and his or her environment is that the "multitudinous affinities between existents are suppressed by the single relation between the subject who bestows meaning and the meaningless object."[36] For Adorno and Horkheimer, the fate of the Enlightenment is to return to mythology: the entrenched separation of the subject from the object and the reduction of the world to classifiable matter ultimately leads to reification, with existence now grasped only as a series of "given" elements:

> What appears to be the triumph of subjective rationality, the subjection of all reality to logical formalism, is paid for by the obedient subjection of reason to what is directly given. What is abandoned is the whole claim and approach to knowledge: to comprehend the given as such; not merely to determine the abstract spatio-temporal relations of the facts which allow them just to be grasped, but on the contrary to conceive them as the superficies, as mediated conceptual moments which come to fulfilment only in the development of their social, historical, and human significance.[37]

The inability to penetrate to the social, historical, and human relations that determine the contours of existence results in these same contours being reproduced as immutable.

The consequences of this inability are illustrated in *The Secret Ladder*, not least by Fenwick's initial attitude to Poseidon and his followers. Take, for example, Fenwick's reaction to the news that they fear the reservoir will flood them out. Gesturing to "his tidal graphs and notebooks," he stresses that the people will be compensated, a desirable outcome in his mind, since "'the land isn't all that rich up here—in fact it's a mess—and they wouldn't want to keep it in face of a scheme that would do untold benefit to the sugar estates and rice-lands of the Courantyne and Berbice coasts'—he found himself speaking as if he were recounting an obsession and a lesson—'which draw their irrigation supplies catch-as-catch-can mostly from an unaided river now'" (381). Fenwick's obsessively scientific apprehension of the landscape prevents him from understanding the project in any other way than as a necessary form of economic progress. He fails to appreciate the human ties to the land established by Poseidon's followers. Such ties contrast markedly with Fenwick's own abstracted stance, emphasized by the instrumental language he employs (though his sense that he is merely "recounting . . . a lesson" suggests a growing awareness of the limitations of his detached position). In trying to facilitate the reorganization of the land in accordance with what he calls "the unadorned facts of science, the plain economic structure of society" (396), Fenwick not only fixes and frames it as beyond human interaction but also seems set to perpetuate the colonial policy of forcibly imposing on communities alien socioeconomic structures. Such problems point to the wider shortcomings of the state development project he is involved in: rather than genuinely integrating all parts of the country and drawing on the resources and traditions of its peoples, the project is geared toward the needs of the coastal dwellers.

Now, integral to all that has just been said is the body: the limitations in Fenwick's apprehension of the world are bound up with the particular form of corporeality with which he is inculcated, one inextricable from the capitalist economic system and the separation of the subject from the object world. The type of contained and regulated body this system strives to impose is of a piece with that which Mikhail Bakhtin contends is consecrated by the Renaissance, one that is "isolated, alone, fenced off from all other bodies." "The accent," argues Bakhtin, "was placed on the completed, self-sufficient individuality of the given body . . . [which] was presented apart from its relation to the ancestral body of the people."[38] This is a corporeality numbed to its sensuous connection to the material world and to the social relations that reproduce its immediate form; it is thus one numbed also to the connections that exist between individuals, to the whole network of human interactions that make up the collectivity. Not only does *The Secret Ladder* dramatize such bodily reification, but it also shows the impact this has in a situation where ethnic differences already divide the populace, where working-class women are treated as commodities to be bought, sold, and gambled for, and where a vexed relationship to an occluded history remains an ongoing issue.

If Fenwick is locked into the monadic sovereignty of the bourgeois subject, his working-class crew bear the disciplined, isolated bodies demanded by capital to render them productive units of exploitable energy. Harris's concept of block function—a uniform identity or mode of operation within which an individual can become trapped—underscores the consequences of capitalism's atomization and rationalization of the labor process; it can usefully be applied to the situation in *The Secret Ladder*, where Fenwick's men are hemmed in by their allotted roles (foreman, boatman, cook, and so on). In this they reflect Harris's own experiences of surveying teams, in which crew members "operated within a rigid function and . . . were excellent within that function," yet to exercise it had to "eclipse a great deal": they "accepted themselves within a certain kind of hierarchy . . . [and] to extend themselves beyond this was a matter that aroused uneasiness."[39] In the novel, the crew's inability to "extend themselves" outward prevents them from grasping the connections that bind them together, and so the totality of social relations that determine their position within the system. Moreover, it renders them susceptible to the kind of divide-and-rule tactics that were deployed by the colonial state,[40] tactics that Fenwick too has been using, a pattern he becomes consciousness of upon realizing that Jordan has served as

> his shield against importunity, an agent of governance to exercise over the men in lieu of a genuine and profoundly human natural understanding he would have given all he possessed to possess. . . . It was always Jordan's head—Medusa-like— that inspired in them a certain cynical helplessness, the helplessness of men who could be contained by forces of greed and self-interest or guile. It was a strange fellowship and barren condition. (378–79)

Jordan, whose name puns on Gorgon, personifies the reifying effect that the dominant power relations have on the men: petrified within the integument of what the crewman Bryant calls their "complacent bod[ies]" (395), they can be manipulated and discouraged from working collectively to challenge their subordinate position.

The "contained" and isolated condition of the men also prevents them from being able to "extend themselves" out to the land and the history it holds. More specifically, it cuts them off from an understanding of Poseidon and the legacy of peasant resistance and communal action he represents. Although Bryant begins to grasp the import of the old man's claim to the land, the crew's attitude generally is best summed up by Jordan's dismissal of Poseidon's followers as a "'pack of crude children. . . . Savages, too!'" (381). Such terms not only recall colonial stereotypes but also emphasize how Jordan is alienated from a history that is his own submerged Guyanese history, too.

The occluded connections that do exist among the surveying team, as well as between the team and Poseidon's followers, are frequently exposed in the novel. However, they are just as frequently reconcealed by capitalist reification. When the foreman Weng visits Fenwick, for example, Fenwick is seized by the impression that he is "regarding himself, not Weng": "In that flash . . . Fenwick had seen Weng focused in the reflection of himself, and being drawn out again from within his own (Fenwick's) eye like a rubber twin turning into substantial alien being—Weng, quite distinctly, after all" (389). Here the isolated, self-sufficient individuality of the modern body is temporarily disrupted by the emergence of what, again following Bakhtin, we might term the grotesque body. "Contrary to modern canons," writes Bakhtin, "the grotesque body is not separated from the rest of the world. It is not a closed, completed unit; it is unfinished, outgrows itself, transgresses its own limits. . . . It is blended with the world, with animals, with objects."[41] The appearance of this form of premodern corporeality momentarily blurs the boundaries between Fenwick and Weng before its modern, sovereign avatar reasserts itself, leaving the two men "quite distinct" again.

The complicity between Fenwick's reified corporeality and his inability to fully comprehend not only the social relations that bind him to his crew but also the "buried community" (389) represented by Poseidon is best illustrated by his first encounter with the old man:

> There was the faint hoarse sound of an approaching body swimming in the un-
> dergrowth. Fenwick adjusted his eyes. He could no longer evade a reality that had
> always escaped him. The strangest figure he had ever seen had appeared in the
> opening of the bush, dressed in a flannel vest, flapping ragged fins of trousers on
> his legs. Fenwick could not help fastening his eyes greedily upon him as if he saw
> down a bottomless gauge and river of reflection. . . . The old man's hair was white
> as wool and his cheeks—covered with wild curling rings—looked like an unkempt
> sheep's back. . . . Poseidon addressed Fenwick at last. His mouth moved and made
> frames which did not correspond to the words he actually uttered. It was like the
> tragic lips of an actor . . . galvanized into comical association with a foreign dub-
> bing and tongue which uttered a mechanical version and translation out of accord
> with the visible features of original expression.

The confrontation between the two men underscores Guyana's uneven development and its corollary, the coexistence of realities from radically different moments of history. Faced with the "reality that had always escaped him," Fenwick's
circumscribed understanding of the world and the enclosed character of his sensorium are made plain. The surveyor continues to exhibit an exclusively ocular
apprehension of existence, his abstracted eye "greedily" consuming all within
its purview, scientifically gauging it on a disembodied conceptual scale ("river
of reflection"). Poseidon, however, represents a distinctly bodily presence, one
that overwhelms Fenwick, leaving him "disturbed to the greatest depth" by his
incapacity to adequately classify the old man (373). The very name Poseidon (the
Greek sea god) indicates a resistance to easy categorization (he is both "Greek"
and "African") while pointing also to the fluidity of his movements (emphasized
by his "body swimming" through the bush). This fluidity and the (to Fenwick's
eyes) wildness of his bearing recall the movements of the enslaved—their gestures, dances, and rituals—and thus the role these practices played as repositories of history. Moreover, Poseidon's corporeality transgresses the limits of the
human subject to merge with the animal and plant worlds. His appearance thus
signals another eruption of a grotesque or premodern body, one that extends
outward and foregrounds (rather than effaces) its connection to material and
social reality.

It is for these reasons that Poseidon appears "out of accord": his lips do not correspond to the words he utters because his habitus is, as Bourdieu would put it,
"out of phase" with the commonsense world imposed by the dominant order and
embodied in Fenwick.[42] Fenwick requires that the "visible features of original expression"—the corporeal element in Poseidon's communication—be translated

into a normative verbal discourse. However, this "mechanical version" cannot articulate the fullness of the old man's expression, becoming a distorted and, to the surveyor, unintelligible form of speech. Yet Fenwick comes to realize that he must overcome his "failure of comprehension" (373), since Poseidon holds the key to that submerged history of enslavement and resistance, of liberation and the dissipation of its promise. As Fenwick muses on the day after the meeting: "In this creature Poseidon, the black man with the European name, drawn out of the depths of time, is the emotional dynamic of liberation that happened a century and a quarter ago [Emancipation]. . . . Something went tragically wrong then. Something was misunderstood and frustrated" (385). The traditions and resources that Poseidon embodies must be integrated both institutionally and at the level of popular consciousness to decolonize both state and mind, as well as to avoid the repetition of past mistakes. Indeed, Poseidon's grotesque or premodern body furnishes an image of the type of social relations that would have to underpin any new state formation. The alternative he represents to a reified monadic subjectivity points to a world in which the contingent relationships between individuals, and between individuals and the environment, are grasped and made visible, allowing for the possibility of the collective reorganization of society.

Fenwick actually begins to move toward this utopian promise: his meeting with Poseidon accelerates a change that the jungle itself seems already to have provoked in him (hinted at earlier by the way its failure to conform to his abstract plans leaves him feeling "as if he were recounting an obsession and a lesson"). The surveyor begins to shed his circumscribed, sovereign carapace. Whereas he had been regarded as "hard as stone" (391) by the crew, his attempt to achieve a "profoundly human natural understanding" of them sees Jordan admonish him for "showing too much real sympathy" (424). Fenwick's alteration in his leadership style indicates a search for a new way of organizing people, one that is not bound to a master-slave structure of command or an authoritarianism exercised through intermediaries. Instead Fenwick seems to be looking for something more inclusive and collective. Jordan's accusation that he is showing too much sympathy is significant, since it directly recalls Fenwick's earlier view of Poseidon as an "ancestral apparition" containing "a new divine promise, born of an underworld of half-forgotten sympathies" (379). The parallel here suggests the way in which the surveyor has begun to integrate the traditions and resources embodied in Poseidon, the changed practice of governance this encourages again intimating the promise of a radically different form of state—a potential imaged also in Poseidon's house, which is described as having "no marks of exclusiveness—rather a spirit of all-inclusive privacy, the most welcome artifice of humanity. . . . It had acquired a special seal and privilege, the stamp of a multiple tradition or heritage" (411).

However, the movement toward these new forms of social relations is ultimately thwarted. Like *Palace of the Peacock*, *The Secret Ladder* is set over seven days, during which a kind of reverse genesis similar to the one in the earlier book takes place: Fenwick is stripped of his reified habitus to be reborn. But instead of the collective rebirth of the whole crew, as happens in the earlier novel, it is Fenwick's expanded consciousness alone that forms the focal point of the novel's conclusion. Moreover, his newfound apprehension of community is already on its way to becoming only a phenomenal legacy. Its promise is being resubmerged by events occurring around the Canje, where a violent incident leads to Poseidon's men mistakenly believing they have killed Weng. Although the return of the men to their camp enables Bryant and Catalena Perez (who have been taken hostage) to escape death at the hands of the old man's followers, the news prompts the group to flee. "And now it was all over," the narrative suggests. "At any moment Weng and his men, followed by the jungle police, would be on their heels" (462). Thus the novel ends as it began, with the state encroaching on the interior and Poseidon's community on the verge of dispossession. That the pursuit is led by Weng, the foreman who earlier declared that he had modeled his leadership style on Fenwick's old "hard as stone" persona (391), indicates that, while the surveyor has divested himself of this disposition, its legacy lives on. A new form of authority has emerged, but far from being the inclusive, collective kind toward which Poseidon's corporeality pointed the way, it is one that perpetuates the dictatorial character of past incarnations.

Emphasizing this dissipation of potential is the text's portrayal of gender relations and of the persistence of patriarchal models of power. Catalena, the novel's only female character, is routinely beaten by her husband, Perez, and even used as a gambling chip. Toward the end of the narrative, she runs away with Bryant, an act that might be taken to prefigure the possibility of new forms of social interaction liberated from patriarchal norms. Significantly, upon learning of Catalena's flight, Fenwick muses:

> Catalena had arrived . . . on the mailboat *Andromeda*. Half-priestess, half-prostitute. Had Andromeda not been saved by Perseus and his perennial agents in history around the globe, around the centuries—had she been left to suffer death, would history have regarded her rock as the true cross, the true death of the gods? (454)

This not only alludes to the motif of tragic sacrifice but also raises the issue of the masculinist quality of that trope. What alternative possibilities might arise, the passage appears to ask, if the woman became the sacrificial actor and was not bound by a framework in which male Perseuses are the agents of history, tasked with redeeming others? We might answer by pointing to the potential for social transformation the sacrifice of Alexis's La Niña seemed to symbolize. But, again, such potential goes unrealized in *The Secret Ladder*: Catalena gets caught up in the events that cause Poseidon's followers to flee and precipitate the rise of Weng as a dictatorial, masculinist successor to Fenwick.

The contrast between the utopian finale of *Palace of the Peacock* and the more pessimistic conclusion to *The Secret Ladder* can be read as registering the changing situation in Guyana in the early 1960s. The later novel appeared at the moment when ethnic violence in the country was intensifying. The inability of the crew to overcome their divisions obviously speaks to this situation. Additionally, the way in which Fenwick's rule—the highly problematic rule, that is, of a bourgeois professional—is succeeded by that of someone apparently closer to the crew (Weng) yet equally authoritarian prefigures the kind of politics that would emerge from the national crisis. The threat of state violence against Poseidon's followers, and the implication that Weng's ascent will mean the continuation of the policy of divide and rule, seem to prefigure the difficulties that beset Guyana under the regime of Forbes Burnham. It would be wrong to read too much into this comparison; after all, Burnham did not come to power until 1964. But it is possible that Harris's novel is registering the ingrained structural problems that contributed to the rise of authoritarianism in Guyana, a process evident also in a number of states across the Caribbean.

In his extensive work on the subject, Clive Thomas argues that due to the underdeveloped economic power of the national bourgeoisie in peripheral societies, the apparatus of the state becomes the "principal instrument of developing a strong class formation": "Traditionally, in the context of highly developed class societies . . . the state [is] the *object* of class conquest and the *instrument* of class rule. In the historical situation that prevails in these [peripheral] countries, it is more correct to argue that the state has become, as it were, an *instrument of class creation*."[43] The ruling class thus depends on the state for its very existence, which in turn breeds a zero-sum politics whereby to lose power is not just to lose control of the state but also to risk being destroyed as a group. Moreover, the importance of the state to the consolidation of economic power leads to "the notion of a 'state for itself,' in other words, a situation in which those controlling the state use it to promote the economic interests of their own group or family, friends, and political allies."[44] The upshot is that the state becomes a breeding ground for socially divisive policies. The desperation of the ruling class to hang on to power frequently results in it encouraging behavior such as ethnic chauvinism to shore up its own political capital in lieu of a genuine ability to foster nationally integrative development. Furthermore, as the repressive tendencies of the state increase, an effort is invariably made "to promote a charismatic leader, in the belief that such a leader will symbolize the unity of the whole people, will stand above class—and even above the government and state machinery—and that this will create a large political space within which the ruling class can manoeuvre."[45] Such tendencies were certainly evident in the evolution of the Burnham administration. That *The Secret Ladder* picks up on the lineaments of these strategies of power—as with Fenwick's use of Jordan as an "agent of governance" behind whose Medusa-like figure he can maneuver, for example—emphasizes how the conditions for the emergence of an authoritarian state were already present in Guyana.

Thomas has also called attention to the way in which ideology in the authoritarian state—often in contradiction to the divisive impact its policies have in reality—encourages "the vigorous promotion of the state as the principal unifying force and unifying symbol of society." "While it is recognised that racial and ethnic contradictions will affect the functioning of the state," argues Thomas, "ruling class ideology presents the *state itself* as a symbol of unity among these contradictory forces."[46] Again, Burnham's regime offers a case in point. In the collection of essays titled *Co-operative Republic, Guyana 1970*, published as part of a propaganda campaign by the PNC government, Burnham's elaboration of a national ideology, as Shona N. Jackson observes, can be seen to be "building on the racial structure that emerged out of plantation-era society in creating 'the small man' as a racial/ethnic hybrid to inherit the narrative of progress and development bequeathed to the nation by British colonialism."[47] This discourse, in which ethnic diversity was to feature as a marker of unity—along with other social factors it was incorporated into "one narrative that the regime could essentially manipulate in a kind of economic egalitarianism that would engender loyalty to the state"[48]—in fact drew on the established colonial paradigm in Guyana whereby ethnic groups were separated out and stereotyped according to perceived physical and cultural differences, their particular position in the socioeconomic order being determined by that group identity.[49] The postindependence model of national citizenship and collectivity was thus one in which discrete communities were to be held together in a single entity, a task that was to be performed by the state as an all-encompassing force operating above society.

We have already seen how Harris's work registers a concern with the way colonial structures might persist in the postcolonial era. The reality of what would come to pass in Guyana under Burnham, however, returns us to the limitations of Harris's vision of liberation, especially as it is articulated in *Palace of the Peacock*. The ending of that novel shows the crew becoming conscious of the "subtle and nebulous links" that bind them together in a cross-cultural community, yet the image of each man as a face at a window within the Palace of the Peacock might easily be read in terms of the idea of a cultural unity forged out of the holding together of otherwise discrete groups—a multicultural rather than cross-cultural vision. This is, of course, far from Harris's intention; he is seeking to unveil the contingency and mutuality of all peoples and cultures. But because of the way in which the narrative moves squarely here into the realm of the metaphysical, having hitherto emphasized the interpenetration of the material and spiritual, a sense of the historicity of these contingencies—of their being part of an active process—is occluded.

Commenting on the depiction of the Indian community in *The Far Journey of Oudin*, Poynting suggests that "though Harris for much of the novel avoids the 'conventional distinctions' and static social stereotypes which he criticizes in the conventional realist novel, there are times when the Indian peasant characters lose the rich concrete particularity of the individual and become emblematic figures, exemplary of particular spiritual tendencies, as reductive in a way as the portrayal of character in terms of traits which Harris so rightly criticizes."[50] Something similar occurs at the end of *Palace of the Peacock*, where the dematerializing trajectory makes it easy to regard the crewmen in the palace not as revealing of a dynamic imbrication of histories but as symbols for cultural substances that can exist outside historical determinations. Indeed, the move toward the metaphysical means that the very idea of cultures intermingling becomes predicated on a prior substantialization of culture as matter (which by extension obscures an understanding of culture as a process bound to the social reproduction of reality). Thus even as it penetrates the reified crust of the given world, the novel is in danger of substituting this for the flux of given cultural forms. This in turn limits any engagement with the historical pressures and power relations that have shaped these forms and contain the key to understanding how they have been construed and manipulated by successive governing regimes.

However, these limitations also form the basis of a wider problem with Harris's philosophical framework. One of the striking features of the final scene in *Palace of the Peacock* is the way the characters are encompassed by the spiritual wholeness they experience in the palace, where each looks through an eye "shared only with the soul, the soul and mother of the universe" (112). This sensation is inextricable from the music they hear, which further binds them together and stimulates the renewal of their sensorium: "One was what I am in the music—buoyed and supported above dreams by the undivided soul and anima in the universe from whom the word of dance and creation first came" (116). It is worth recalling here Bakhtin's conception of the grotesque body, which not only transgresses the limits of the isolated modern body but is also "something universal, representing all the people." "The body and bodily life have here," argues Bakhtin, "a cosmic and at the same time an all-people's character; this is not the body and its physiology in the modern sense of these words, because it is not individualized. The material bodily principle is contained not in the biological individual, not in the bourgeois ego, but in the people, a people who are continually growing and renewed."[51] Harris is clearly looking to evoke something similar to this "collective ancestral body of the people." Within the Palace of the Peacock, the crew acquire a decidedly "cosmic" sense of the interrelatedness of their histories and unbounded bodies—only here the emphasis falls more heavily on the spiritual as a collective binding agent. Yet it is again precisely with this shift toward the metaphysical that difficulties arise. Whereas the grotesque, collective body for Bakhtin is the proliferating and immeasurable mass of the material linkages between people and between their bodies and the earth, the actuality of such linkages is lost when seen exclusively through Harris's spiritual optic. As a result, rather than the collective being apprehended as the totality of active and mutating interconnections, it appears as differentiated within itself but discrete and inevitable—even timeless—as a structure (a quality emphasized by the way the discovery of cross-cultural community is said to be that which each crewman had "for ever been seeking and what he had eternally possessed" [117]). In other words, the unified ego of the isolated individual is broken apart, only for the ideological image of an unmediated unity to be resuscitated in communal form—a community that is diverse or cross-cultural to be sure, but one where the connection to particular social relations is in danger of being erased.

It is in moving away from historicizing the collectivity, therefore, that Harris's vision of liberation runs into most difficulties. While the collectivity is vital to securing meaningful freedom, it is not inherently emancipatory: it only becomes so when organized in a way conducive to the needs of the poor and the powerless, or yoked to a specific, politically progressive project. Indeed, we have already seen how the ideology of the collective can be used just as easily by authoritarian regimes for pernicious and regressive purposes, a possibility that the ambivalent finale of *The Secret Ladder* points up.[52] The issue is more clearly illustrated, however, by texts that explicitly engage with the various dictatorships under which Caribbean countries have suffered. Discussing the use of free indirect style in Latin American "dictator novels" such as Augusto Roa Bastos's *I the Supreme* (1974) and Alejo Carpentier's *Reasons of State* (1975), Franco Moretti observes how "in place of a third-person narrative modulating into a first-person monologue, we see the dictator's attempt to objectify his private (and pathological) self into the monumental poses of a public persona."[53] This stylistic shift registers the tendency for the authoritarian state to become identified with the (masculine) body of the dictator—for the dictator to become the embodiment of the nation as an all-encompassing figure simultaneously standing above society. Significantly, the image of an enveloping corporeality recalls Bakhtin's grotesque, proliferating body of the people. Here, however, it becomes the sign of the repressive encirclement of, and intrusion into, all aspects of social life by the state. Indeed, the sovereign body of the individual now reappears, albeit as an individuality that, in the form of the dictator, extends throughout the public sphere.

One can see this, for example, in *The Labyrinth* (1959), Enrique Laguerre's novel about the Trujillo dictatorship in the Dominican Republic. The first time the protagonist, Porfirio Uribe, witnesses the president close at hand, he is attending an official ceremony, decked out in full military regalia:

The "monster" seemed very human—indeed, Porfirio had an inclination to laugh. But this was no place for laughter, and he tried to repress the impish thoughts that danced through his brain. Was it possible that His Excellency, the President of the Republic, Don Augusto C. Luna del Valle, had once been known as the ranch-foreman, Ursulino Cachola? The most illustrious historians had invented the greatest battles and the most unforgettable feats of courage for him. Diplomats had announced triumphant proposals for international peace in his name. The most powerful nations had decorated him or allowed him to bestow decorations upon their chiefs of state. He even overshadowed nature itself.

Porfirio was now bursting with repressed laughter. Could it be that the fiction created by historians and biographers was actually this man of flesh and blood, with a face bloated as if were blowing into an imaginary *bombardino*?[54]

Porfirio's recognition of the discrepancy between myth and reality emphasizes the way in which the dictator's "flesh-and-blood" body has been monumentalized as the embodiment of an all-powerful state: he now even "overshadow[s] nature itself." This excessive, public body, which transgresses its own limits to stamp itself on the rest of society, has elements of the grotesque about it. Indeed, Porfirio's description conveys an air of the carnivalesque with its emphasis on the president's bloated features and extravagant costume. This is accentuated by the way Porfirio is on the verge of laughter—the laughter of the people being a key component of the culture of folk carnival humor (which generates the image of the grotesque body), and one of the means by which the high are brought low and the abstract made bodily. The logic of carnival, writes Bakhtin, is that of "the 'inside out' . . . of the 'turnabout,' of a continual shifting from top to bottom, from front to rear, of numerous parodies and travesties."[55] Here, however, the carnivalized body of the president is not about to open on to the possibility of liberation; rather, its grotesqueness registers only the perversity of authoritarian power, a power that ultimately causes the repression of Porfirio's laughter, not its release. Underscoring this point, later in the same scene the president is charged by a heifer from the ceremony. Again, the incident has all the qualities of the carnivalesque, with the president falling over as he runs to safety and an officer demanding absurdly that the beast be shot for not showing "the proper respect." But the upshot is an "all-pervading silence," one "more than weighty, it was bone-crushing," as the crowd stifle any laughter for fear of reprisals.[56]

A similar motif is evident in the series of novellas that make up *Amour, colère, et folie* (1968), Marie Chauvet's literary indictment of the Duvalier regime in Haiti. The disturbing opening of *Folie*, for instance, highlights the way in which the authoritarian state encroaches on every area of existence. A grandfather comes downstairs one morning to find some "men in black" (Duvalier's *tonton-*

macoutes) surrounding his family's home. Each day the men get closer, their occupation of the land producing a sense of claustrophobia that leads to the eruption of repressed hostilities that fracture the family unit. The same atmosphere
of suppressed violence and explosive release is evident, too, at a collective level.
One notable example comes when the mother of the family gets caught up in a
carnival band while walking down the street. "Manhandled by the crowd" (mal-
menée par la foule), she feels herself a "prisoner of its exuberance" (prisonnière
de son effervescence): "The people in a frenzy, eyes closed, howled louder and
louder, possessed by the sound of the tambour . . . taking refuge in ancestral
customs which, for a moment, gave [them] the illusory sensation of freedom."[57]
Here the mad *défoulement* of carnival generates a sense of imprisonment rather
than emancipation in the mother while offering only the illusion of liberty to
the crowd. The carnivalesque travesty does not imply the inversion of power relations in this context of all-pervasive authoritarian control; instead it signals a
frenzied manifestation of the madness induced by living under such constraints.
Far from presaging the rebirth of the community, this degraded expression
seems to register its disintegration.

The works of Laguerre and Chauvet not only underscore the necessity of
historicizing appeals to collectivity, therefore, but also point to a fundamental
blockage in attempts at articulating social emancipation in the types of societies they depict. The communicative difficulties dramatized in both texts—
Laguerre's "bone-crushing" silence, Chauvet's frenzied howling—are symptomatic of an underlying lack of collective control over the material conditions of
existence. The issue here is one of structuration, to borrow Glissant's phrase.
"Every community," he writes, "lives a space-time that is *more or less* socially
mediated, and . . . this relationship structures the behaviour of each member of
the community 'through' episodes of individual history and physiological determinants."[58] Collective control over the principles of the construction of social
reality (division of labor, kinship patterns, property rights) enables a community to constitute itself in relation to its surroundings—the process of "structuration."[59] When this control is absent, however, a traumatic disjunction arises
between the needs and practices of the people and the institutions that organize
the social world. Moreover, a controlled or mediated relationship to the land is
necessary for the elaboration of a history coincident with the collectivity. "The
individual, the community, the land are inextricable in the process of creating
history," maintains Glissant.[60] A community that is unable to structure its material reality autonomously is in danger of being unable to structure its history
autonomously or to give voice to it in a coherent and explicit manner. Such was
the case, of course, for the colonized, who were subject to the repressive frameworks imposed by colonialism. But such is also the case for the majority of people in the postcolonial situations described by Laguerre and Chauvet. Here the
authoritarian state, which focuses power ever more narrowly on the ruling class

while working to demobilize the masses, continues to frustrate genuine collective control over material reality.[61] The result is precisely the arrested expression of collectivity represented by Chauvet's carnival revelers, where the grotesque body, which has the capacity to prefigure a liberated community, becomes the sign of a victimized and disfigured group.

If thus far I have focused on authoritarian or dictatorial states, that is not to say that similar issues are not at stake in those countries marked by less extreme processes of constitutionalist decolonization and bourgeois nationalism. Indeed, while the worst features of an invasive authoritarianism are absent here, comparable problems arise in terms of elite power and the continued marginalization of the masses. The difficulty remains of how the habitus inculcated by imperialism is to be overthrown and the social order restructured in accordance with the needs of the poor and the powerless. At the end of the previous chapter, I noted the way in which a number of Anglophone and Francophone Caribbean novels from the 1950s evoked the potential for such transformation. This potential was inseparable from the gains made by burgeoning nationalist movements that drew their strength from progressive alliances between the middle and working classes. However, we also saw how many of the same novels foreshadowed the dissipation of this potential, a phenomenon I connected to the topos of the tragic sacrifice. I suggested that the crisis this motif undergoes—its inability to figure the renewal of the community in the way that it had in Roumain's *Masters of the Dew*, for instance—represented the translation into the logic of the literary field of a crisis besetting the political field. In the remainder of this chapter, I want to expand on this contention, using Lovelace's *The Wine of Astonishment* to suggest that the crisis mediated by this malfunctioning topos is that of the breakdown of the alliance between the middle and working classes as a result of the failures of the national bourgeoisie.

Although published in 1982, *The Wine of Astonishment* was written directly after Lovelace's 1968 novel *The Schoolmaster*.[62] Hence the backdrop to its creation was the tumultuous late sixties and early seventies period in the Caribbean, when a tide of radicalism swept the region. Events such as the 1968 Rodney Affair in Jamaica and the so-called Black Power Revolution of 1970 in Trinidad demonstrated the disillusionment of the masses with the postindependence political settlement.[63] Set in the middle decades of the twentieth century, *The Wine of Astonishment* does not treat this later era explicitly. However, through its presentation of the travails of a Spiritual Baptist community in the Trinidadian village of Bonasse, the text offers a complex mediation on issues of resistance and collective consciousness.

The Bonasse villagers, we should note immediately, have managed to maintain an alternative habitus to that imposed by the colonial order, their cultural practices the repository of a countermemory of collective struggle. Rituals such as the stickfight not only replay in symbolic form the violence of the plantation system but also, through the dances and gestures of the stickfighter, transfigure such violence into an assertion of communal identity. Thus, when the village champion Bolo enters the ring, performing "the dance, the adventure, the ceremony to show off the beauty of the warrior," it is as if he is "offering himself up with his quick speed and rhythm, as if what he really want was for people to see in him a beauty that wasn't his alone, was theirs, ours, to let us know that we . . . was people too."[64] The ability to structure and articulate their history autonomously in this manner is inextricable from the degree of control the villagers exert over the structuration of their material and social reality. Nowhere is this more evident than with the Spiritual Baptist Church.

The Spiritual Baptists were a revivalist Christian sect born from "a cultural transaction between the African inheritance of the slaves and the new religion acquired in the new world."[65] In 1917 the sect was banned: its manner of worship, which included "handclapping, dancing, stamping and loud singing of hymns all leading to possession by the spirit," was considered to violate norms of respectability; the colonial authorities desired that people should attend more conventional Anglican or Roman Catholic ceremonies.[66] But as *The Wine of Astonishment*'s narrator, Eva, explains, the Spiritual Baptist Church offers the villagers a sense of community that the Catholic Church cannot. Unlike the Catholic Church, says Eva, where one must "kneel down in front of white saints," the Baptists' church has no "white priests or latin ceremonies. But is our own. Black people own it. Government ain't spent one cent helping us to build it" (32). Such control over the structuration process strengthens collective expression, reflected in the "we" of Eva's narration. Unlike the isolated individuals of *The Secret Ladder*, the Bonasse villagers recognize their interconnectedness, out of which emerges the distinct yet—because entwined with all—omnipresent voice of Eva.

The conjunction between the material reality of the community and the cultural forms through which it represents itself is underlined by the description of the Baptists' worship:

> The rain was falling and the church was leaking and the brethren was humming deep in soft rhythm to Bee preaching, and all of us was moving and the church was a sea and we was the boats rocking sweet. . . . And in between the humming and the jumping, Sister Lucas . . . get up trembling, walk to them and she balance on one leg and she step off in that sweet, graceful, noble walk that black women alone have from generations of carrying on their head buckets of water and baskets of cocoa, and she go to the Centre Post. (61–62)

The ceremony is striking in its physicality: as with the stickfight ritual, the body becomes the vessel of communication, as emphasized by the image of the congregation as "boats rocking sweet." Indeed, the service allows for both the release and the transformative rearticulation on a collective level of the memories carried by the body. Sister Lucas, for example, enacts the toil that black women have been forced to undertake for centuries, manifesting this past for the community while simultaneously turning it into something "sweet, graceful, noble." The smooth, rolling cadences of the narrative—its undulating syntactical patterns ("was falling . . . was leaking . . . was humming")—register and reinforce the sense of bodily movement, the tripping meter ("and she balance . . . and she step . . . and she go") suggesting the graceful steps of Sister Lucas. Thus the passage dramatizes the way in which the cultural practices and alter/native habitus of the villagers open on to a different understanding of history and society. The church becomes the synecdoche for a form of collective organization adjusted to the needs and experiences of the majority. It does not just represent a cultural identity but also figures new, egalitarian social structures via the nonhierarchical character of the Baptist ceremony, wherein all can be touched by the Spirit and may dance around the center post.

However, although it stands as a bastion of resistant history and autonomous structuration, the form of collectivity embodied in the church has not been generalized to the rest of society, which remains structured along imperialist lines. Set in this context, the Baptists are not as strong or as independent as they first appear, as evidenced by their response to being banned. The uncertainty of the worshippers when confronted by the authorities points to the power still exerted by the colonial legacy. Often they are reduced to inaction: the men fail to help Bolo when he is beaten by the police, for instance, and Eva's husband Bee hesitates so long over his stated aim to break the ban that he "make a fool of himself" (51). In part, such behavior has its roots in the equally ambivalent nature of their religion, the residue of Christian doctrine it contains continuing to exert, in some respects, the same pernicious impact it did when used by the colonizers to enforce control. This is especially so with regard to the notion of suffering as a prelude to future release. When Eva asserts that the community has been made to suffer by God because the "strong suffer most" and "we could bear it" (2), her beliefs appear to encourage only acquiescence to the constraints imposed by the ruling class. But there also persists a debilitating, inculcated reliance on the "mother-country." "We will have to talk to the authorities," claims Brother Oswald with respect to the ban. "Let them know that we is British citizens too. . . . We have to get a man they will listen to, a man who they respect and who could talk for us" (38). It is thus not just a case of restructuring society along different lines. The consciousness of the villagers must first also be heightened: the sense of solidarity that the church grants them has to be yoked to a greater awareness of the sociopolitical bases of their oppression.

As it is, the community turns to a man who "could talk for us," in Brother Oswald's words. This is the villager Ivan Morton, the schoolteacher educated in Port of Spain and elected to the Legislative Council as representative for Bonasse. The relationship between Morton and the other villagers figures the alliance between the middle and working classes that was so crucial to the nationalist movements of the time. The struggle over the church becomes a microcosm of the struggle for independence, when the inroads made by the bourgeoisie into the institutions of power seemed to hold out the potential for progressive change. As we saw in the previous chapter, these transformations were bound up with a general process of modernization in the region, something alluded to here also:

> The government had some people from England making a report to give teachers and civil servants more pay, and a lot of Americans was coming in to put up industries in the island with a tax holiday.
>
> New schools was building, giving children more places in high school, and we was hearing that soon there would be free secondary education on the whole island. (6)

This promise, however, was offset by the regressive effects of modernization in a context where it remained tied to imperial imperatives (not only those of Britain but increasingly also those of the United States). In *The Wine of Astonishment*, these issues are dramatized through Morton's behavior. Educated within the colonial system, he is not only incapable of raising the villagers' consciousness to the underlying causes of their subjugation but also dismisses the significance of the church as a bulwark of cultural memory and collective identity. Indeed, at one point Bee reveals that Morton has told him that "he not against the principle of the freedom of worship but what worrying him is that I, we should still be in the dark ages in these modern times when we could settle down and be civilize" (13). Aside from the repetition of the colonial discourse of the civilizing mission, Morton singularly fails to grasp that the Baptists do represent a form of modernity, one that is inflected by their own lived experience and the particular responses they have elaborated to the Caribbean's irruption into modernity. By contrast, Morton's model for "these modern times" is an imported one that will only foster long-term underdevelopment.

This lack of understanding on the part of the schoolmaster-turned-politician is but one shortcoming in a character who will come to display all the limitations of the national bourgeoisie in colonial and postcolonial countries. Deprived of genuine control over an externally dominated economic system, he acts as an agent for foreign capital. Rather than helping a local shopkeeper obtain a loan, his energies are spent securing tax breaks for incoming U.S. industries. Like the political mimic men of V. S. Naipaul's novel of that name—men who become merely symbols displaying "the trappings of power: the motor car marked M, the suits on the hottest days, the attendant white men and women"[67]—Morton assiduously cultivates the postures of power, including moving into the former house of a white estate owner and repeatedly holding up "the fingers of his right hand in a V for victory sign, like Winston Churchill" (84), without once exercising his influence on behalf of the people.

In fact, Morton seems to become locked in these postures, the narrative illustrating his alienation from the community by way of the gradual stiffening of his body. The jacket and tie he wears to project an air of "civility" constrict his movement and force him to walk slowly in the heat. Alongside him walks his wife, a "starched, tall, light-skin lady" (49). She is contrasted unfavorably with the village girl Eulalie, whom Morton earlier abandoned. "If it was Eulalie walking by the side of Ivan Morton," muses Eva, "her chest woulda been jumping and her bodyline rolling to make that white dress dance and sing" (50). The petrifaction of Morton's gestures manifests his suppression of the very history that defines the people he is there to speak for, a history that—as we saw with the Baptists' worship—is tied to the polyrhythmic movements of the body. More broadly, his disconnection comes to stand as a warning about a certain way of articulating the link between intellectuals and the masses in the context of the nationalist struggle. For Fanon, this link had to be dialectical: "To educate the masses politically," he wrote, "does not mean, cannot mean making a political speech. What it means is to try, relentlessly and passionately, to teach the masses that everything depends on them; that if we stagnate it is their responsibility, and that if we go forward it is due to them too, that there is no such thing as a demiurge, that there is no famous man who will take the responsibility for everything, but that the demiurge is the people themselves and the magic hands are finally only the hands of the people."[68] But insofar as Morton "educates" the masses, it is to encourage precisely the view of himself as the "famous man" who will solve all their problems.

Yet the villagers themselves are complicit in this deification of the intellectual. Even when Morton was a young boy, they had him marked down as the one who would "rise to take up the greater burden to lead his people out of the hands of the Pharaoh" (40). "When he pass us in the street," recounts Eva, "his chin up, scenting another air and his gaze far away as if he wasn't here in Bonasse, not seeing the people or the place, we nod our heads and smile: we understand. We understand that a boy with all that brain and that great burden on him at such a early age, wouldn't have time to see people" (41). The rush to anoint Morton as the savior blinds the community to his inadequacies. More fundamentally, they fail to grasp that, far from marking out his suitability for leadership, his inability to "see people" should disqualify him from the task.

The tendency to exalt an individual as a Christlike hero come to save the community is an understandable one in circumstances where people suffer under enslavement or imperial domination, and as we saw previously, representations of such figures are common in Caribbean literature.[69] Clearly the influence of

Christian teaching and iconography plays a crucial role in generating such perceptions. Shiva Naipaul has written of his "sense of shock when, in 1955 or 1956, I saw a group of black women parading with placards that proclaimed Dr. Eric Williams—our future Prime Minister—as the Messiah appointed to lead his people out of bondage. It was my introduction to the idea that the language of religion could be transformed into the language of politics."[70] Of course, politicians have proved themselves adept at cultivating such religious parallels. The need to do so has often derived from a lack of real control over economic structures still dominated by foreign capital. This lack of control mediates against the instigation of social programs that could truly change the condition of the poor. In lieu of such programs, the strategy of playing on religious identifications is a useful way of shoring up popular support.

The structural weaknesses this reveals, however, are partly responsible for the rise of such demiurgic leaders in the first place. They create the conditions for a highly individualized form of politics wherein the party is reduced to the successes and failures of one charismatic hero. Glissant has noted how, in Martinique, the fact that the elite do not exert meaningful control over the economy means that even when this class does seek to resist, it cannot do so structurally. Its radicalization will instead take place in relation to "selected individuals." Through education or exposure to the realities of decolonization, contends Glissant, these individuals accede to "a critical but always personalized vision of the ensemble of the system. This strongly individualized (non-total) aspect of resistance among the middle 'class' . . . will reinforce the tendency for the adoption of charismatic, popular leaders issued from this class."[71] Though Glissant's arguments refer to the extreme situation that obtains in Martinique, where the elite have been reduced to a chronic nonfunctionalism by departmentalization, similar problems are evident in other Caribbean societies saddled with comprador bourgeoisies. Writing about Trinidad, for instance, Gordon Lewis identifies the antecedents of this kind of personalized national politics in the various struggles for office waged during the 1940s and 1950s.[72]

The danger of such individualism, then, is its tendency to divert attention away from collective action. The elevation of leaders into messianic figures may be useful in creating a point of identification or stimulating immediate engagement on the part of the masses. But unless the people come to recognize that, as Fanon put it, "the demiurge is the people themselves," the ability to effect long-term structural change coincident with the needs of the majority will be limited. Moreover, should the all-too-human messiah fail to live up to expectations, supporters may sink into despair. In *The Wine of Astonishment*, the faith placed in Morton results in just these kinds of problems: the villagers' initial reliance on him contributes to their indecision over whether to act collectively against the ban on the church, and his frequent disappointment of their hopes intensifies their sense of helplessness.

Ultimately Eva and Bee realize that in Morton "is not a leader we choose . . . but a star, a star to be alone" (136). Their recognition is prompted in large part by the actions of the stickfight champion Bolo. His attempts to resist not only the ban but also many of the other changes the village is undergoing do, to some extent, raise the collective consciousness of the community. Unlike the mimic man Morton, moreover, Bolo is far more connected to the villagers and actively fights for their rights. But questions remain as to whether his efforts to move the community to action also furnish a vision of a radically different form of collectivity. Does he project a solution to the structural inarticulacy that increasingly besets the villagers (something best exemplified by the way the ban reduces the Baptists to worshipping in a "dead way, without bellringing or handclapping or shouting" [17])? I end this chapter by suggesting that he does not—that his rebellion contains fundamental problems that limit its potential. Moreover, the formal means by which the narrative represents Bolo's struggle, in which he takes on the role of the tragic hero and sacrificial scapegoat, reemphasizes the problem with a form of political representation predicated on the Christlike elevation of certain individuals above the masses.

Although they stand in absolute opposition to each other, Bolo and Morton nevertheless appear as twinned protagonists. Both misunderstand the possibilities inherent in the cultural practices of the community they seek to save, for example. In Morton's case, as noted earlier, the misunderstanding results from his adherence to colonial ideology and his belief that modernization means paying obeisance to foreign models. Bolo, of course, is very different: he not only opposes the latter kind of modernization but is suspicious of any sort of change, fearing its impact on the community. Yet his desire to hold on to what he considers the purity of the village's traditions undermines his resistance. Once again, these issues are figured through the body. In the stickfight ritual, Bolo's fluid movements are a conduit for the embodied cultural memory of the people, manifesting a history of collective struggle. But in trying to bring this struggle into the present, he seems to lose touch with something fundamental to its vitality. As he assumes a rebellious posture in response to the persecution of the Baptists, his movements harden: whereas he once had "that free easy stride, that smooth fluent joyful walk," now a "stiffness come over him" (27). The echo of the way Morton's body petrifies under the weight of his own mimicry is clear. With Bolo, however, the issue is that of the necessity of modifying cultural practice, as well as the modalities of resistance, to respond to changing circumstances.

Early in the novel it is clear that this will be a problem for the village champion. When a ban on Carnival reduces stickfighting to a series of mock battles, Bolo worries that he is becoming "a clown performing for a drink of rum" (25). The singer Clem advises him to remember whom the ritual is really for, even as he makes a show of it: "What you worrying yourself for? . . . When I take up my guitar, I don't sing for them, I sing for me; and when you dance in the stickfight ring, you dance for you" (25). For Clem, no matter how much he "play the clown, nothing could make him less than himself" (25). Bolo, though, is less adaptable. While his refusal to bow to the folklorization of the stickfight is a necessary one, his refusal also to contemplate how the ritual could be made to engage the contemporary situation is ultimately regressive. In wanting to shield such cultural forms from the "corrupting" influence of the modern world, he blunts their power to resist the conditions that foster such folklorization. By contrast, Clem recognizes that, with modernization, things "had to change": he begins "taking the old music, stickfight tunes, and bongo songs and putting words to them and singing them as calypso" (28). Calypso, by melding the "old music" with new forms, becomes the means to articulate the resistant identity of a community confronted by new social conditions in a way that Bolo's frozen gestures cannot. Indeed, at the end of the novel, the Spirit lacking in the church during the first Baptist ceremony after the ban is lifted is heard by Eva in the music of a steel band. Tellingly, the steel pan is an eloquent example of how practices or objects associated with a foreign-dominated process of modernization—in this case, empty oil drums from the U.S. military bases on Trinidad—can be reappropriated, indigenized, and used to express radically new meanings.

Bolo, it seems, is stuck in a mind-set geared toward a time when issues of domination and resistance were more clear-cut, when his enemy was the obvious target of the white colonist rather than the more insidious violence of commercialization. The campaign he undertakes to make the community reflect on itself and resist its own disintegration, for all its importance in demonstrating the necessity of combating the hollowing out of indigenous cultural practices, does not offer a way forward or a sense of how these practices might be regrounded and renewed in light of the social transformations that have already taken place. His attempt to unite the villagers by violently provoking them into action only leads to their alienation without initiating a dialectical movement toward a greater understanding of reality. Bolo's actions gradually become "a kinda joke" (109) before climaxing in tragedy. He does not succeed in penetrating the immediate form of the forces that menace the community to grasp the underlying power relations that structure these. To some degree, in fact, he replicates Morton in diverting attention away from such structures.

Moreover, Bolo also mirrors the councilor in seeking to separate himself from the collectivity and to cultivate a messianic individualism. As Bee puts it, Bolo "choose out himself . . . to be the sacrifice. To be the one terrible enough and strong enough and close enough to our heart to drive us to take up our manhood challenge that we turn away from for too long" (122). Whereas in *Masters of the Dew*, however, Manuel was able to refashion the group by stepping outside of it and performing the representative deed of self-sacrifice, here Bolo's attempt at playing the sacrificial victim only seems set to perpetuate a cycle of violence.

Part of the reason for this is the impact of that same process of modernization Bolo tries not to engage with. In contrast to Roumain's Fonds Rouge, where the villagers retained control over their immediate material reality and the threat represented by Hilarion's scheme to expropriate the land seemed a distant one, Bonasse's integrity as a community is progressively eroded. Social bonds are dissolved by the corrosive power of capital—"I guess you could say we was changing," admits Eva, "with the Yankees in the island and the hustlers in the village and the gayappe and lend-hand dying and the people living a life every man for himself" (78)—and the power the villagers did have to autonomously structure their social reality wanes over the course of the novel. It is this underlying lack of control that renders the act of sacrifice problematic as a means to renew the collectivity. Indeed, in this context, violence "ceases to be simply an instrument for effecting change—it becomes a desired end in itself, an expression of the tragic resignation of the people to their fate."[73]

To understand why this might be so, I want to turn briefly to René Girard's *Violence and the Sacred*. Analyzing the historical role of ritual sacrifice in a number of societies and works of literature, Girard argues that the death of a sacrificial victim can serve not only to resolve feuding but also as the basis on which collective history is founded. Should reciprocal violence take hold of a people, he contends, it will spread throughout the community with disastrous effect; the "role of sacrifice is to stem this rising tide of indiscriminate substitutions and redirect violence into 'proper' channels."[74] These "indiscriminate substitutions" are the result of the tragic symmetry that grips those involved in such violence. For Girard it is not the difference between individuals that perpetuates their feud but its effacement. This effacement disrupts the stability imposed by the demarcations of the social order and enables the constant reversals in position that lock people into a cycle of vengeance. However, it is precisely this symmetry that will also allow for the resolution of the crisis, since once a unanimity of violence exists, society can recompose itself around the belief that one among them is alone responsible.[75] The death of this scapegoat provides a conduit for hatred that breaks reciprocity. Hence in subsequent sacrificial rituals, this death is reenacted to affirm the social order. Just as the scapegoat is transformed into the cause of disorder, so his or her exit is mythified as the moment when the community was restored. Such rituals thereby make visible one form of violence but conceal the deeper conflict at the core of society, as well as the inequities of the social demarcations that enforced the original stability before the crisis. As Girard argues, a "particular version of events succeeds in imposing itself; it loses its polemical nature in becoming the acknowledged basis of the myth, in becoming the myth itself."[76] The community thus narrates back to a founding act, establishing a line of filiation down to what will become the bedrock of collective identity.

The problem when it comes to the situation dramatized in *The Wine of As-*

tonishment is that where the community lacks collective control over the social order, the victimization and death of the scapegoat will either merely inflame violence or, in restoring the social order, reinforce that initial lack of control. Indeed, insofar as the scapegoat's death imposes one particular narrative of the restoration of the community over the complexity of the struggles that preceded the sacrifice, it obscures the underlying—in this instance, imperial—violence that had structured society unevenly in the first place. The events around Bolo bear this out. His initial violent behavior does not have the effect he intends due to the difficulty of uniting a community increasingly fragmented by not only immediate, internal pressures but also wider external ones to which—as will become clear in a moment—the scapegoat does not really respond. Then when he does sacrifice himself, the narrative of his martyrdom—though drawing attention to those internal pressures—actually imposes itself over a more subtle and comprehensive understanding of the social totality. These limitations would again seem to be inseparable from Bolo's assumption of an individualized, messianic posture. As Eva recognizes, Bolo's death in fact enables the villagers to abnegate responsibility for the struggle for freedom: "It just give us the chance," she muses, "to put aside our human challenge and blame it all on Bolo, make him the victim and the sacrifice, make him Christ . . . [and] pretend that his death solve the problem" (129).

The idea that Bolo's actions remain bounded by an underlying framework of power, one that his sacrifice is unable to penetrate, is reinforced formally in the text by the way he gets sucked into the space-time structures of the colonial order and its particular scripts of reality. When he first confronts the policeman Prince—a native instrument of colonial power—after the arrest of the Baptists for breaking the ban on worship, their encounter assumes a ritual character: "Slow, stiff-leg like one dog inspecting another, Prince walk up to Bolo and look him over from head to toe. . . . And Bolo stand up there in the middle of the road, tall, stiff, his mouth half open as the other fighting dog" (67). The situation may bear comparison to the stickfight, but the flowing gestures of that ceremony are here replaced by petrified postures that bespeak a tragic symmetry. As Bolo and Prince oppose one another, the differences between them are effaced. Just as the warring protagonists in Greek tragedy become interchangeable as their accusations fly back and forth,[77] so the two exchange repetitious dialogue:

"Listen," Prince say, and Prince still cool, still calm, still comfortable in his own power, "you obstructing the law. If you don't move . . ."

"If I don't move?" Bolo ask. "If I don't move?" Bolo ask again.

"You *want* me to arrest you?" Prince ask. . . .

"You want to arrest me?" Bolo ask, his voice so polite and soft. . . .

"You want me to arrest you?" Prince ask again, in his softest words, wondering a little. (69)

There is an infectiousness about this theatrical standoff as each character gets caught up in the other's speech. But it is Bolo who at the outset is drawn into the official, declaratory discourse of "the law" as voiced by Prince. Bolo's echoing of Prince emphasizes his inability to break through the ruling structuration of reality. The conflict generates an order of symmetry that appears absolute, the cyclical syntax through which it is articulated creating the impression of an unalterable progression toward disaster.

This becomes evident as the novel reaches its climax and Bolo's attempted heroic sacrifice fails to go to plan. Having taken two village girls hostage, he waits, hoping that the people will "go against him with strength and anger" and so awaken to their own power (121). All that occurs, however, is a sterile ritual. The police are called by the girls' father, which thwarts Bolo's plan, since it reintroduces the external discourse of colonial law. The scene at Bolo's house again has an air of static theatricality, with the "six policemen spread out in a circle with their guns on Bolo who stand up on the steps with the girls in front of him" (127). The actions of the characters appear predetermined: the police sergeant talks to Bee "like he know already just what he going to do no matter what Bee say" (123); Bolo's response to the gathering at his house is dictated by an absolute logic: "'You come for the girls?' Bolo turn now to the sergeant. 'Then you come to kill me,' he say in a matter-of-fact way" (126). This cause-and-effect fatalism once more manifests an incapacity to articulate a position beyond the dominant organization of society. Bolo's speech reinforces the paralysis, beginning to conform always to an apparently unalterable position, best exemplified by his greeting to Bee: "'You bring police for me,' he say, not questioning it but fixing it as a fact in his brain" (125).

The standoff at Bolo's house ends bloodily: not only is Bolo shot by the police, but one of the hostages is killed also. The outcome underscores the limitations of the sacrificial rite in this context: whereas it might have worked if the conflict was only an internal matter, here the police, who serve as agents for the external force of imperialism and usurp the role meant for a united group of villagers, short-circuit the dialectic of sacrifice. Moreover, it is precisely that external imperial force that must be consciously grasped and its structures of power mapped, something Bolo's actions seem incapable of facilitating. While they draw attention to the *individual* tyranny of Prince, they do not give on to a coherent vision of how the power relations that permitted him to gain ascendancy in the first place might be overturned and replaced by a new social order. The needs of the masses in this sense are overlooked. This gap in understanding can be seen as being mediated formally by an interesting lacuna in the text: the youngest hostage, who is shot and killed alongside Bolo, is never mentioned again after the incident, as if she has been erased from the text. Her effacement, moreover, points to the masculinism of this tragic narrative, its exclusive organization around the actions of a male hero.

More generally, the manner in which the sacrificial topos breaks down here can be read not just as indicating the problems with Bolo's approach to instigating a collective response to oppression but also as figuring, on some more abstract level, the breakdown of the political dispensation that underpinned the process of constitutionalist decolonization in Trinidad as in, for example, Jamaica and Barbados. In other words, this crisis of representation translates into the logic of the literary field the crisis in the nationalist alliance between the middle and working classes in the late 1960s and 1970s. The failure of the sacrificial act to provide the community with a sense of how they might assume control over the construction of social reality mediates the failure of bourgeois nationalism to dismantle the socioeconomic structures inherited from the colonial state. The connection we have noted between the persistence of patriarchal gender relations and the recurrence of the motif of the tragic male hero can be read along similar lines. The masculinist character of this motif refracts the way bourgeois nationalist movements perpetuated colonialist frameworks with regard to gender identities and female sexuality. Hence the breakdown of the topos mediates also the limitations the retention of such patriarchal models placed on efforts at social transformation.

If Bolo's actions do not have the desired effect on the community, then, nevertheless this failure at least shows up the malfunctioning of the link between the "leader" and the "led," thereby suggesting the need for a different articulation of the relationship between the people and those who seek to represent them. These new relations must form the basis of original modalities of collectivity capable of wresting back control of the structuration of reality.

A number of critics point to what appear to be the seeds of this development in the final scene when the Spirit is heard in the steel band.[78] I want to suggest, however, that a vision of collective renewal also arises in the middle of the narrative of sacrifice, revealing a submerged alternative to the dominant understanding of the social world. From the moment Bolo abducts the village girls, the text hurtles inexorably toward its bloody finale. But in the middle of this sequence, an interlude disrupts the flow of action. Eva has just watched the men depart, and the expectation is that she will now recount, via Bee, the confrontation with Bolo. Instead the text remains focused on her private thoughts for a brief period:

> I remain there at the window long after [Bee] gone, watching outside, watching the marigolds . . . with their yellow flowers like turn up parasols catching the white rain and above them the coconut tree with its trunk straight and its head leaning to one side in the slow wind and its branches stretch out like two arms making a cross under the sky, and coming down the road is Brother Christopher and his son in their donkey cart rolling on their way to work the piece of land Brother Christopher have. . . . I stay there by the window, forgetting time, forgetting everything. (125)

This lyrical passage breaks into the account of tragic sacrifice and offers a sense of depth and possibility different to the linear momentum that defines Bolo's last hours. Eva dips into what seems like another reality when set against the events unfolding elsewhere, a reality in which the rejuvenation of the community can be conceived otherwise. The focus on her perceptions highlights the feminine in contradistinction to the masculinism of Bolo's sacrificial narrative and suggests a potential for moving away from patriarchal social models. Although the passage is loaded with imagery tied to the crucifixion, its effect diverges from that produced by Bolo's death. There the cross is the rebel's lifeless body, lying on the ground with "feet close together" and "arms stretch[ed] out" (128). Here the cross is also the tree of life, the link made in Eva's consciousness between this resurrection symbol and her surroundings emphasizing how the villagers must assume control over material reality if their "resurrection" is not to be stillborn like Bolo's. By crafting a coincidence between lived experience and the environment—symbolized by Brother *Christ*opher's working the soil—they can inscribe themselves on the land. That this connection to the land should recognize a cross-cultural heritage is underscored by the allusiveness of the passage. The Christian legacy, placed in relation to the specificity of the Caribbean landscape, is, via the fluid, rolling rhythm of the text, connected to the bodily movements and ritualized practice through which the Baptists maintain their history. (Indeed, the style of the passage recalls the earlier account of their worship.) Moreover, the juxtaposition of images such as "yellow flowers like turn up parasols" points beyond the culture-nature dichotomy (which was so detrimental to Fenwick's apprehension of reality in *The Secret Ladder*) while also suggesting the conjunction of disjunctive elements that characterizes the marvelous real, thereby invoking something of the specificity of Caribbean experience.

In that it interrupts the expected trajectory of the narrative, therefore, this passage is a diversionary one. But it is also diversionary in the sense meant by Glissant when he uses the term in conjunction with the idea of a "return to the point of entanglement." Referring to Fanon's involvement in the Algerian struggle, he argues that this "diversion"—Fanon's commitment to acting on his ideas—enabled the development of new, concrete possibilities that could be brought to bear on the Caribbean situation. "It is clear," he asserts, "that in this case *to act on one's ideas* does not only mean to fight, to make demands, to give free rein to the language of defiance, but to take full responsibility for *a complete break*. The radical break is the extreme edge of the process of diversion."[79] Following this radical break, one can return to one's problems and seek to implement a radically new solution. For Glissant, as noted earlier, it is at the point of entanglement that "we must ultimately put to work the forces of creolization" as part of an attempt to negate the existing social unity and initiate an emancipatory future. The diversion that appears in the climactic scenes of *The Wine of Astonishment* suggests the radical break that is required from the space-time structuration imposed by imperialism, as well as the need to "put to work" the entangled legacies alluded to in the passage to construct a new social order. The way in which this diversion is occulted by the dominant narrative paradigm of the tragic sacrifice, however, indicates that not only is such an order still to be actualized but even its very articulation poses problems; new forms of political expression and representation are necessary for its elaboration, just as new narrative forms will have to be invented for its translation into the logic of the literary field.

3

Literary Deliriums: Cultural Expression, Commodity Fetishism, and the Search for Community

In Patrick Chamoiseau's 1986 novel *Chronique des sept misères* (Chronicle of the Seven Sorrows), the decline of the Fort-de-France market in Martinique is signaled by the descent into madness of its *djobeurs* (market porters or odd-job men). When one among them, Bidjoule, suffers the loss of a wheel from his barrow, for instance, he becomes delirious, "rubbing the same ten words together in a furious discussion with himself." Later he is discovered "in the brushwood of Bois-de-Boulogne . . . buried up to the waist and claiming to be a yam."[1] Underlying this insanity is the destruction of the *djobeurs'* social world in the postwar years with the increase in imported French produce and the construction of modern supermarkets. Bidjoule's condition is symptomatic of a people whose "relation with its surroundings (what we would call its nature) is in a discontinuous relation to its accumulation of experiences (what we would call its culture)."[2] Unable to structure its history autonomously, the community suffers the past as a series of convulsions that it cannot bring to light on a collective basis. The *djobeur's* actions manifest this lack of control over social reality, yet they can also be regarded in Glissant's terms as an unconscious refusal of the "historically imposed structuration" that reflects also a "negative, unconscious, traumatic search for a sense of security in lived space-time."[3] Bidjoule's burying himself in the ground, in other words, could be understood as a delirious attempt to claim that which is denied him: a real connection to the Martinican landscape and its history.

We have already encountered similar difficulties in *The Wine of Astonishment*. There, an externally driven modernization process, alongside the meretricious actions of a comprador bourgeoisie, divided and devitalized the villagers of Bonasse. The shortcomings of the new elite, and the problem of identifying the oppressor as the more obvious manifestations of colonial violence are replaced by the insidious menace of commercialization, resulted in a crisis of political representation. This, I argued, was mediated as a crisis of aesthetic representation, most notably through the malfunctioning of the topos of the tragic sacrifice. I also pointed to passages toward the end of Lovelace's novel when the outlines of a different form of structuration appear, figuring the promise of a social world reorganized in relation to the local environment and the lived experience of the community.

The need for a radical break with the structures and habitus implanted by imperialism found popular expression in the protests that swept across the Caribbean in the late sixties and early seventies. These reflected increasing frustration
with the limited progress made by a number of nationalist projects. The growing
strength of revolutionary ideologies such as Black Power underscored the desire
for a more thoroughgoing transformation of society in the interests of the poor
and powerless. In this chapter, I explore further this desire for change by considering Lovelace's *The Dragon Can't Dance*, which includes a fictionalized account of
the 1970 Black Power Revolution in Trinidad. I also examine the continuing difficulties with both articulating and instantiating such change. In many ways, the
problems identified in the previous chapter have intensified, the relentless commodification of social relations accelerating the erosion of resistant habitus and
the histories they embody. Far from it seeming likely that alternative modalities
of structuration will be installed, the very foundations of these emergent formations are under threat.

In this respect, I consider two novels emanating from islands that represent
something of an extreme insofar as they remain nonindependent. Chamoiseau's
Solibo Magnifique (1988) and Luis Rafael Sánchez's *La guaracha del Macho Camacho* (Macho Camacho's Beat) (1976) engage with the fallout from, respectively,
Martinique's position as a *département* of France and Puerto Rico's subordination to U.S. imperial hegemony. Despite their emphasis on the difficulties of
cultural expression, however, both novels (and the same is true for *The Dragon
Can't Dance*) suggest that new social relations and forms of collectivity can be
articulated, though they embed that suggestion less in any explicit avowal than
in the challenges and innovations of their aesthetics.

In terms of thinking about the literary encoding of struggles over political
representation, *Solibo Magnifique* offers a good starting point. In recounting
the police investigation into the death of the titular storyteller (he has been
"snickt by the word," or choked by the sounds caught in his throat), the narrative dramatizes the issue of representation through the inclusion of Chamoiseau as a character in the text—indeed, as a writer hoping to document Solibo's
life.[4] Moreover, the relationship between the French and Creole languages in
Martinique provides a striking illustration of the inseparability of linguistic antagonisms from contests over power. Like *Chronicle of the Seven Sorrows* before
it, the novel portrays the clash and coexistence of realities from radically different moments in history, the result of the imperial imposition of late capitalist modes and structures on Martinique, a condition that departmentalization
only intensified. The resulting disjunction between competing understandings
of space and time is neatly staged during Chief Inspector Pilon's investigation
into what he believes is Solibo's murder. Take this scene, for instance, in which
he interrogates the witness Bête-Longue:

—Monsieur Bête-Longue, what is your age, profession, and permanent address?

—Huh?

—The Inspector asks you what hurricane you were born after, what you do for the béké, and what side of town you sleep at night? Bouaffesse specifies.

—I was born right before Admiral Robert, I fish with Kokomerlo on Rive-Droite, and I stay at Texaco, by the fountain. (95–96)

To classify his suspect, Pilon employs the language of state bureaucracy and the principles of social construction on which it is predicated. As a member of the elite, he has internalized a perceptual schema adjusted to norms and models originating in the metropole. Bête-Longue's initial incomprehension and eventual response indicate his rather different grasp of reality, one grounded in his practical experience of the landscape. Yet it is Pilon's abstract framework that counts as legitimate, tied as it is to the ruling political dispensation. The power of the law here is inextricable from its ability to inscribe people within categories sanctioned by a state structurally integrated into a foreign system of government.

The departmentalization of Martinique, Guadeloupe, and French Guiana in 1946 had at first been welcomed broadly as a step on the road to decolonization. It quickly became apparent, however, that the consequences were in fact greater dependency and simultaneous over- and underdevelopment. As Richard D. E. Burton notes, French manufactured goods flooded into the departments, "displacing locally made goods and undermining the very real degree of economic self-sufficiency that had obtained under the former dispensation." "Scarcely 25 years after departmentalization," continues Burton, "French West Indians were confronted by the effective erosion of the traditional economic base (agriculture, fishing, craft industries) and its replacement by a top-heavy service economy dependent on imported goods, themselves purchased by transfers of public and private funds from France."[5] *Solibo Magnifique* captures the destabilizing effect of the disintegration of the occupations and crafts that once provided the community with a mediating link to the environment. As the witnesses to Solibo's death contemplate how the island has changed—

Richard Coeurillon and Zaboca spoke of a time of harvests and smokestack factories, at that time one man handled a machine, the other a scythe, that was time, but now if the fields are deserted and the factory whistles no longer give rhythm to the day, now that your hands no longer know how to lash a rope, braid, nail, cut anything, where does time happen, Inspekder? Some say it's France, that there, there is time. (98)

—it becomes clear that if the modern service economy has freed people from laboring in fields and factories, it has also divorced them from any sense of control over reality: time itself is suffered; it is only meaningful elsewhere. In such circumstances, the whole community could go the way of Bidjoule in *Chronicle of the Seven Sorrows*.

In this respect, *Solibo Magnifique* develops a concern that dominated many Francophone Caribbean novels in the 1970s, when recognition of the "cultural impoverishment" wrought by departmentalization resulted in a series of protagonists "whose personal alienation [was] suggestive of national confusion and distress regarding cultural identity."[6] Characters like the titular antihero of Vincent Placoly's *La vie et la mort de Marcel Gonstran* (1971) found themselves locked in a world of madness and sterility, the history of their fractured communities as exhausted as the despoiled landscape. Such themes perhaps found fullest expression in Glissant's seminal novel *Malemort* (1975). Here the obscuration of the community's history has reduced people to a zombified or schizophrenic state, made viscerally evident in the final chapter when the protagonist Silacier splits into two parts. Repeatedly, the inability to articulate a cultural memory is manifested in a corporeal tension: "The jerking of the body suddenly arched in the impossibility of saying anything."[7] We can clearly see similarities here to the petrifaction of Bolo's movements, and of the history they embody, in *The Wine of Astonishment*.

Indeed, the extent to which the motifs of madness, ennui, and nihilism common in Francophone Caribbean literature of the 1970s pervade a series of contemporaneous texts from the Anglophone territories demands consideration. While clearly the impact of departmentalization is not at issue in these works, a sense of frustration with both the political impasses of the period and the imposed social structures maintained by the elite results in a similar emphasis on mad or arrested forms of expression. One thinks, for example, of Roy Heath's novel *The Murderer* (1978), in which the stifling norms and constraints of lower-middle-class life contribute to the gradual derangement of the protagonist Galton Flood, whose repressed rage eventually overflows in an act of callous brutality when he batters his wife to death. Or take John Stewart's *Last Cool Days* (1971), in which another unhinged character, Marcus Shepard, murders the son of the overseer from the estate on which they both grew up. What is intriguing about this work is that, like a number of the texts I considered in the first chapter, it is set in the middle decades of the twentieth century; but whereas many of those earlier novels treated the period as one of great difficulties but also of great potential, *Last Cool Days*, looking back from the 1970s, is infused with the despair and insecurity that characterize its psychologically damaged narrator. In Lamming's *In the Castle of My Skin* (1953), the atmosphere of fragmentation and arrested development is offset by what Rohlehr calls "choric integrative passages" and moments when "all voices, natives of the author's person, meet and melt into the single voice of history."[8] The narrative in Stewart's novel, by contrast, is mediated predominantly through the alienated consciousness of

Marcus, who admits to being unable to integrate and articulate his fragmented history—those "states of myself," as he puts it, "scattered in more or less a triangle from West Africa to Europe to America."[9] The text marks this instability formally, switching from an opening section narrated in the third person to Marcus's own diary entries, which are punctuated at one point by a kind of editorial commentary that questions their veracity. That Marcus has only produced an irregular journal itself becomes testament to his inability to express the past that weighs on him. Marcus's grandfather, who declares that "Black man needs a book of truth about himself," encourages his grandson to use his superior education to write such a book, a task Marcus promises to undertake yet fails to achieve.[10]

Switching linguistic traditions once more, the same incapacity to articulate a coherent history is present in Sánchez's *Macho Camacho's Beat*. Set over the course of one day, the novel uses the paralysis caused by a huge traffic jam in San Juan to symbolize the impact of U.S. imperialism on Puerto Rico. Not just the character Senator Vicente Reinosa but society itself is, so to speak, "tied up, held up, caught up in a traffic jam as phenomenal as life, Made in Puerto Rico."[11] (In the Spanish original—"está atrapado, apresado, agarrado por un tapón fenomenal como la vida made in Puerto Rico"—the switch to English for the phrase normally found stamped on merchandise better emphasizes the reifying effect of U.S.-driven commercialization.)[12] This sense of clogging up is reinforced by the way both the public sphere and individual lifeworlds have become saturated with commodities. The signs, images, and gobbets of information pumped out by the mass media have penetrated and transformed people's habitus: "Did she learn the sweet charm of pretence from the mannerisms that reverberate out of the magnificent snake-long soap opera *The Son of Ángela María* that had turned the island's heart to honey?" asks the narrator of one character (13). Another is shown communicating through a delirious regurgitation of advertising slogans:

> In Manatí she took two Cortals and with an artificial relaxation announced, singing and trilling like an announcer for Colgate: *Cortal, when taken, stops the achin'*. From Manatí to Arecibo she didn't say boo. Once in Arecibo she opened her mouth again to proclaim with great wisdom: *Arecibo is Captain Correa's town* and to the genteel approval of her husband repeated, merry, witty, jovial, talkative: *Cortal, when taken, stops the achin'*. (83)

The degraded manner in which the verbal relationship between husband and wife is mediated through commercial jingles bespeaks a reprogramming of subjectivities that bears comparison with the way, in *Solibo Magnifique*, characters are shown to have been shoehorned into state-sanctioned norms that likewise distort expression.

With regard to Sánchez's novel, Lizabeth Paravisini-Gebert observes that the "language of the characters is as empty and alienating as the mass-media models it emulates, a language laden with clichés . . . an alienated language seemingly devoid of power to serve as a vehicle for growth and rebirth."[13] Indeed, this language seems to trap people in the present, numbing them to social realities and hence to the possibility of effecting change. The most obvious example is Macho Camacho's guaracha itself, *Life Is a Phenomenal Thing* (guaracha is a popular music style with lyrics, introduced to Puerto Rico from Cuba in the nineteenth century). The repetition of its refrain throughout the novel accentuates the sense of stasis. At the same time, the song serves to divert attention away from the island's problems. When a set of traffic lights fails, for instance, and a man on a bus declares that "the country doesn't work," the other passengers form

> two opposing parties: one a minority of timid people in agreement and the other a vociferous majority who proceeded to intone with a verve reserved for national anthems Macho Camacho's irrepressible guaracha *Life is a Phenomenal Thing*, the deeper tones provided by the driver . . . the bus afire with the torches of happiness held high by the passengers of the vociferous majority party: happy because with a neat swipe of a guaracha they had crushed the attempt at dissidence. (11–12)

Public criticism is thereby drowned out by the hysterical repetition of the guaracha. Similarly, the text refers several times to protests against the material conditions on the island but never elaborates further on these strikes, since almost as soon as they are mentioned, they are swept back up in the rush of products and media-related discourses. Through its own silences and thwarted narratives, then, the text conveys a sense of a society in which the superstructure is becoming unmoored from the base, while the possibility of a public sphere in which arguments about society might be articulated is blocked off by the commodification of the civic domain.

Something similar is evident in *Solibo Magnifique*. Here the very grounds of expression are being lost with the erosion of the material base: increasingly, what is at stake is no longer simply a disjunction between realities but the wholesale obliteration of one of them. As occupations and crafts disappear, so too does the social history they kept in view. Discussing the character Congo, who makes manioc graters, the narrator expands on the relationship between certain foods, their methods of preparation, and the particular historical eras they evoke. During the "manioc epoch," Congo was able to make a living selling or bartering his graters. However, the "Made-in-France stuff undid the manioc, putting it out of our way and even our memory. Now, wheat flour was needed for bread. Eating well meant eating steak and french fries" (142). Congo continues to make graters, but his "anachronistic silhouette" has become a "hopeless symbol of those epochs when we had been different and from which now everyone turned away" (142). The waning of Congo's craft thus signals the waning of historical memory;

replacing the manioc are imported foodstuffs that, prepackaged and sold in supermarkets, no longer bear the traces of the material practice required to produce them or of the social relations determining their distribution.

If such is the fate of artisan crafts, then it should come as no surprise that Solibo's occupation as a storyteller is similarly on the verge of extinction. In his well-known ruminations on storytelling, Walter Benjamin observes that this practice is itself "an artisan form of communication." "It does not aim to convey the pure essence of the thing, like information or a report," he argues. "It sinks the thing into the life of the storyteller, in order to bring it out of him again. Thus traces of the storyteller cling to the story the way the handprints of the potter cling to the clay vessel."[14] That in Martinique Solibo has "seen the tales die, Creole lose its strength" (156) testifies not just to the loss of stories and memories but to "the suffering pulse of a world coming to an end" (159). Solibo's death is inevitable in this sense, since he exists as a storyteller only in his connection to that world. Indeed, his stiffened corpse is emblematic of the reification and cadaverization of society as a whole as it confronts what Glissant called the "cultural genocide" of assimilation.[15] Tellingly, under the ruling political and socioeconomic dispensation, the only way put forward to preserve the history that Solibo and his tales embody is to turn it into a commodity; yet to do so only hastens its corrosion.

Solibo is well aware of this. He seeks to "inscribe his words in our ordinary life" but sees that besides "a few out-of-the-way places . . . the space for this folklore was dwindling. Organizers of the cultural festival had often solicited him for storytelling bits, but Solibo, dreading these kinds of conservation measures where you left life's theatre to stand within an artificial frame, had given mysterious excuses" (156). The danger with such displays is that they abstract the storytelling performance from its social context. It becomes severed from lived experience and is gradually made over into a commercial spectacle. A process that Richard Price has termed the "postcarding of the past" occurs, whereby embedded historical and social meanings are leeched out of the cultural object or act, reducing it to an ornamental husk fit only to be marketed to tourists.[16] Moreover, the way in which storytelling is confined to officially sanctioned folkloric festivals resonates with what we saw in Sánchez's novel regarding the erosion of the public sphere owing to the saturation of the civic domain by the commodity form. In *Solibo Magnifique*, what was an open, publicly accessible communicative practice that engaged with contemporary society is being fenced off as picturesque heritage. (It is significant, too, in this regard that the location of Solibo's final performance is ultimately cordoned off by the police, colonized by the state.)

Glissant has written extensively on the pernicious influence of such "folklorization." He is particularly concerned with the way that in Martinique, folklorization is inextricably bound up with the status of the Creole language. "[A] national language is the one in which a people produces," he argues.[17] To articulate the community, effectively structuring its relationship to a reality ordered symbolically by this same representation, a language must be bound to the practices and institutions through which space-time structuration is effected and the rapport to the environment mediated. The difficulty for Creole is that both the system of production in which it was forged (the plantation) and the crafts to which it was later connected have disappeared. Replacing them is an imposed system of exchange (between French goods and Martinican services). And "with the standardization of business . . . with the importation of all natural and manufactured products . . . Creole in fact, in the logic of this system, no longer has a *raison d'être*. . . . A language *in which* one no longer makes anything (so to speak) is a threatened language. A folkloric language."[18] The dangers of folklorization are acute for a mode of expression that has not been "structured" in relation to a system of production and so lacks the dialectical connection to the world that would enable it to provide a reflection on the history that has shaped it. These concerns can be extended to cultural practice in general. For Glissant, the "folkloric background represented, reflected on, given a cultural thrust, is raised to the level of consciousness, shapes it, and—strengthened by the very action of reinforcing consciousness—criticizes itself as a consciousness in its new 'form' as 'culture.'"[19] In Martinique, however, the community has been denied the resources to reinforce its cultural articulation and initiate a self-reflexive critique, while the elite, who might have taken charge of guiding the move from folklore to consciousness, are "precisely that part of the social body whose function here is to be both alienated and alienating."[20]

The inability to reestablish a connection between a cultural form and the material reality of the social world reinforces the reification of the cultural form, neutralizing its potential to interrogate the received contours of the social world. It was for this reason that, as Fanon observed with respect to the Algerian situation, when new kinds of engaged arts and practices emerged during the liberation struggle, it was the colonialists who rushed "to the help of the traditions of the indigenous society" to ensure they remained locked in a devitalizing aspic.[21] Thus similarly in Martinique, writes Glissant, the "first official who comes along will defend indigenous cultural manifestations, and their 'enchanting' quality. . . . Folkloric displays are therefore never part of a program of self-expression, which is what paralyses them."[22]

Such reification needs to be understood also within the wider context of the generalization of commodity production under capitalism. Indeed, to theorize explicitly what has already been hinted at, the fetishism of the commodity is centrally important to the attenuation of a sense of history we have observed. For Marx, commodity fetishism arose from the peculiar social character of labor under capitalism, whereby the "labour of private individuals manifests itself as an element of the total labour of society only through the relations which the act of exchange establishes between the products, and, through their mediation, between the producers." The result is that to the producers, "the social relations between their private labours appear as what they are, i.e., they do not appear as direct social relations between persons in their work, but rather as material [*dinglich*] relations between persons and social relations between things."[23] Hence the commodity now confronts the producer as an alien object, with the labor stored within it concealed from view and the social relations between individuals that determine its production eclipsed. What Chamoiseau's and Sánchez's portrayals of Martinique and Puerto Rico emphasize is the way this effacement of social relations, and the nullification of an individual's sensuous connection to material reality, can extend right across the social world, entailing the commodification of the past and the traversing of subjectivities by the logic of capital (the trajectory of any number of societies under the social imperialism of late capitalism). Thus there emerges what begins to feel like a perpetual present as antecedents are obscured and the possibility of alternative futures forgotten.[24]

From this perspective, one can not only better understand the sense of stasis in Sánchez's novel but also account more fully for the delirium of those characters apparently overcome by commodities, like the wife who regurgitates commercial jingles. In *Postmodernism, or, The Cultural Logic of Late Capitalism*, Fredric Jameson remarks that the crisis in historicity associated with late capitalism raises in a new way the question of temporal organization. If the "subject has lost its capacity to extend its pro-tensions and re-tensions across the temporal manifold and to organize its past and future into coherent experience," he asks, what are the implications for cultural production?[25] Jameson suggests that a kind of schizophrenic aesthetic might be one consequence, the impossibility of unifying the past, present, and future of biographical or psychic experience generating a "series of pure and unrelated presents in time." These presents come before the subject "with heightened intensity, bearing a mysterious charge of affect, here described in the negative terms of anxiety and loss of reality, but which one could just as well imagine in the positive terms of euphoria, a high, an intoxicatory or hallucinogenic intensity."[26] Something like this is evident in *Macho Camacho's Beat*. Take the wife with her giddy repetition of advertising slogans. These infuse her with an artificial euphoria that matches the "artificial relaxation" brought on by consuming the advertised products (in this instance, painkillers). Later she suffers a breakdown at her psychiatrist's clinic, during which she becomes lost in a series of presents that she cannot structure coherently—presents, moreover, that are not even anchored in her own experience but refer to images of celebrity lives she has imbibed from glossy magazines:

> Graciela stops fas-ci-na-ted, en-chan-ted, be-wit-ched, looking at the fascinating, enchanting, bewitching photograph of Liz and Richard's house in Puerto Vallarta

published as a graphic supplement of *Time*. . . . Graciela turns another page. . . .
Once upon a time there was a little princess named Jacqueline who married the
King of Scorpion Island. . . . Graciela edits out unedited orgasms, Graciela edits
out uterine heat waves, Graciela edits out mucous secretions: Princess Jacqueline
dressed to ride a wild boar, Princess Jacqueline dressed to eat French fries, Princess Jacqueline dressed to give alms to the poor. . . . Graciela Alcántara y López de
Montefrío, pricked and pricked and pricked by the painful pleasure of the pins of
pleasure, throws *Time* into the air, flings *Time* into the air, hurls *Time* into the air,
shrieks with pain, shrieks with resentment, shrieks with shrieking: that's living.
(131–32)

The repetitive, fractured syntax bespeaks Graciela's frantic efforts to organize
a biographical narrative; yet as she displaces her life story with those of foreign
film stars and royalty, her own experiences manifest themselves only through
her symptomatic repression of bodily functions.

That we have here not only the kind of schizophrenia Jameson speaks of in
connection with a crisis in historicity but also the added problem of misidenti-
fication with presents that are not one's own underscores the necessity of fore-
grounding the specificity of the colonial experience. Colonialism has its own
devastating impact on the psyche and, materially speaking, underpins the way
that certain cultural products are imported for consumption. For this reason, I
will come back to the topic of schizophrenia and think it through from a slightly
different, Glissantian perspective. Before that, however, there is the issue of the
vexed relationship to the body that Graciela's breakdown reveals. This is partly
the product of her sexual neuroses. But it would also seem to have wider significance in terms of a general alienation from the body and the senses observable
in the characters in Sánchez's novel who belong to the elite class. Graciela's son
Benny, for instance, takes after his mother in lacking a real sensuous grip on
the world: he floats in a kind of surreality, swaddled by commodities. Moreover,
for him too what would appear to be an unconscious desire to surmount this
ultimately debilitating alienation manifests itself pathologically. The vision he
has of himself shitting on "the maternal relations of a considerable number of
virgins and saints" (52) can be read as a delirious and displaced expression of an
impulse to rematerialize his relationship to the world.

In the *Economic and Philosophic Manuscripts of 1844*, Marx theorized the connection between the commodity form, the body, and the senses. Not only does
capitalism entail the producer's estrangement from his or her body (in the sense
that human labor is invested in an object that then returns as an alien commodity), but private property also leads to the nullification of the senses, of
those "*human* relations to the world—seeing, hearing, smelling, tasting, feeling, thinking, being aware, sensing, wanting, acting, loving."[27] "In place of *all*

these physical and mental senses," argues Marx, "there has therefore come the sheer estrangement of *all* these senses—[by] the sense of *having*."[28] Crucially, the senses have a history: they are conditioned by the object before them. Under the aegis of commodity production, when the thing they relate themselves to is a nonsocial object (insofar as its social character is occulted), the senses become lost in the object; they are themselves objectified. Thus the eye, for example, will become a *human* eye only when "its *object* has become a social, *human* object."[29] The reification of the senses affects both the capitalist and the worker. The worker, in being reduced "to the barest and most miserable level of physical subsistence," is rendered an "insensible being."[30] But, as Terry Eagleton puts it, paraphrasing Marx's argument, "if the capitalist strips the worker of his senses, he equally confiscates his own."[31] The capitalist saves himself from undertaking any sensuous activities in the pursuit of capital, but having "alienated his sensory life to capital, he is then able vicariously to recuperate that estranged sensuality by the power of capital itself."[32] It is thus capital that actively consumes those pleasures for the otherwise benumbed capitalist, with the result that both are "images of the living dead, the one animate yet anaesthetised, the other inanimate yet active."[33]

As we have seen, such estranged sensuality—the tendency to live vicariously through commodities—is evident among the elite figures in *Macho Camacho's Beat*, perhaps finding its ultimate expression in Benny's progression from being interested in girls to becoming obsessed with pornography to pleasuring himself over his Ferrari. But a similar dulling of the senses can also be observed in *Solibo Magnifique*. For the poor, it is bound up with the reduction of their lives to mere survival and the distance from reality that opens up as their trades become obsolete and local produce is replaced by imported French merchandise. For example, whereas Sidonise the sherbet maker used to grasp the world via her practice, "today the sherbet was made elsewhere, she bought it in plastic boxes and put it in her sherbet maker for style, [and] since then she glided over the hours and everything else" (98). For the elite, this distance is already embedded in their structural dislocation from the Martinican milieu, symbolized by the senior police officers' inability even to understand the existence of Solibo and his craft. Pilon, for instance, upon hearing from one witness how the storyteller's speech is inextricable from his other sensory faculties—"[it's] the sound from his throat, but it's also his sweat, the rolling of his eyes, his belly, the gestures he draws with his hands, his smell"—can only grumble that "this doesn't make any sense!" (99). Tellingly, his approach to investigating Solibo's death is to draw a geometric plan designed to unlock the mystery. Yet by reducing every event and person into an abstract point on the diagram, he succeeds only in obscuring the significance of the storyteller's being "snickt by the word." Pilon's methodology, moreover, owes much to the French detective novels he enjoys, emphasizing the overdetermined quality of alienation in the colonial context: weighing on the characters is not only the reification of a sensorium confronted by an equally reified object world, but also the imported character of that object world.

Taken together, these examples highlight the way the effects of late capitalism often resemble more insidious versions of those felt under colonialism. "In the pit of colonial domination," writes E. San Juan Jr., "the native's senses, no longer effective powers of worldly intervention, are mystified and estranged until she/he is finally deprived of any awareness of identity as producer, as the motive force of history."[34] This could just as well serve as a description of that nullification of sensory plenitude we have seen achieved through commercialization and folklorization. Indeed, the way these occult the historical processes that structure the social world, preventing it from being grasped as something that can be acted on, suggests the continuation (again albeit in more surreptitious guise) of what Amilcar Cabral described as the "essential characteristic of imperialist domination": the "negation of the historical process of the dominated people."[35]

For Glissant, in fact, Martinique represents something like the extreme edge of this negation: its trajectory from colony to département has meant social relations on the island have continued to be structured directly by external forces, while the internal class struggle, which should have served as the driver of an autonomously determined history, has been distorted and eclipsed. "When, in a society, the relations of production and exchange (which 'determine' class relations) are *dominated* by an outside factor," writes Glissant, "class relations in turn are obscured, becoming artificial *in terms of the social connection*, that is, the given society becomes incapable of finding in itself the 'motive' of its development."[36] The short-circuiting of class relations that conform to norms not of the Martinican milieu thus bestows on the island a "nonhistory," the persistence of this disjunction between social forms and a social dynamic making it the "only extreme (or successful?) colonization in modern history" (la seule colonisation extrême [ou réussie?] de l'histoire moderne).[37] In addition, since the distortions in relations of production and class cannot be elucidated politically (precisely because of these same alienating distortions), the society lives this nonhistory at a latent level, manifesting it only through what Glissant calls "routine verbal delirium."

Thus might we return to the issue of schizophrenia, approaching it from the slightly different angle that Glissant opens up here. In Martinique, he argues, the short-circuiting of collective political action and the absence of a mediated relationship to the environment mean that sociohistorical factors can act immediately on the unconscious.[38] Consequently individual pathology becomes a direct response to the social situation. However, this pathology or delirium is not felt as abnormal by the community but is accepted as everyday—the result of its being manifested "in the very texture of daily existence, through the absence of any reference to oneself" (dans la texture même de l'existence quotidienne, par absence de référence à soi-même).[39] The imposition of, and the accession of people to, norms that do not coincide with Martinican sociohistorical realities have reached such a pitch that the perversity of these distorted identifications is accepted as normal. In other words, since the norms themselves are alienated or abnormal, the manifestations of madness (which frequently take the form of a delirious use of language) are not grasped as such and instead appear routine. Hence routine verbal delirium, whereby the contradiction between what one is supposed to be (according to the imported French models) and what one is, is lived in traumatic fashion at the level of an instinctive attempt to resolve this irresolvable opposition.[40] Glissant identifies four types of such delirium, those of representation, persuasion, communication, and dramatization (*théâtralisation*). The first two are elite forms, the second two popular; the first three are "depropriating," the last "repropriating." I will come back to the repropriating form in a moment. Suffice it to say for now that the depropriating forms seek to "confirm in an obsessive and reassuring manner . . . the general ideological alienation" (à confirmer de manière obsessionnelle et rassurante . . . l'aliénation idéologique générale), that is, to corroborate the imposed norm by consolidating an alienated pseudo-French identity.[41]

Before examining *Solibo Magnifique*'s treatment of verbal delirium, it is worth looking again at the behavior of the characters in Sánchez's novel. Take Graciela, for instance, with her frantic babbling about the lives of celebrities in Europe and the United States: it is hard not to see her relentless yet always frustrated (mis)identification with these figures as a delirious manifestation of the elite's agony at not being what it believes itself to be, its simultaneous refusal to discover this, and its powerlessness to cease attempting such a discovery (here represented by the compulsive naming of celebrities, which only underscores Graciela's *difference* from them). A similar theme is evident in what Gerald Guinness calls the "linguistic mishmash" of Benny's and his father's speech: "Papito Papitín decía: celebrar en fecha a convenir un get together de maestros en el molto bello jardino de tu Mamá: get together con mozos uniformados, cold cuts, a La Rotisserie, toneles de Beaujolais y Lambrusco espumoso: get together que carga a mis gastos de representación senatorial."[42] This deranged mix of Spanish, English, French, and Italian not only testifies to the "linguistic foreign interference" that José Luis González claims affects the "educated classes" in Puerto Rico.[43] It also signifies the compulsive desire to identify with the elite European lifestyle that those languages are here associated with, the resulting incoherent medley emphasizing the disjunctive nature of this identification.

The issue of linguistic competence is similarly fraught in *Solibo Magnifique*. The vexed relationship in Martinique between French and Creole impacts greatly on the articulation of the power relations between classes. French has been installed as the universal standard for society: used in institutional spaces, it is construed as the language of education, economics, civility, and the law—discourses in relation to which Creole has been marginalized. Creole is thus made synonymous with powerlessness, while French is able to confer legitimacy and status on its speakers. The connection between French and power is made explicit in *Solibo Magnifique*: French not only is the language of official police procedure but is also used to intimidate interviewees. Bouaffesse, for example, muses that the "best way to corner this vicious old blackman [Congo] was to track him down with French. The French language makes their heads swim, grips their guts" (66). Later, Congo, who speaks only an old-fashioned Creole, is beaten with a French logbook.

Such violence, however, in revealing the physical oppression that underpins linguistic domination, unravels the pernicious cloak of legitimacy cast over it by its objectification in institutional structures. The position of French as the linguistic norm is thus shown to be unstable, a perception reinforced by the frenzied madness that seizes the police officers during their interrogations. Once more it is the external provenance of the norm and its lack of grounding in the local milieu that lie at the heart of this instability. French has not been indigenized in Martinique as the language of production (in contrast to the way that, as Glissant suggests, Spanish has in Cuba, for example).[44] Thus, whereas Creole has become nonfunctional in relation to the modern economic system, French is inextricable from it but in consequence is structured (at least when used uncritically) in relation to that regime of nonproductive exchange imposed by the metropole. The elite's deployment of French thereby enables it to assert its circumscribed authority, reassuring its members that they are what they think they are, that is, French (even white) and in full control; yet at the same time, the ungrounded, external orientation of this language ensures that its usage also points up the elite's alienation and lack of genuine autonomous power over the structuration of Martinican reality. Out of this tension arises behavior unconsciously geared toward defusing it. But due to the irresolvable nature of the contradiction between (French) appearance and (Martinican) reality, such behavior becomes increasingly manic, spilling over into delirium.

Take Pilon, for instance, who displays a compulsive need to reassure himself of his official status. His verbal contortions suggest the delirium of persuasion: the deployment of facts and statistics, garnered from "commonsense" observation, to camouflage "the deliberate refusal of one's history, the panic of finding oneself but not *as one believes oneself to be*" (le refus délibéré de sa propre histoire, la panique d'avoir à se trouver mais non pas *tel qu'on se dit être*).[45] In his report into the Solibo affair, Pilon introduces himself as an "officer of the Police of Urban Safety of Fort-de-France, Criminal Brigade, officer of the Department of Criminal Investigation" (3). This obsession with status is echoed in his meticulous citation of legal regulations: "I am from the Department of Criminal Investigation. . . . Per Articles 76, 77 and 78 of the Code of Penal Procedure, you are in custody for the purposes of a preliminary inquiry" (94). Pilon, educated in "the land of Descartes" (75), seeks to make reality comply with the French symbolic structures that legitimize his identity. However, his attempts to apply "cold logic" to the "irrational side of 'cases' in this country"—at "the price of a rather disagreeable mental exertion"—frequently flounder (75). We have already noted his ill-fated effort at explaining Solibo's death via the geometric plan, the "scientific" appearance of which conceals the (normative) madness of its unreal deductions. Eventually the material violence that underpins its imposition of imported codes erupts into view, with those deemed guilty by its diagrammatic logic assaulted in a manner far removed from legal propriety.

For those outside the elite—but especially those who nevertheless have some access to official status (due to their job, for example)—the pressure of living the disjunction between norms and reality can manifest itself in even more visceral fashion. When officer Diab-Anba-Feuilles becomes embroiled in a fight with the market vendor Doudou-Ménar, for instance, his state-sanctioned identity is split apart by an eruptive, Creole-speaking Martinican selfhood. Confronting the vendor, he begins to hit himself in a show of strength, biting and tearing his own flesh. As if sloughing off his inculcated French habitus, he enacts a violent return of the repressed: "His eyes were swirling, and his frothy mouth let out a torrent of ever-vibrant curses in a Creole he could no longer hold back" (58). Such behavior recalls Glissant's description of the delirium of communication, which is characterized by "an agonized search for oneself that collides with an irrepressible tendency to destroy oneself" (une recherche angoissée de soi boutée sur un penchant irrepressible à se détruire).[46] Significantly, Bouaffesse can reassert control over his fellow officer only by recourse to the "official civil status of the crazed one and a French-French (Monsieur Figaro Paul, if-you-pleeze, you are forgetting yourself!), at which sound Diab-Anba-Feuilles became a statue" (59). By way of the standard language and the symbolic weight attached to proper names, Bouaffesse reimposes the legitimate French norm.

Nevertheless, Diab-Anba-Feuilles's highly visible pathological breakdown suggests a kind of madness that goes beyond the everyday madness of the Martinican situation. Indeed, the officer's frenzied actions begin to resemble the fourth type of verbal delirium, that of dramatization. This delirium is the closest to the pathological kind, since it refuses the abnormal norms of reality; it is the "*torment of history*, whereas the other routine deliriums signal the absence of history or its refusal" (*tourment d'histoire*, là où les autres délires coutumiers signalent l'absence à l'histoire ou son refus).[47] Hence is it repropriating: externalizing and restaging the conflicts in society, the *délirant de théâtralisation* "tries dramatically to reappropriate through the word" (essaie dramatiquement de réapproprier par le verbe), that is, to reconnect with a history that has the potential to generate social forms structured by an internal dynamic.[48] The visible performance of social contradictions this delirium enacts means that, in contrast to the other types, the sufferer is perceived by the community "as mad (he forces it to really look at itself), but as a spectacular and important madman (for it has need of this look)" (comme fou [il l'oblige à se regarder vraiment], mais comme un fou spectaculaire et important [car elle a besoin de ce regard]).[49]

It is Solibo who most clearly exhibits the delirium of dramatization. With the disintegration of the material basis of his craft and the saturation of society with French modes and structures, the storyteller finds himself "submerged by the reality he had thought he could vanquish": "So he spoke to the only one who could understand him, and we saw him go by with his lips beating out a silence, talking to himself. There were two of him, but out of tune with each other: abruptly stopping too many times while walking, arms flying in the air too many times, too much hesitation choosing the path at the crossroads" (157). Solibo's madness—his being out of phase with the social world after its metropolitan-driven modernization—is played out on the street. His schizophrenic behavior, which theatrically manifests the tensions within himself as well as the phenomenon of split identities, is not just seen by the public; more importantly, it is recognized as mad. It is this visibility that helps bring to consciousness the trauma experienced by society as a whole. Through his words and dramatic silences, Solibo forces the community to reflect on its precarious position and to grasp that another history is, or at least was, in existence—in contradistinction to the perpetual present established by the commodification of social relations under the current dispensation. In this way, the hold of the abnormal norms that produce the delirious status quo might be weakened, allowing the community to look beyond the consolidation of alienated identities toward the only action that could extricate it from such behavior—the economic and political transformation of society.

However, if Solibo begins the process of raising consciousness, neither he nor the novel *directly* articulates what new social and representational forms might emerge with any such transformation. Solibo's delirious communication must itself be restructured if it is to give on to a coherent vision of a revitalized society. Yet it seems that his constitutive connection to a vanishing artisan world means the storyteller can only go so far in this respect. He dramatizes the disintegration of collective representation with the decline of his own and related cultural practices, but the forging of a new mode of articulation that could both draw on these older practices and engage with contemporary conditions is a task he leaves to a younger generation. Indeed, the necessity but also the difficulty of fulfilling this task is staged in the narrative through the interaction between Solibo and the character of the writer "Patrick Chamoiseau," who is positioned as the successor to the oral storyteller. The appearance of the author in the text could be viewed as a literary form of dramatizing delirium that acts out publicly, as it were, the novelist's attempts to continue Solibo's craft in the form of the novel. However, confronted by the difficulty of representing the community in writing with the same immediacy with which the storyteller represented it in speech, Chamoiseau, in his fictional guise as the *marqueur de paroles*, or "word-scratcher," begins to question the efficacy of his practice.

Solibo himself offers a barrage of advice and criticism. Crucially, he is wary of the difference between orality—the word, or *la parole*—and writing. He understands that the *marqueur de paroles* wants to carry on his craft, yet he also recognizes that this cannot be done by simply appropriating the written and deploying it in place of the oral. Writing is not speech, and to treat it as such risks stifling the reality one aims to describe: "One writes but words, not the word [*la parole*], you should have spoken," he counsels. "To write is to take the conch out of the sea to shout: here's the conch! The word replies: Where's the sea?" (28). Indeed, the manner in which writing abstracts its subject from a living context and fixes it on the page is reminiscent of the impact of folklorization. The mimetic re-creation of the oral in the written is liable to turn the oral into a picturesque ornament of the past. Yet Solibo knows that times have changed. He does not "grieve for tradition" (105): although he distrusts writing, he accepts that because he is "going" and the writer is "staying," writing should be used as the means to represent the community (28). To do so, though, it must be transformed, reconciled with the word but not reduced to a facile reproduction.

Against Solibo's advice, however, the character Chamoiseau does try to re-create the word directly, assembling "a reduced, organised, *written* version, a sort of ersatz" of the storyteller's final performance (159). This reproduction, which forms the novel's final section, defies grammatical convention to approximate Solibo's speech; yet compared to the main body of the text, it feels relatively drained of vitality and exuberance. The word here is in danger of being embalmed, with the character Chamoiseau's attempt to bridge "the distance" (as Solibo puts it [28]) between orality and writing failing to attend to the specificities that differentiate one from the other. Consequently the resulting "Document of the Memory" appears as a kind of inverted version of the official police report into Solibo's death that opens the novel, the legal discourse of which dissects the particulars of the case while missing its wider significance. The possibility that the ersatz of the storyteller's performance will preserve his speech, but only by making of it a folkloric relic, is emphasized when the police, having had the document read to them by "Chamoiseau," conclude their investigation by filing everything in a dossier and consigning it to the archive.

The issues raised by the attempt to transcribe Solibo's performance are germane also to the effort made by the *marqueur de paroles* to represent the collectivity more generally. "Chamoiseau" the character conceives of himself as a kind of ethnographer but admits that his approach is highly problematic. In trying to record the culture of the marketplace, for instance, he becomes so immersed in his surroundings that he forgets his task: "I would yell, gesticulate like everybody else . . . no longer caring to listen, to scrutinise or understand life around here, or even . . . the things I scribbled to cheat my remorse" (21). Dissolution in the collective is thus by itself unproductive, since it does not allow for the sort of engaged and self-conscious writing required to grasp the social world. The idea that the logic and modalities of communal life can simply be transferred in unmediated fashion to the page is shown to be misleading. It is interesting in this regard how *Solibo Magnifique* differs from *Chronicle of the Seven Sorrows*. The earlier novel did seem to suggest that a collective oral discourse could be transposed fairly straightforwardly into writing, its narration provided by the undifferentiated *nous* of the *djobeurs*. The appearance of "Chamoiseau" as the *marqueur de paroles* in the later work, alongside the evident anxieties over representation, indicate that Chamoiseau is no longer satisfied with that transposed *nous*. Something of the specificity of writing has to be taken into account. At the same time, this specificity must be interrogated and many of its manifestations reworked if the representation is to avoid distorting or silencing those it seeks to represent (not least because writing in this context is an elite discourse that has been used as a means to further the marginalization of large sections of society). If in this search for a narrative mode that will provide representational adequacy the character "Chamoiseau" appears at something of an impasse, the author himself might be said to come close to adumbrating its outlines via the very form of the novel. This is a theme to which I will return toward the end of the chapter. At present I remain focused on the difficulties that surround writing as representation, examining how they intersect with concerns about both specific kinds of political representation and representational politics in general.

In the context of the colonization of the Americas, writing was construed as a sign of civility in contradistinction to those peoples perceived to be still "trapped" in an oral culture. Thus bound up with the so-called civilizing mission and the legitimation of colonial power, writing itself became a trope, a sign of its own quasi-magical capacity to confer on people a recognized identity. This trope finds its way into the work of some of the earliest black writers in the Americas, one variant being the image of the talking book that crops up in a number of slave narratives, such as Olaudah Equiano's.[50] Indeed, writing was to become deeply enmeshed in a network of socio-symbolic struggles. To write was to appropriate the power invested in the word, which meant that for the colonized, it became a way to demonstrate their equality and to lay claim to a "civility" that had been denied them.

The difficulty with such a form of self-assertion is immediately obvious: it remains tied to the underlying colonialist indices of civility and the superiority or otherwise of certain discourses. Yet even as later authors in the Caribbean successfully challenged and overturned such hierarchies, reappropriating and redeploying the written word on their own terms, uneasiness remained over writing as a means to represent the history of the dominated classes. Its long-standing imbrication in the mechanics of exploitation (from slave inventories and colonial proclamations to exclusive educational systems and the consolidation of elite power over the masses) meant it was frequently treated with ambivalence. Moreover, in the Enlightenment dichotomy in which culture and the mind were opposed to nature and the corporeal, writing was ranged alongside mind and culture. Hence writing was situated as antagonistic to not only orality but also the body. Given the historical importance of the body in the Caribbean as a repository of memory and a means of self-expression, this antagonism presented a real problem. To continue to locate writing within a framework of civility (in which the "profanity" of the corp/oral is excised) risked reducing it to a circumscribed or distorting mouthpiece.

On a related if slightly different note, Chamoiseau has spoken of the specific problems that surround the creation of an I-narrator in circumstances where the community is imperiled. "The 'I' intervenes when the community is more or less clear," he suggests, "but when the community is problematic, the 'I' becomes artificial. When you meet a premature 'I' in our books, it is the occidental 'I' that is pasted over our reality."[51] In other words, the collectivity must first be secured and structured autonomously before it can generate an individual "I" that would then be able to emerge from the group and yet remain contiguous with it.

Wilson Harris has similarly been interested in the connection between literary forms and sociocultural structures. The daSilva twin in *Palace of the Peacock*, for example, neatly images something akin to Chamoiseau's point in the foregoing paragraph, as well as the disquiet over the relationship between writing and the body. Toward the end of the novel, daSilva becomes encased in print:

> His flesh was newspaper, drab, wet until the lines and markings had run fantastically together. His hair stood flat on his brow like ink. He nodded precariously and one marvelled how he preserved his appearance without disintegrating into soggy lumps and patches. . . . He shook his head again but not a word blew from his lips.[52]

This bodily metamorphosis, which precedes daSilva's death, suggests the damaging impact of material and discursive frameworks that bind the individual to an artificial model of subjectivity. The twin is rendered a hollow shell, the decaying reminder—the other daSilva views him as "his own sogging fool's life"[53]—of an identity defined by the imposed colonial habitus. Circumscribing communication ("not a word blew from his lips"), it must be sloughed off if the collectivity is to reestablish structures capable of supporting nonalienated forms of expression. These ideas offer a way to understand the disappearance and return of the I-narrator in the novel. As an artificial "I" dislocated from any form of collectivity, he must first be decomposed and can be restored only at the climax of the narrative with the return to "the folk," that is, with the renewal of the community via its reconnection to a collective history.

Harris's theoretical writings elaborate such concerns more systematically. As is now well documented, he calls for a revolution in the novel form, its transformation into something that "seeks to visualise a *fulfilment* of character . . . rather than [a] *consolidation*."[54] The tendency toward consolidation, he argues (in somewhat general terms), is typical of conventional nineteenth-century realism, which "coincides in Europe with states of society which were involved in consolidating their class and other vested interests."[55] Consequently, "character" in the novel comes to rest "more or less on the self-sufficient individual—on elements of 'persuasion' . . . rather than 'dialogue' or 'dialectic.'"[56] Harris thus underscores how the socioeconomic and intellectual transformations wrought by the emergence and entrenchment of the capitalist mode of production—in particular, the containment of the body and the production of the monadic subject—play out also on the level of literary form. His central reservation is with the way the consolidation of characters as sovereign monads, which entails also "persuading" the reader to view as inevitable the plane of existence or historical situation these characters occupy, obscures the mediations and connections that exist between individuals, and between individuals and society. For the Caribbean specifically, the adoption of this formal logic results in the eclipse of "the series of subtle and nebulous links which are latent within [the West Indian]."[57]

The task, then, is to develop an aesthetic that can articulate such linkages, enabling them to "act on each other in a manner which fulfils *in the person* the most nebulous instinct for a vocation of being and independent spirit."[58] However, Harris goes on to reinforce the point that this task is hampered by the way writing itself (particularly insofar as it has been construed as a transcendent act set in opposition to the body and separated from the chaotic matter of nature) can distort the world it seeks to represent, shoehorning experience into narrative structures and topoi that occlude constitutive relations between objects, practices, and subjects. He argues that "the convolutions of image, whether clear or grotesque, are related as diverse rooms, capacities expanding or contracting within one field of consciousness. To prise these images apart is in fact to lose the dialectical field in which they stand or move."[59] The problem Harris identifies with forms of writing thus unable to grasp such dialectical fields is related to the point I touched on in the previous chapter with respect to *The Secret Ladder*: the alienation of subject from object and the reduction of the world to classifiable elements, leading ultimately to reification and an inability to penetrate the given forms of social reality. (The issue of the senses returns here too—the conditioning of a now atomized sensorium, so that the social character of the object remains obscured.) Harris, moreover, connects these difficulties to the position conventionally ascribed to the author. The idea of writing as a transcendent act—as an ordering and a genesis[60]—turns the writer into an elevated, sovereign creator, an isolated individual who shapes the profuse matter of the object world through authorial (authoritative) intention. This "authorizing" of the one who writes reinforces the disconnection of subject from object, heightening the possibility that the author will eclipse his or her own interrelation to the world.

Thus it is not surprising that so many of Harris's novels involve the deconstruction of the figure of the author. I do not have space here to explore this motif in detail, but Harris's own commentary on *The Far Journey of Oudin* deserves attention. Toward the end of *The Far Journey of Oudin*, in a manner similar to *Palace of the Peacock*, the ruling space-time structuration of reality collapses, and eclipsed histories and cultural traditions become visible. The subjectivity of the protagonist Oudin is displaced by these legacies, his body channeling them like a superconductor. Subsequently it is his lover Beti who must take responsibility for him. As Harris puts it: "All these seeds [legacies] come with him, so that suddenly he is reduced and helpless, he's like a dead man at a certain stage whom she has to carry, whom she has to sustain, even as she *reads* him, *writes* him into herself in a new way."[61] Significantly, Beti's rewriting of Oudin—her "translation" of the heritages being made manifest in him—occurs via the body: "What she had to do was to make her kind of secret mark on him—the obvious mark an illiterate person must make in lieu of a signature and name. With her toes she drew in the sand an incomprehensible fertile figure within a hollow cage at Oudin's feet."[62] With this overwhelming of the narrative by a multiplicity of histories rewritten through the characters, it is as if, contends Harris, "the author ceases to be the kind of realistic author which one usually looks for . . . [and] becomes himself a fiction created by his own characters."[63] Harris is keen to stress, however, that this transformation is not reducible to the postmodernist notion of "the death of the author." For Harris, what is at stake here (and, too, in the death of that transcendent author/ity figure God) is a "replay of forces that may revive the drive and dynamism of creation so that the Creator is there within some complex, thrusting, marvellous tradition."[64] The death of the elevated, sovereign author thus forms the prelude not to the complete unmooring of all meaning but to the emergence of a new form of representation that, attentive to the specificities of cultural history (hence Beti's "bodily writing"), attempts to mediate the heterogeneous determinations of reality.

While Harris's arguments on this issue are typically esoteric, they nevertheless resonate with the concerns and strategies of a number of other Caribbean writers. We have already seen how Chamoiseau turns himself into a character in *Solibo Magnifique*, dramatizing his struggles over representing the collectivity. And depictions of author figures and the problems they encounter are widespread in novels by the likes of Glissant, Raphaël Confiant, Maryse Condé, Xavier Orville, and Sam Selvon. In Confiant's *Eau de café* (1991), for instance, the narrator is an aspiring novelist who returns to his hometown, only to be scorned by a community fearful of anyone probing its repressed past. Condé's *Traversée de la mangrove* (1989) features a mysterious character, Francis Sancher, who is attempting to write a book called "Traversée de la mangrove." In Selvon's

Moses Ascending (1975), the protagonist's literary pretensions are subject to re-morseless parody, his authorial malapropisms used to undermine his author/ity. More overtly, both Glissant in *Mahogany* (1987) and Orville in *Laissez brûler Laventurcia* (1989) have their protagonists challenge the writer over how they are portrayed. In Glissant's text, Mathieu liberates himself from what he feels is the falsifying character figure he has been assigned, seeking to become his own "all-powerful creator" (créateur tout-puissant).[65] But in retaining the idea of the author as an elevated sovereign individual, he repeats what he denounces: the disconnection from, and reductive telescoping of, experience. The narrative itself tries to counter this problem by establishing a relay between one character and the next, with each offering his or her own perspective on events. Once more, then, the challenge to the status of the author does not entail abandoning representation altogether.

Like Harris, in fact, Glissant has been concerned to distinguish his thinking on such matters from apparently similar ideas in postmodernist-poststructur-alist discourse. In *Caribbean Discourse* he notes "the very interesting work being done on a theoretical level in the West . . . on the subject of the destabilizing of the text and 'its' author."[66] He goes on to suggest, however, that such theories as they are formulated in the West are unsuited to a situation in which "we need to develop a poetics of the 'subject,' if only because we have been too long 'objecti-fied' or rather 'objected to'":

> The text must for us (in our lived experience) be destabilized, because it must be-long to a shared reality, and it is perhaps at this point that we actually relate to these ideas that have emerged elsewhere. The author must be demythified, cer-tainly, because he must be integrated into a common resolve. The collective "We" becomes the site of the generative system [of the text], and the true subject. Our critique of the act and the idea of literary creation is not derived from a "reaction" to theories which are proposed to us, but from a burning need for *modification*.[67]

The struggles that these writers stage with their own practice must be seen as indicative of the *importance* of representation, of the necessity of finding ways to articulate a "shared reality." The uncertain or dominated position of the col-lectivity means that, as Glissant makes clear, destabilizing or demythifying rep-resentation to the point where one repudiates any claim to be able to represent social reality or to speak for the "we" of the community is unhelpful. Articulating the collectivity must be attempted as part of the drive against oppression, even as the position of the one representing and the efficacy and impact of the repre-sentation are constantly interrogated and revised.

The struggles over literary representation, then, are inextricable from politi-cal considerations; indeed, they pose questions for the very idea of a represen-tationalist politics. Such are the connections that I want to explore by way of

Lovelace's *The Dragon Can't Dance*, which develops themes already encountered in *The Wine of Astonishment* and *Solibo Magnifique* regarding both cultural practice and political representation—specifically, the commodification of cultural practice and the shortcomings of the elite when it comes to political representation.

At first glance, *The Dragon Can't Dance* would seem to suggest that the vitality of popular cultural practice in Trinidad is such that the articulation of an identity and history grounded in lived experience remains achievable in a way that in *Solibo Magnifique* it increasingly is not. The most significant cultural form in the novel is Carnival, which emerged on the island after the enslaved reappropriated a custom brought over by French Creole planters. Carnival's subsequent creolization with elements of African ritual means the ceremony now "goes back centuries for its beginnings, back across the Middle Passage, back to Mali and to Guinea and Dahomey and Congo."[68] The yearly Carnival rites reenact the struggle of the oppressed to maintain their personhood in the face of the dehumanizing force of colonialism. As they seek to keep alive the past in the present, emphasis again falls on the body as a crucial repository of memory. For the dragon maker Aldrick, fashioning his costume on Calvary Hill, "every thread he sewed, every scale he put on the body of the dragon, was a thought, a gesture, an adventure. . . . He worked, as it were, in a flood of memories, . . . letting them soak him through and through; and his life grew before him, in the texture of his paint and the angles of his dragon's scales" (28). Aldrick's craftsmanship establishes a sensuous connection to his materials that at the same time mediates a connection to a social history.

Nevertheless the manifestation of a resistant selfhood permitted by this practice is not without its problems. The rapid socioeconomic changes of the postwar years are leading to the gradual commodification of Carnival. Once "the entire Carnival was expressions of rebellion," with "stickfighters who assembled each year to keep alive in battles between themselves the practice of warriorhood" and "black men who blackened themselves further with black grease to make of their very blackness a menace, a threat" (113). Now, though, such figures are "all gone, outlawed from the city or just died"; and Aldrick worries that their "message" too will be lost "among the fancy robbers and fantasy presentations that were steadily entering Carnival; drowned amidst the satin and silks and the beads and feathers and rhinestones" (113). Carnival is being sanitized: in a process akin to folklorization, its commercialization is stripping it of its dynamic connection to history. What had been serious play—a release of energies that actively confronted both past and present—is reduced to just play. The Carnival masks become ornamental spectacles, the legacies they do signify now reified as images to be consumed rather than revivified and made meaningful in relation to the contemporary situation. Whereas in Aldrick's workshop his costume had come before him visibly invested with his own labor and the history that informed it, the new costumes appear only as objects, denuded of social significance.

In fact, Aldrick begins to suspect that even his own practice is losing its meaning. He worries that "he didn't believe in the dragon any more" (113), recognizing that both it and the tradition of warriorhood it represents are becoming separated from the Calvary Hill community. Wrapped up in the task of costume making, he has failed to grasp the increasing inability of the dragon to articulate the collective identity of the Hill, an inability arising in part from the way that this identity is being transformed—indeed, rapidly eroded—by the penetration of capital, its dissolution of social bonds and fostering of possessive individualism. Moreover, the type of resistance the dragon embodies seems flat-footed when confronted by the more insidious forms of domination that have emerged in the era of independence. The straightforwardly oppositional—or "purer" (151)—stance of warriorhood looks less able to unmask the complex vectors of power that now organize social relations. Hence the dragon can't dance, its immobility reflecting its disconnection from a history that is itself being reified.

Similar themes are dramatized via other characters in the novel. The calypsonian Philo, for instance, begins to make increasingly commercial music, his success threatening to drive a wedge between him and Aldrick. For the dragon maker, Philo's new calypsos represent a betrayal of the legacy of resistance that Aldrick tries to uphold against a social order that has failed to deliver on its emancipatory promises. The confusion he feels over Philo, his "inability to hold the two ideas in his brain—Philo as a friend, and Philo as threat" (151), illustrates the uncertainties of that resistance when confronted by the capacity of commercialization to co-opt once critical discourses.

In her separate way, Sylvia, the young woman from the Hill with whom Aldrick falls in love, is in danger of being similarly co-opted by the dominant order. At first the movement of her body associates her with the collective history that has been sustained through subaltern cultural practices. At Carnival, dressed as a slave girl, she dances "with all her dizzying aliveness, . . . leaping as if she wanted to leap out of herself into her self, a self in which she could stay forever, in which she could *be* forever . . . her whole self a shout, a bawl, a cry, a scream, a cyclone of tears rejoicing in a self and praying for a self to live in beyond Carnival and her slave girl costume" (119). The sensuous plenitude Sylvia exhibits is inextricable from the community's historical opposition to colonialist efforts to repress the energies of the colonized and regulate the "transgressive" bodies of black women. It underscores, too, a continuing desire to remake selfhood, which, by implication, means remaking society in such a way as to enable the full expression of that emergent subjectivity.

However, Sylvia is taken under the wing of Miss Cleothilda, the Hill's light-skinned shopkeeper, and Guy, the rent collector who becomes her lover, both of whom, as Aaron Love puts it, "attempt to cannibalise Sylvia's energy under the old, symbolic order, in order to shore up their own social authority."[69] These petit bourgeois characters encourage Sylvia to abjure the emancipatory forces her own libidinal vitality embodies (which they connect, disparagingly, to the resistant posture of Aldrick and other rebellious figures on the Hill). They clearly stand for the attempted inculcation of the colonialist and patriarchal model of the "respectable" female body, which bourgeois nationalist elites sought to impose as part of the limited social and political settlements they implemented.[70] Aldrick, meanwhile, is left

> helpless as Sylvia surrendered herself to Guy and Cleothilda, surrendering not only her own body and time of her own, but surrendering in herself that thing in herself that was not hers alone, that others—the whole Hill—could lay claim to; that spirit, that hope that had lived in the Yard . . . that belief that there was ahead a better life, a nobler life, for which they, the whole Yard, were candidates out of their steadfast insistence on their right to a humanness unlinked to the possession of any goods or property, arrived at, realized, born to, in consequence of their being. (143)

As she surrenders herself to the ethos of private property represented by Guy and Cleothilda, Sylvia begins to change physically. Aldrick watches her "going by forcing that tall swing of her young limbs into that brisk mincing gait of one of those office ladies" (159).

The struggles of Fisheye, meanwhile, the local badjohn, foreground the search for adequate structures in which to ground selfhood. Frequenting the cinema to watch Hollywood Westerns, for instance, he models himself on a cowboy: "He began to develop a crawl, a way of walking that was kinda dragging and slow . . . his legs spread apart to give the appearance of being bow-legged from riding a horse. He walked, crawled to and from work, to and from the cinema, tall, slow, a bow-legged cowboy" (43). His changed gait not only emphasizes the impact of imported cultural forms in terms of restructuring habitus but also, as with Sylvia, signals his potential disconnection from a collective history associated with bodily movement, a history linked explicitly to Fisheye's family: his father was a Baptist preacher and a stickfighter who passed this art on to his children (40). Reduced to a cartoonish "spectacle" by the posture he adopts (43), his frustration at the inadequacy of his chosen model leads to a madness similar to that seen in *Solibo Magnifique*. When the streets of Port of Spain fail to live up to his cowboy-inflected imaginings—"he would pick his way between the garbage and dog shit with his secret power and invisible guns, his eyes searching the shadows for a hidden gunman . . . but all he saw was maybe a few fellars gambling" (42)—he returns home and smashes up his room. His desire for expression can manifest itself only in a frenzied rush: walking the streets after being freed from jail, he senses "his own strength stifling him. He wanted to burst out of himself, to fly out and become himself" (45). Society, it seems, is unable to provide the framework in which he can just *be*.

On joining the steel band, however, Fisheye temporarily discovers a "place where he could be a man, where his strength and quickness had meaning and he could feel pride in belonging and purpose to his living" (46). Like the dragon, the band enables its participants to reconnect with a history of "warriorhood" (47). Melding people together, the band permits Fisheye to express himself as an integral member in a social organism coincident with his own habitus. Even the battles between bands from different districts of the city are for Fisheye a "celebration and consecration of a greater brotherhood" (51). The novel suggests, though, that such battles are becoming a comforting, unthinking custom rather than a challenging affirmation of identity. Fisheye, for all the "love and power" he receives from the steel band community, makes "no move to go beyond living his warriorhood; and he went into battle after battle with that dull, triumphing might" (50). When his girlfriend Yvonne points out that rather than fighting each other, the bands should fight those "who keeping down black people. Fight the government" (51), Fisheye recognizes the sense in it. The other bandsmen, however, remain unable to "turn their eyes away from each other outwards to the world . . . where resided the levers of power that moved people, that moved them. It was as if they were purposively blind to this world" (53).

This failure to abandon their habitual postures and challenge the status quo is cemented by the bands' eventual co-option by the ruling order. The peace between rival groups that Fisheye sought as the prelude to their unification in one rebel army is achieved, but the cessation of hostilities is brought about by its being a precondition for corporate sponsorship. Subsequently, commercialization neutralizes the sociopolitical significance of the bands, inveigling them into the ambit of official culture, so that they become an affirmation of the capitalist values they once opposed. Fisheye watches as the Desperadoes band is rebranded "Sampoco Oil Company Gay Desperadoes," and "instead of the little fellars pushing the pans, you had the sponsors: the sponsor's wife and the sponsor's daughter and the sponsor's friends . . . their faces reddened by the excitement and the sun, . . . singing, All Ah We Is One" (60). Even as they celebrate the island's supposed unity-in-diversity, the sponsors marginalize the lower classes, the "little fellars" from the slums. In this respect, the "All o' we is one" mantra—Trinidad's official national motto—is an empty and invidious slogan. It serves only as a means to preempt any real interrogation of the interrelated issues of ethnic division and class inequality. Indeed, it is part of what Stefano Harney calls Trinidad's metadiscourse of race, which "masks deep economic and political stratification and limits all discourses to the boosterism of racial harmony."[71] The slogan's empty rhetoric is exposed in the novel by the way the lighter-skinned continue to exert disproportionate power. It is no surprise that one of its greatest advocates is the shopkeeper Cleothilda. Her incessant cries of "All o' we is one" not only are contradicted by her "hostile, superior and unaccommodating" attitude to her neighbors (10) but also distract from the fact that the position of superiority she claims for herself in the Yard stems not from her role as Carnival Queen but from her skin tone and her proprietorship of the shop. Her economic position, in fact, is a good part of the reason for her prejudice toward Pariag, the Indian, whom she views as a potential threat. When she encourages the vandalizing of his bicycle, it has little to do with her supposed commitment to preserving equality and resisting materialism, and more to do with a desire to safeguard her own propertied status.

The degeneration of a progressive ideal into an ideology of collective identity that only helps buttress bourgeois interests reflects something of the trajectory of the People's National Movement (PNM) as it is represented in the novel. Initially the PNM (the nationalist party which under Eric Williams led Trinidad to independence in 1962) rekindles Fisheye's enthusiasm for social change. In "joining people to people and people to dreams and dreams to hope that man would battle for more than to proclaim the strength of his arms" (57), the movement holds out the potential for the creation of a society that will at last provide the means to fully express the collective history of the masses. Significantly, with his involvement in the PNM, Fisheye's "gestures were beginning to flow again, his rhythm came back" (58). Through his excited response to the party, however, he unconsciously reveals incipient problems with its political program: "Fellars was talking. He couldn't understand the words. He doubted that they could explain them; but you didn't really need words to understand. . . . Words were just a kind of background dressing, a kinda screen, a sound, the sounds. Manifesto, Nationhood, Culture, Colonialism" (57). While these rallying cries are essential for rousing supporters, Fisheye's incomprehension, and the fact that the people shouting such slogans cannot explain what they mean, portends the forthcoming split between the national bourgeoisie, who seize power on the back of such declarations, and the masses supporting them. The "screen" generated by the slogans, rather than providing a background to the interrogation of the issues they raise in the specific context of Trinidad, will come to function only as a means to mask the PNM's subsequent failure to implement the necessary changes. This, in fact, has proved a durable tactic for a number of postcolonial national elites, both across the Caribbean and elsewhere in the Third World: political debate is framed in terms of epic battles over cultural identity so as to delay dealing with structurally embedded social problems. Lovelace has characterized this tendency as the "displacement and postponement of crucial national business . . . [arising] because many people have been persuaded that they are fighting not simply for political change but for their political and racial life and social life."[72]

In light of the failings of many such nationalist movements, much postcolonial (specifically postcolonialist-poststructuralist) theory has been moved to disavow all forms of nationalism. As Neil Larsen observes, the "governing impulse of postcolonialism . . . is clearly one of hostility to nationa*lism*, in implicit recognition of its betrayal of those who once saw in it the emancipatory alternative to colonialism and imperialism."[73] He goes on to argue, however, that what should be the next step—a class critique of Third Worldist cultural nationalism—typically remains deferred. Instead nationalism and the nation are treated almost exclusively as textual or narrative phenomena, enabling them to be subjected to a deconstructionist reading that exposes the inherent instability of these phenomena—an instability supposedly generated by a constitutive yet disavowed ambivalence. This ambivalence is subsequently converted into a form of agency (often designated "hybridity") and a site from which to resist oppressive power relations. But the effect is "simply to equate the *historical crisis* of cultural nationalism with the *fait accompli* of its transcendence."[74] The idealism of this theoretical maneuver is reinforced by the way the undifferentiating disavowal of all nationalisms and the rewriting of the social as the textual (which usually corresponds to a de-emphasis on the concept of the state) obscure the determinate grounds on which any emancipatory transformation could be enacted.

As the foregoing discussion suggests, underlying both this lack of attention to the state and the conflation of different types of nationalism (say, bourgeois nationalist and national liberationist) is what Neil Lazarus identifies as "a culturalist emphasis on nationalism as *a mode of representation*."[75] This emphasis, in turn, lies behind perhaps the key charge that postcolonialist-poststructuralist critics lay at the door of nationalism: its appropriative character. Lazarus summarizes the charge thus:

> All nationalisms, it is suggested, strive to represent themselves as the true—the legitimate—voice of the people-as-nation. All nationalisms are therefore appropriative, since they claim unisonance, and since these claims necessarily involve speaking for—and therefore silencing—others. Specifically, nationalism is viewed as an *elitist* cultural practice in which subaltern classes are represented—spoken for—in the name of the nation which is, supposedly, themselves.[76]

Thereby refused is the idea that some kind of dialectical link could exist between the subaltern classes and those representing them. Lazarus critically dissects this line of thought, which frequently leads to the disparagement or even jettisoning of representationalist politics per se. He emphasizes the necessity not only of acknowledging that some representations might be more adequate to their object than others, but also of recognizing that by dismissing the prospect of subaltern identification (however partial and mediated) with nationalist representations, it becomes "impossible to account plausibly for the investment of the masses of the colonized historically in various kinds of nationalist struggle."[77]

Rather than rehearse the particulars of this debate here, I want to turn back to the writers studied in this chapter. We have already heard the explicit concerns voiced by Harris and Glissant that their interrogation of literary representation should not be confused with its endless deconstruction. Indeed, Glissant made clear that such a luxury, so to speak, is not an option for Caribbean writers when the collectivity remains imperiled or subjectivity has been wrenched from an imposed objecthood only relatively recently. The dramatization of the act of writing evident in Chamoiseau's work further reinforced the sense that at stake was a struggle to establish a dialectical link between the writer and society, to elaborate an adequate representational form—albeit one that will be subject to constant critique and recalibration. Significantly, however, the political concerns of these writers with regard to literary practice also carry over into their thinking about political representation itself.

Lovelace's work is especially instructive in this regard. He is clear about his desire to represent what he calls the "ordinary people" in his fiction. "The struggle for narrative voice," he writes, "is the struggle to elevate and utilise the voice of the ordinary people or, at least, a voice that reflects the rhythms, vocabulary and imagery of the ordinary people, their sensibility and achievements whether they realise them consciously or not."[78] I also noted in the introduction how Lovelace insists on the continued relevance of national independence as an unfinished project, one necessary to prevent the "real possibility of being diffused into an impotent individualism by the workings of forces alive in the postcolonial world."[79] Underlying these sentiments we can discern an attentiveness to the need to establish the determinate grounds on which a fully emancipatory social order could be erected. Essential to this is the creation of institutions and organizations that would allow individuals and communities to have their concerns rearticulated at a national level: "The key, one of the keys to our future, to liberation is to help us to involve ourselves in it. Local government and community representation and organization and involvement assume a particularly important role in any planning for our society for the reason that there are so many communities unrepresented to speak."[80] Lovelace thus commits himself to a representationalist and nationalist politics. The problem is not representation or nationalism as such but the specific forms they have taken in Trinidad; and the way forward, as he sees it, is to reorganize or reinvent these forms in such a way that they are embedded in, and ultimately controlled by, the people. "The people must realise," he argues, "that the only power is the power they, the people, give to the leaders. The people must realise as they very well do that when they appoint anybody to power they, the people, must share in that power, must in fact be really the final holders of that, living and constant keepers of that power, for only in that way is power safe from ill use by those who seek after it."[81]

The issue of political representation and how it relates to the so-called ordinary people moves to center stage in *The Dragon Can't Dance* after Aldrick, Fisheye, and a number of other badjohns from the Hill attempt to start a popular rebellion, hijacking a police jeep and driving to Woodford Square, exhorting the people to revolt. (As noted earlier, the novel here draws on the events surrounding the Black Power Revolution in Trinidad in 1970.) Despairing at both conventional political structures and the commodity culture that has permeated the community, the rebels look to keep alive a history of resistance oriented around reclaiming a personhood defined other than by the possession of things (a direct response to their ancestors' having been treated as property). However, while such resistance remains unforgoable, their understanding and articulation of its significance is insufficient to move others on the Hill to action. Before the jeep episode, they try to convince the people to continue fighting against the status quo. Standing at the Corner, they harass passersby going to work, their eyes "challeng[ing], accus[ing] them of abandoning their sacred war" (158). Predictably, these tactics only alienate those they are meant to radicalize. The rebels' mind-set, typified by Fisheye's fantasies of an all-out war, limits their ability to respond effectively to the subtle constraints of the postindependence socioeconomic order. "People had jobs now," muses the more thoughtful Aldrick, "had responsibility now for the surviving of families, they could no longer afford rebellion at the Corner" (156). In such circumstances, while the posture of warriorhood might be "purer," it isn't "the truth" (151).

When their revolt climaxes with the protest in Woodford Square, the rebels again fail to convey coherently the import of their actions. The uprising is described in a chapter titled "The Dragon Dance," underscoring how it too is in danger of becoming an unavailing gesture. As they drive across town, declaiming slogans through a megaphone and encouraging onlookers to rise up, Aldrick thinks back to his father, Sam, who upheld a tacit resistance to the colonial system through a stubborn irresponsibility. For all that it rebuffed the dominant order, however, this defiance could not provide a model for collective action, its impotence reflected in the image of Sam dying—still stuck in the same unsatisfying jobs—with his "hands in his pockets" (165). Aldrick repeats this stance during the rebellion, again indicating the entrenched postures into which the resistance has sunk; indeed, circling with the others in the jeep, Aldrick has a "feeling of being imprisoned in a dragon costume on Carnival Tuesday" (169). The rebels' shortcomings are confirmed by what at first appears to be their victory. The police do not try to stop them; yet far from a capitulation to the gang, such inaction is designed to allow them to undermine themselves. "The authorities trusted these men to fail," says the defense lawyer at the rebels' trial. "They trusted that they would be unable to make of their frustration anything better than a dragon dance, a threatening gesture" (175). The attempted revolution collapses because the rebels are unable to universalize their struggle, to rearticulate it for the watching masses and elaborate a program for transforming society grounded in popular practice and responsive to popular wants.

Later Aldrick will come to realize this. "We couldn'ta enter where we had no vision to go," he explains, and without this vision, the tendency to seek validation in imposed structures will continue: "How come everything we do we have to be appealing to somebody else? . . . Is like we ain't have no self. I mean, we have a self but the self we have is for somebody else. Is like even when we acting we ain't the actor" (179–80). Aldrick had sought in the rebellion an alternative to the dragon costume as a means to embody the collective hopes of the people, his performance that of an engaged, revolutionary artist. During the uprising, he takes over the megaphone and begins to speak to the gathering crowds. Freed from the dragon mask, he seems to find his voice (as Sylvia informs him later: "Everybody was surprised you coulda talk so" [188]). Ultimately, however, his speech does not give on to a transformative vision. As David Williams observes, all he "can offer the waiting audience as a revolutionary message is a deterministic statement of the powerlessness that he shares with them."[82] Indeed, to the questions Aldrick poses the crowd—"How can you rise with rent to pay and children to school, and watch hunger march across your yard and camp inside your house? How can you not make peace?"—he too has no answers: "He had wanted to stir them up, to help, to make people know, to strengthen them. He felt very disappointed at himself" (171). His attempt to play the revolutionary artist thus falters, but as his emphasis on the need for a vision implies, the importance of political representation remains. If the changes required to fulfill the aspirations of the people are to be grasped and acted on, then they need individuals or groups capable of appealing to and raising popular consciousness.

The crowd's responses to the rebellion, moreover, demonstrate that they are awaiting just this kind of intervention. When Aldrick begins speaking over the megaphone, the listeners take up his chant of "Pow-er!": "People were shouting, crying out. They were looking to them in the jeep, expecting something" (167). Later, as the rebels continue to talk, the crowd stands there "waiting for something else, some kind of redemption, some saving" (172). The people are looking for leadership that will show them how they can rise up and tackle the constraints ("rent to pay," "hunger") that currently force them to "make peace" with their condition. Yet as we have seen, the rebels fall short in this respect.

Nevertheless Aldrick, upon returning to the Hill after serving time in prison, is sufficiently changed by his experiences to be able to grasp the world in a new way. His comments on the manner in which the rebels had appealed "to somebody else" indicate his growing understanding of how society must be restructured. And integral to this, it is suggested, is his deeper apprehension of the social relations between people. Musing on Pariag and his harsh treatment by the others, Aldrick realizes that "he did not really know Pariag," but also that he "might have known him if he had known himself" (196). He comes to the conclusion that "each man . . . had responsibility for his own living, had the responsibility for the world he lived in" (196). Harney views this declaration (and indeed the tenor of the novel's ending as a whole) as an assertion of individualism over group identity.[83] I would argue, however, that it points in the opposite direction: it is a recognition of the need for a more self-reflexive understanding of selfhood, which necessarily involves a more comprehensive understanding of how one relates to society. To know oneself properly is a social issue: individuals are not isolated monads (which Aldrick initially seemed to want to believe, attempting to keep his distance from others as he labored in his workshop) but bound together and constituted through social relations. At stake is a group identity that allows people to be their full selves, whether that is Aldrick, Sylvia, or Pariag (Pariag having been marginalized so that, as he puts it, the Hill "see[s] one part of me and they take that to be the whole me" [203]). To remake selfhood and to remake society, as dialectically linked processes, must thus entail exploding the integument of the isolated individual and establishing a new transparency in human relations.

This, I submit, is the implication for social practice behind the new aesthetic practices Aldrick begins to conceive at the end of the novel. Considering his future, he wonders whether he might become a sign painter: "He thought of some signs he could paint: Beware of the dog! No spitting! Trespassers will be prosecuted according to the Law! No obscene language! Wet Paint! Men at Work! Maybe he could paint some new signs, signs of life, of hope, of love, of affirming, and let his own living match and mirror them" (197). Having been a Carnival artist and a would-be revolutionary artist, Aldrick moves here toward something like a combination of the two. The new signs he imagines bespeak the possibility of a transformed social world. Integral to the consolidation of the ruling socioeconomic order, I have argued throughout this chapter, is the nullification of the senses imposed by colonialism and capitalism, this nullification helping to prevent the social relations that structure reality from being grasped and acted on. For Marx, who viewed the senses as historically conditioned by the world before them, the reification of the sensorium could be overcome only by challenging the reified condition of the object world. If private property has led to the estrangement of all the other senses by "the sense of *having*," then the "transcendence of private property is . . . the complete *emancipation* of all human senses and attributes; but it is this emancipation precisely because these senses and attributes have become, subjectively and objectively, *human*."[84] Once the object world becomes a social, human object world, then the senses relate themselves to that world as social, human senses—the "senses have therefore become directly in their practice *theoreticians*," writes Marx.[85] The new signs Aldrick intends to paint would seem to presuppose just this kind of liberation and humanization of the senses: not only do they celebrate life and promise sensory renewal, but they do so in opposition to those old signs—commandments, rather—which upheld the law and private property ("Trespassers will be prosecuted").

Aldrick's new aesthetic practice, then, can be read as figuring social relations yet to come, as translating the utopian hope for a social world in which the sentiments of those signs could find objective expression. A similar pattern is evident with Pariag, whose own utopian vision of a different form of society is likewise bound up with the potential of new kinds of aesthetic practice. Reflecting on his hitherto marginal position, he wishes:

> I was just beginning now, just coming into the Yard. . . . I wish I had choose myself to represent myself. . . . I wish I did walk with a flute or a sitar, and walk in right there in the middle of the steelband yard where they was making new drums, new sounds, a new music from rubbish tins and bits of steel and oil drums, bending the iron over fire, chiselling out new notes. . . . I wish I woulda go in there where they was making their life anew in fire, with chisel and hammer, and sit down with my sitar on my knee and say: Fellars, this is me, Pariag from New Lands. Gimme the key! . . . And let his music cry too, and join in the crying. (202)

The original musical combinations of which Pariag dreams thus register his desire to be integrated on his own terms into a society simultaneously being made anew. Crucial to this remaking is a revitalized sensorium: the new instruments and identities being forged in the yard are inextricable from an emphasis on bodily practice and the material process of reworking received forms. Such transformations, moreover, can clearly be understood in terms of creolization, and in particular of creolization grasped not simply as the interaction of cultural legacies but as a process that is folded into the social reproduction of material reality.

In sum, then, the passage once more implies the necessity of cracking open inculcated monadic identities, recognizing or *resensing* the linkages that mediate between people as the prelude to being able to reorganize social relations. Indeed, in its emphasis on the bodilyness of the new sound that Pariag envisions being created—its notes being chiseled out, extruded from lived corporeal experience—the text indirectly posits the possibility of an as-yet-unrealized social world that would be adjusted to the practices and needs of the mass of the people.

An explicit imagining of that world remains beyond the scope of *The Dragon Can't Dance*, however, which ends with Aldrick leaving still in search of a space in which he can claim his full selfhood. Nevertheless that world's potential lineaments are underscored by the form of the text, which simultaneously points also to the need for new modalities of literary representation. The novel reproduces structurally the disjunction between the prevailing social structures and individual habitus. In the first five and the last two chapters, it narrates the lives of the major protagonists by dedicating a chapter to each, designating their role via headings such as "The Princess," "The Dragon," and "The Bad John." In so doing, it suggests something like Harris's conventional "novel of persuasion," in which individual identities are consolidated through the selection of details and situations that work to render those identities apparently self-sufficient and inevitable. But the narrative subsequently undermines this formal logic, for in each instance the role allotted by the chapter heading does not fully coincide with the behavior and needs of the character. Thus, for example, Aldrick must move beyond the dragon mask if he is to satisfy his growing desire for change, while Fisheye is shown to be uncomfortable with his tough-guy posture, at least initially when its limitations contribute to the maddened frustration he feels at his inability to just *be* in society.

The accent this places on the necessity of breaking out of these fixed, isolated carapaces is further underlined by the book's distinctive spiraling trajectory. The novel seems set to climax with Aldrick's encounter with Sylvia after his return from prison, the scene apparently signaling the closure of a narrative arc opened near the beginning of the book when Sylvia first visits Aldrick in his workshop. Yet instead of drawing to a close, the text kicks on again, revisiting Pariag and, most strikingly, devoting a chapter to Philo that elaborates on the calypsonian's past and his rise to fame. By continuing to expand outward, as it were, rather than contracting into a neat resolution, the narrative structure generates a sense of overspill, of the bursting of the arcs through which it might conventionally be channeled. The same thing is evident at the level of syntax, with Lovelace frequently constructing long, spiraling, clause-laden sentences (see, for example, the openings of chapters 1 and 8). Married to the exuberance of his writing and the fluid shifting between linguistic registers, this again gestures indirectly to the requirements of a transformative politics in terms of cracking open reified social structures and reorganizing the power relations they contain.

I will have more to say about the spiraling quality of Lovelace's narrative in the next chapter when examining *Salt* (1996), where that distinctive formal aesthetic is more obviously linked to the explicit articulation of a political program. As indicated previously, the novels on which this chapter has focused do not offer such explicit projections. Although *The Dragon Can't Dance* certainly moves in this direction, both *Solibo Magnifique* and *Macho Camacho's Beat* are permeated by an air of pessimism when it comes to overcoming the alienation they identify. Yet here too the forms of both texts implicitly point beyond the political impasses registered in their content. In Sánchez's novel, the same frenzied energy that infuses the writing as it reproduces the delirium and volatility of its protagonists also becomes potentially destabilizing of the reification and anesthetization that contribute so significantly to these problems. Like Solibo's schizophrenic breakdown, the language of the text, even as it figures the inability to structure time and space coherently, does manifest the "torment of history," in Glissant's words. And in its vibrancy, excess, and at times grotesque, carnivalesque character, it begins to strain toward the change that would achieve the negation of this torment: not the (impossible) reconciliation with an alienated identity but the resensing of the materiality of the social world so that it can be grasped as a construct subject to change.

In *Solibo Magnifique*, Chamoiseau's creolized writing style, with its energetic mixture of Creole and French, the oral and the written, performs a similar function. The sinuosity and dynamism of the novel's middle section, which sits between the cold, abstract language of the opening police report and the slightly stilted "ersatz" reproduction of Solibo's speech that closes the book, becomes the formal mediation of a sensory plenitude to come. It gestures beyond a reified sensorium, serving implicitly as a utopian sign for the as-yet-unrealized social order that would be the precondition for achieving such plenitude; it marks, in other words, the faint, shimmering outlines of an alternative reality to the perpetual present established by the imperialist obscuration of history. Significant here is both Chamoiseau's attempt to bring the body back into the text with his emphasis on orality and the part played in his representation and understanding of the social world by creolization (as noted earlier, these things are also integral, in different ways, to Pariag's vision of a new aesthetic practice in *The Dragon Can't Dance*). In the introduction, I argued that the concepts of transculturation and creolization could be viewed as offering an optic on commodity fetishism, one that in "bringing into the open concealed exchanges between peoples and releasing histories buried within fixed identities," as Fernando Coronil put it, helps unmask the social relations and structural determinants such fetishism occludes. The emphasis on creolization in these texts seems to be working to similar ends, functioning as a way to map the social totality so as to penetrate reified forms and provide a vital resource for elaborating a political project aimed at transforming society. In the next chapter, we will see how these ideas are developed and deployed in varying ways by a number of writers as part of original philosophies of history. The result is the emergence of new literary forms able to express the lineaments of a nation-state reorganized in relation to the needs and habitus of the people.

4

From Breakdown to Rebirth: Ritual Reconfigurations of the Nation-State

Toward the end of *A Singular Modernity*, Fredric Jameson calls for the continuation of attempts to elaborate an ontology of the present, remarking that a "true ontology would not only wish to register the forces of past and future within that present; but would also be intent on diagnosing . . . the enfeeblement and virtual eclipse of those forces within our current present."[1] Recalling the way both Ezra Pound and Walter Benjamin scrutinized the public sphere for signs of modernist energies, Jameson concludes: "We need to combine a Poundian mission to identify Utopian tendencies with a Benjaminian geography of their sources and a gauging of their pressure at what are now multiple sea levels. Ontologies of the present demand archaeologies of the future, not forecasts of the past."[2] The previous chapter examined the attenuation of the forces of past and future under imperialism and late capitalism, but it also considered the countervailing impulse in the novels I discussed to project the possibility of as-yet-unrealized social formations. The distinctive formal aesthetics evident in the work of Lovelace, Sánchez, and Chamoiseau, I argued, created a disturbance in the field whereby the faint outlines of an emergent reality hove into view amid a reified social world. These moments of disturbance correspond to Jameson's utopian tendencies, representing pressure points that mark the potential for the total transformation of society. They are in that sense also the headwaters of archaeologies of the future—projections of what might be that allow one to rehistoricize an enfeebled present, reading back into it radically other futures that shed new light on the problems of the here and now.[3]

In this chapter, I explore how those stylistic innovations and glimpses of utopian potential are extended by Chamoiseau, Lovelace, and Erna Brodber, among others, into whole aesthetic programs that flesh out projected new modes of collectivity. As these writers develop original approaches to history, they fashion something like a new kind of epic form. This form refracts the potential lineaments of a reconfigured nation-state. It seeks to respond to the crises suffered by various nationalist projects from the independence era, crises I have analyzed in terms of their textual mediation through the topos of the tragic sacrifice. I return to that topos here insofar as it is now completely transformed, being replaced by a new set of images and motifs that stand as the literary translation of a political and social dispensation yet to come. We will thus be concerned with archaeologies of the future, but we will also be considering reconstructions of the past in light of the deformations wrought on history by colonialism. In this sense, Jameson's injunction regarding ontologies of the present might require some modification, for while *forecasts* of the past are not helpful, *restagings* of it are required as part of the attempt to rethink the future.

It will be clear from the foregoing that the utopian dimension of artworks will be of central importance in this chapter. It is hence worth returning for a moment to the issue of the relationship between empirical reality and the literary object. This study has sought to emphasize both the relative autonomy of the literary field and its inescapably social dimension. Earlier we had recourse to Bourdieu's notion of homologous fields. Without wishing to suggest that their theories are synonymous, I turn now to Adorno's concept of the autonomy of the aesthetic—albeit with the proviso that (as noted in chapter 1) when it comes to the relative autonomy of the literary sphere in the Caribbean context, its aesthetic mediations do not involve only strictly "literary" forms; it also uses non-canonical and popular cultural forms, as well as drawing on other fields of social life.[4] Commenting on artworks, Adorno writes that "it is precisely as artefacts, as products of social labour, that they also communicate with the empirical experience that they reject and from which they draw their content [*Inhalt*]. Art negates the categorical determinations stamped on the empirical world and yet harbours what is empirically existing in its own substance."[5] This mediating of the social world within the art object itself means that the "unsolved antagonisms of reality return in artworks as immanent problems of form."[6]

But the double character of art is key also to its utopian promise: in seeking to free itself from an empirical world into which it might at any moment fall back, art constantly posits the negation of that world and the possibility of one that is radically other. Indeed, it is the distance of the aesthetic sphere from society, and the transformative effect worked on empirical matter by form, that allows for the articulation of something so absolutely different it cannot be assimilated to the governing logic of the status quo. As Adorno contends:

> Even the contemplative attitude to artworks, wrested from objects of action, is felt as the announcement of an immediate praxis and—to this extent itself practical—as a refusal to play along. Only artworks that are to be sensed as a form of comportment have a raison d'être. Art is not only the plenipotentiary of a better praxis than that which has to date predominated, but is equally the critique of praxis as the rule of brutal self-preservation at the heart of the status quo and in its service. It gives the lie to production for production's sake and opts for a form of praxis beyond the spell of labour.[7]

If art's utopian dimension lies in its negation of the existing world, however, this negation is also the source of a subsequent ambivalence in its indictment of this world; for as Jameson has observed with regard to utopian texts specifically, "The more surely a given Utopia asserts its radical difference from what currently is, to that very degree it becomes, not merely unrealisable but, what is worse, unimaginable."[8]

I have already touched on the issue of utopian visions of transformation in chapter 1, where I considered the possibility of a "dialectical image" that could project the unity of an existence in a state of disparity. This disparity was the result of the uneven development engendered by imperialism, whereby some areas of a country undergo rapid modernization while others remain locked into archaic forms of economic and social relations. Such unevenness, with different sections of the population living (in one sense at least) in different historical moments, impedes social mobilization and entrenches inequality. The purpose of a dialectical image would be not only to capture the reality of this divided condition but also to articulate its unity, to reveal its nonsynchronous modalities to be nevertheless synchronous insofar as they are the product of a total, unitary historical process. By thus restoring a sense of historicity to the symptoms of unevenness, enabling one to grasp its causal basis in imperialist exploitation, the image also gestures toward the possibility of a future in which such exploitation is negated. In Adorno's terms, then, the dialectical image can be viewed as drawing the empirical antagonisms of uneven development and multiple temporalities into the aesthetic sphere, where, once mediated as formal antagonisms, they are reorganized and transformed into a representation governed by a new logic—a representation, that is, which serves as the utopian anticipation of a future, emancipated society.

The examples of marvelous realism I considered in the first chapter, as well as Selvon's more social realist narrative style, go some way toward producing a dialectical image for the period in the 1940s and 1950s when the possibility of a society liberated from colonial domination became an increasingly tangible prospect. With their combination of local and imported contents and styles, these texts not only pointed up the Caribbean's structurally dependent position within the capitalist world system but also began to establish the coordinates of a literary form congruent with their own social and historical context. The writers studied in the present section build on these earlier formal developments. They do so, however, in light not only of the political gains and disappointments of the intervening years but also of the intensification of uneven development, and its attendant juxtaposing of nonsynchronous realities, as a result of the increased penetration of transnational finance capital.

To speak of the synchronicity of the nonsynchronous is to recall the work of Ernst Bloch, who coined this seemingly oxymoronic formula in *Erbschaft dieser Zeit* (1935).[9] Bloch distinguishes between synchronous contradictions (those that are posited in and grow with present-day capitalism, most obviously the contradictions that hold between capital and labor) and nonsynchronous contradictions (those that are "far from and alien to the present," including "both *declining remnants* and, above all, [the] uncompleted *past*, which has not yet been 'sublated' by capitalism").[10] Bloch is clear that the second type constitutes a problem for society, retarding agency and rendering certain groups vulnerable to manipulation by reactionary forces.[11] Nevertheless he also suggests that the nonsynchronous holdover from the past can deliver "a part of that matter which seeks a life not destroyed by capital."[12] In particular, it can furnish a sense of a time when human relationships were "relatively more lively and intact" and "relatively more immediate than those in capitalism"; and while such "immediacy was only seemingly closer in earlier forms," this residual structure of feeling can be set against capitalism and its baleful social consequences.[13] For Bloch, the task "is to extrapolate the elements of the nonsynchronous contradiction which are capable of antipathy and transformation, that is, those hostile to capitalism and [that] are homeless in it, and to refit them to function in a different context."[14] To be clear, then, the past itself is not the solution: "Even the possible late ripening of what is actually incomplete in this past can never turn into a new quality of its own accord, one that is not already known from the past. That end could be served at best by an alliance, which liberates the still *possible future* from the *past* only by putting both in the present."[15]

If Bloch's theories provide a way of approaching uneven and combined development as a condition intrinsic to global capitalist modernity—a condition that assumes a specific and particularly acute configuration in the Caribbean—his view on nonsynchronicity also finds a counterpart in various Caribbean engagements with the issue. Indeed, his emphasis on the need to liberate the future from the past is striking for the way it recalls the philosophy of history elaborated by Harris, whose own ideas reflect in addition his having to deal with the legacies of colonialism and the collision of peoples it engendered. We have already encountered (in the discussion of *Palace of the Peacock*) Harris's concept of a return to an unfinished past that is pregnant with a "phenomenal legacy" yet to come to fruition. The most systematic exegesis of this position is given in *Tradition, the Writer, and Society*. Here Harris poses the question of how one can let the variable parts of a cross-cultural past "act on each other in a manner that fulfils *in the person* the most nebulous instinct for a vocation of being."[16] His solution requires that "the monument of consolidation breaks down and becomes the need for a vision of consciousness."[17] The monument of consolidation is the dominant narrative of history; it is by way of a vision of consciousness that one begins to look through this reified structure and to perceive the unconsummated possibilities buried within it.

Thus, turning to the colonial conquest and, in particular, the search for El Dorado, Harris suggests that in examining this monumentalized history of violence, one should not dismiss the "instinctive idealism" associated with the pursuit of the City of Gold, an idealism ultimately overwhelmed by the reality of exploitation and greed.

The substance of this adventure, involving men of all races, past and present conditions, has begun to acquire a residual pattern of illuminating correspondences. El
Dorado, City of Gold, City of God, grotesque, unique coincidence, another window
within upon the Universe. . . . in terms of the novel the distribution of a frail moment of illuminating adjustments within a long succession and grotesque series of
adventures, past and present, capable *now* of discovering themselves and continuing to discover themselves so that in one sense one relives and reverses the "given"
conditions of the past, freeing oneself from catastrophic idolatry and blindness to
one's own historical and philosophical conceptions and misconceptions which may
bind one within a statuesque present or a false future.[18]

The key to Harris's thinking here is his emphasis on the need to return to or,
better, reanimate the past via an imaginative rehearsal that opens it up to an
interpretation beyond its historical limits. The narrative fictions through which
history is replayed enable original correspondences to be uncovered. For Harris,
images and symbols (especially mythic motifs) provide a means to link otherwise
opposed events and thereby illuminate unseen connections that evolve beneath
the surface of reality. Hence the historical experience of colonial conquest might
now be sifted for signs of its obviously unrealized utopian negation: within the
ruins of a quest "involving men of all races" may lie not only the self-evident
cleavages between these races but also, paradoxically, the unborn potential of a
new architecture of cultures harbored in an unconscious striving to process the
shattering impact of the collision of so many lives and traditions.

Harris's approach to history, then, aims to unblock the utopian energies
dammed up within its sedimented layers. These unfulfilled or phenomenal currents are brought, imaginatively, into the present, where they are converted into
a means of electrifying our understanding of reality. Like Bloch, Harris looks
to recuperate from a nonsynchronous past something—typically, the ideal of
cross-cultural community, considered to be implicit in the creolization of cultural forms—that can be used against the debilitating conditions of the present;
only he is not so much calling up a residual idea of, or structure of feeling from,
the past as attempting to redeem from it resources that never existed concretely
in the first place.

Harris's ideas undoubtedly provide a challenging and far-reaching means of
rethinking the contours of Caribbean experience. They are properly utopian in
the sense that they open the way to imagining a radically other world not reducible to the ruling conventions of the status quo; indeed, we have here also
the production of a radically other past, one not reducible—precisely because
it was unborn—to the received narratives of history. However, his theories also
display the ambivalence I alluded to earlier as being common to utopian visions;
that is, in their radical difference, they risk appearing unrealizable and even
merely fantastical. Perhaps the most significant accusation one could level at

Harris's project is that, in suggesting that the recognition of hitherto eclipsed cross-culturality might help convert a legacy of conflict into a future of reconciled community, it offers little more than an imaginary resolution of the social contradiction between oppressor and oppressed. Such a resolution, insofar as it is activated on the level of cultural forms, would seem to disengage these forms from their more intransigent socioeconomic contexts as the condition for construing cultural imbrication as a catalyst for transformation. This risks displacing and even occluding the structural inequalities and asymmetrical power relations that are central to the reproduction of unevenness and nonsynchronicity.

But if Harris's vision risks becoming little more than a benign celebration of cultural dialogue, it is also possible to place a slightly different slant on his approach to history, one that ensures it retains its utopian dimensions by shifting our understanding of where their power lies. This book has sought to apprehend creolization not simply as the result of flows of culture meeting and mingling—as a phenomenon that occurs independently of social reality—but rather as a process folded into the very production of that reality. Creolization originates and develops within the total context of the collision, opposition, and indigenization of different economic modes and structures, social relations, habitus, and lifeways. From this perspective, what is most compelling is not any claim to the supposedly inherent emancipatory properties of creolization but rather the way the concept can be used as an optic by which to read back through the process of social reproduction. Under capitalism, the relations between people that determine this process are eclipsed by commodity fetishism, making it hard to grasp the structures of power and domination that regulate existence. By pointing to the cultural exchanges and linkages that are an integral part of the history of the present, creolization can be made to function as a means of opening up the reified social world, restoring a sense of the human agency and structural determinations that shape its contours. In other words, it can be deployed as a mapping device by which one can move from an apprehension of the interconnection and interpenetration of cultural forms to a perception of the social relations with which they are necessarily imbricated.

From this perspective, the concept of creolization might be understood as furnishing us with an allegory of the social totality. Turning back to Harris, it becomes possible to view his cross-cultural revisioning of history as working in a similar way, seeking as it does to map unseen connections between people, or between events, through imagistic correspondences. It is not too much of a leap to make of this mapping an allegorical means of grasping the totality of relations and mediations that constitute society. Indeed, this leap is given impetus by Harris's work itself, by the way it construes the movement of history as being predicated on such interactions and connections. (It is worth noting, too, how Harris frequently stresses the need to pursue "wholeness"; see, for example, *The Infinite Rehearsal* [1987], in which he insists on wholeness as a kind of impossible perspective that we must nonetheless seek to bring to bear on reality.)[19] Harris's imaginative rehearsals of the past thus also become restagings of history on the level of the collective: by emphasizing the entanglements and collisions that characterize its unfolding—those "grotesque" adventures involving "men of all races"—Harris aims to break down the static monumentality of history and resink it into the teeming mass of humanity. And it is here that we might relocate the utopian content of his work: in its desire to negate reified categories and in its impulse toward the collective. It is by grasping the constitutive relations of the collective and imagining them otherwise that one lays the foundations for projections of the world that retain a properly radical otherness.

But what the foregoing also underscores is that just to identify the presence of creolization cannot be an end point in itself. Rather, it must be considered an integral part of an ongoing process to construct a path toward new futures. The still vital question is how the reigning structures of power are to be dismantled and those futures materialized. In the remainder of this chapter, I consider the ways in which other writers have engaged with the question of what it might mean for the nation-state if the original approaches to history, society, and subject relations they elaborate were to become concrete practice.

I turn first to Brodber's *Jane and Louisa Will Soon Come Home* (1980). In its portrayal of psychic trauma alongside social frustration with the postindependence political settlement, this novel again raises the issue of allegory and its mediation of the individual and collective. Moreover, the experimental form of the text and the particular way in which it refracts and registers history offer a striking illustration of how socioeconomic unevenness is reworked in the aesthetic sphere in terms of an overlap and clash of literary styles.

Set in Jamaica and featuring characters who move between rural and urban worlds, as well as between bourgeois households and working-class tenement yards, *Jane and Louisa Will Soon Come Home* displays, as Carolyn Cooper puts it, "an interpenetration of scribal and oral literary forms: a modernist, stream-of-consciousness narrative voice holds easy dialogue with the traditional teller of tales, the transmitter of anansi story, proverb, folk song and dance."[20] In fact, the novel began life outside a strictly literary field, its initial purpose being "to serve as a case study of the dissociative personality for [Brodber's] social work students."[21] It thus exemplifies the tendency for cultural, social, and intellectual fields to overlap in the Caribbean, bearing out Glissant's claim that "literature for us will not be divided into genres but will implicate all the perspectives of the human sciences."[22] Such catholicity, Glissant argues, is the only way to properly register a history so grossly mutilated by colonial forces. "Because the collective memory was too often wiped out," he contends, "the Caribbean writer must 'dig deep' into this memory, following the latent signs that he has picked up in the everyday world."[23] These latent signs might be detected in routine cultural practices, for example. However, the imprint of the history they contain may be so faint as to be imperceptible to conventional historiography; hence for Glissant (as for Harris), the significance of fiction to history as a means to imaginatively reconstruct inaccessible pasts. Brodber too, in her role as a social anthropologist, has stressed the importance of extending historiographic methodologies in new directions for the purposes of creating a social history of the Caribbean.[24] *Jane and Louisa Will Soon Come Home* can be viewed in this context. As Evelyn O'Callaghan notes, in one sense the novel is "a therapeutic exercise, a case-study of sorts, with the therapeutic tool being the process of 'going back' to the past."[25] It is engaged in an imaginative excavation of the collective memory of the community, using cultural practices such as folk song and dance to unearth perspectives that might otherwise have remained concealed.

In this regard, the body once again assumes a particular significance, given its centrality to many of these practices. Indeed, the novel is very much concerned with the female body, which has been the site of an especially intense negotiation of the pressures generated by colonial domination (most obviously in terms of the sexual abuse and attempted control of the reproductive powers of enslaved women). It is concerned, too, with the attitude toward gender relations within nationalist movements. We have already seen how many bourgeois nationalist political settlements perpetuated inherited patriarchal models. In fact, in the Anglophone Caribbean, during the period of agitation leading up to independence, a tendency already existed for gender concerns to be marginalized as not integral to the national struggle—as something separate to be dealt with later, lest they distort the nationalist focus. As Hilary Beckles observes, even some feminist historians "were swept along by the compelling tide of a hegemonic male representation of the nationalist project. While their participation in the discourse was guided by considerations of intellectual decolonization and nation-building, they applied brakes to the advancing theoretical critique of patriarchy in order to facilitate the suppression of political dissonance."[26] This masculinist framework obscured "the fact that for Caribbean women as historical subjects the struggles of nationalism were always gendered and the struggles of women's rights were always informed by the politics of race and colonialism."[27]

Jane and Louisa Will Soon Come Home foregrounds and interrogates this connection between gender relations and national politics, with Brodber's rearticulation of collectivity and nationhood highlighting the shortcomings of anticolonial ideologies that perpetuate the positioning of women according to patriarchal categorizations. In so doing, the novel deals in a more explicit way with issues that were only implicitly touched on in some of the texts we have considered previously, while also providing a counterpoint to those narratives wherein the articulation of the possibility of radical social transformation nevertheless continued to be mediated through masculinist tropes.

Brodber's novel describes the protagonist Nellie's attempts to reconstruct her family history and, more generally, to reconnect to a social world from which she has become alienated. Structurally, the book is organized around lines from the children's ring game alluded to in the title. In the first section, "My Dear Will You Allow Me," the narrative records fragmentary voices and snippets of childhood experience. The second section, "To Waltz with You," is a more chronologically straightforward account of Nellie's involvement in radical politics and her traumatic breakdown. The third and fourth sections, "Into This Beautiful Garden" and "Jane and Louisa Will Soon Come Home," return to the events and experiences introduced in the first section as Nellie seeks to come to terms with her past.

The central image in the text is that of the kumbla, a kind of protective casing variously described as "like a beach ball," "an egg-shell," and a "round seamless calabash that protects you without caring."[28] The kumbla serves as the metaphorical embodiment of the strategies by which women have shielded themselves against the pressures of colonial domination and, in particular, the repressive gender and sexual identities thrust upon them. As Rhonda Cobham observes:

> Historically, the Black woman in the New World has always been associated with qualities such as physical strength, sexual independence, and economic resourcefulness. These qualities were imposed on her as part of her status as non-person (and therefore non-woman) during slavery but, like the kumblas of Brodber's vision, the disfigurement functioned dialectically to protect and extend African traditions of female independence and physical prowess.[29]

However, emphasizing the ambivalence of such protective strategies, the kumbla in Brodber's novel also signifies the detrimental impact that they can have on subjectivity and the body: "The trouble with the kumbla is the getting out of the kumbla. . . . If you dwell too long in it, it makes you delicate. Makes you albino: skin white but not by genes" (130). This tendency toward repressing a black corporeality again has its roots in the physical and ideological violence perpetrated by colonialism, which inculcated the colonized with a schema wherein "the vulgar body of knowledge produced by the people . . . [was] devalued."[30] In this schema, the "vulgar" black female body was doubly stigmatized.[31] Brodber's novel dramatizes this double bind, revealing how the self-denial it fosters is especially virulent among the bourgeoisie.

The character of Aunt Becca is exemplary in this respect. She rules over Nellie's family with a "shaming eye" (92), on the lookout for any perceived (especially sexual) impropriety. Her strict and censorious manner is reflected in her buttoned-down appearance: her "crinkly hair scooped away from her face" and "her thin lips pursed together like a shrivelled star apple" (93). The pinched posture of her body indicates the level of censure she works on herself. Indeed, it emerges that her self-denial has left her literally sterile: she has become infertile after aborting a child by Mass Tanny so as to be able to marry the more "respect-able" schoolteacher Pinnock. Having gone to live with Aunt Becca in town, Nellie is exposed to her aunt's way of thinking. She is shown "where to find and how to wear my kumbla" (142). "Those people," says Aunt Becca, meaning the poorer classes and men in particular, "will drag you down child. You have to be careful of them" (142). While such advice and the refuge provided by her aunt's home al-low Nellie to concentrate on her education, they also contribute to her becoming alienated from her own body:

> So the black womb is a maw. Disinfect its fruits with fine sterilised white lint if you can. You suck a wasp's sting from a child's hand, clear its nose of the bluish green blockage and spit. The black womb sucks grief and anger and shame but it does not spit. It absorbs them into its body. Take an antidote. Silence it. Best pretend it doesn't exist. Give it a cap of darkness, take a pill. (143)

The consequence of such internal self-mutilation is neurosis, registered in Nel-lie's own eventual breakdown.

Emphasizing that any resolution to these problems must be sought on a po-litical and social level, and not just in the domain of individual psychology, Brod-ber weaves the story of Nellie's traumatic collapse into an account of her involve-ment with a group committed to a form of radical politics. Although events in the novel are not dated explicitly, the group's enthusiasm for Marxism and Black Power suggests the context is that of Jamaica in the late 1960s and early 1970s. Despite their radicalism, however, the would-be revolutionaries are revealed to be as alienated from the community they seek to represent as Nellie is from her cultural background. They live in a tenement yard among the working classes, but their attitude only emphasizes their distance from the yard dwellers: "We have unfortunately to make a distinction between them and us. Those people throw dice, slam dominoes and give-laugh-for-peasoup all day long. . . . They have no culture at all. No interest in helping their leaders keep their heads up high. We get no co-operation from them. How will we ever lead them out in the right and proper way?" (51). Thus the novel confronts us with the now familiar image of the failure of a radicalized bourgeoisie to establish a dialectical link to the masses.

However, the group's shortcomings also point to the limitations of any na-tionalist project that does not tackle the issue of gender relations. Nellie begins to grasp this problem after the death of her lover Robin, whose radical fervor causes him to self-combust. She recognizes that the group's very approach to the social world leads to disconnection and "desiccation": "We were bent on ex-terminating water. . . . Robin had reached our highest phase of evolution: he had become a dried up bird and could only crumble into dust" (53). Robin's fate connects him to the topos of the tragic male sacrifice, and hence to its problematic masculinism, while the emphasis on the dryness and sterility of the group's politics establishes a connection to the denial of the female body, and in particular to the literal sterility of Aunt Becca. In so doing, it underscores how Aunt Becca's psychopathological relationship to her body is also a political problem to be addressed as part of the nationalist project: full decolonization and the total reorganization of the nation-state must include not only the revalorization of the vulgar popular body of the people but also the dismantling of the patriarchal frameworks imposed on the doubly stigmatized female body.

In this regard, Brodber's emphasis on the tenement yard as a microcosm of political relations is significant, given the literary history of this space. As Cobham points out, a number of the Jamaican and Trinidadian barrack-yard stories from the 1930s feature strong, independent female characters whose "masculine" traits serve to erode gender boundaries. "The existence of such representations," argues Cobham, "acknowledges the tenacity with which the first generation of Black women after emancipation fought for the right to an independent and emotionally satisfying existence for themselves."[32] However, she goes on to note their "disappearance from later Caribbean fiction, or their truncation into stereotypes in the work of the nationalist writers of the 1950s and 1960s."[33] This did not mean they had ceased to exist, Cobham points out, but rather "reflects the ambivalence of the emergent Black elite, from whose ranks these writers were drawn, about their connection with a female tradition so at odds with the normative gender roles of their new class."[34] Thus the image of the tenement yard in Brodber's novel stands for the fluctuating fortunes of the literary figuration of a history of female agency, with the failure of Nellie's political group to connect to the yard dwellers mediating the failure of the bourgeois nationalist project to incorporate and build on that history.

Accordingly, the necessity of doing so to achieve the progressive transformation of the personal and the political is figured by Nellie's reconciliation with the inhabitants of the yard. Her reintegration into the community (the vulgar popular body), which ultimately enables her to overcome her psychic fragmentation, is achieved via Baba Ruddock. He is one of those vulgar boys stigmatized by Aunt Becca when Nellie was young as likely to "drag you down child." When Baba and Nellie meet as adults, she recognizes that in contrast to the dried up members of her political group, he "still had oodles of moisture" (68). Crucially, he does not "save" Nellie as such—he is not a sacrificial male hero, nor is he a conventionally masculine one: he appears before Nellie "straight and tall in a long white gown. He was the bride" (63). He is also notably diffident when Nellie tries to instigate a sexual relationship, telling her, "'That will come later. After I have met you'" (69), the implication being that (like La Niña) Nellie must first secure her autonomy on her own terms. Baba's role is more like that of a mediator, helping to pave the way for Nellie's being healed by the yard community. Central to this healing process is her coming to terms with her own repressed vulgar corporeality, while central to the way the narrative stages the related transformation of self and society is how it uses forms and practices from cultural fields and areas of social life usually positioned outside a strictly literary field. These include not just the oral traditions and folk dances mentioned earlier but also elements of religious and ritual practice.

The novel not only shows the importance of such practices to the life of the community but also registers the influence of the religious field formally: the resources and traditions connected to it provide a means to unbind Nellie from the once protective but now inhibiting integument of the kumbla, as well as a strategy by which the text can narrate the resolution of the contradiction the kumbla foregrounds between security and freedom. Nellie's experiences take the form of a descent into madness wherein her body is felt as a constrictive husk, which she scratches at until tearing her skin. But her breakdown is also an opportunity to break out of the kumbla. After losing consciousness at the height of her mania, Nellie awakens with a new sense of the people around her, of the texture of life in the yard. Her convalescence "amid the smell of beef soup and ginger tea, the commotion of tipping toes and tired thoughts" (67), allows for the rediscovery of her body and a renewal of her muted sensorium. At the same time, it signals the start of a return to, and reexamination of, the past. One of the defining moments of this "physical and spiritual rebirth," observes Cobham, comes when Nellie ventures into a dance hall and the sounds of the voices and movements of the people around her "merge into a seamless fabric of humanity in which the lines of demarcation between human bodies are no longer of importance."[35] It is after Nellie establishes this sensual, bodily connection to the community that the novel circles back to those incidents alluded to in the fractured prose of the first section, seeking at last to make sense of their implications.

On the level of structure, Nellie's path from psychic disintegration to rebirth can be read as patterned on the trajectory marked out in various Afro-Caribbean religious practices. Central to a number of these practices, including vodun, Santeria, and—most pertinently in the context of Jamaica—Myal, is the temporary displacement of an individual's consciousness as part of rites of possession, a voiding of the self aimed at opening up a gateway to the spirit world and enabling the manifestation of the ancestors. In Myal, the "ecstatic trance" of possession "allows for the possibility of a direct interaction between ancestral spirits and the living, who in turn become the spirits' vehicles for prophecy, healing, advice, and revenge."[36] Drawing on these resources, *Jane and Louisa Will Soon Come Home* finds a way to organize the painful shards of experience that punctuate Nellie and her family's history but point also to the conditions incubated by colonial domination.

What I am suggesting, then, is that the novel's form works this ritual practice on its content. It turns Nellie's madness, which significantly sees her become a "public spectacle" (65), into a voiding of consciousness that renders her a vessel through which (like the possessed in Myal) the past is manifested. By way of this rite, she is reconnected to her own and a collective history: the immersion in the past facilitated by ritual—during which "linear time dips down into the reservoir of collective experience and repairs the apparent fissure between then and now"[37]—allows Nellie to bring to light the repressed legacies of her childhood and organize them into a coherent structure in which the problems of the present can be made sense of now in relation to the pressures of history. This means of organizing the past pulls that personal world into the communal: it of necessity motivates the working out of conflicts in the social domain as opposed to reprivatizing them in the realm of individual psychology (which only reinforces the normative status of the monadic subject of capitalist modernity). As the public nature of her breakdown emphasizes, Nellie's disintegration and recovery become a restaging for the whole community of the difficulties from which it suffers; the working through of her vexed history entails the working through of a vexed collective history.

There are clear affinities here with what in the previous chapter I identified, pace Glissant, as the delirium of dramatization, a condition exemplified by Solibo's equally public and "spectacular" breakdown. The difference now is that whereas the storyteller's delirium remained unstructured and frenzied, the framework provided by the ritual act permits Nellie's individual delirium to be restructured and converted into a creative potential on a collective level. Discussing the displacement of the ego of the *serviteur* during possession rites in vodun, Maya Deren notes that "in the growing control accomplished by the ordeals and instructions of initiation, and in the prospective vigilance of houngan and *societé*, he [the *serviteur*] is reassured that the personal price need not be unpredictable or excessive. In the principle of collective participation is the guarantee that the burden shall, in turn, be distributed and shared."[38] The ritual act reaffirms the dialectical link between individual and community: the individual is temporarily lost with the voiding of the ego but simultaneously gained by the community, leading to a renewal of the self through the support of the collective, itself strengthened in the process.

It is in the light of this particular mediation between the individual and the collective that we must understand the allegorical dimension of *Jane and Louisa Will Soon Come Home*. The reciprocal revitalization of Nellie and the yard community can be read as standing for the possibility of reconfiguring the nation-state and of overcoming the problems associated with the bourgeois nationalist project, an interpretation given weight by the explicit referencing of these problems through the failings of Nellie's political group. But we must not assume that allegory refers here to a crude one-to-one or typifying correspondence between characters and events or social forms. Rather, recalling the discussion of national allegory in Selvon's work, we should conceive of the allegorical relationship as a dialectical one, whereby the transformations in Nellie's psyche and habitus necessarily figure in some way transformations in society precisely because the individual is connected concretely to the community as a whole. In other words, the remaking of individual subjectivity will register the remaking of the collectivity and vice versa, since each presupposes, acts on, and is mediated in the other. The ritual movement on which the text is patterned provides the template for the allegorical movement of the narrative, therefore, with both seeking to break down the division between public and private—to break through the reification of the social world and the individual—so as to foreground the social relations that the collectivity must act on if emancipatory changes to individual habitus are to be fully realized.

In sum, then, Brodber's use of ritual forms in *Jane and Louisa Will Soon Come Home* can be seen on the one hand as a further refraction of uneven development. If, as Jameson observes, the novel form in Europe had as its "historic function" the "secular 'decoding' of those pre-existing inherited traditional or sacred narrative paradigms that are its initial givens," then in Brodber's text that "novelistic' secular decoding coexists with just such sacred paradigms, with narrative patterns derived from forms of religious experience.[39] On the other hand, it is precisely this combination that allows the novel not only to restructure histories that might otherwise have remained fractured and incoherent, but also to project the utopian possibility of transforming a restrictive social world (figured in the kumbla) by staging the ritual displacement of sovereign individuality as a prelude to grasping the potential for collective, emancipatory practice. Indeed, insofar as Nellie's reintegration into the community resolves the contradiction between individual ontological security and freedom among others, it points to the concrete changes required in society as a whole. The social order must be able to reproduce and institutionalize the kind of secure freedom offered by the yard community. To do so, its structures and organizing protocols must be made to coincide with the vulgar popular body of the people, itself now revalorized. And for such reconstruction to truly succeed, Brodber's novel suggests, the doubly stigmatized vulgar female body must be able to claim an equal and independent place within the new society.

The key to the transformative vision elaborated in *Jane and Louisa Will Soon Come Home* is the conversion of Nellie's traumatic breakdown—the collapse of her ego—into a moment of creative potential. That collapse is brought on by an accumulation of personal and social pressures, all of which in some way bear the imprint of the fallout from colonial domination. It can be understood in relation to the kinds of ontological crises described by Fanon in *Black Skin, White Masks*, crises triggered by the objectifying, racist gaze of the white:

"Dirty nigger!" Or simply, "Look, a Negro!"
I came into the world imbued with the will to find a meaning in things, my

spirit filled with the desire to attain to the source of the world, and then I found that I was an object in the midst of other objects.

Sealed into that crushing objecthood, I turned beseechingly to others. Their attention was a liberation, running over my body suddenly abraded into nonbeing, endowing me once more with an agility that I had thought lost, and by taking me out of the world, restoring me to it. But just as I reached the other side, I stumbled, and the movements, the attitudes, the glances of the other fixed me there. . . . I was indignant; I demanded an explanation. Nothing happened. I burst apart. Now the fragments have been put back together again by another self.[40]

In *Jane and Louisa Will Soon Come Home*, the kumbla helps guard against such crises. However, since it also fosters self-denial, Nellie has to be rid of it, and despite the problems this causes, her subsequent confrontation with her repressed corporeality opens the way to the rehabilitation of her traumatized psyche. Fanon too, as Paget Henry has shown, looks to rescue the creative possibilities from the zone of nonbeing one enters during collapses of the ego. Noting that Fanon speaks of this zone as "an extraordinarily sterile and arid region, an utterly naked declivity where an authentic upheaval can be born," Henry cites the following passage as another moment of ego collapse, but one that gives Fanon "more than just exposure to nonbeing with its paralysing silence":

I feel in myself a soul as immense as the world, truly a soul as deep as the deepest of rivers, my chest has the power to expand without limit. I am a master and I am advised to adopt the humility of a cripple. Yesterday, awakening to the world, I saw the sky turn upon itself utterly and wholly. I wanted to rise, but the disembowelled silence fell back upon me, its wings paralysed. Without responsibility, straddling Nothingness and Infinity, I began to weep.[41]

For Henry, this experience offers Fanon "a glimpse of the infinity that includes but extends beyond the zone of nonbeing. This infinite oceanic consciousness can genuinely transform any complex-ridden ego, if only it can conquer its fear and creatively negotiate its way in the zone of nonbeing."[42]

Henry's reading of this zone forms part of his wider attempt to locate the influence of African philosophical traditions within the work of various Caribbean writers and thinkers. His suggestion that creative possibilities can emerge out of the trauma of ego collapse derives from his emphasis on the importance of such experiences to traditional African existentialism, itself inextricable from traditional African religious beliefs. "The primary project of traditional African religion," asserts Henry, "is the transcending of the everyday ego in a search for balance and harmony with the creative womb or original matrix of forms and energies."[43] Consequently, at its heart lies an existential critique of egoism: it seeks to challenge the ego's tendency to enclose and consolidate itself, to absolutize the reality it has constructed and thus exclude other possibilities inherent in the spiritual ground that surrounds it. The solution to such blind fixity is for the ego to be disrupted or voided, for it to temporarily let go "its self-positing and centring activities and surrender to the correctives and directives of the deities and ancestors."[44] These "periodic baptisms in the waters of spirit" reconnect the ego to the larger spirit world, leaving it "more fully aware . . . of the whole range of spiritual claims for which one is responsible."[45] In this context, then, the temporary voiding of the ego is a traumatic but necessary process to enable the full realization of selfhood. The primary means for activating this process are rituals whereby, through drumming and dancing, a trance state is induced in individuals, suspending the ego and opening the body to possession by the deities, who then speak or act through the possessed. In the Caribbean, the influence of this worldview and its associated practices is most clearly evident in the creole religions mentioned earlier, such as vodun and Myal.

Henry argues that Fanon ultimately turns away from considering what the African philosophical tradition could add to his take on nonbeing, suggesting that the peripheral position of this tradition in the (European-dominated) field leads him to continue using the language of European existentialism.[46] In discussing how these African worldviews were indigenized and creolized in the Caribbean, however, Henry points out that, as well as mixing with other religious belief systems, they were also often historicized and combined with secular ideologies of liberation. I want to suggest that in *The Wretched of the Earth*, Fanon does elaborate something like a historicized, liberationist version of the descent into, and creative negotiation of, the zone of nonbeing, here become the "zone of occult instability" that is the emerging ground of the collective potential of the people to transform social reality:

> It is not enough to try to get back to the people in that past out of which they have already emerged; rather we must join them in that fluctuating movement which they are just giving shape to, and which, as soon as it has started, will be the signal for everything to be called in question. Let there be no mistake about it; it is to this zone of occult instability where the people dwell that we must come; and it is there that our souls are crystallized and that our perceptions and our lives are transfused with light.[47]

To expand on these issues, I will first explore how rituals of ego displacement and possession—and hence worldviews that uphold the necessity for periodic voidings of the ego as a means of opening oneself to a whole range of spiritual and ancestral claims—have imprinted themselves (albeit often in their more historicized or secular guise) on the content and form of novels by a number of Caribbean writers in addition to Brodber.[48]

Not surprisingly, given his emphasis on the transformative power of myth and consciousness, as well as his attention to popular rituals and arts, Harris's work provides a convenient starting point. His concept of a vision of consciousness, by way of which one looks through the monument of received history to the unconsummated possibilities contained therein, is analogous to the ritual process whereby the voided ego is made to surrender to the possibilities contained within its spiritual ground. That the example Harris's uses to illustrate his approach is the possessed body of the vodun dancer only emphasizes this connection. The dancer whose ego is voided replays the traumatic collapse of stable identity caused by the Middle Passage and colonial domination. Harris suggests, however, that the same ontological collapse might also open the way to establishing new connections between individuals, and between individuals and the environment: the erosion of the consolidated outlines of sovereign individuality generates a kind of porosity that enables multiple histories and identities to overlap and interact, which in turn provides the foundations for a new architecture of cultures. For Harris, the dancer's movements in space embody this otherwise phenomenal potential through the relationships they establish with their surroundings: "The dancer moves in a trance and the interior mode of the drama is exteriorised into a medium inseparable from his trance and invocation. He is a dramatic agent of subconsciousness. The life from within and the life from without now truly overlap."[49] In other words, the actions of the possessed body temporarily devoid of its ego make visible a collective drama of consciousness.

If Harris's work lends itself fairly obviously to such a reading, I want to turn now to a more unlikely example of the impact of these ritual patterns on Caribbean thought. In their manifesto *Éloge de la créolité*, Chamoiseau, Confiant, and Bernabé conceptualize what they regard as the underlying creoleness of Caribbean society in terms of the "*interactional and transactional aggregate* of Caribbean, European, African, Asian, and Levantine cultural elements, which the yoke of History has reunited on the same soil."[50] It is noteworthy that this theory of créolité exhibits the same kind of totalizing perspective that I have argued is characteristic of a number of other theorizations of the creolization process, where it reflects the need to find some way of mapping the social totality. "Créolité," maintain the Créolistes, "is '*the world diffracted but recomposed*,' a maelstrom of signifieds in a single signifier: a Totality."[51] However, the social dimension of the manifesto is problematic: political issues are treated explicitly only in a short appendix; and as Shalini Puri points out, the work as a whole offers little in the way of "a project for social, political, and economic regeneration," which would be necessary to ground the linguistic and cultural ideals the Créolistes espouse.[52]

The manifesto has been criticized on a number of other fronts also, which I will not go into here.[53] What interests me are the terms used by the Créolistes when arguing that créolité, which they present as a substrate of identity, must be apprehended through an "interior vision" (*la vision intérieure*). Their phrasing is suggestive of the rite of ego displacement and the descent into a spiritual ground wherein one can achieve, in Henry's words, "harmony with the creative womb or original matrix of forms and energies." The difference is that this process has been recoded in terms of cultural influences, with the spiritual ground replaced by créolité's mangrovelike mass of entangled histories. The unfolding of the manifesto's argument, its reappraisal of past models of identity and its drive toward a new vision of subjectivity, follows a pattern whereby those past self-understandings are constantly dissolved by immersion in the depths of oneself, of one's créolité. It is necessary, write the Créolistes, "to break up what we are" (décomposer ce que nous sommes) and simultaneously "to plunge . . . into the chaos of this new humanity that we are" (plonger . . . dans le chaos de cette humanité nouvelle que nous sommes).[54] Though Mary Gallagher has suggested that this trajectory might be considered Hegelian in the sense that each position is progressively superseded through a "narrative of transcendence" that culminates in créolité,[55] it is also reminiscent of the periodic baptisms in the waters of spirit found in traditional African religions. Moreover, the manifesto's imagery recalls elements of vodun cosmography, in which the world is a crossroads with a vertical axis that extends from the heavens above to the watery depths below the earth.[56] In the death rite of *dessounin* (a "ritual of 'degradation,'" whose purpose is to detach from the body both the *gros-bon-ange*—the personal soul or self—and the loa *maît-tête*—the divine loa which is the 'master of the head'"),[57] the *gros-bon-ange* is freed to descend into the waters as a prelude to rebirth, just as the depths of créolité function in *Éloge* as a source of renewal for a self-understanding that has been degraded and decomposed.

To gain a better sense of how this way of conceiving transformations in subjectivity might be extended beyond the limited identity politics of the manifesto, I want to turn to Chamoiseau's novel *Texaco* (1992). Here, as in *Jane and Louisa Will Soon Come Home*, the convulsions of individual consciousness are linked explicitly to social upheavals and struggles over the reorganization of the state. In recounting the epic battles of Marie-Sophie and her ancestors to stake a claim to the Martinican land on their own terms, the narrative stages a number of scenes of ego collapse, which in different ways bespeak the pressures exerted on the colonized by the colonial system.

There is the aspiring mulatto Gros-Joseph, for instance, who is fixated on acceptance by the white world, and whose house, named "Little France," contains a library stuffed with classical French literature. Seeking to enter into the colonial economy, he eschews subsistence farming to sell crops to an army barracks. However, he lacks the requisite resources and has to rely financially on the discovery of buried treasure—a fantastical occurrence belonging to the world of folklore and indicative of the underdevelopment of society. When later Gros-Joseph is denied the opportunity to travel to France, the realization that his white mask will never obliterate his black skin drives him mad.[58] Locking himself in his library, he spends two days "raving beneath a mound of Montaigne, Descartes, and Montesquieu."[59] Subsequently, he "pissed and shat on his own books, then ate them" (223), his actions a pathological attempt to achieve a white body by literally ingesting French culture. As Mireille Rosello observes, the motifs of swallowing, ingestion, and force-feeding have served as privileged metaphors for the process of cultural assimilation in the Francophone Caribbean. But they have also been reversed by writers such as Césaire, who makes eruptive vomiting the sign of revolt against the colonial authorities.[60] When Gros-Joseph, still eating his books, begins exclaiming manically, "Ah Zola taste of shit, Ah Daudet taste of shit" (224), it seems as if a similar reversal has taken place, the mulatto's frenzied behavior becoming a violent repudiation of colonial values. Indeed, his incarceration in the library so decomposes the former mimic man that even his wife, "trying to find her husband in a look, in a familiar gesture," sees "nothing in that degenerate [that] evoked Gros-Joseph" (223).

His breakdown thus exposes the racist limit of the "civilizing mission," revealing the barrier that his black or "degenerate" body will always pose to his being accepted as an equal by the colonizer. But it also points in two other related directions. First, his delirious consumption of books covered in bodily fluids can be read (like Benny's shitting fantasies in *Macho Camacho's Beat*) as the displaced and pathological expression of an unconscious desire to overcome his corporeal alienation. Second, the frail, degenerate body that is all that is left of him after his disintegration becomes prospective of a new form of subjectivity and, by extension, new kinds of social relations, whereby not only the mask of mimicry but also the integument of the isolated individual is exploded. Like Fanon's sense of the creative possibilities of the zone of nonbeing, Gros-Joseph's decomposed remainder can be seen as figuring the potential for a selfhood beyond monadic enclosure, one sensitive to the contingencies and mediations that bind it to the social totality.

For Gros-Joseph himself, however, this potential will remain unfulfilled: the mutilation of his psyche is such that he cannot be rescued from his delirium and ends his days locked in an asylum. Later in the novel, something similar occurs to another of Marie-Sophie's employers, Monsieur Alcibiade. Not only does this later episode explicitly reinforce the connection gestured to obliquely in the Gros-Joseph affair between isolated individuality and private space (the library, in that instance). It is also significant because Marie-Sophie now also suffers a breakdown, only her disintegration becomes the prelude to a rebirth that sets her on her way to founding Texaco.

Alcibiade is a black civil servant who venerates colonialism. His initial distress is caused by the news that Césaire has been elected to Fort-de-France's town council. In response to her husband's increasing delirium, Alcibiade's wife locks him up in the family home along with herself and Marie-Sophie, who has been raped by Alcibiade. Subsequently all three sink into madness. They lose any coherent, structured perception of the world and experience only a confused, unprocessed series of sensations: Marie-Sophie, for example, "wades about in hazes of images," hearing "unspeakable sounds" and smelling a plethora of odors that "became tastes" (261, 260). What is striking about this episode is that it suggests the enclosed, private environment of the bourgeois family home is itself partly responsible for fostering the kind of alienation and delirium exhibited by Alcibiade. The issue, in other words, is not just the socio-psychological one of mimicry and self-denial but also that of how these attitudes and habitus are consolidated by the organization of land and space.

This is underlined by the description of the Fort-de-France cityscape: not only is the urban space a mimetic phenomenon in its own right (the inner city is shaped by "an occidental urban logic" [220] and seeks to dress the poorer quarters in "materials from other lands" [172]); it also institutes a system of land-ownership based on private property, one that has a detrimental effect on its inhabitants: "City: that crumbled solitude, that withdrawal inside the house, these millstones of silence on the pain next door, this civilized indifference. Everything that made the hills (the heart, the flesh, the touching, the solidarity, the gossips, the jealous butting into others' business) would fade before the coldness of City's centre" (256–57). Driven by the imperatives of market capitalism, this spatial formation reinforces both the reification of the sensorium and the prevailing economic and class relations. To transform society thus requires that the distribution and organization of the land be completely overhauled as part of the construction of a different kind of economic system.

The squatter settlement of Texaco founded by Marie-Sophie represents just such an attempt to ground a new social order, even as it emerges in relation to the dominant mode of production in the city center. Texaco looks to recover and orient itself around the bodily, sensuous, relational qualities—"the heart, the flesh, the touching, the solidarity"—that defined the understanding of space and community in the Hills. It is fitting, then, that the antecedents to Texaco's creation include the renewal of Marie-Sophie's own sensorium after the brutalization of her body and the scrambling of her senses inside Alcibiade's home. She is finally broken out of that "tomb" by her lover Nelta, who takes her to the Morne Abélard Quarter. There, "surrounded by that solicitude which Quarters breed," she is given "reinvigorating teas, hardy soups, bay rum rubs" (263). This episode is reminiscent of the way Nellie in *Jane and Louisa Will Soon Come Home* is healed and reborn within the yard community after her breakdown has prised open the kumbla. Marie-Sophie's rebirth is mediated through the intervention of the local healer, or *mentô*, Papa Totone.[61] When he appears, he simply brushes her forehead: "Life returned to my eyes. I began to look, to feel, to want to get up and live again" (265). The tactile connection to the body and the environment that Marie-Sophie rediscovers at this point inspires her subsequent drive to found Texaco.

Before examining the specific qualities of this settlement, however, I want to consider how the novel itself, in narrating the history and landscape of Martinique, performs a similar recovery of lost bodies and occluded material relations. Indeed, the text can be seen to enact something like Harris's imaginative rehearsal of history, albeit in more materially grounded fashion. The past and the spaces in which it has been embedded are revisited and, as it were, subject to a ritualistic restaging that rearticulates history on the level of the collective—in terms, that is, of the mass of interactions and sensuous activities that produce social reality. In this sense, the novel becomes an epic of the Martinican nation, but, necessarily, a new kind of epic.

The traditional function of works such as the *Iliad* and the *Aeneid* has been to act as the poetic expression of the collective memory and emergent consciousness of a community.[62] As Glissant has remarked, however, insofar as epic form looks to invoke "the principle of a Genesis and of a filiation with the aim of establishing a legitimate right to a land which from that moment becomes a territory," it becomes problematic when transplanted to the Caribbean.[63] Here, successive waves of forced and voluntary immigration from around the globe, and the ethnic and cultural diversity those movements have engendered, have made appeals to a singular, lineal, and exclusive genesis impossible (not to say dangerous). Moreover, the conventional epic conception of the past is unhelpful in this context. "Absolute conclusiveness and closedness is the outstanding feature of the temporally valorized epic past," argues Mikhail Bakhtin. "The epic world is an utterly finished thing, not only as an authentic event of the distant past but also on its own terms and by its own standards; it is impossible to change, to re-think, to re-evaluate anything in it."[64] Clearly this sits awkwardly with the attempt, evident in the work of so many Caribbean authors, to reengage and rethink history, to discover within it new possibilities.

Yet epic form has been appropriated and deployed by these authors time and again (suffice it to mention here, from among any number that could be cited, the names of Harris, Walcott, Brathwaite, Condé, Simone Schwarz-Bart, Carpentier, and Lezama Lima). Undoubtedly, the very demand to recover submerged histories and to forge a sense of community from a mass of fractured, diverse traditions is a good part of the reason for epic's appeal, as well as for the transformations it subsequently undergoes in being remade in the Caribbean. However, I want to suggest that the resonance of epic is due also to the way its form can serve as a utopian resource in such circumstances. Traditional epic stands on the basis of an organic unity between part and whole, between Being and the world. "It is traditionally thought," Lukács has observed, that one of the essential characteristics of the epic is the fact that its theme is not a personal destiny but the destiny of a community. And rightly so, for the completeness, the roundness of the value system which determines the epic cosmos creates a whole which is too organic for any part of it to become so enclosed within itself, so dependent upon itself, as to find itself as an interiority.[65]

Returning to this organic unity is impossible, for it would require a return to the determinate historical conditions out of which traditional epic arose. But the image of the coincidence between the personal and the communal, between the individual (as far as one can speak of individuals in the epic cosmos) and the structures of the world, could be made to stand, in the Caribbean context, as the utopian figure for the overcoming of the disjunction between, on the one hand, the experiences and practices of the (to use Lovelace's phrase) ordinary people and, on the other, the structures and institutions of the social world. Epic, in other words, is a potent form on which to draw because embedded within it is an idea of integratedness that can be translated into the radical hope for new, more representative social configurations.

The epic quality with which Chamoiseau invests *Texaco* is not only made to articulate an entanglement of histories rather than an exclusive filiation but also bears that desire to project original modes of collectivity. Walcott has suggested that *Texaco*, "like *Ulysses*, is a large prose-poem that devours the structure of narrative fiction."[66] This epic cannibalism is central to the way the novel reworks epic form, for instead of allowing the past to remain as "an utterly finished thing" sealed off from the present, the narrative draws it close, consumes it, and in so doing rematerializes it. For Bakhtin, it is laughter that destroys epic and its distanced, completed past: "Laughter demolishes fear and piety before an object, before a world, making of it an object of familiar contact and thus clearing the ground for an absolutely free investigation of it."[67] What distinguishes the novel from epic, he argues, is the way the novel brings such comic familiarity to bear on the world and humanity, restoring both to a contradictory, inconclusive reality pregnant with multiple possibilities. In this light, one could read *Texaco* as restaging a series of epic moments, ritualistically summoning up certain epic narratives—the Christian one that frames Marie-Sophie's story, for example, or the *Aeneid* in terms of the founding of a settlement, or the negritude-like epic of the Noutéka section—which it then consumes within novelistic discourse, parodying them, profaning them, but also opening them up and excavating new possibilities that could be brought into the present to transformative effect.

More specifically, the text subjects those narratives—and, indeed, dominant histories and canonical literary discourses in general—to something like the carnivalesque laughter that Bakhtin contends is characteristic of the culture of folk humor in the Renaissance and Middle Ages. Such laughter, exemplified by

Rabelais, was inextricable from an understanding of the body as unfinished and open. This is a body different from the monadic, modern one produced under capitalism: it is not "a private, egoistic form, severed from the other spheres of life, but . . . something universal, representing all the people"; it is "blended with the world, with animals, with objects. It is cosmic, it represents the entire material bodily world in all its elements."[68] Carnival laughter degrades an object and sinks it into this corporeal world, exposing the suppressed material relations constitutive of its form. "Rabelaisian laughter," comments Bakhtin, "not only destroys traditional connections and abolishes idealized strata; it also brings out the crude, unmediated connections between things that people otherwise seek to keep separate."[69] The renewed emphasis on concrete human corporeality means "the entire remaining world also takes on new meaning and concrete reality, a new materiality; it enters into a contact with human beings that is no longer symbolic but material."[70] *Texaco*, in cannibalizing other discourses, plunges the dominant constructs of history and society into the material bodily stratum, laying bare all the sensuous connections between people, and between people and things, that underpin them. It reveals, in other words, the profane mass of interactions and of laboring bodies that produce social reality and yet are occluded as society is reified.

But if we can understand the novel's epic cannibalism in terms of Bakhtin's carnivalesque laughter, we can also understand it in relation to the rites of degradation and renewal found in creole religions such as vodun.[71] Indeed, the complement to the vodun death rite of *dessounin* mentioned earlier is the ceremony of *retirer d'en bas de l'eau*, the "reclamation of the soul of the deceased from the waters of the abyss."[72] As Deren notes, this ceremony is not "a moment of return to the past; it is the procedure by which the race reincorporates the fruit of previous life-processes into the contemporary moment, and so retains the past as a ground gained, upon and from which it moves forward to the future."[73] Moreover, the rite "restores the disembodied soul *to* the physical, living universe."[74] This, just as much as Bakhtin's rematerializing plunge into the bodily stratum, provides a model for the way *Texaco* consumes the past, rebirthing it, as it were, in the service of rethinking the present and future.

It is worth underscoring here what such epic cannibalism shares with Césaire's poetic "vomiting up" of the colonial culture force-fed to the colonized. There is, in the way *Texaco* ingests various imported literary forms and voices, a recognition that it is impossible simply to shrug off that history as if it never happened (just as in Selvon's *A Brighter Sun* the imported modernist form had to be incorporated even as its inadequacy vis- à-vis local content was flagged up). However, having consumed these discourses, the novel then spews them back out in transfigured guise, the ritual debasements it subjects them to disintegrating their "sacred" status and forcing them to speak in new, "profane" ways.

Let us look at a few concrete examples of this cannibalizing narrative style. In the episodes recounting life on the plantation, *Texaco* appears at times to allude to the work of Saint-John Perse, consuming what Walcott has called the "incantatory memory" found in the litanies of the Guadeloupean-born white creole poet.[75] For instance, Perse's nostalgic evocation of his childhood in what, from his privileged position, was an Edenic island space—

> Palms! And the sweetness
> of age-old roots . . . ! The breath of the trade winds, the woodpigeons and the chest-
> nut brown cat
> furrowed the bitter foliage where, in the harshness of an evening in the perfume
> of the Flood,
> the pink and green moons hung like mangoes.[76]

—finds an echo in *Texaco*'s otherwise very different portrayal of the landscape:

> It was the month of the digging for the planting of the cane, and in the digging one
> weeded the mad grasses. The fine-fine rain dug its heels in, hypnotising the work,
> forcing the men to watch out for its moods, to count the lost time in the prolonged
> evenings. Then the rain took the bad path of a perennial waterfall until it reached
> an orchestra of winds, patient trumpets full of nine thunderous blows [neuf ton-
> nerres du sort].[77]

Perse's rhythmic chronicling of bygone days ("in the harshness of an evening in the perfume of the Flood") returns in Chamoiseau's text, which uses the same kinds of lexical repetitions ("the month of the digging for the planting of the cane") to convey a similar sense of fecund nature. But what in Perse is paradisiacal in Chamoiseau is inseparable from the inferno of exploitation. Where Perse presents an immutable landscape emptied of any human presence, Chamoiseau shows it being produced through sensuous labor. In consuming Perse's discourse, *Texaco* releases and materializes the specter of the enslaved bodies that, as an absent or marginalized presence, so often haunt colonialist representations of plantation life. This is replicated at the level of syntax as Chamoiseau's narrative moves from a register akin to Perse's "high" poetic style to the "profanity" of the creole vernacular: witness the descent at the end of the passage from the high-sounding "orchestra of winds" to the "low" creole of the trumpets' *neuf tonnerres du sort*, an arcane folk exclamation incorporating the superstition of numerical luck. The text thus performs the ritualistic restaging and degradation of the colonial discourse, exposing as it does so the mass of material and bodily relations that seethe beneath Perse's sacred Eden.

What Graham Huggan has said of Harris—that he "plays on the fears of his European ancestors, 'inhabiting' their texts, preying upon them like a ghost"[78]— might therefore be applied to Chamoiseau, who similarly haunts and, in a manner reminiscent of a vodun rite, possesses his literary forebears. This is again evident when *Texaco* switches to narrating life in the city. If Perse was made the *serviteur* for the text's restaging of the rural world of the plantation, then when it comes to evoking Saint-Pierre, it is the voice of the great poet of the modern cityscape—Baudelaire—that Chamoiseau chooses to mount.

Take the following episode, for example, in which Marie-Sophie's father, Esternome, and his lover Ninon wander through the urban labyrinth:

> In the depth of dark shops he showed her strange objects from other countries. The least storefront window held unexpected treasures. Carafes of misty porcelain at a cloth salesman's. Pans with guaiac handles at an angelical haberdasher's. Portuguese lace inside a jewellery store. Silver spoons. Intricate bottles made of thin and whistling glass. Where a witch [*sorcière*] was filtering aromas, he found Judean balm, double-rose water, raw mint water, templar water, epicurean water which smelled like marjoram, and maiden water. Proud, he would point to the bits of arches he had replaced at the bottom of the façades. He showed her the balcony guardrail he had replaced and on which, forgetful of him, some dreamy mulatto girls rested elbows and sighs. Through louvered shutters he pointed out to her portraits of ancestors slashed with light. . . . He made her listen to the distant piano sounds coming from deep courtyards, catch a glimpse of the peculiar flowers on some dining room tile. She saw in a backyard, near a basin made of bricks, somnambulant black mammies sleep-rocking suckling angels. (106)

This litany of images recalls the lyrical cadences and accumulation of sensory stimuli that characterize Baudelaire's evocations of nineteenth-century Paris:

> Reveille sang its call among the barracks' paths
> And moving air disturbed the tall, commanding lamps.
>
> It was the time when dreams of lust and swarming heat
> Set brown young adolescents twisting in their sheets;
> When, like a bloody eye that pulses as it stares,
> The lamp will cast a stain of red throughout the air;
> line of ellipses
> Like a wild sob cut short by foaming blood, somewhere
> A distant rooster's cry tore through the misty air,
> A sea of fogs that bathed the buildings and the streets,
> And dying poorhouse wretches from their sad retreats
> Rattled away their lives in strangulated coughs.[79]

It is entirely apposite that in depicting Saint-Pierre, *Texaco* should consume this poetic discourse. The novel confronts us with a similarly modernizing urban landscape. We have moved away from the site of production—the fields and laboring bodies of the plantation—to a site of consumption. The commodities that catch the eye in shop windows are tantalizing objects of desire for Esternome and Ninon, holding out the promise of vicariously recuperating a sensory plenitude alienated by capital. They are, however, out of reach for the couple: Esternome might have helped build the city, but its "treasures" are reserved for the delectation of the mulatto bourgeoisie and white elite. This disparity is emphasized by the fleeting glimpse we catch of a copresent yet nonsynchronous reality: among the accumulated "objects from other countries" that testify to Saint-Pierre's integration into the economic circuits of the capitalist world system, we see that sorceress from the world of creole folklore—a world increasingly occluded by the externally driven modernization of the city.

But it is not just the sorceress who signals the shadowy presence of another history; so too do the bits of architecture that Esternome has had a hand in. These recall a phenomenon described earlier in the novel during the construction of Saint-Pierre. There, Esternome witnessed the white elite demand "houses like the ones in their original province," but also observed how "the spirit of the blackworkers undid and reinvented the dwelling" (77). Like history, then, the dominant organization of space not only rests on a mass of suppressed interactions and sensuous labor but also is pregnant with the potential for radically other ways of organizing the material world. Of course, as *Texaco* constantly underscores, the colonial structuration of the urban landscape is designed to neutralize such potential, thwarting any claim to control over the land by the oppressed.

When Esternome first reaches Saint-Pierre, he encounters a space reminiscent of Fanon's description of the typical colonial city as a Manichaean "world divided into compartments," a world split between the "settler's . . . strongly-built town, all made of stone and steel" and the "native town" where people live "on top of each other."[80] While Saint-Pierre's salubrious center is home to the white elite, the black working classes are sequestered in run-down shacks on the outskirts. Esternome notes the ostentatious fashion in which "Békés and france-whites went around in carriages, dined on dinner on the top floors of restaurants, and paraded on the steps of the theatre or the cathedral whose creamy white stone broke up the shadows" (69). By flaunting their status in public spaces redolent of power and culture, the elite concretizes its ascendant social position: the city center is marked out as both a "white" space and (since it is the site of the institutions of authority) the locus of official history. This territorial inscription ensures that, for the black working classes, this is a city "from whose memory they were excluded": "For them City remained impenetrable. Smooth. Waxed. What to read in this wrought iron, these painted wood shutters, these enormous cut stones?" (80).

The way the architecture of Saint-Pierre rejects and devalues the history and lived experience of the colonized is evident, too, in Fort-de-France. I have already touched on the mimetic quality of Fort-de-France and the manner in which its spatial organization reinforces the isolation of individuals and suppresses the kinds of social and physical connectivity found in the Hills. In fact, the very founding of the city is predicated on a denial of the body and of the practical experience of space. It is built on a strict geometric grid system in accordance with an a priori plan, thus embedding as a basic organizational principle the division of subject (mind) from object (body). From the outset, therefore, the cityscape is reified as an immutable formation: its spatial order appears as *the* order of reality, since it presents itself as the logical fulfillment of the plan, as the inevitable manifestation of a concept.[81] The result is a space the meaning of which is defined by the group or class that did the planning, in this instance the colonial army: "They say: old swamp but pretty site. They set up the Fort there. Then the Army spoke its law. A checkerboard stretch-strung from the Fort. Businesses here. Houses there. Depots here. . . . Batteries were set on the hills. . . . One battery, one house. Ten houses, a quarter" (175).

As alluded to earlier, this parceling out of the land facilitates the production of the kinds of subjects and bodily dispositions required to satisfy the economic demands of the dominant order. It helps inculcate the city's inhabitants with the perception of private property as a necessary and inevitable feature of social organization. Simultaneously, the striated, checkerboard-like landscape contributes to the enclosure of individuals, who are converted into monadic units of energy to be shunted around in the service of capital. It restricts interpersonal contact and impedes the emergence of a sense of collectivity, something Fanon noted when describing the Fort-de-France Savannah in *Black Skin, White Masks*:

> Imagine a square about 600 feet long and 125 feet wide, its sides bounded by worm-eaten tamarind trees, one end marked by the huge war memorial (the nation's gratitude to its children), the other by the Central Hotel; a miserable tract of uneven cobbles . . . and, amid all this, three or four hundred young fellows walking up and down, greeting one another, grouping—no, they never form groups, they go on walking.[82]

Fanon's reference here to the war memorial highlights perhaps one of the most significant architectural contributions to the inscription of a particular history or set of power relations into a specific space: statuary.

The traditional statue can be seen to embody a monumentalized history. It is the material equivalent of traditional epic, valorizing a heroic past presented as closed off and complete while concretizing a claim to an area of land by a specific group or community. The statue, observes Nathaniel Mackey, appropriates "the solidity and durability of stone to give a look of permanence . . . to what is merely a regime."[83] Hence its utility for the colonizer: as Fanon noted, the colonial world is a "world of statues: the statue of the general who carried out the conquest, the statue of the engineer who built the bridge; a world which is sure of itself, which crushes with its stones the backs flayed by whips."[84]

This issue is especially pertinent to Fort-de-France. Here four statues in particular—those of Napoléon's wife Joséphine de Beauharnais, the colonizer Desnambuc, the abolitionist Schoecher, and the aforementioned war memorial—have excited critical comment as monuments that enshrine Martinique's colonial relationship to France.[85] Césaire, at the beginning of *Cahier d'un retour au pays natal*, associates these statues with what he perceives as the general air of oppressive fixity that besets the city: "This sorry crowd under the sun, taking part in nothing which expresses, asserts, frees itself in the broad daylight of its own land. Nor in Empress Joséphine of the French dreaming high, high above negridom. Nor in the liberator rigidified in its liberation of whitened stone."[86] In Confiant's *L'allée des soupirs* (1994), Cicéron Nestorin's decision to "stand at attention for three weeks in front of the war memorial," his "right hand frozen in an impeccable military salute," dramatizes the psychological petrifaction engendered by assimilation and enforced by the codification of space performed by statuary.[87] At one point, Cicéron removes "some papers covered in scribble from [a] bag crammed with French dictionaries" and declaims: "I have suffered the presence of the White in my most intimate self. . . . I felt as if I was inhabited by some interior spy, some Trojan horse that concealed from me what was most mine."[88] His complaint underscores how the ideologies given concrete form by the city's monuments are internalized. Indeed, his bag "crammed" with French dictionaries symbolizes his being crammed with imported values, and so establishes an indirect link between statuary and the motif of force-feeding.

Significantly, however, what I have characterized as the "revolting" reversal of that motif has also featured in connection with statues. In Alfred Parépou's novel *Atipa* (1885), the eponymous hero recounts a story that has become part of the lore surrounding the monument of Empress Joséphine: on the day it was raised to the wife of the man who "re-established slavery so that the blacks wouldn't stop working in the canefields of his father-in-law . . . a blackman covered it all over with shit. It was the only thing he could think of doing."[89] These actions can be read not just as an expression of disgust at the power relations the statue embodies but also as a ritual degradation, that is, as part of a desire to rematerialize a reified order of reality, to sink it back into the bodily stratum so as to lay bare the mass of material relationships and collective sensuous labor undergirding it. Statuary, then, draws attention to the way that space, like history, might also be ritualistically restaged to release from beneath its dominant configuration the "profane" bodies it conceals.

Texaco takes up this challenge, performing the systematic remapping of the urban environment. The text consumes the topography of Fort-de-France, feeding it into the material bodily stratum by renarrating it in terms of the corporeal movements and practices enacted within it. The effect is to suggest the possibility of breaking out of the order sanctified by the plan: as space is re-staged through the body, suppressed histories are sensed beneath its rigidified contours and buried realities are brought to the surface. Through its aesthetic reconfiguration of the cityscape, then, the novel projects the utopian image of a world transformed.

This is most evident, on one level at least, in Marie-Sophie's description of the lanes that run through Morne Abélard. As noted earlier, it is in this quarter that Marie-Sophie experiences the reawakening of her sensorium before going on to found Texaco. Her incantatory litany of the lanes reveals a new appre-hension of space, foreshadowing the principles she will instantiate in the later settlement:

> There was . . . the lane where hunger whittled teeth. The calanda lane where one starts lurching, dancing the cossack, the guiomba, and the bombé serré. The pious lane from where the white whales sparkle at night. The lane where dawn's black-birds learn a lot of things. The lane of forgotten mysteries where old blackmen look like Carib warriors. The lane of black maroons twisting ferns while speaking other tongues. . . . The lane of the syrians going through with their big bundles on Saturdays. The lane of holy water sprinkled on each Friday the thirteenth. The lane of drying laundry clothing the wind. The lane of slops smelling of bitter old age . . . . The lane of Adventists gathering on Saturdays on red numbered cafeteria chairs to read the Bible's songs in some other way. The lane where the general coun-cilman held his meetings about the idea of happiness. . . . All of that mingled, shifted, depending on who died, on the hours, on success, and joined us like true ox yokes. (279)

In contrast to the staccato account of the construction of the city center on the basis of the plan, Marie-Sophie's ritualistic inventory is a dense mass of rhyth-mic sentences that narrate space as an entangled accumulation of practices, in-teractions, and memories. What was monumentalized, striated, and sterile in the center is in the quarter an overflowing carnival of sights and sensations. Textually speaking, the passage again exhibits *Texaco*'s epic cannibalism. There is clearly something of the oral storytelling performance about Marie-Sophie's topographical incantation. But her repetition of "the lane" also recalls Césaire's refrain of "the morne" in his less celebratory evocation of Martinican space at the beginning of *Cahier*: "At the brink of dawn . . . the morne alone and its spilt blood, the morne with its bandages of shade, the morne with its rivulets of fear, the morne with its great hands of wind."[90] At the same time, the passage's juxta-position of imagery and its emphasis on sensory perception seem to nod toward the symbolist poetry of Rimbaud (whom Marie-Sophie acknowledges as an in-fluence on her own writing elsewhere in the novel).[91]

This trelliswork of literary voices functions as the formal mediation of the multiple nodes of different realities that make up the space of the quarter. Indeed, the narrative produces a dialectical image of the unity of an existence in a state of disparity. First, it registers the heterogeneity engendered by uneven development and the creolization of cultural practices. In the lanes, creole dances overlap with the rituals of Adventists, who themselves read the Bible's songs "some other way" in a setting (with "its numbered cafeteria chairs") distinctly marked by modern consumer culture. Similarly, Christian beliefs are entwined with folklore ("holy water sprinkled on each Friday the thirteenth"), while traditional craftwork (the maroons "twisting ferns") overlaps with the mercantile activities of the Syrians as well as the economic demands of the city's new industries, which are the reason that so many people are migrating to the outlying quarters. Crucially, the narrative's form then ensures that this heterogeneity is articulated as a unity, as one simultaneous albeit nonsynchronous phenomenon. In addition to the sense of connectedness created by the repetition of "the lane," the images in the passage become a series of relays, linking the nodes of the different realities from which they spring. Thus we start with the deprivation ("hunger") of the first lane, which then leads to the marginalized existences and subaltern practices of the lanes where live the maroons "speaking other tongues" and the black men who look like Carib warriors. We then encounter the petit bourgeois Syrian traders, who in "going through" the quarter take us closer to the civic institutions of the more developed center (prefigured here by the councilman). By stitching these radically different worlds together, the text underscores how they are nevertheless all part of the same historical process.

But in so mapping the social totality, this dialectical image points in turn to its complete reorganization. Crucial in this respect is the emphasis on bodily movement in the description of the quarter, the text leading us step by step through Morne Abélard's lanes, registering their topography in experiential terms. Unlike the false totality presented by the plan, which in imposing the geometric striation of space made it graspable as a whole only by abstracting from the real relations undergirding it, the totality presented by the passage is one mapped from below, emerging precisely out of the social, material, and bodily relations that determine the spatial and socioeconomic contours of the quarter. This thereby raises the possibility of instantiating a new kind of spatial formation, one reorganized around a liberated sensorium, around bodies freed from the integument of the isolated individual. And this in turn implies a shift toward a different kind of economic system. Indeed, what that liberated sensorium prefigures is the transcendence of private property, since (pace Marx) such transcendence will mean "the complete *emancipation* of all human senses and attributes."[92]

The passage, then, can be viewed as a microcosm of all that *Texaco*'s epic cannibalism entails. Offering something like a socialized equivalent of the rite of ego displacement, the text's consumption of the various enclosed, monumental-ized forms of the dominant order (space, history, subjectivity) results in their being restaged, degraded, and broken apart, releasing new possibilities for the future. Those new possibilities are contained in the descent into the seething mass of bodies, histories, practices, and interactions that fill the lanes and, in Marie-Sophie's words, "joined us like true ox yokes." In fact, what the narrative could be said to reach down to here is Fanon's "zone of occult instability where the people dwell." In this zone (which, as suggested earlier, might be consid-ered a historicized, liberationist version of the zone of nonbeing accessed via ego collapse), the potential for transformation resides in the approbation of col-lectivity, and in the recognition of the power of the people, on whose labor and exploitation the social order rests, to reshape the present.

The emergence of Texaco represents the crystallization of this consciousness and a concomitant attempt to reorganize social reality, the settlement concretiz-ing the utopian possibilities implicit in the narration of the lanes. Hence space in Texaco is structured around bodily practice, around the communal experience of its inhabitants and the practical relationships they establish both to each other and to the land:

> Our hutches sat on the soil, espousing its contours. . . . Our light house frames (tested in the Noutéka of the Hills) allowed us to hook on to the most extreme points of the cliff. We knew that this way would promise each hutch almost direct access to the wind, a panoramic opening on sky and sea. . . . No private land, no col-lective land, we weren't the landowners, so no one could pride himself on anything besides the number of hours, minutes, seconds of his arrival. . . . If the first one had a good spot, he could only, on that good God's land, contemplate the settlement of the other; he even had to help him. . . . Each hutch, day after day, supported the other and so on. The same went for the lives that reached out to each other over the ghost fences writhing on the ground. (318–19)

Despite developing in the shadow of the socioeconomic demands of the modern-ized city center, Texaco, in drawing on the past—on the memory and knowledge preserved from the Hills—produces a space that transcends the determinations of the dominant order, most notably by abolishing private property. It is the materialization of a form of structuration coincident with its inhabitants' social and cultural practices.[93] As such, it figures the cornerstone of a projected new kind of nation-state, one restructured along different lines both internally and externally: internally, insofar as the settlement represents a form of society or-ganized in accordance with the needs of the people; externally, insofar as the de-gree of self-sufficiency secured by the settlers, as well as their reappropriation of the land from Texaco, the multinational oil company, symbolizes independence from France and resistance to capitalist imperialism more generally.[94]

The novel also makes plain, however, that with respect to such restructuring, Texaco is not an end point in itself. The material relations and collective practices on which it is predicated must be universalized. As it is, the quarter remains an illegitimate site in constant danger of being razed on the orders of the ruling class. If its promise is to be made good for society as a whole, then the institutions of the state must also be reappropriated. Marie-Sophie recognizes this; hence her decision to relate her "poor epic" (388) to the urban planner. The planner enters Texaco initially as part of a council project to demolish the settlement. However, Marie-Sophie's story radically alters his way of thinking. It "gave me new eyes," he claims. "I suddenly got the feeling that Texaco came from the deepest reaches of ourselves and that I had to learn everything. And even: to relearn everything" (165–66). Subsequently he becomes something like Fanon's "native intellectual" at the third stage, converted to the cause and seeking to "become the mouthpiece of a new reality in action."[95] He fights not just to protect the quarter but also to ensure that "City would integrate Texaco's soul" so that the city might be remade in accordance with the organizing logic of the quarter (381). He serves as the kind of representative whose importance we saw Lovelace stress in the preceding chapter, someone who is dialectically linked to the people and can aid in the generalization of their struggle, rearticulating it at a national and institutional level. At the end of *Texaco*, Marie-Sophie assures the planner: "We were going to fight alongside him to advance what he was proposing for us, but that the essential thing was that we would enter City by his side, rich with what we were and strong with a legend that was becoming clearer and clearer for us" (381). Her declaration thus emphasizes how the relationship established between the "native intellectual" and the "masses" (whose "legend" is "becoming clearer" to themselves) engenders a reciprocal raising of consciousness, heralding the emergence of a fully articulated liberationist movement geared toward social transformation.

I want to conclude this chapter by looking at Lovelace's *Salt* (1996). This novel allows me to draw together many of the themes I have touched on thus far, including epic form, ego displacement, representationalist politics, and the relationship between nationalist and feminist concerns. It will also enable us to revisit the trope of the tragic sacrifice and to observe how it is transformed as part of the struggle to elaborate a different kind of narrative form expressive of a different kind of nation-state. *Salt* is immediately arresting in this respect, since it opens with two competing epic discourses. The first chapter begins with Bango reciting the tale of the slave Guinea John, who one day mounted a cliff and "flew away to Africa, taking with him the mysteries of levitation and flight, leaving the rest of his family still in captivity mourning over his selfishness."[96] The story recalls traditional epic insofar as it deals with the possibility of reestablishing a connection to a homeland and to a "pure" identity, both of which are then sealed off in the past; for by taking the mysteries of flight with him to Africa, Guinea John ensures that his family's "future would be in the islands" (3). This bracketing of the past is in fact consolidated by Guinea John's own descendants, who seem to prefer that it be forgotten altogether. Indeed, Bango's insistence on recounting the tale causes his relatives to construe him as dangerous. As his nephew observes, "There was nothing I could identify as threatening [in Bango]. And I knew of no possession of his, or of any previous differences between either my mother and him, or him and my father, no family quarrel. All that I could see separating him from my other uncles was this story that he was ever willing to tell. So it had to be his story" (4).

But if Bango's story is regarded with suspicion, many are only too willing to subscribe to its alternative: the epic of the flight to the promised land of the colonial "mother-country." Echoing the Guinea John episode, chapter 2 begins on the "morning of the day that Alford George was to discover that he wasn't going to be leaving the island" (8). For Alford the blow is immense, since for him all that is of value lies outside Trinidad. The ships in the Port of Spain harbor fascinate him, for example, because they sail "to England, out into the world, *the world*, already to him more than a place, a mission, a Sacred Order that brought him into meaning, into Life" (26–27). As with the Guinea John story, the true home of identity is located elsewhere: the world is the sacred, Trinidad only a profane dot on a map, as Alford tells his pupils when he becomes a schoolmaster (72). He comes to believe, in fact, that it is his mission to protect others from this profanity. Asked by his lover Gloria why he will not follow her by leaving the island when he again has the chance, he replies that he must stay to "save" his pupils. To Gloria's query "Save them for what?" he responds: "Not save them *for*; save them *from*" (69–70). The Caribbean past is once more treated as anathema, then, as a traumatic legacy to be disavowed rather than revisited and confronted.

Salt thus presents us with two protagonists who parallel the would-be saviors from *The Wine of Astonishment*: Alford, like Morton, is a schoolmaster-turned-politician who becomes increasingly alienated from those he supposedly represents; Bango, like Bolo, is a rebel and martyr who is unwilling to deviate from his stance of heroic and isolated resistance. Now, Bango's refusal to accept the compromises of the postemancipation and postindependence political settlements is a necessary one. The problem is that this refusal seems to have congealed into a repetitive harking back to an African past, the significance of which he is incapable of conveying to those around him. He never ceases to reiterate his story, yet he cannot articulate what a different kind of Caribbean present and future might look like. Nevertheless, though his tale seems to replicate traditional epic in its apparent privileging of a finished and distant era, there is another way of approaching it that uncovers an alternative history, one present less in the literal content of the story than in the style of its narration.

Bango's physical style is the first indication of this possibility. In fact, the negative attitude some have toward him comes in part from the way in which he carries his body. His nephew, for example, watches him "come into our front yard with the brawling parrot-toed sure-footed walk with which I had seen him step on to the cricket field and into the stickfight ring, grand and compelling, making my mother step back, draw away as in the face of some danger" (4). Bango's movement thus expresses an identity linked both to the subversive reappropriation of imported colonial culture (cricket) and to the indigenous traditions (stickfighting) that embody the historical memory of the community. The novel emphasizes how this particular bodily disposition conflicts with the habitus that the colonial education system attempts to instill into people. Tellingly, Alford has been one of the most "successful" products of that system, as exemplified by the way he feels compelled to develop "a new walk," adopting "slower, more leisurely steps that gave him time in which to work out his translations from his thinking into what he saw now as proper English" (33–34). Against this is Bango's style, which we can use as an optic through which to reread the tale of Guinea John.

This tale can be seen not simply as an epic lament for the break with the African past but also as an indigenized piece of storytelling—a ritual act—that in its performance revisions the surface meaning of loss and flight:

> Two months after they hanged his brother Gregoire, king of the Dreadnoughts band, and Louis and Nanton and Man Man, the other three leaders of African secret societies, who Hislop the governor claimed to be ringleaders of an insurrection that had a plan, according to the testimony of a mad white woman, to use the cover of the festivities of Christmas day to massacre the white and free coloured people of the island, Jo-Jo's great-grandfather, Guinea John, with his black jacket on and a price of two hundred pounds sterling on his head, made his way to the East Coast, mounted the cliff at Manzanilla, put two corn cobs under his armpits and flew away to Africa, taking with him the mysteries of levitation and flight, leaving the rest of his family still in captivity mourning over his selfishness. (3)

The linearity of traditional epic—the return through a filiation to a sacred origin—is disturbed here by the very style or movement of the recital. The single sentence that unfolds the action in a meandering stream full of diversions recalls the spiraling form of folktales. This is not the consecrated narrative of received history but an unstable and entangled story woven from rumor and "mad" testimony. As such it appears as unfinished and open to reinterpretation, unlike the completed past of conventional epic. Moreover, the rhythm of the language creates a sense of excess that fractures closure and unity. Epic discourse, argues Bakhtin, is based on the direct word: the purity of the national myth is reinforced by a language whose meaning emerges "as a single intentional whole."[97]

Here, however, the relentless cadence engenders a sense that the reader is always about to stumble into another story. Indeed, the narrative's incantatory style points toward an alternative repository of history. "The rhythm is meaning too," Lovelace has said of writing. "We have tended to look at language in terms of its linear aspect, its logic, and that logic as meaning. But sound itself, after it is repeated, has an accumulated effect of communicating a deeper meaning. What we are really translating with words is not words, it is meaning."[98] The repetitions of the passage, its rolling, exuberant stride, recall Bango's own rhythm and style of movement, and thus the indigenous history this embodies. An overspill of meaning occurs beyond the literal content of the text: Bango's story, despite its theme of a return to Africa, contains the seeds of an original Caribbean epic bound to the creolization of tradition and an alternative conception of the nation grounded in an entanglement of histories (indeed, this is "only one of the beginnings of the story" that Bango will tell [3]).

Nevertheless these seeds appear destined not to come to fruition. Bango is unable to communicate the deeper meaning of his narrative to those around him, who read his actions as a retrograde obsession with "a past that everybody gone past" (49). Related to this is his inability to explain why he refuses to accept the distribution of land as sanctioned by the state. Bango continues to live on the plantation where his ancestors worked, since like them he believes "that somebody owe them something. It have something to do with land that they waiting on Government to give them; but they have no papers and no claim" (139). This belief goes back to emancipation, which, as Bango's grandfather Jo-Jo realized at the time, condemned the formerly enslaved to "second-classness." Not only did it fail to acknowledge the injustices they had suffered; it also instituted an inimical land settlement policy in which one either had to buy land, and thus accept that it was the planter's to sell, or squat on it illegally. The resistance upheld from Jo-Jo through to Bango reflects the demand for the more equitable redistribution of land on the basis of the rights and interests of the people, and not that of its being the private property of the ruling classes to do with as they see fit.

When it comes to his difficulties in expressing the reasons for his behavior, Bango's predicament is similar to that of the rebels in *The Dragon Can't Dance*. He lacks the requisite resources to generalize his struggle into a whole program for progressive transformation. But not only does this result from the lack of adequate institutional structures in which to anchor his inchoate demands; equally problematic is the way that, like Bolo, Bango adopts the role of the sacrificial savior and scapegoat. In chapter 2, I explored the problems with this position, so I will not reiterate them here. Nevertheless, bearing in mind the issues around gender I considered earlier, I do want to examine the way *Salt* uses the shortfalls in the male protagonists' relationships with women to interrogate the position of the martyred hero.

Take, for example, Alford's father, Dixon, who refuses all offers to better his post as a laborer, since he does not want "to be beholden to Carabon [the estate owner], not for house or land or anything" (20). Like Jo-Jo and Bango, then, Dixon resists a "gift" of freedom that in reality would reduce him to a dependent status. Gradually, however, his behavior begins to perpetuate the underlying dynamics of this supposed gift. His wife observes that Dixon's "way to feel himself the equal of if not the superior to anybody was to give more and more of himself, this giving making him more martyred and heroic" (19). His act of giving remains tied to the cultivation of debt, while he is unable to "receive" anything for fear of being obligated to someone. He thus seems to deny the possibility of engaging with others on an equitable or reciprocal basis, and by locking himself into the posture of the sacrificial victim, he replicates the kind of isolated individualism that underpins the socioeconomic order he is resisting. This is highlighted by the ritual he performs during the courtship of his wife. On spying her at a dance with a group of girls, he approaches. But instead of going directly to May, he first asks each of the other girls onto the floor, all of whom refuse: "He continued down the row of them, with . . . the martyred smile, holding himself with a pained haughtiness as each one turned away, not as if he was the one rejected, was the one doing them a favour, or was it putting them to a test?" (14). The fruitless requests become part of a sacrificial act for Dixon, one that leaves his intended with a sense of debt. When she sees behind his smile "the wound, the bleeding, his desperate appeal," she feels obliged to dance; and Dixon, having given so much of himself, believes he now has a right to her, standing guard over the "space in front of her, so that fellows approaching her to dance felt it necessary first to ask his permission" (14).

Bango exhibits similar behavior. The belief that he must always be the one to give, and that to receive or to open himself up to others is to compromise the purity of his resistance, prevents him from establishing a productive dialogue either with his wife or with the community. Concerned to maintain his heroic, martyred posture of "undefeat" (155), he isolates himself and fails to account for his actions. "You never tell me why," says Myrtle, his spouse. "If somebody was to ask me, I wouldn't know what to say" (164). Moreover, his all-or-nothing mind-set encourages him to carry as his burden the needs of the village, which "woulda been all right," observes Myrtle, "if people pull together and share the responsibility; but like the knowledge he was there leave them free to do as they please" (147). His organization of the Independence Day parade is a case in point. The first year is a success: "Whatever was his point Bango had made it alone. . . . Everybody was witness. And right there he shoulda stop, invite other people in and if they wanted to carry it on, OK. He had done his part" (161). But he is back every year thereafter, without asking others to join in. Soon he is marching not just for independence but "for any and every cause, once The People were involved" (161). The lack of real engagement, however, between him and what he confronts precisely as an abstract agglomeration—"The People"—renders his actions hollow: "Every protest, every celebration, he was there. . . . And why is he marching? Nobody ever ask him a word. Sometimes they bring him on the stage with them like a clown, like a puppet show, on parade. They giving the speeches and not asking him to say a word" (161).

While Bango's actions are thus in danger of becoming as unproductive as those of Bolo in *The Wine of Astonishment*, Alford seems on course to replicate the failures of Morton. Unlike Bango, Alford's political career grants him access to, and a degree of control over, institutional frameworks through which to effect change. Yet he fails to pursue the radical transformation of the structures inherited from the colonial state. Soon caught up in the "tapestry of pretence of power" (130), he becomes emblematic of the general dissipation of the emancipatory potential of the nationalist project, a dissipation *Salt* captures most strikingly through the implicit contrast drawn between two key scenes in the novel.

One of these relates Myrtle's experience of a National Party rally held before its electoral victory (the National Party is a fictionalized version of the PNM). Here she is made to "see the world afresh" by energetic speeches that narrate five hundred years of Caribbean history (152). However, the images summoned up by the speeches recall a real painting seen in the prime minister's office earlier in the novel (though chronologically at a later date), at a time when the party is ensconced in power. The history presented at the rally is reiterated in the mural, but it has been transformed into a series of visual platitudes that evoke a feeling of stasis rather than dynamism. Emphasizing this shift, the language deployed in the two passages differs markedly despite the overlap in content. The account of the mural is a fairly straightforward depiction of its subject matter:

> There it was. Native Indians in a ballet of welcome offering gifts to Columbus, who stands with imperial nonchalance, one hand on his hip, the other holding a lance as if deciding whether he should accept their offering. . . . Africans are dancing to their jungle tom-toms. . . . Toussaint L'Ouverture in the dress of a general is on horseback at the head of a ragged army swooping down upon burning plantations. (126)

In contrast, the description of Myrtle's reaction to the speeches repeats, expands, and reanimates these events:

> She see the Indians of the Indies in a ballet of welcome, offering gifts to Columbus who stand up disguising his wonder with a pose of imperial nonchalance, one hand on his hip, the other holding a lance. . . . She see Africans in Demerara with lithe limbs of dancers and teeth of ivory and torsos of gymnasts hanging on gibbets from their waists. . . . She witness the grand uprisings in Haiti with Toussaint

L'Ouverture and Dessalines and the plague of freedom beginning to spread fear of retribution, planters leaving Grenada, St Lucia, Martinique, heading for Trinidad. (152–53)

While the first version is immediately fixed in the past ("There it was"), the second suggests an active awakening to history ("She see . . . She see . . . She witness") as the rhythm of the passage conveys a sense of rising excitement and a rapid expansion in perception. Indeed, as in Bango's story, this rhythmic excess seems to cause an overspill in content that opens up new perspectives. The painting offers only a stereotypical portrait of Columbus standing "with imperial nonchalance." In the second scene, however, the surging energy of the line—"Columbus who stand up disguising his wonder with a pose of imperial nonchalance"—unleashes (in Harrisian fashion) an extra dimension whose utopian potential might be recuperated: here the sense of wonderment that ran in parallel with the sterile greed of conquest. Similarly, while the painting sports the cliché of "Africans" with "their jungle tom-toms," the verbal picture with its poetic cadences—"limbs of dancers and teeth of ivory and torsos of gymnasts"—becomes a celebration of vitality even in the midst of barbaric "gibbets."

Through the contrast that the novel stages between these two scenes, the failings of the National Party are made clear: the potential it had to rouse the people, and to evoke the possibility of a change that might redeem a brutal past and fashion a new future, has congealed; the energy of those early rallies has evaporated in the Eric Williams–like prime minister's stifling office space where the painting hangs. The question, then, is how to unlock this shackled potential. It is worth recalling here Lovelace's emphasis on the promise of national independence as a potential that remains unfulfilled but is also worth struggling for in the postcolonial world. Both Alford and Bango, the elite politician and the working-class rebel, appear unable to prosecute this struggle in such a way as to ensure that it once more connects with the people. Nevertheless the novel ends with the significance of Bango's resistance finally being recognized, and with Alford, who is made to understand the need to tackle the entrenched power relations concretized in the landownership system, finding his way back to the community. How are these changes brought about and narrated? The answer is connected to the way the text circles back to restage the history contained in the painting, a point to which I return in a moment.

Equally pertinent, however, is the sentiment expressed by the first-person narrator toward the end of the novel that "if what distinguishes us as humans is our stupidity, what might redeem us was our grace" (259). This aphorism sums up a central theme in the novel, its emphasis on what might be termed the beautiful stupidity of humanity, and the need to learn to recognize the frailty and contingency of oneself and others. "Grace" here refers to a willingness to accept the world, not in acquiescing to the status quo but in recognizing one's entangled relationship to it as the basis from which to effect change. In this respect, epic form once more serves as a utopian resource, foreshadowing the kind of subjectivity such grace will entail. As Lukács notes, the "paradox of the subjectivity of the great epic" is "its 'throwing away in order to win': creative subjectivity becomes lyrical, but, exceptionally, the subjectivity which simply accepts, which humbly transforms itself into a purely receptive organ of the world, can partake of the grace of having the whole revealed to it."[99] Thus we come back to the need to divest oneself of an enclosed, monadic selfhood to be able to grasp the world anew.

What is at stake here can be illuminated by considering Jameson's gloss on Adorno's construal of humanity's history of "mutual aggressivity, inevitable misery and unwarranted triumph" as "grounded in the seemingly biological and Darwinian instinct of self-preservation." The "philosophical subtext of this startling suggestion," notes Jameson, "lies in the proposition that 'self-preservation' is not an instinct at all, but rather something like an ideology, or at the very least an ideological mechanism":

> All human societies, necessarily organized around scarcity and power, have had to program their subjects in such a way as to construct some seemingly primordial effort to preserve one's self at all costs, which is to say at the cost of other people. This "self," which one then jealously hoards and protects against incursion, is something like a form of property, the very first form perhaps, around which all our personal and social struggles are organized. Adorno's speculations thereby unexpectedly renew their ties with the oldest and most tenaciously rooted Utopian traditions: to abolish private property. Yet it is now the private property of the self which is to be abolished.[100]

As this suggests, the abolition of the private property of the self implies the transformation of societies organized in such a way as to produce the ideological mechanism of self-preservation in the first place. Thus we can read Lovelace's emphasis on grace—on freeing oneself from an isolated individualism—as the utopian prefiguration of a radically different social order. The persistent motif of characters being divested of a monadic subjectivity becomes the translation into the logic of the literary sphere of a political dispensation yet to come. It replaces the motif of the tragic sacrificial hero and so mediates a shift away from the idea of the individual who steps outside the group to refashion it, pointing instead toward a transformative dynamic grounded in the collectivity, in Fanon's "zone of occult instability." If this dynamic implies the necessity of recognizing the interconnectedness of all that constitutes the social totality, its emancipatory potential rests on the possibility of reorganizing that network of relations on the basis of equality and reciprocity.

It is therefore unsurprising that the moment Bango opens himself and his struggle to others, moving beyond his isolated martyrdom, is the moment his character trajectory swerves decisively away from that of Bolo's. It is also the moment when new political possibilities emerge and, significantly, when his relationship to his wife changes. Hitherto Myrtle has not been able to understand why Bango insists that Alford's offer of land must be given as a public form of reparation or not at all. Exasperated with what she sees as a vainglorious martyrdom, she complains: "If I miss the point, then why you don't tell me the point" (164). Bango realizes he has never finished his story, never explained the history he protests against. This realization and the subsequent openness it encourages allow him to appreciate the sacrifices Myrtle has made, to see how she has played an equal and integral role in the fight against dispossession. For Myrtle (her being acknowledged now as central to this history emphasized by a shift from third- to first-person narration), there is a sense of "triumphant peace" because "she could see that Bango had recognized her. He had made me out. All at once he realize that in the journey he thought he had made alone, I had been with him the whole way" (165). Their relationship is thus freed from the dynamics of gift and debt to become one based on an open and equal engagement with each other.

To the extent that the scene thereby underscores the necessity for any new national project to involve the recalibration of gender relations, it also reinforces why the narrative must break here with the topos of the tragic sacrifice. The masculinism of that topos, as we saw in the earlier chapters, mediated the limitations of the political projects it encoded insofar as it bespoke the continuance of patriarchal power relations, which themselves testified to the persistence of preexisting forms of economic organization. In this sense, too, the move away from the topos underlines how the changes in Bango and Myrtle's personal relations point forward to a change in political relations. Confirming this, the next chapter opens with Bango and Myrtle entering the offices of the National Party, with Bango ready now to tell his story not just to his family but, thanks to Myrtle's encouragement, to Alford and, via him, the nation.[101] Divested of his egoism and sense of heroic isolation, Bango recognizes he can do so without compromising the purity of his resistance. Like Marie-Sophie, he grasps the necessity of reappropriating institutional organs to rearticulate his struggle on a national level. In so doing, he bears out Lovelace's injunction to "reclaim institutions that can carry us forward, make us new."[102] Once Bango is in the prime minister's office, the space of which materializes the official story of independence as told by the National Party, he consumes this sacred history, plunging it into his own more profane tale that stretches back to the toils of Guinea John and Jo-Jo.

Tellingly, the way in which Bango restages the past for Alford can be seen once more in terms of possession rites and ego displacement. Funso Aiyejina argues that Lovelace's frequent switching between narrative consciousnesses is a form of "narrative possession or narrative ventriloquism, a process that allows for the primary narrator to be invaded/mounted and controlled, or relieved of the task of narration, by the subject of the narration who temporarily takes over the task."[103] This is certainly the case here. It is Bango who begins telling the story, only for the narration to be mounted by Jo-Jo. However, the passages focalized through his consciousness assume a literary poeticism that suggests that they too are being mediated through another consciousness, one that "translates" Jo-Jo's story into the kind of discourse that resonates with the native intellectual and former schoolteacher Alford. The ritualistic voiding and possession of narrative viewpoint not only enable the past to be reenacted on a collective level, insofar as it is rearticulated through a polyphony of voices, but also provide a model for a new form of political dialogue and representation.

The story of Bango and his ancestors converts Alford to the cause of publicly redistributing the land. Crucially, what leads him to listen properly to the story in the first place is the way Bango now speaks from a position of grace. Expecting a sterile tragedy "of self-pity and martyrdom," Alford has to admit that this is "not what I got from Bango." "Understand from the start," says Bango, "I ain't come here to make the Whiteman the devil. I not here to make him into another creature inhabiting another world outside the human order. . . . I come to call him to account, as a brother, to ask him to take responsibility for his humanness, just as I have to take responsibility for mine. . . . This business of being human is tougher than being the devil, or being God for that matter. And it doesn't matter whether in the role of brutalized or brutalizer" (167–68). Bango's emphasis is on engaging the world: he seeks not to set his antagonists apart but to understand the respective positions he and they occupy within a network of relations. The task is then to change the very basis of this network, that is, to project the possibility of a world in which genuine equality and reciprocity will enable the transcendence of the brutalized-brutalizer dichotomy. Stirred both by the story and by its telling, Alford is not only persuaded to identify with Bango's struggle but also converted in terms of *how* he identifies with it. He too divests himself of the elevated, egoistic posture he had assumed—the political martyr come to save the islanders—and opens himself up as a vehicle or mount for the collective history invoked by Bango. His subsequent political actions (speaking out on the land issue, joining the Independence Day parade) reflect his mediation of this history. Thus we have here the image of a different form of political representation to that of the isolated leader set over and separate from the masses. What Alford's possession by Bango's story suggests is the achievement of that dialectical link, sought after but ultimately lacking in *The Dragon Can't Dance*, between the represented and the institutional representative.

If both Alford and the history materialized in the prime minister's office are reanimated by contact with Bango and his story, the novel at the level of form similarly reanimates the idea of the nation and the nationalist project. We have already seen how the dissipation of the National Party's potential is conveyed through the contrast implied between the official mural depicting Caribbean history and the narration of that same history at the pre-election rally. That this chronologically prior event is placed after the first appearance of the mural, so that what we seem to see is the revitalization of a narrative that has congealed into cliché, suggests that it is precisely a reengagement with the nationalist project that is required, its being returned to afresh to redeem the promise it contained. In other words, the nationalist project must be submitted to the same epic cannibalism as history, releasing its unfinished potentials. The failure of the bourgeois nationalism of the National Party should not be cause to repudiate nationalism per se. For Lovelace, "what we stand to lose, should we not take the side of National Independence as the rallying point, is a perspective of ourselves as being able to do anything in the world. . . . We stand to see ourselves truly as simply enduring, as individuals consuming what is fed us in the vastness of the global village."[104] In this view, then, the nation-state and an *ongoing* anti-imperialist national liberationist movement remain the basis on which to struggle for internal social transformation and against external domination.

But the novel's nonlinear, spiraling form also contributes to its articulation of a way of thinking about nationhood in terms of the challenges posed by an ethnically diverse populace. To illustrate this point, I want to turn briefly to Confiant's *Le nègre et l'amiral* (1988), which shares certain structural similarities with *Salt*. Like many of Confiant's novels, it is split into nonchronological but intersecting narrative "circles." Typical is the section detailing the life of the Indian character Vidrassamy. It opens with the protagonist Rigobert trying to deduce who has betrayed him to the authorities. The chapter then circles back to a past *damier* confrontation between Rigobert and Barbe-Sale, the event that prompted Barbe-Sale to inform on his old rival. However, in the middle of the account of this ritual combat-dance, the text switches focus to Vidrassamy after he attempts to intervene in the confrontation. Subsequently we are plunged into a story about his childhood in which his parents, recognizing their son's creolization, decide he should remain in Martinique rather than return with them to India.[105] Through this narrative detour into Vidrassamy's past, the novel enacts a kind of temporary displacement of the consolidated or enclosed identity of Martinican society. Another cultural history is uncovered, one nevertheless bound to a collective, protonational experience (indeed, in addition to confronting the trials of establishing a place for himself within island society, Vidrassamy in later life will help to organize numerous cross-racial, anticolonial strikes).

Now, the novel as a whole uses this spiraling form to evoke the very idea of a Martinican nation in the context of departmentalization. It circles back to resurrect a past—the period under Admiral Robert during World War II—when Martinique was forced into a degree of self-sufficiency; or at least Confiant fictively reimagines this past, using it as a kind of memory of the future (like Harris's imaginative resuscitation of unborn histories) to summon up the possibility of an independent, national alternative to departmental status.[106] In this connection, the particular narrative spiral concerning Vidrassamy emphasizes how any projected nation-state cannot close ranks around an exclusive, singular notion of identity. Rather, it must remain open to the multiplicity of histories present on the island, even while attempting to articulate them within a wider collective project. In other words, a nationalist discourse should be predicated not on closure but on constant revision; it would require (in an echo of the way ritual displacement serves as a periodic corrective to the absolutizing propensities of the ego) that the process of restaging the nation be built into its very articulation, so that its scope and meaning remain subject to regular recalibration.

Salt employs a similar narrative form for similar ends. Alongside the multiple histories that infuse its wandering sentences, the novel (like *The Dragon Can't Dance*, only more so) has a burgeoning trajectory that defies the conventions of narrative closure. Once Bango has told his story to Alford and the politician has committed himself to land reform, a conclusion seems imminent. Yet the novel then opens back up with chapters on the white creole Carabon and the Indian Lochan family, each of which replays earlier episodes from a new perspective. This spiraling narrative arc again underscores the need for a national discourse open to constant revision, one that is expansive and inclusive, seeking (like Bango) not to ostracize anyone but to map the totality of positions, contingencies, and relationships that constitute the social whole, and thence to remake this whole on the basis of equality, reciprocity, and acceptance (or grace). The climax of *Salt*, the Independence Day parade in which various characters come together, hoping that Carabon and Lochan will join them, serves as the figure for this utopian national project. Nevertheless the novel is far from naive when it comes to the likelihood of achieving real change. Indeed, it continues to highlight the problems surrounding attempts to articulate new forms of nationalist discourse and to concretize new kinds of social relations, especially against a backdrop of persistent ethnic tensions. And it is to these difficulties, as well as to the more general crisis that has beset nation-states in the era of neoliberal globalization, that I turn in the final chapter.

5

"No Pain like This Body": Race, Gender, and Sexuality in a Time of Crisis

Although Lovelace's *Salt* concludes with the Independence Day parade and the utopian desire for a new, genuinely inclusive form of nationalism, it is nevertheless careful to highlight the ongoing difficulties with achieving this goal.[1] Even as the narrator expresses his hope that the white creole farmer Carabon and the Indo-Trinidadian politician Sonan Lochan will join Alford and Bango on the march, the reader has already witnessed Sonan's attempts to articulate a less narrowly identitarian style of politics eclipsed by a rising tide of ethnic triumphalism. Sonan has long exhibited discomfort with the idea of representing Indian interests alone: during his early years on the Hindu School cricket team, the sense that he was batting not merely for himself but as "an Indian" prevented him from playing freely. Now that he is a politician, he tells supporters at a rally, using his childhood experiences as an analogy for his antisectarian perspective, he wants to "bat for something bigger."[2] But his efforts to cultivate a broad-based nationalism by bringing Afro-Trinidadians into the Indian-dominated Democratic Party are met with censure by Mr. Bissoon, his campaign manager. Mr. Bissoon holds that it "is our time now" (241) and is initially horrified when, on the eve of the elections, Sonan delivers a speech emphasizing the need for the island's different ethnic groups to "welcome each other" (243). The campaign manager's horror turns to joy, however, when he realizes that "with all the noise in the square, nobody was hearing a word he, Sonan, was saying. What he was saying was drowned out by the chutney tassa calypso music, coming from the enthusiasm of a people who would not be denied the victory there were scenting for the first time" (243).

Despite his best intentions, therefore, Sonan finds himself in a position similar to that which we saw Bango escape from in the previous chapter: the elevated, almost messianic individual to whom the hopes of the people are transferred. That the crowd cannot hear Sonan's speech emphasizes that the dialectical link between himself and those he supposedly represents remains problematic. Moreover, the drowning out of Sonan's inclusive sentiments points to the persistence of an ethnically charged, zero-sum form of politics in Trinidad. Indeed, Lovelace's narrative alludes specifically to political events in the island during the 1980s and 1990s, which underscored the tenacity of such problems. The attempt by Alford, Sonan, and others to form a political party representative of a wide cross section of society recalls the emergence of the National Alliance for Reconstruction (NAR), which came to power in 1986. The difficulties the characters encounter, however, gesture to the NAR's collapse in 1991 and the subsequent domination of Trinidadian politics by the rivalry between the largely Indian-backed UNC and the largely African-backed PNM.[3]

If Lovelace's utopian projection of a reorganized nation-state subtending a new kind of nationalist discourse has not been realized, the same could be said for Chamoiseau's depiction of the emancipatory potential of Marie-Sophie's Texaco. The quarter concretized emergent forms of social and economic relations and figured the cornerstone of a future independent polity. But where *Texaco* ended with the possibility that the alliance between the urban planner and Marie-Sophie might precipitate the transformation of society, Chamoiseau's later work, *Biblique des derniers gestes* (2002), emphasizes Martinique's continued subordination to France and to the power of global capital. Indeed, the novel shows the island having to face up to new challenges in the shape of organized crime and drug trafficking. Meanwhile the inimical effects of mass-market tourism and folklorization appear to have intensified. Developers now swarm across the land:

> They wanted to transform each district into a hotel. Install travel agencies at the entrance of churches. Build holiday cottages beneath the great trees. Train butterflies so that they danced around the open-air cafes. . . . The tourist boards proposed painting the blackbirds blue, perfuming the manicous, and rewarding youths capable of smiling at groups of tourists. . . . The country's agricultural lands, more or less paralysed, suffered an unprecedented assault. No more need to cultivate or produce anything. Just put up hotels, swimming pools and marinas, touring-clubs and youth hostels, holiday villages and casinos. . . .[4]

The issues highlighted in Chamoiseau's and Lovelace's novels are far from unique to Martinique and Trinidad. Across the Caribbean, societies have had to confront the fallout from rising rates of criminality, ethnic tensions, the social and environmental costs of tourism, increased unemployment, and the changing demands of the global economy. In many cases, governments have struggled to cope. In a brief survey, Evelyn O'Callaghan suggests that violence is "reaching epidemic proportions in the region": "Domestic violence, male on male gang violence, hate crimes against racial groups and non-heterosexuals—it is the stuff of everyday reporting. In Jamaica, the exceptional nature of a 'Murder Free Day' makes the headlines of the national newspaper."[5] Anthony Bogues, meanwhile, notes:

> Politics and the anglophone Caribbean nation-states are in acute crisis, from where there seems no easy exit. This crisis pervades the intellectual climate. Brian Meeks suggests that perhaps we are in a stage of "terminal meltdown," David Scott argues

that "there is scarcely a postcolonial society that is not in fundamental crisis," and Selwyn Ryan opines that the "tensions between economic distress and democratic governance" engender regional political instability. In the contemporary period, "crisis" is a much overworked label. As a political term it is a sign of instability, of chaos, of disorder, and broken social bonds. Clearly the Caribbean nation-states constructed from 1938 onward are in crisis.[6]

The specific coordinates and manifestations of this crisis vary from state to state, but its long-term trajectory needs to be seen in the context of a broader structural crisis in the capitalist world system that began in the 1970s. In response to this crisis, which resulted from the shrinking availability of "financially profitable new outlets [for capital] capable of expanding productive capacity," the main global powers implemented a management strategy aimed at "finding alternative new investments for excess short-term capital."[7] "Crisis management by national governments," argues Samir Amin, "proceeds by policies of deregulation designed both to weaken the rigidities of trade unionism and dismantle and liberalize prices and wages; reduce public expenditure (principally subsidies and social services); and privatize and liberalize external transactions."[8] These policies reflect neoliberal economic thinking and underpin what is today commonly referred to as globalization. As Amin makes clear, however, such liberalization ensnares the economy "into deflationist spirals of stagnation, unmanageable at the international level, multiplying conflicts which cannot be mediated, against the empty promise of future 'healthy' development."[9]

On one level, then, the troubles in the Caribbean are testament to the adverse effects of the neoliberal restructuring of the world system. In some instances, as indicated earlier, the increasing instability of already economically precarious societies has raised the prospect of their disintegrating as nation-states. Unable to function as sites for capital accumulation, they become incapable of launching the kinds of nationally integrative modernization projects that characterized many postindependence rebuilding programs.[10] At the same time, support for institutional political structures is ebbing as cuts in public expenditure worsen poverty and leave political parties "no longer able to deliver the benefits of the system of spoils and political patronage."[11] In this context, ruling elites often resort to manipulating ethnic divisions to shore up political capital among certain segments of the population, thereby causing further social fragmentation.

In this chapter, I examine how novelists writing in the 1980s, 1990s, and the first decade of the twenty-first century have sought to engage with the crises affecting the Caribbean. Many of the texts studied here are by women, reflecting the increase in, and greater visibility of, female authors after 1980.[12] As Helen Scott observes, "This generation of writers reached maturity in a period characterized by the failure of political independence to deliver the freedom, equality and liberation it had promised."

No longer saturated with the political optimism of the earlier age, late century Caribbean literature (which is much more visibly female, though contemporaneous male writers exhibit the same trends) is more likely to be marked by a mood of disillusion or even despair. What hope remains is confined to the individual realm; women may "make it" by leaving their home country to seek opportunities abroad or by freeing themselves from oppressive family situations, but the victory is tainted by an awareness of those left behind.[13]

The issues Scott raises—disenchantment with nationalist discourses, emigration, the role of the family, the relationship between the diaspora and those that remained in the region—will all feature in my analysis of novels by, among others, Oonya Kempadoo, Margaret Cezair-Thompson, Michelle Cliff, and Shani Mootoo. I will also draw a comparison with the treatment of crisis in the work of Pedro Juan Gutiérrez, whose portrayal of the problems confronting the national project in Cuba, particularly since the collapse of the Soviet Union after 1989, reflects the distinctive socioeconomic and political trajectory of that island. Finally, I return to some of the concerns outlined in my introduction regarding the frequent emphasis in postcolonial studies on hybridity, diaspora, and postnationalism and consider why the nation-state has not yet been rendered obsolete as a site of emancipatory possibility.

Before all of this, however, I revisit the issue of creating a nationalist discourse capable both of remaining open to a multiplicity of cultural legacies and of rearticulating them within a wider collective project. In the previous chapter, I explored the ways in which writers drew on Afro-Caribbean rituals as they sought to elaborate such a discourse. Here I examine how Indo-Caribbean rituals have been used to similar ends. Efforts by some authors to establish a framework in which an Indian heritage can be proclaimed as part of an assertion of Caribbeanness reflect a desire to project the resolution of the tensions between Afro- and Indo-Caribbean peoples. I touched briefly on these matters in the first chapter when looking at Selvon's *A Brighter Sun*. There the development of Tiger's consciousness entailed the incorporation of his Indian inheritance into a wider Trinidadian identity, one defined in political terms across ethnic lines. But the underlying assumption of the narrative seemed to be that the emergence of a national consciousness would in itself solve the dilemma of multiple identifications. Later novels, written in the shadow of the disappointments of independence and the persistence of ethnic conflict, have engaged with this theme in far more explicit and critical fashion. With this in mind, I examine a selection of works from a relatively understudied body of Caribbean literature—that produced by Francophone Indo-Caribbean authors. Lacking visibility in the literary field and occupying a minority status in Martinique and Guadeloupe, these authors have tackled very directly the question of what it means to be both Indian and Caribbean.[14]

The first novel by a Francophone Indo-Caribbean writer did not appear until 1972. Maurice Virassamy's *Le petit coolie noir*, based on the author's childhood in Martinique, details the hostility experienced by Indians on the island. For Chamoiseau and Confiant, its bitter tone reflects a "distaste for Martinican society."[15] Subsequent writers, however, have sought not only to celebrate their Indian inheritance but to do so as part of an affirmation of Caribbeanness. The Guadeloupean novelist Ernest Moutoussamy, for instance, argues that "when today the young speak of a pilgrimage to the source, it is not a question of a return to the country of the ancestors, but of drawing from there the elements indispensable to the understanding and consolidation of an Antillean Indianité." Hence, he adds, it is "a matter of resuscitating the past, of maintaining the collective memory, of enabling the appropriation of aesthetic values in order to authenticate an Antillean identity."[16] The resuscitation of the ancestral past as, paradoxically, a way to negotiate the Caribbean present and to inscribe into its history an Indian heritage (which in turn becomes "authentically" Antillean) is at the heart of Moutoussamy's fiction. Arguably, however, the formal devices through which he attempts to stage this reconciliation often fail to sustain his intentions.

Take, for example, his novel *Aurore* (1987). Set in India and the Caribbean, it tells the story of Râma, a young Brahmin expelled from his family home and brought to Guadeloupe on board the *Aurélie* in 1885 as an indentured laborer. The narrative details the brutality of plantation life and the methods by which control was exerted over the indentured, including the suppression of the Tamil language and the promotion of Christianity over Hinduism. Against this, Râma seeks to revitalize Indian culture. This revitalization, however, is also intended to enable the community to begin to assert itself in Guadeloupean society: "With their Tamil spoken at night, which, in order to banish, the tyrants had in times gone by cut out the tongues of those refusing capitulation and betrayal, they revived India, fought against the forgetting, inspired the young while turning them resolutely towards Guadeloupe. . . . They thus fertilized the future, searching for a solution to their integration into this hostile world."[17] Tamil religious rites become integral to this struggle, with the performance of sacred texts and the manifestation of the gods in possession rites allowing for the restaging of the ancestral past within the new environment.[18]

On a more explicitly political level, Moutoussamy's text suggests that the parallel demands of identifying both as Indian and Guadeloupean can be reconciled in the arena of the class struggle. To challenge the dominance of the planters and maintain their cultural inheritance, the Indian laborers must unite with their black counterparts, the two communities having been deliberately divided by the planters to forestall such an alliance. In this context, Râma and the Afro-Caribbean Vitalien come to an economic arrangement designed to secure for their peoples a degree of self-sufficiency in the face of the plantation regime:

> To break, link by link, the chain of serfdom surrounding his companions, Râma proposed to Vitalien a system of barter. He delivered to him some rice . . . in exchange for some salt, fat, and fish. . . . All this was done in confidence, with both sides respecting the quantities. This new relationship had a profound effect on behaviour. The plantation, shaken by the wind of independence, saw arise from this depth of fraternity another kind of man. . . . The exchange system defied the law of servitude. The hands joined in the darkness menaced the affluence and power of [the planter]. (141)[19]

Through this alternative economy, Râma and Vitalien lay the foundations for a challenge to the power of the plantocracy. The emergence of "another kind of man" from the confluence of each group's specific contribution to the system symbolizes the potential for the emergence of a new social order, one in which Indianness is secured as part of the assertion of an emergent, popular national identity.

Such symbolism reappears in the romantic plots that infuse the novel. Râma's initial plan for forging an alliance with the black community involves cultivating a relationship with Maya, the black mistress of the plantation manager. Later he determines to propose to her, wishing to start a family on the island. By so doing, he muses, "Guadeloupe would truly become his homeland. This union would put a definitive end to the temptation to return, would transform exile into sanctuary, and would increase further the prospect of integration into the local society" (145).[20] However, this symbolically freighted coupling fails to materialize. Instead, at the end of the novel, Râma marries Aurore, his bride-to-be back in India before the break with his family. Aurore, it transpires, had followed Râma to Guadeloupe twenty years earlier but had been unable to find him. Râma locates his former lover, who has been forced to serve as the mistress of a planter, and flees with her and her child. The pair's subsequent betrothal becomes emblematic of Râma's (India's) definitive implantation in the Caribbean.

However, it is with this romance narrative that problems arise in the text's attempt to reconcile a demand for cultural specificity with a collective social project bound to the assertion of a national (Antillean) identity. The denouement of the Râma-Aurore story line occurs against the backdrop of a riot on the plantation. The riot follows a strike by black factory workers, which the Indian laborers oppose, since they believe (due to misinformation spread by the planters) that "*Grève*" [strike] refers to the leader of a mob intent on rape and murder. Râma uncovers the real meaning of the strike and tries to convince his companions not to defy it. He fails, and a fight breaks out between blacks and Indians, with casualties on both sides. However, the text does not expand on this incident and its implications for that hitherto central theme of the possibility of a class-based alliance between the two communities. Instead the narrative switches focus, concentrating exclusively at its conclusion on Râma's reunion with Aurore. Thus the two plotlines—the romantic and the political—finish by falling away from each other.

This formal disjunction permeates the novel in other ways. The section set in India recounts Râma's experiences and feelings, the difficulties of his everyday life, in detail to produce a concrete sense of character. Here the romantic (his entanglement with the untouchable Sarah, which precipitates his expulsion from the family home) does overlap with the political (the caste system, colonization, and economic hardship). But once the story moves to Guadeloupe, Râma loses much of his complexity, increasingly resembling a one-dimensional savior figure. Many of his relationships, such as those with Vitalien or Maya, assume a schematic quality, distinguished more by their symbolism than by a sense of genuine interaction. Indeed, as the political program of staking a claim to Guadeloupean society begins to dominate the text, the concreteness and depth of the human drama diminish. At the end of the novel, the complexity seemingly returns: Râma again appears a more rounded character, beset by contradictions and desires. But these arise only in relation to his search for Aurore, emphasizing how the political plot is here pushed into the background by the romance narrative. As indicated earlier, the romance narrative seems designed to provide a kind of imaginary or aesthetic resolution to the political conflict, with Râma's marriage to Aurore, who now possesses a mixed-race child born in Guadeloupe, figuring the emergence of a fully articulated Indo-Caribbean identity.[21] But its symbolism is no longer coherent, given the events of the strike: the union of the two individuals loses its referent as political allegory when read against the backdrop of the ethnic division engulfing the plantation. Indeed, the romance plot now merely serves to occult the gap that opens up between, on the one hand, the projected reconciliation of Indianness with Caribbeanness and, on the other, its achievement via the class struggle.

The reasons for this formal short circuit, I would argue, have to do with the relationship between the individual and the collective that the romance paradigm sets up. Romance ultimately seeks to reprivatize experience in the libidinal body, thereby excluding the messier precincts of collective history. In other words, what we have is something like the reversal of the allegorical connection between the public and the private that I noted in the novels of, for example, Selvon and Brodber. Whereas there the individual's struggle opened on to the wider social struggle, being dialectically linked to transformations in the community, here the individual becomes separated and sealed off from the collective with the unfolding of the romance plot. This is not to say that subsequently Râma's experiences are wholly unable to symbolize the wider struggle, but they can do so now only insofar as it is recontained within the image of the individual. That Râma's allegorical dimension is thus of a more typifying as opposed to dialectical sort is what occasions the novel's disjunctive climax: without that dialectical link, it is all too easy for the narrative to escape into the romantic fantasy of married bliss even as the political dream of social change falls apart.

To counter such a tendency would require a narrative form that explodes the monadic integument of the isolated individual, reestablishing a connection to collective history and the social totality. In the case of *Aurore*, this would have prevented the abrupt termination of the political story line with the riot, the complex, mass-historical character of which does not fit easily with the individualized, moral dichotomies of the romantic paradigm. The narrative could instead have penetrated the disturbances, exploring how the emancipatory project they have disrupted might yet be rebuilt (rather than abandoned for the realms of privatized desire). It will be clear by now that the form I have in mind would be something like the narratives discussed in the previous chapter, which sought a descent into Fanon's "zone of occult instability where the people dwell." In this connection, I want to turn to *Dérive de Josaphat* (1991), by the Indo-Martinican novelist Michel Ponnamah.

Ponnamah's narrative is structured around the meandering journey of its title character, a former agricultural laborer, as he walks across an abandoned plantation. Encountering various material or sensual traces of the old system of production (rusted train tracks, for example, or the smell of particular plants), Josaphat is called back to past incidents and events, one recollection the spur to another until the text becomes a web of memories. However, the way in which these memories erupt into the former laborer's thoughts suggests the past is far from a benign force. Rather, it manifests itself as a violent return of the repressed. Indeed, the landscape is revealed to be imbued with unresolved histories that Josaphat experiences as nightmarish visions. In addition to his own disturbing recollections, he details the various reports he has heard of ghosts from the past (such as dead slaves) or fantastical monsters (representative of various oppressors) terrorizing the present. Such phenomena are symptomatic of the condition Glissant described wherein a community is unable to structure its history autonomously, causing it to suffer the past as a series of convulsions that it cannot bring to light on a collective basis.

For Josaphat, this convulsive pressure exacts not only a psychic toll but a physical one, too. In fact, it contributes considerably to the pain that wracks his body. Upon being plunged into a recollection of plantation life after detecting the odor of cut cane, for example, he is "suddenly overcome with a feeling of faintness, a tiredness that spread throughout his body and made him yawn. He swayed. The air was charged with the noise of straw being trampled on, the hiss of leaves from coconut palms, and snatches of voices. Josaphat reopened his eyes. His heartbeat had accelerated. His chest vibrated."[22] Later, when similarly tormented, he emits "an odour of putrefaction that seemed to spread over his entire body" (une odeur de putréfaction qui semblaient gagner tout son corps) (49). The impression that Josaphat is disintegrating under the weight of repressed history is heightened by the images of liquefaction that attend his descents into memory. He appears increasingly swamped by the past: after he is overcome by one recollection, for instance, the narrative describes how he "shook his head as if freeing himself from immersion" (secoua la tête comme s'il se dégageait d'une immersion) (39). Seeming almost to dissolve in the stream of his memories, Josaphat at times enters a state of near delirium, unable to distinguish reminiscence from reality.

But this breakdown also contains the germ of a productive response to the trauma of history. To posit such a reversal brings us back to the thematic and formal preoccupations of the texts examined in chapter 4, to which the narrative structure of Ponnamah's work can now be compared: once again we have a character suffering from a delirium that becomes something like a rite of ego displacement, eroding the boundaries of the isolated individual and opening up the possibility of grasping a collective history—here one embedded in a landscape that has been produced by, and still bears the material traces of, the labor of the dominated classes, both African and Indian. In this connection, we have again that image of a "degrading" descent (figured in the motifs of decomposition and submersion), which we earlier associated with the descent into the "waters of spirit" in traditional African religion. *Texaco*, it was suggested, drew on this ritual pattern, historicizing it as a descent into the mass of human interactions and material relations that shape the social world. *Dérive de Josaphat* does something similar, with Josaphat's immersions in memory being inextricable from the sensuous connection he establishes both to the environment and to the history it contains.

More pertinently, however, one could also view the novel in relation to Indo-Caribbean religious practices. The form of Hinduism present in the Antilles has its own rites of possession. In these ceremonies, the priest, or *pousali*, enters a trance to be possessed by a god from India. The god speaks through the human vessel in Tamil, with his or her spiritual demands then translated into creole by the *vatialou*, the teacher or spiritual master.[23] Thus this act of ego displacement—the temporary voiding of the *pousali's* consciousness—permits the manifestation of the Indian heritage. With this in mind, it would not seem too far-fetched to reread Ponnamah's novel as an extended rite of possession, one in which Josaphat, adrift in a trancelike delirium, is continually displaced as the central consciousness by a stream of memories and histories. Crucially, however, he channels not only his own but also those other pasts sedimented in the landscape. Like the *pousali*, Josaphat becomes a medium for expression; but just as the priest's words must be translated from the ancestral Tamil into Creole, so Josaphat's memories are no longer exclusively "Indian," as it were, but rather "Martinican," since they invoke the experiences of all those, blacks and Indians alike, who have worked on and humanized the land. The Indian specificity represented by Josaphat is thus rearticulated as part of a totality of legacies grounded collectively in the Martinican environment in terms of the labors of the oppressed.

In this respect, Ponnamah's narrative gestures toward the kind of class-based approach to cultural reconciliation and integration elaborated in Moutoussamy's novel. Unlike *Aurore*, however, *Dérive de Josaphat* does not express this in an overtly political fashion; and at least in terms of content, it tends to emphasize the still often ambivalent position of Indians in Martinican society (the novel ends with Josaphat being knocked over by a van, with one onlooker commenting "An Cooli?" [It was only a Coolie?] [109]). But whereas *Aurore* was unable to hold to a confrontation with such political problems and at the same time pursue the utopian thrust of its romance narrative, Ponnamah's text succeeds in dissecting the continued sufferings of Indo-Martinicans while simultaneously projecting—implicitly, through its "ritualistic" formal structure—a utopian resolution. Crucial in this regard is its displacement of the isolated individual and the descent this enables into the mass of material and social relations that undergird reality. Even if the novel does not demarcate explicitly the contours of some new socioeconomic and political order, the very fact that it descends into the ground of collective history points to the necessity and possibility of transforming this ground to realize the ideal of community emitted by the narrative's form. It is this same ground that *Aurore* ultimately abandons for the strictly cultural(ist) resolution of the romance plot. Ponnamah's novel, by contrast, keeps in view not only the pessimism and hope surrounding the potential for a new architecture of cultures, but also the material foundations required for its construction.

It is, as noted earlier, pessimism rather than hope that has come to dominate attitudes toward the possibility of reconciling multiple cultural legacies—indeed, toward transformative collective projects in general—as nation-states have run into crisis. We have already observed how ethnic tensions continue to distort the political landscape in Trinidad. The same is true in Guyana, where the antagonisms between the Afro- and Indo-Guyanese communities, which preceded independence in 1966, continued throughout the 1970s and 1980s under the increasingly corrupt and authoritarian regime of Forbes Burnham. These hostilities form the backdrop to Oonya Kempadoo's 1998 novel *Buxton Spice*, which narrates the coming of age of a mixed-race girl, Lula, in the village of Tamarind Grove. Here the strains of racial conflict permeate everyday life: "Up by the seawall was the ruins of an old mosque. Wasn't ancient ruins, just a few years old . . . . Mums said it was Riots made it so. Race Riots before we moved in. Fires and Bombs chasing Indians out. Now Tamarind Grove was black race people, strong PNC party people. Dads, Bunty family and Aunty Babe was the only East Indians."[24] By the end of the novel, Lula's family too have been forced to leave the village.

Most striking is the way the text folds these political events into its exploration of sexual and familial relations. Lula's own burgeoning sexuality is a central theme of the book. Her early erotic experiences are generally a source of pleasure. However, as Alison Donnell observes, with the unfolding of the political narrative, "the free space of sexual experimentation and pure sensation rubs up against the fixed matrix of racial and gender configurations where sexuality is again implicated in conflicts over ethnic identity. . . . Initiation into the adult world is painful, not because sex itself is difficult or traumatic, but because sex inevitably becomes political in divided societies."[25] This is borne out when the white-skinned village girl Judy is accused publicly by her mother of having had sex with a black man, and then examined for signs of sexual activity. As Donnell puts it, the "privacy and intimacy of Judy's sexual life [are] destroyed by the public scrutiny of her body and the policing of racial, as well as sexual, contamination."[26] Such policing not only reflects national pressures around ethnicity but also disrupts ideological constructions of the body politic as unified and harmonious. Specifically, it undermines the discourse elaborated by Burnham's PNC in the 1970s, which proclaimed the diversity of Guyana as a marker of unity insofar as distinct ethnic groups were to be brought together under the banner of the Cooperative Republic. This discourse, in fact, relied on the hierarchical separation and stereotyping of those groups as the precondition for their subsequent rearticulation as a totality.[27] The efforts of Judy's mother to police the boundaries of her daughter's personal relations point figuratively to the coercive underside of that discourse, its basis in the policing of ethnic boundaries by the state.

On the one hand, then, *Buxton Spice* highlights the regulation of gender and ethnic norms implemented through the institution of the patriarchal family, though it is the mother here who assumes the role of the patriarch (the monitoring of sexual activity being a traditional means of preserving "the security of the male conjugal sphere").[28] On the other, the implicit connection the novel draws between familial power relations and the regulative behavior of the state indicates the historical tendency for nationalist discourse and policy in many Caribbean countries to assume a patriarchal character. Although women "were crucially involved with national liberation struggles, and independence at least initially raised greater possibilities for sexual equality in spheres such as education, employment and social services," national liberation did not make good on this promise, just as it fell short in other areas for both men and women.[29] In fact, postindependence ruling elites have often deployed patriarchal discourse to shore up the social order when unable to achieve stability through economic or political development. Images of the family and of the nation-as-family become crucial in this regard, helping to mystify and naturalize exploitative power relations by recoding them in terms of the loyalties and obligations of kinship.[30]

Kempadoo's novel provides a sharp illustration of this process during a scene

in which Burnham visits Tamarind Grove. Speaking to two female PNC supporters, he adopts a familiar tone that is part paternal, part flirtatious:

> "Mrs Sampson, ah see you ain lose no size even with all dis hot sun. Yuh husband
> must'e strong! Heh. He don' need some help?" . . . "And Mrs Bee," he went on, "you
> did some good work de other day fuh Tamarind Grove. What *else* you does so good?
> What kind'a *work* you could do fuh me? Ah like a woman does *hard* work."
>
> A couple'a women around Mrs Bee laughed and slapped her. Mrs Bee and Mrs
> Sampson was respected leaders in the village. I'd never seen them get like children
> so, shuffling around.[31]

The infantilizing effect Burnham has on the women emphasizes how the discursive framework that underpins his dialogue—or rather monologue, for the
women remain silent—not only works to construct them as submissive but also
diverts attention from the political power that enables such domination, pack-
aging it instead as familial affection. Tellingly, Aunt Ruth, the only person who
stands up to Burnham, is already positioned outside the norms of female behavior by virtue of being an obeah woman. Refusing to conform to the patriarchal
model of dutiful child-wife, she insults the president over the lack of basic goods
in the co-op store.

This resistance to gender stereotypes resurfaces in less overt form in Lula,
who develops a conception of herself as possessing a "man-self" and a "she-self,"
either of which can come to the fore depending on the circumstances. Thus, as
O'Callaghan observes, "normative concepts of male and female are defamiliar-
ized."[32] It is in this connection that the novel perhaps retains something like
a utopian horizon, with the refusal to be limited by regulative gender categories bespeaking the possibility of resistance to the political structures that manipulate such categories for their own ends. The sense of a body unbounded by
normative constraints, meanwhile, might easily be projected into a figure for a
liberated body politic.

Ultimately this does not happen, and the novel's final image is of Lula's family preparing to migrate to Britain. In equally pessimistic vein, Narmala Shewcharan's *Tomorrow Is Another Day* (1994), which is similarly set amid the political
and social turmoil of Burnham's Guyana, chronicles the struggles of the Indo-
Guyanese politician Jagru Persaud, as well as the suffering and eventual suicide
of Chandi Panday. Once more the predatory character of the state is reflected
in predatory personal relationships. The family unit again functions as a site of
patriarchal oppression, most glaringly when Chandi is raped by her husband,
Lal. After the assault, Lal breaks down, and it is left to Chandi to comfort him:

> Awkwardly, she got up from the floor. She could not bear to listen to his sobbing
> and between anger and pity went to sit next to him. They sat together for a long

moment, the bitterness and anger which he had forced into the atmosphere dis-
sipating in the silence. He placed his hands around her tenderly. Chandi did not
resist his embrace. She was a good woman, had always been a good woman. How
could he have thought otherwise? She did not put the thought into words.[33]

Even now Chandi finds herself adopting the role of the submissive "good
woman" who offers only silent support to her husband. This image, however,
contrasts with the agency she otherwise displays throughout the novel as she
strives to raise her children. Her efforts culminate in her committing suicide
so that the family can claim the insurance money, a desperate act that clearly
signals the limits imposed on female action by society. It also stands in illuminating contrast to Lal's political career, in which the sacrifice he boasts of having
made as the price for his commitment to the Workers Party is the well-being of
his family: "How could I allow myself to be fed and housed and to be a cog in a
system which was allowing so many others to starve? . . . I have forgotten my
own tomorrows and those of my children."[34] As noble as these sentiments are,
they also suggest a dangerous separation of the party political battle from the
everyday battle for survival: caught up in the righteousness of his martyrdom,
Lal overlooks the added pressure that his behavior places on his wife. The novel
thus underscores the shortcomings of a nationalist politics that fails to address
wider issues of social equality.

The oppressiveness of the patriarchal family is also a central theme in Shani
Mootoo's *Cereus Blooms at Night* (1996), where it governs a whole series of enforced position takings and exclusions (in terms of ethnicity, gender, and sexuality) while also housing violently deformed sexual relations—here Chandin
Ramchandin's incestuous abuse of his daughter Mala. I will return to this novel
in detail later; suffice to say for now that it is set on a fictionalized version of
Trinidad (Lantanacamara), and that many of its concerns mediate the political
issues surrounding ethnic stereotyping and the attitude toward sexual minorities on that island. In particular, the prejudice and marginalization experienced
by the novel's gay characters—including Mala's mother and her lover Lavinia,
and Tyler, the nurse who cares for Mala in her old age—reflect a hostility toward homosexuality that many Caribbean governments have only reinforced,
criminalizing same-sex acts through legislation such as Trinidad and Tobago's
Sexual Offences Act of 1986 (which "effectively made lesbian sex a crime for the
first time, as well as re-inscribing the illegality of and harsh punishment for male
same-sex relations").[35] As M. Jacqui Alexander has shown, this state-sanctioned
discrimination is often the product of a desire by the ruling elite to strengthen
its authority by scapegoating minorities. Referring specifically to the 1986 act,
she notes that the state "moves to police the sexual and reinscribe inherited and
more recently constructed meanings of masculinity and femininity, while simultaneously mediating a political economy of desire in tourism that relies on the

sexualization and commodification of women's bodies. Further, the nationalist state mediates the massive entry of transnational capital within national borders, but blames sexual decadence (lesbian and gay sex and prostitution) for the dissolution of the nation."[36]

Let us turn now to Jamaica and the political and economic crises that took hold there during the 1970s. In 1972 the People's National Party (PNP) came to power under Michael Manley, raising hopes of a better future that were soon dashed as the country descended into turmoil. Promoting democratic socialism, the PNP sought to create a more equal society (and indeed had some early successes in this regard).[37] However, the opposition Jamaica Labour Party (JLP) launched a campaign to destabilize Manley, allegedly with the support of the CIA. As Brian Meeks describes it:

> In a series of sustained and increasingly heinous attacks, armed and trained gunmen, largely from the Opposition JLP, were able to undermine the rule of law and bring Jamaica to the brink of civil war. It is true that the PNP, with its significant mass base in the city, did indeed join battle, but . . . the brunt of the offensive was against PNP strongholds, with the twin purposes of demoralizing the hardcore democratic socialist support and discrediting Manley's ability to govern.[38]

Moreover, with the Jamaican economy suffering the effects of capital flight, Manley was forced to go to the IMF for a loan. The loan conditions became increasingly stringent after the initial test of compliance was failed on a technicality: "In May 1978 the new Extended Fund Facility was implemented and the real economic contraction began. Between 1978 and 1980, under the aegis of the IMF programme, the Cost of Living Index increased by some 40 percent; real wages declined by 20 to 30 percent and unemployment again began to increase."[39] Defeat followed for the PNP in the 1980 election. Under Manley's successor, the JLP's Edward Seaga, further IMF loans were contracted, and the adverse effects of structural adjustment programs more keenly felt.

A number of novels return to the events of this era. In Patricia Powell's *A Small Gathering of Bones* (1994), which deals with the impact of HIV/AIDS on Jamaica's gay community in the late 1970s, the political turmoil punctuates the text only at a few key moments. Nevertheless this is enough to imply a kind of parallel between the fragmentation of the nation-state and the decimation of the gay community, which in turn points obliquely to the pattern Alexander describes wherein the worsening of politico-economic conditions leads to greater discrimination against minorities. Far more explicitly, Margaret Cezair-Thompson's *The True History of Paradise* (1999), which is structured around the flight from Kingston of the middle-class Jean Landing in 1981, describes the violence that engulfs society as rival political supporters do battle and the poor and the dispossessed rail against their plight. As the conflict rages, women and minority groups again become the target for displaced anger at the social situation. "Rape had become so prevalent in the island," muses Jean, "it was beginning to seem like a war against women; rape of the nation's women, rich and poor, had become a casual and ubiquitous weapon, like stones in the hands of bad boys."[40] Later we see threats being directed at the theater company run by Jean's lesbian friend Faye, and then the murder of Faye's lover Pat.

But if *The True History of Paradise* offers a compelling portrait of the crisis tearing the Jamaican nation-state apart, its perspective on the underlying causes of this crisis is problematic. While it refers to socioeconomic and political factors like IMF loan conditions, U.S. interference, and capital flight, the novel also appears to intimate that the situation is somehow fated rather than historically contingent. As Helen Scott puts it, at some points the narrative suggests that "Jamaica's perennial problems are the inevitable product of a violent national personality," while at others "cultural creolization . . . is held responsible" (though this is quickly reevaluated as a positive influence). "In these ways," continues Scott, "it could be said that the novel mystifies social conditions—they are inexplicable and inevitable—and expresses the jaded perspective of the Jamaican bourgeoisie. The violence of slavery is equated with the violence of dispossessed youth; the novel's central identification is not with the hungry and homeless masses but with the elite whose luxury homes have become fortresses gated against them."[41] This circumscribed viewpoint is reinforced on a formal level, I would argue, by the narrative device through which a wider account is given of Jamaica's history—the series of first-person passages, voiced by Jean's ancestors, which are interspersed throughout the text. These record the lives and loves, the genealogical and romantic entanglements, of the speakers. However, they tend to privatize history back into individual biography (indeed, each flashback is headed by the speaker's name and dates of birth and death, recalling a biographical entry in an encyclopedia). The effect is to diminish a sense of the more complex, transindividual forces operating in society. This, I think, is decisive when it comes to the text's inability to articulate a way out of the political impasse of the narrative present: without that exploration of the structural factors at work in the crisis, or of the systematic oppression of the poorer classes that fuels their violent reprisals, it is impossible for the novel to move beyond the limited bourgeois perspective of its central characters and to project the kind of mass-based systemic change that might put an end to the cycle of misery and violence.

In this respect, *The True History of Paradise* compares unfavorably with Michelle Cliff's *No Telephone to Heaven*, published twelve years earlier. Set over much the same period, and drawing on several of the same historical incidents, Cliff's novel is more formally inventive and provides a much broader set of perspectives on the crisis gripping Jamaica. Through the character of Christopher in particular, we get an insight into the experiences and motivations of those "hungry and homeless masses" who tend to be viewed in Cezair-Thompson's text from the vantage point of the gated home. Moreover, *No Telephone to Heaven* is able to offer some sense of a possible response to the turmoil beyond despair or exile, precisely because of its attention to the structural and class coordinates of the conflict. Whereas the narrative of *The True History of Paradise* is spun out around that central thread of Jean fleeing the island, Cliff's text has running through it the activities of a group of guerrilla fighters, among them the pro-tagonist Clare Savage. At the end of the novel, the group prepares to launch an assault on a film set where a pseudohistorical movie about the Maroons is being shot by a joint American-British production company, the activities of which serve as a synecdoche for the baleful impact of transnational capital in Jamaica. The guerrillas' actions, which cause them eventually to be massacred by the army, reflect a desire to keep alive the possibility of revolutionizing society. The camp the fighters set up around the former home of Clare's grandmother, in the forests of the Cockpit Country, becomes a site in which socioeconomic relations different from those currently dominant can be maintained. The group culti-vates the land to achieve a level of self-sufficiency, bartering surplus goods for what they cannot produce and distributing the rest "to people around who did not have enough land to support them."[42] The guerrillas thus retain a commit-ment to an alternative form of social organization, itself inextricable from the continued pursuit of what is for them an as yet unrealized national liberationist struggle (as is implied by Clare's conversation with one of the guerrilla leaders before she joins up [189–96]).

This emphasis on the possibility of fulfilling the promise of national liberation is obviously very different from the thrust of *The True History of Paradise*, where the nation-state is abandoned altogether. In this regard, Cezair-Thompson's novel fits comfortably into the critical moment of postcolonial studies, which (in its dominant institutional avatar) has typically demonstrated an "undifferen-tiating disavowal of all forms of nationalism and a corresponding exaltation of migrancy, liminality, hybridity, and multiculturality."[43] I will return to this point in more detail later. But it is worth noting here that such disavowal rests in part on the idea put forward by a number of critics that nationalism will tend always toward patriarchy and heteronormativity, since as a totalizing discourse, it of necessity entails the marginalization of "others" as a way to preserve its singu-larity (such thinking being heavily influenced by poststructuralist theory and its general hostility to totalities).[44] Cliff's novel, however, implies that a national-ism could still be constructed wherein the freedom it promises would include freedom from patriarchy and heteronormativity. For example, it is a woman who assesses Clare's suitability to join the guerrillas, and the movement includes the transgendered Harry/Harriet, for whom gender realignment surgery might be possible only "when de revolution come" (168). This is a nationalism that looks to preserve Fanon's ideal of the national struggle as a gateway to social revolution, therefore, while also upholding the nation as a bulwark against the pressures of transnational capital.

However, as is made clear by the killing of the guerrillas by the army (who serve the interests not of their fellow citizens but of the filmmakers and foreign capital), resisting such pressures is extremely difficult. Oonya Kempadoo's more recent novel *Tide Running* (2001) underscores the far-reaching impact of the ever-deeper integration of the Caribbean into the world market. The book focuses on the friendship that a husband and wife, Englishman Peter and Trinidadian Bella, establish in Tobago with two local brothers, Ossi and Cliff. Cliff begins a casual sexual relationship with the couple, who now live permanently on the island, having previously visited as tourists: "The house, our holiday haven from Trinidad city life, seduced us into its womb, promising peace of mind, crime-free living and the blue Caribbean sea."[45] Their view of Tobago as a benign paradise is mirrored in their view of the relationship with Cliff as a harmless bit of fun between equals. In reality, both the island and the affair are marked by relations of domination and class inequality. Kempadoo's novel, then, raises issues around the impact of tourism, sexual exploitation, and intraregional power imbalances (in terms both of class and of nation insofar as Trinidad is shown to dominate over Tobago). But it also points to the persistence of imperialism under the new guise of globalization, the effects of which are most visible in everyday life in terms of the penetration of the "culture-ideology of consumption."[46]

Thus in *Tide Running* we see the saturation of Tobago with imported goods and multinational brand names to the extent that the "national dress . . . for old and young alike, rich and poor [was] Fila, Hilfiger, Adidas and now FUBU" (125). Likewise, imported cultural products, especially films and TV shows from the United States, encourage Tobagonians to identify with the lifestyles, values, and patterns of consumption that the imports glamorize. Cliff's sister Lynette, for instance, is in thrall to foreign food:

> In foreign they don't eat real food, that is why they look so, like dolly. Is only clean, wrap-up package food they does eat. Never see them cut up bloody meat or clean a chicken, just take out a thing from the freezer and *pop* it in the microwave and *wallah*. And Big Mac and KFC. All'a that does make them big-up and shine, skin smooth and fair, not a black hole in they teeth. Lynette feel if she really try, if she had money, she could make Baby Keisha look like foreign. (165)

The changes thereby wrought on habits, body image, and language ("*pop*," "*wallah*") are in evidence throughout the novel; they suggest a more intense version of the cultural imperialism we saw in *The Dragon Can't Dance* in the form of Fisheye's obsession with Hollywood Westerns. For example, the perception local young men have of themselves and their surroundings is shown to be mediated through the stereotypes of gangster life they have imbibed from cop shows and gangsta rap videos. One youth, Dobermann, acts as a bodyguard for a local criminal not because the man needs protection but because "Dobermann like to move like how he see on TV with them gangs, and real big-city blocks and alleyways, and police cars chasing you" (28).

Similarly, ideals of female beauty are increasingly being shaped by MTV videos and advertising visuals. When Bella's Trinidadian friend "Small Clit" arrives at the airport, Cliff and Ossi perceive her as a "Black Entertainment Princess come true":

> Visions of African Coca-Cola-bottle figures revolved in their eyeballs, curves with ball bearings for joints, firm flesh bouncing. Tall, neck long and straight, they didn't even have to see her face before the close-up of chocolatey-smooth full features smooched onto their screens. Eye-shadow-dark eyes flicking, mascara lashes on matt brown skin, glistening maroon lips parting. Till she cut the Toni Braxton video playing in their heads with a ice-water look and a long steups. (122–23)

The colonization of the lifeworld by imported commodities not only helps naturalize the systemic economic domination of peripheral nations by the core capitalist powers but also engenders, as Jennifer Rahim observes, quoting Merle Hodge, the "'mental desertion' of our environment."[47] Indeed, the novel describes something approaching the extreme dissociation from immediate reality we saw in Sánchez's *Macho Camacho's Beat* in the context of Puerto Rico's subordination to U.S. hegemony, suggesting that neoliberal globalization has enabled the extension of that level of domination (albeit on a more "informal" basis) to otherwise independent states.

This, however, is not to say that we are presented only with a straightforward antagonism between the global and the local. *Tide Running* shows clearly how international vectors of power intersect with national and regional ones. Signal in this regard is the way in which local elites can integrate profitably into the circuits of transnational capital, as well as appropriate global products as a means of reinforcing their position nationally. While far from the kind of jet-set VIP this description perhaps conjures up, Bella (who "used to work in film" [64]) nevertheless enjoys a certain elevated status in relation to the locals around her. While Cliff and his peers aspire to the lifestyles they see on TV, Bella lives a version of one of those lifestyles: she has the "film-style house" (49), the "car with a phone" (46), and other such luxuries. The prestige this bestows on her and Peter, moreover, is inextricable from their ability to seduce Cliff.

As the increasing penetration of transnational capital exacerbates these kinds of differentials in the integration of different classes and segments of the nation-state into the world economy, the state becomes ever more fragmented. The impact of export-processing zones (EPZs) in the Caribbean epitomizes such trends. Typically these zones involve transnational corporations subcontracting a segment of the production process to a local firm or subsidiary, taking advantage of exemptions granted by governments on taxes and levies. As Clive Thomas explains, the zones are "literal enclaves set aside exclusively for processing imported inputs for direct re-export to Western Europe, North America and Japan and, as enclaves, they fall outside the jurisdiction of the various national customs authorities."[48] They effectively split part of the island off from the wider body politic, thus rendering it an externally orientated hub locked into the imperial circuits of the global economy.

Such issues are mediated indirectly in Kempadoo's novel through the portrayal of Bella and Peter's house. This too is an enclave, differently integrated into the world market in comparison with the surrounding town of Plymouth: it is a place outside everyday Tobago life, one that makes you "feel like you on TV" (51), a place associated with the "foreign" or the global, a place in which leisure pursuits and fantasies can be indulged. Cliff is allowed temporary access to this space, but his admittance depends on his occupying a specific role: he must be "street" enough to generate the thrill of class difference in Bella and Peter's erotic play, but not threatening in the way other local young men are perceived to be. As Peter puts it when first evaluating Cliff and Ossi: "I like their slanty style! Couldn't see a trace of 'attitude,' even though they're from Plymouth. When you think of the kind of fellas you usually see hanging around there . . ." (58). Once the pressures of Cliff's social situation begin to tell and he starts stealing from the house, his privileges are terminated. While Bella and Peter retreat into the safety of their class, Cliff is sentenced to jail. Thus the inequalities that underlie the fantasy of equality and mutual recognition staged by their ménage à trois are exposed. The house is revealed as a space in which the bodies of the poor become resources to be consumed by the elite, just as global capital consumes the laboring bodies of the poor through operations such as EPZs.

The incarceration of Cliff, with which the novel ends, seems to confirm a pessimistic view of the island's future, for it suggests that there are few options beyond either succumbing to exploitative commercialization (becoming a playground for tourists, in other words) or falling into ruin. The way in which Cliff's body is imaged in the text figures this predicament. The sculpture of the "Little Black Boy" that Bella and Peter have in their bedroom—a "racially constructed prototype that marries aesthetic pleasure to the reification of the body as sexual commodity and plaything," as Rahim puts it—is the double of Cliff, whose own body is similarly aestheticized and sexualized under the couple's gaze.[49] When he can no longer be contained within this stereotype, that is, when his behavior disrupts the relationship with Bella and Peter, it is telling that he is quickly recontained, literally, in a prison cell, his body now battered and broken: "Is scraps I feel like too. Beat-up hand-me-down police scraps. How you does feel when the swelling gone down from a bruise—a shadow'a real pain left in your flesh" (200). The cell, moreover, evokes "the black holes of slave ships crossing the Atlantic" and thus the violated bodies of the enslaved.[50] This contrast in the different bodily images Cliff seems constrained to move between not only emphasizes how the old imperialist power relations still subsist under the more glossy economy of tourism, with its images of shiny, happy "natives," but also underscores the difficulty of exiting from such relations for fear of retribution and further immiseration.

I turn now to Cuba, a country that did delink itself from the global capitalist economy and suffered retribution in return—principally at the hands of the United States via its long-standing trade embargo. If many of the Anglophone Caribbean novels we have looked at reflect popular disappointment with the unfulfilled promises of national liberation, Cuba for a time represented "a rough facsimile of what Utopia might look like."[51] Indeed, Cuba seemed destined to realize the kinds of transformations that constitute the utopian horizon of the texts discussed in the previous chapter. It pursued the kind of social revolution at which elites in newly independent nations elsewhere in the Caribbean balked. Moreover, its reconstruction of society was meant to involve the total liberation of the body—the complete emancipation of all human senses and attributes— as a necessary step toward breaking decisively with the structures of imperialism. Hence Che Guevara's emphasis on the "new man and woman" to be created by the revolution: "The individual under socialism," he wrote, "despite apparent standardization, is more complete. . . . The individual will reach total consciousness as a social being, which is equivalent to the full realization as a human creature, once the chains of alienation are broken."[52]

Of course, the revolution's utopian project has experienced a sizable number of setbacks and shortfalls over the years. In fact, just as the nation-states evoked in texts like those of Cezair-Thompson and Kempadoo are beset by crises that threaten the integrity of the body politic, so Cuba, in the context of its very different relationship to the world system, has increasingly had to confront similar pressures.

The key reference point here obviously is the onset of the Período Especial in the early 1990s after the demise of the Soviet Union. Economic and political problems had been mounting in Cuba since the mid-1980s, but they came to a head once its main communist ally had collapsed.[53] Pedro Juan Gutiérrez's *Trilogía sucia de La Habana* (Dirty Havana Trilogy) (1998) begins in 1991 and covers the impact of the early years of the so-called Special Period. The novel is divided into three sections, the titles of which—"Marooned in No-Man's-Land," "Nothing to Do," and "Essence of Me"—give some indication of the sense of desperation that pervades the narrative, as well as of its emphasis on the progressive reduction of individuals to a basic instinct for self-preservation. Each section comprises a series of vignettes, fragmentary sketches, and stories that follow no linear narrative arc and are held together loosely only by the central presence of the narrator Pedro Juan (although even he is absent from some of the chapters, especially in the final section). This disjunctive, fractured form registers the increasing fragmentation of the state with the intensification of the crisis. Indeed, not only does it point to the crumbling of the planned economy, but the ad hoc and seemingly arbitrary narrative structure can be read also as mediating the contours of the ever more dominant informal economy, which is characterized by barter, insecure supply lines, and erratic exchanges.

Against this backdrop, the novel shows people struggling to satisfy the elementary demands of bodies that, lacking nourishment and stimulation, increasingly resemble little more than insentient matter:

> Everybody's always waiting, day after day. Nobody knows what they're waiting for. Time passes, and your brain goes numb, which is a good thing. When you don't want to think, it helps if your brain is numb. . . . I used to study, work hard, set goals for myself, and try to make my way in the world. Then everything fell apart and I ended up in this pigsty. Some people have scabies, others have lice or crabs. There's no food or money or work, and everyday there are more people.[54]

In this brutal environment, it seems to Pedro Juan that, ironically, a kind of primitive capitalism and a ruthless individuality have come to predominate, signaling the collapse of the heroic ideals of the revolution:

> There's no heroism in me, or in anybody else anymore. These days, no one is as stubborn as he was or has such a sense of duty or devotion to their work. The spirit of the age is commercial. Money. And if it's dollars, all the better. The stuff heroes are made of gets scarcer every day.
>
> That's why politicians and clergymen talk themselves hoarse urging loyalty and solidarity. . . . They think they can make everything change by sheer force of will, by spontaneous generation. But that's not the way things work. We human beings are still savages, treacherous and egotistical. We like to break off from the pack and keep watch from a distance, eluding the snapping jaws of our fellows. (354–55)

Tellingly, this passage appears in a chapter titled "The Cannibals," in which a neighbor of Pablo Juan's, recently arrived from the countryside, manages to establish himself in the city by selling pork liver. Only later is it discovered that the man actually works at the morgue and has been peddling human organs. Such accounts of degradation and of the reduction of the populace to brute, bodily necessity draw attention to the dystopian reality that has replaced the utopian ideal of liberating the senses and fully realizing the human being. The novel, in fact, is a scatological riot of corporeal activities and emissions, particularly shit and semen; there are constant references to the way people live surrounded by the sight and smell of excrement, especially from the animals kept in housing blocks as a source of food.[55] But this kind of carnivalesque excess reflects only lack and suffering.

It is interesting in this regard to compare Gutiérrez's work with an earlier Cuban novel, written just a few years after the revolution. Edmundo Desnoes's *Memorias del subdesarrollo* (Memories of Underdevelopment) (1967) explores the experiences of a middle-class writer struggling to adapt to life under socialism. Here we get some sense of the kind of alienated, reified body the revolution sets itself against. Referring to his ex-wife, who has fled the island, the narrator describes how she has left her things behind, her "clothes and shoes scattered about the closet": "It's almost as if I still had her here with me. She was actually made out of all those things she owned and wore. The objects that she used and was surrounded by were as much a part of Laura as her own body."[56] Similarly, he recognizes how his own corporeality has been molded by his class background: "I felt like puking, throwing up all my family, my business; the mediocrity of my class had been rammed into my stomach" (34). Throughout the novel, in fact, he is extremely conscious of the materiality of his body. Indeed, while less pronounced than in Gutiérrez's text, a narrative seam of scatological imagery is associated with the narrator, from the "sonorous belch" he emits at breakfast (20) to his frank admission "Feel like taking a crap" (73). The impression created is of the disruption and degradation of his hitherto contained, disciplined bourgeois habitus under the new socialist dispensation. "I'm turning into an animal" (20), he remarks after the aforementioned belch. Bearing in mind the middle-class identifications of the narrator, however, and his apparent distaste for the "rabble" who "have some money in their pockets now" (18–19), what he views as an encroaching animality can be read from another perspective as signaling the fall of the iniquitous social structures that enabled him to cultivate the patina of bourgeois distinction in the first place. In other words, despite his own skepticism, it is still possible to grasp the changes he refers to in terms of the utopian desire to construct the liberated "New Man" of the revolution.

In *Dirty Havana Trilogy*, by contrast, the fear of "turning into an animal" has moved from being an expression of disquiet at the loss of middle-class status to representing something more literal in the context of the general populace's desperate struggle for survival. The transformations in the body evident now are produced by malnourishment. In such circumstances, Pedro Juan suggests, the ideal of the New Man is nothing more than an anachronism: "It's a new era. All of a sudden, money is necessary. As always, money crushes everything in its path. Thirty-five years spent constructing the new man. And now it's all over. Now we've got to make ourselves into something different, and fast" (99). The novel also serves as a reminder, then, that the kinds of ideas we examined in the preceding chapter, such as the significance of religio-cultural rituals of degradation to the production of a narrative form capable of articulating an emancipatory break with a reified reality, must always be read back into their historical and sociopolitical context. It would not be hard to envisage, in a situation like the one described by Gutiérrez, an appeal to collectivity that, as it were, celebrated degradation—in the need for austerity and sacrifices on the part of the masses—in the interests of maintaining a faltering status quo rather than exploding it.

So have the aesthetics of the body, of the descent into the massy depths of material reality, lost their utopian dimension in Gutiérrez's novel? Do they now register only a dystopia of suffering flesh? Not quite, I would argue. The carnality, the sheer sense of corporeality, that permeates *Dirty Havana Trilogy* can be read also as an indication of a continued investment in the ideal of freedom from domination. Guillermina de Ferrari's discussion of the novel's "dirty realist" style is helpful here. Drawing on Bourdieu's critique of Kant's notion of pure aesthetics (in which Bourdieu argues that insofar as aesthetic contemplation rests on freedom from necessity, it can be used in the service of reinforcing class distinction), she asserts: "If behind the denial of corporeality implied in the notion of pure aesthetic appreciation lies the legitimate claim to dominate a social order, what we find in Gutiérrez's writing is precisely the impossibility of sustaining such a claim. For the political value of *Trilogía sucia de la Habana* resides in its abolition of the distinctions between nature and culture, thus redefining the assumptions that inform—and are informed by—aesthetic judgment."[57] Gutiérrez's emphasis on bodilyness and animality, then, upholds a resistance to the reifying effect induced by the separation of culture from nature. By so doing, it projects, implicitly, the possibility of renewing a revolutionary politics capable of confronting the current crisis and liberating individuals from the grip of sheer necessity and the all-consuming struggle for self-preservation.

If nation-states of different kinds across the Caribbean are so beset by difficulties—internally divided on the one hand, and battered from without by the vagaries of the capitalist world system on the other—should the modern nation-state project as a whole be abandoned? This, as has been suggested, seems to be the implication behind Cezair-Thompson's *The True History of Paradise*, an impulse that positions it neatly in relation to the dominant assumptions of postcolonialist-poststructuralist theory. That theory has tended not only to disavow all forms of nationalism but also to construe the migrant, the nomad, the exile, and the diasporic subject as paradigmatic of the postcolonial condition—not least because such figures are viewed as disrupting national boundaries and subverting the "unisonant discourse" of nationalism.[58] As noted in the introduction, the concept of hybridity is frequently invoked in these formulations, where it is used to name the ability of the marginal to destabilize the self-proclaimed unity and originality of social identities. In this way, hybridity is made consonant with postnationalism, itself often understood as corresponding to a world in which globalization has rendered the nation-state obsolete. It is with this in mind that I return to Shani Mootoo's *Cereus Blooms at Night*. The central concerns of Mootoo's narrative—hybridity, marginality, exile, the discursive construction of history, the relationship between the oral and the written—are of the kind that tend to appeal to postcolonial criticism. But the way in which the text deals with the idea of the nation and of national community raises the most interesting questions.

In this context, it is worth looking first at a reading of *Cereus Blooms at Night* that to some extent conforms to the protocols of postcolonialist-poststructuralist theory. Grace Kyungwon Hong's "'A Shared Queerness': Colonialism, Transnationalism, and Sexuality in Shani Mootoo's *Cereus Blooms at Night*" is an insightful commentary on the novel's staging of queerness and its implications for rethinking relations of gender, sexuality, race, and power. Referencing M. Jacqui Alexander (whose work was cited to similar ends in my own earlier discussion of *Cereus*), Hong succinctly delineates the connection between state economic interests and the production of "deviancy":

> In the contemporary era, Caribbean nation-states attempt to reconsolidate a sense of national identity undermined by transnational economic restructuring. They do so by blaming the dissolution of the nation-state not on such processes as structural adjustment, privatization, and international investment but on those figures that are defined as deviant and threatening because of their lack of "propriety" and "morality," such as women, prostitutes, and homosexuals.[59]

This, I think, provides an excellent overview of the way in which a particular form of nationalism—its trajectory inseparable from the impact that specific international pressures have on the state—descends into exclusivity and chauvinism as the ruling elite struggles to maintain its position. But Hong moves immediately from this nuanced critique to a disavowal of nationalism as such:

> If propriety and morality as mechanisms of discipline reproduce the variety of nationalisms that sustains the transnational economic restructuring of Trinidad and Tobago, [*Cereus*] . . . is evidence of the impossibility of such a nationalist project. This impossibility is registered in the fact that such processes must also create deviant, disorderly subjects who cannot fit a nationalist definition of morality and thus must imagine new modes of affiliation than that of nationalism.[60]

The poststructuralist inflection of this argument is driven home a few lines later when Hong makes clear that what really tells against nationalism is the totalizing quality of its discourse. Hong writes that her essay approaches *Cereus Blooms at Night* as "identifying the desire for totality, resolution, or wholeness as fundamentally nationalist and colonial."[61] Such a formulation, which implies that nationalism will only ever be colonial, recalls the tendency among many postcolonialist critics to view "anti-colonial nationalism (whether bourgeois or liberationist) as . . . a *mimetic* discourse—that is, as a metapractice, one modeled—in certain key aspects, at least—on diverse metropolitan nation-projects and subordinate, for this reason, to their forms and protocols."[62]

If nationalism and the nation are anathema, then, what are those "new modes of affiliation" Hong speaks of? And where are they to be grounded? It is here that the problems with Hong's position become most apparent. The new modes of affiliation she discerns in *Cereus Blooms at Night* are defined as "existing in the interstices of colonial and neocolonial regimes of rule," and as resisting (here she cites Gayatri Gopinath) "the logic of blood, patrilineality, and patriarchal authority."[63] However, their most important feature, repeatedly emphasized in the essay, is that of their falling outside national modes of belonging. But this does not answer the question of how they might become nonmarginalized phenomena, embedded in collectively recognized structures that would allow those who identify with them to do so freely. Without such structures, what is to stop their continued repression by "colonial and neocolonial regimes of rule"? These issues are not addressed: having begun by identifying the socioeconomic factors contributing to the state's production and regulation of deviant subjects, what should be the next step—a class critique of the type of nationalism promulgated by the ruling elite and its connection to their comprador status within the capitalist world system—is forgone by Hong in favor of a repudiation of nationalism *tout court* on discursive grounds. Consequently she gives no sense of what might negate the material conditions that incubate oppressive attitudes toward certain groups in the first place. Hong frequently gives the impression that the discursive destabilization of nationalist representations alone would be sufficient. Though she remarks in the conclusion that "'queer' in and of itself does not necessarily disrupt national modes of belonging," she does not follow through on this point, so that the social and economic dimensions of the struggle remain in suspension.[64]

A good part of the reason for this impasse, I suggest, is that one of the key grounds on which such issues might have been worked out has already been foreclosed. The nation-state as a site in which the poor and the marginalized can potentially make some claim on power—a site that does allow for the possibility of instantiating an emancipatory social order and for transforming local or embodied subaltern (or in this case "deviant') knowledge into a wider collective consciousness—is renounced, without anything that possesses the same kind of capacity for popular empowerment being put forward in its place.[65] Moreover, to return to a point reiterated throughout this study, insofar as imperialism continues to operate in terms of a hierarchically structured world system of nation-states, it is "only on the basis of nationalitarian struggle—that is, of a (global) struggle for socialist internationalism, but one centred (locally) on the nation—that the overthrow of imperialist social relations can plausibly be envisaged."[66] Simply to jettison the nation-state in light of its shortcomings, then, is not only idealist but also exacerbates the uncertainties around how any new form of community might be realized; for even if it is not an end point in itself, the nation-state at least provides the grounds on which to resist the imperialist machinations that Hong pointed to initially as central to the oppressive power relations maintained by the ruling elite.

If I find Hong's essay problematic on these terms, however, that is not to say I think her reading of Mootoo's novel is wholly inaccurate. Indeed, her theoretical preconceptions, and her dismissal of nationalism in particular, would seem at first glance to find a ready ally in *Cereus Blooms at Night*. But to the extent that she gets the latter right, as it were, she inadvertently reveals a dilemma the text itself in fact tries to resolve in its narrative unconscious. That it attempts such a resolution, moreover, again raises questions about Hong's approach.

Now, certainly she is correct when she argues that the novel proposes new modes of affiliation. These are linked to the notion of hybridity via the image of botanical transplantation. Throughout the book there are instances when plant cuttings (usually cereus clippings) are transferred between places and people, with each exchange marking the formation of an alliance between those possessing marginalized identities. So, for example, we have Lavinia, the daughter of the white missionary Reverend Thoroughly, taking cuttings from her garden for Sarah Ramchandin to plant in hers. The subsequent hybridization of Sarah's garden foreshadows the eventual relationship between Lavinia and Sarah, a cross-race, cross-class, same-sex alliance that stands in opposition to the prevailing social norms. Equally important is the cereus clipping planted in the yard of the almshouse where Mala Ramchandin lives. This comes to symbolize the nexus of connections that develop between Mala and Tyler, her cross-dressing gay nurse; between Mala and her rediscovered childhood sweetheart Ambrose; between Tyler and Ambrose's daughter Otoh, who lives as a man; and between Mala, Tyler, and Mr. Hector, the almshouse's gardener, whose brother was sent away on account of his homosexuality. In all these examples, the (racial, sexual, gender, class) hybrids or affiliations that emerge suggest the possibility of a new kind of collectivity. But we have here also two different ways of understanding hybridity and community. On the one hand, Lavinia and Sarah's hybrid relationship is about mobility, about the necessity of leaving the garden (a symbol of rootedness and emplacement) and moving away from the island. Hybridity in this instance is associated with migration and diaspora, just as it tends to be in postcolonialist-poststructuralist discourse. On the other hand, the series of hybrid associations that cluster around the characters linked to the almshouse suggest something closer to hybridity as indigenization, as a process inextricable from adaptation to, and implantation in, a particular environment.

In the novel, the latter kind of hybridity is presented as highly precarious. Indeed, for the most part it appears something of an impossibility, since staying in a place frequently results only in ruin: Mala and her sister Asha are left behind when their mother elopes with Lavinia, and the consequence is Chandin's abuse of Mala; Mala remains in her home after the death of her father and descends into madness. By contrast, flight from the island is presented as synonymous with liberty and with the potential fulfillment of hybrid identities, as in the case of Lavinia and Sarah's migration to the "Shivering Northern Wetlands" (England). We see this also in the sequence in which Mala's reminiscences of her childhood escapades of sneaking into other people's houses are interwoven with the invasion of her garden by the police. Encouraging her childhood self to flee her pursuers, she imagines soaring into the air and away from her troubles: "Down below, her island was soon lost among others, all as shapeless as specks of dust adrift on a vast turquoise sea."[67] On one level, then, it is possible to read these examples as evidence of the way the text registers current concerns over the nation-state and the problematic position of certain groups within it, the implication seemingly being—in line with Hong's interpretation—that the nation-state must ultimately be abandoned if freedom from oppression is to be secured.

And yet, staying with the example of Mala, though she might dream of flight, in reality she remains rooted in her garden (almost literally, given the way she merges or hybridizes with the plant life). Even when she is removed, a new community coalesces around her at the almshouse, reflected in the implanting of the cereus clipping. The hybrid relationships that make up this community, therefore, imply the necessity not of abandoning a locality but of staking a claim to it on the terms of the otherwise excluded, thereby raising the possibility of overturning the dominant order (symbolized by the way Tyler at the almshouse becomes increasingly ostentatious in the display of his gay identity). In this context, moreover, the nation-state surreptitiously enters back into the equation. It reemerges, I would argue, as the never explicitly articulated answer to an unspoken question: that is, how is that claim of belonging to be articulated and sustained? In other words, how might all those hybrid alliances the text depicts be freed from victimization and marginality to become the grounds of a new social order? The political unconscious of the text attempts to solve this dilemma, generating a series of images that seem to serve as figures for the nation-state as the arena through which any struggle of this kind must pass.

The almshouse itself is one such figure: it is a world within a world, in which characters can begin to express previously repressed identities. Here, for instance, Tyler can explore his feminine side and pursue a relationship with the transgendered Otoh. The family is another example: if Mala's family home in which she is abused by her father mediates the nation-state as oppressor—as purveyor of institutionalized discrimination via legislation such as Trinidad and Tobago's Sexual Offences Act—then the adoptive family gathered around her by the end of the novel could be said to mediate the potential for a different sort of national project, one predicated on an openness to marginal subjects. Shalini Puri's analysis of Erna Brodber's novel *Myal* (1988) offers an interesting point of comparison here. "The national community imagined by *Myal*," writes Puri,

> disrupts pure lines of descent and filiation, . . . [replacing] conventional patriarchal narratives of the nation-as-family with a feminist narrative of the nation-as-*adoptive*-family. . . . What are the stakes of this recasting? Despite its vigorous critique of exclusionary forms of black nationalism, *Myal*'s continuing interest in nationalism is signalled by its adherence to the nationalist trope of the family—which it transforms. Instead of serving as the fundamental building block of national sameness (or alternatively as the transcendence of difference), the family in *Myal* becomes itself a unit of difference upon which the nation is built.[68]

Mootoo's novel, then, with its insistent return to the trope of the family, seems unconsciously to be registering the necessity of reckoning with the nation-state insofar as some ground must be located on which the struggle for equality can be prosecuted. Hong's "new modes of affiliation" are certainly present here, reflected in the image of a new kind of family. But this image emphasizes too how such modalities cannot simply fall outside national forms of belonging; they will at least have to engage with them, even if their terminus lies in some other type of social formation.

The abiding significance of the nation-state in this regard has been evident in a range of Caribbean novels since the 1980s, despite the fashion for de-emphasizing nationalist concerns in much postcolonial criticism. We have already observed its import in Cliff's *No Telephone to Heaven*, where a renewed liberationist movement is to make room for previously marginalized identities like that of Harry/Harriet. In Chamoiseau's *Biblique des derniers gestes*, the unforgoability of national liberation struggle is affirmed via the protagonist Balthazar Bodule-Jules, a guerrilla fighter who has participated in anticolonial resistance worldwide. But here too there is recognition that the nationalist project must be reconfigured, especially along the axes of sexuality and gender. The point is neatly summarized by Balthazar's remark that in fighting for various causes, he has not always managed to identify sufficiently with those he is fighting for, and that in particular he has been "not woman enough everywhere" (Pas assez femme un peu partout).[69] Similarly, Lawrence Scott's *Witchbroom* (1992) is very much an epic of the nation, but a revisionary one aimed at projecting a more expansive Trinidadian identity. Narrated by the hermaphrodite Lavren (who "levitated between worlds. S/he hung between genders. . . . S/he was pigmented between races"),[70] the novel underscores the necessity of uncovering the multiplicity of histories and voices present in Trinidad. Indeed, we find diversity and hybridity and ambivalence enough here to satisfy the most ardent of postmodernist critics; and yet the text's final concern is how to articulate those differences together, in a totality, as a whole, as a national community—something the utopian vision of carnival near the close of the book makes clear by way of its riotous celebration of Trinidadian history, geography, and culture.

It is also worth mentioning again Brodber's *Myal*, which, as Puri's comments cited earlier suggest, is equally concerned with rethinking the nationalist project. And there is the work of Lovelace, too, whose emphasis on holding to the promise of national independence I discussed in chapter 3. Significantly, Brodber and Lovelace have been accorded relatively little attention in postcolonial studies, and it would seem that a good part of the reason for this is their continued concern with nationalism and the nation, with locality and emplacement.[71]

In this context, it is interesting to consider a recent novel that has garnered much critical acclaim and might appear at first to fit more readily with the theoretical paradigms of global mobility, migration, diaspora, and postnationalism. Junot Díaz's *The Brief Wondrous Life of Oscar Wao* (2008), written in English by a U.S.-Dominican, recounts the struggles of the titular Oscar, a socially awkward sci-fi obsessive, as he negotiates life as part of the Dominican diaspora in New York. From the outset, however, it is clear that the Dominican nation-state remains integral to the narrative. The book's second epigraph is taken from Derek Walcott's "The Schooner *Flight*" and quotes its well-known line "either I'm nobody, or I'm a nation." This proposition resonates throughout the novel as Oscar's attempts to realize his desires become increasingly inseparable from a confrontation with the traumatic history of the Dominican Republic.

Haunting the text, in particular, is the imprint left by the violence and repression of the Trujillo dictatorship, figured in the image of the faceless man glimpsed at key points in the story, and interpreted colloquially in terms of the force of *fukú*—a "curse or a doom of some kind; specifically the Curse and the Doom of the New World."[72] The silences imposed by the dictatorship are symbolized by a book with blank pages, which appears in Oscar's dreams after he is badly beaten by thugs working for a Dominican police officer whose girlfriend Oscar has latched on to. The blank book surfaces again at the end of the novel as part of a recurring dream had by one of the narrators, Yunior. In the dream, Oscar (wearing a mask but sometimes pictured as having no face) holds the book up to Yunior, the implication being that the story of the nation must be written if the disfiguring effects of the past are to be overcome. Tellingly, the novel adopts something like the spiraling form I discussed in the previous chapter: even before Oscar returns to the island, the narrative (via the stories of other members of his family) has repeatedly circled back over Dominican history, restaging it to show its continuing import for understanding the present.

As with all the novels discussed here, this emphasis on the nation-state does not preclude or lessen the importance of the international context, nor of the impact of migration or diaspora. Indeed, Díaz's novel is explicit in drawing attention to the interconnectedness of these phenomena, both in politico-economic terms and with respect to the collective imaginary. Moreover, *The Brief Wondrous Life of Oscar Wao* illustrates clearly how modalities of national belonging are not necessarily incompatible with ideas of global hybridity or transnational creolization. The novel mediates the twin heritages of a hyphenated U.S.-Dominican identity: Caribbean myths and legends are articulated alongside references to U.S. pop culture, particularly comic books and graphic novels; Dominican phrases and inflections pepper the text just as much as North American slang. But these intermixtures become a means to retell the history of the Dominican nation, recoding historical discourse in such a way as to reinvent how the past is understood. Thus, living in Santo Domingo during the Trujillo era is described as "a lot like being in that famous *Twilight Zone* episode that Oscar loved so much, the one where the monstrous white kid with the godlike powers rules over a town" (224); popular accounts of Trujillo's power are alternately referred to as resembling "some New Age Lovecraft shit" and a "figment of our Island's hypertrophied voodoo imagination" (246); while Haiti's François "Papa Doc" Duvalier becomes "P.Daddy" (111). Unlike in, say, *Macho Camacho's Beat*, where U.S. mass culture is experienced as an overwhelming deluge engendering only alienation from local reality, here it is subject to creolization as indigenization (the difference stemming in part perhaps from the position of Díaz's characters within the United States, which enables them to reappropriate such culture more easily). Thus the national history dramatized through these refunctioned cultural forms and discourses stages in its very articulation the imbrication of island and diaspora.

The nation-state therefore remains both a social and political reality to be reckoned with, as well as a site of emancipatory possibility. Yet it is also undoubtedly in crisis, weakened by the restructuring of the global economic system. Where, then, does one go from here? I want to conclude this study by considering a third term that interposes itself between the nation-state and the world system: the region. For many Caribbean writers and thinkers, the region stands as an important reference point. Politically speaking, regional unity offers one possible means by which a framework—more powerful than anything small island states could construct individually—might be created to provide protection from external interference. As it is, balkanization and the playing off of one state against another have been consistent features of imperialist policy in the region. To take just one example: the Caribbean Basin Initiative launched by President Reagan in the early 1980s, which afforded preferential trade benefits to Caribbean countries in return for opening up markets to private capital from the United States, fostered beggar-thy-neighbor economic policies that worked against the long-term interests of the broad mass of Caribbean peoples.[73]

The idea of cultivating pan-Caribbean unity as a means of better protecting collective interests is a long-standing one. As far back as 1722, Père Labat was describing the Caribbean islands as "all together, in the same boat, sailing on the same uncertain sea."[74] In the nineteenth century, thinkers from the Hispanic Caribbean including José Martí, Antonio Maceo, Eugenio María de Hostos, Ramón Eneterio Betances, and Gregorio Luperón sought to establish an Antillean Confederation, comprising Hispaniola, Cuba, and Puerto Rico, as a bulwark against U.S. and Spanish imperialism. For Luperón, it was "senseless" to be "Dominican but not Antillean, to know our destiny and to divorce it from the destiny of the Antilles."[75] The same emphasis on realizing national goals through regional cooperation resurfaced in the Anglophone Caribbean in the mid-twentieth century as part of the drive for independence. Writers and activists at the time like C. L. R. James and Eric Williams promoted "a vision of the Caribbean as a single region with a shared historical experience of genocide, metropolitan rivalry and wars, the plantation system, slavery and indentureship."[76] Economists such as Arthur Lewis, meanwhile, were advocating economic integration as a means of overcoming the problems of size and scale associated with small island states.

This period of regionalist enthusiasm culminated in the establishment of the West Indian Federation in 1958. The federation collapsed after just four years, however, as more narrowly insular interests reasserted themselves. For the governments of Jamaica and Trinidad, the two largest islands involved, it was felt that national independence could best be achieved alone (they were particularly concerned that their greater wealth would be used to subsidize the poorer states). But for the prominent federation advocate C. L. R. James, such thinking was flawed: the problem was that the federation had not dared be regional enough; only a commitment to a genuine pan-Caribbean unity could break the imperial fetters that still bound the islands to the metropole and guarantee national liberation in the fullest sense.[77] Moreover, James considered that the development of a national consciousness would of necessity involve the development of a regional consciousness, since the national would find its ultimate expression only in the regional. In short, a regional Caribbean identity was essential for any individual country to possess a fully national identity.

This imbrication of nation and region is discernible across a broad swath of Caribbean literature: writing that aims to give full expression to a specific place frequently becomes inscribed with an impulse to look out to the region to achieve that expression. The examples are numerous—we might cite here work by Alexis, Carpentier, Condé, Guillén, Luis Palés Matos, Pedro Mir, Kamau Brathwaite, Daniel Maximin, Merle Collins, and Ana Lydia Vega—but let us take just two from Glissant's oeuvre. Unsurprisingly given his theorization of Antillanité, Glissant's novels are marked by the centrifugal pull of the region even as—or rather precisely because—they seek to uncover a national, Martinican history. In *Malemort* (1975), Dlan, Médellus, and Silacier, struggling against the corrosive impact of departmentalization, look out to sea to the surrounding islands and begin to grasp the progressive potential of intra-Caribbean relationships, a potential hitherto untapped due to an inability to hear "the scratching of so many lands around, who we do not know are calling out to us" (le grattement de tant de terres alentour dont nous ne savons pas que le cri nous hèle).[78] In *La case du commandeur* (1981), Marie Celat responds to that call, attempting to establish a dialogue with the archipelago: "Marie Celat ran to places on the sea shore from where on a clear day you could make out Dominica to the north . . . or Saint Lucia to the south. . . . She called out to the islands. Respond, Dominica. I call you to a conference. . . . Ho, respond Jamaica. Come to the birth and call in dancing, Haiti ho Haiti."[79] Significantly, Glissant was responding to a period of crisis (the "cultural genocide" of assimilation), and in this his work resonates with a point Selvon made regarding popular expressions of Caribbeanness, namely, that "the dream of a common nation is not only grass-rooted in the masses, but that it persists in manifesting itself at critical times in our history."[80]

This has been borne out more recently by a growing emphasis on the potential advantages of regional unity in the context of the destabilizing impact of the transformations in the world economy. Among political commentators, Andrés Serbin has spoken of the need for a "regional epistemic community" as part of any strategy for dealing with the consequences of globalization.[81] Brian Meeks, meanwhile, has argued for "deeper regional integration" as one of a series of measures for future development. He stresses the greater clout the region would have on the world stage if "some national sovereignty is shared in the interest of a larger Caribbean of some thirty-five million persons . . . which could then speak more cohesively about human resources and market share."[82]

At the same time, many novelists have been moved to restate the connections and commonalities that exist between Caribbean peoples. We have seen renewed efforts to think the area from a regional perspective (often via the optic of creolization) and to underscore the significance of a pan-Caribbean identity to national and local forms. Thus Mayra Montero, whose works "endeavour to expand trans-Caribbean consciousness," points to "Afro-Caribbean spirituality" as a potential "unifying dimension of Caribbean cultural identity."[83] In the Dutch Caribbean, the Curaçaoan author Frank Martinus Arion has declared "Caribbeanness" to be "our first hope and goal," and for writers like Lasana Sekou, Drisana Deborah Jack, and Esther Grumbs from the Dutch Windward Islands, "Caribbean unity, a pan-Caribbean outlook, is a constant."[84] In the Francophone Caribbean, where the Créolistes had concluded *Éloge de la créolité* by calling for the creation of a "Caribbean confederation," a group of writers (including Chamoiseau and Glissant) published in 2000 the "Manifeste pour un projet global" (Manifesto for a Global Project). This ambitious proposal, responding to both economic and environmental concerns, called for the transformation of the French *départements* into a regional green zone, specializing in the production of high-quality organic products. The project inevitably has wider pan-Caribbean implications, for as the manifesto's signatories note, it could not be developed "without the effort and support of the other countries of the Caribbean or of the continental neighbours of French Guiana. This new space of solidarity should constitute itself into one of the blue [that is, unpolluted] zones of the world."[85]

Now, in all these formulations, the affirmation of a regional identity does not mean local and national forms are superseded. Rather, each is seen as imbricated in—and as capable of functioning as a particular form of expression of—the other. Aimed at helping to shore up resistance to global imperialism, these broader identifications or alliances nevertheless work on the basis of valorizing and securing the equality of the social units on which they are built. To not do so is to risk the assertion of solidarity becoming, at best, expressive only of the interests of the more powerful groups involved, and, at worst, an empty gesture. This returns us, then, to the injunction that any conception of how the broad mass of Caribbean peoples might be empowered must be predicated on some material ground, on some real or possible social unity, if it is to carry any progressive weight. In this context, the nation-state again presents itself as an indispensable site of struggle. The emphasis in much contemporary theory on rootlessness, nomadism, migrancy, and postnationalism seems to do away with such grounds before many states have even achieved political sovereignty in any meaningful sense.

The same issues pertain when it comes to broader, global forms of association and affiliation. Despite some calls for a new cosmopolitanism predicated on postnational perspectives, the nation-state will of necessity remain integral to the construction of genuinely progressive forms of transnational solidarity—to internationalism, in other words. As Timothy Brennan has noted, "internationalism seeks to establish global relations of respect and cooperation, based on acceptances of differences in polity as well as culture. It does not aim to erase such differences juridically, before material conditions exist for doing so equitably. *Inter*nationalism does not quarrel with the principle of *national* sovereignty, for there is no other way under modern conditions to secure respect for weaker societies or peoples."[86]

Fanon brings this point home in the conclusion to his chapter on national culture in *The Wretched of the Earth*: it is, he writes, "at the heart of national consciousness that international consciousness lives and grows."[87] Four years before this,[88] Selvon too had deftly highlighted the issues at stake here when, in *An Island Is a World* (1955), the protagonist Foster ponders the limitations of his earlier belief that he could live as a kind of detached global citizen, free in his unbelonging: "You can't belong to the world, because the world won't have you. The world is made up of different nations, and you've got to belong to one of them."[89] So long as this remains the case, the nation-state will remain an unforgoable "transitional arena" in the struggle against imperialism.[90] As such it will continue to be mediated in Caribbean literature concerned with projecting the possibility of reconfiguring social relations. And insofar as the body remains a key medium through which power relations are both consolidated and contested, it too will continue to occupy a privileged position in this literature, imaging the effects of domination, but also figuring the potential for the utopian transformation of the social world.

Notes

Introduction

1. See René Dépestre, *Le métier à metisser* (Paris: Éditions Stock, 1998), 49–55. See also Michael Richardson, ed., *Refusal of the Shadow: Surrealism and the Caribbean* (New York: Verso, 1996).

2. J. Michael Dash, *Literature and Ideology in Haiti, 1915–1961* (London: Macmillan, 1981), 160.

3. Michel-Rolph Trouillot, *Haiti: State against Nation: The Origins and Legacy of Duvalier* (New York: Monthly Review Press, 1990), 133.

4. Martin Munro, *Exile and Post-1946 Haitian Literature* (Liverpool: Liverpool University Press, 2007), 25.

5. "Des espoirs démocratiques et décoloniaux que l'immédiat après-guerre avait allumés sur tous les continents. . . . Nous voulions . . . démystifier une société encore profondément tributaire d'un héritage colonial que la *Révolution haïtienne* (1791–1804) n'était pas parvenue à effacer de notre vie nationale." Dépestre, *Le métier*, 50; translation mine. Unless otherwise stated, all translations are my own. For ease and consistency, where English translations of works are available, I have tried to use them (except in instances where I felt a particular point of language use was better served in an alternative translation). The source language quotations for my own translations are given in the notes.

6. On the fallout from the 1946 revolution, see David Nicholls, *From Dessalines to Duvalier: Race, Colour, and National Independence in Haiti* (London: Macmillan Caribbean, 1996), 183–90; and Trouillot, *Haiti: State against Nation*, 13–36.

7. By "Caribbean" I mean not only the islands of the archipelago and the continental enclaves of Belize and the Guyanas but also the circum-Caribbean coastal zones. In this I follow the lead of theorists like Édouard Glissant and Rex Nettleford, whose conceptions of, respectively, the "Other America" and "Plantation America" map an area stretching from the southern United States, down through the archipelago, and into Brazil. See Édouard Glissant, *Caribbean Discourse: Selected Essays*, trans. J. Michael Dash (Charlottesville: University Press of Virginia, 1989), 114–17, 144–50; Rex Nettleford, *Caribbean Cultural Identity* (Kingston, Jamaica: Ian Randle, 2003), 114–15, 197n252.

My intention in this book is to approach Caribbean literature as much as possible from a comparative regional perspective, examining work from across its linguistically diverse literary traditions. While the world-historical forces that have affected the Caribbean (colonialism, imperialism, and neoliberal globalization, for example) have been differentially articulated and unevenly registered across and within societies in the region, at the same time certain similarities or likenesses of the unlike can be detected in the effects of, and responses or opposition to, such phenomena. I am interested not only in the varied ways Caribbean novels encode these same forces, with differences evident in relation to the specificity of different social instances, national contexts, cultural or literary traditions, and so forth, but also, again, in the similarities or likenesses of the unlike found in literary production from across the region. Regrettably, however, my own linguistic shortcomings mean work from the Dutch Caribbean receives relatively less attention, as does literature produced in a number of the region's creole and indigenous languages (Haitian creole being an obvious omission, for example).

8. In taking 1945 as the start point for this study, I do not wish to minimize the importance of Caribbean literature written before this date or to suggest that it marks some kind of absolute break with what went before. Indeed, I draw on works from this earlier period, albeit in arguing that important formal differences are evident in many of the post-1945 novels as they respond, in however mediated a fashion, to changing social and political circumstances. Nevertheless I recognize and hope to avoid the danger (particularly where the Anglophone Caribbean is concerned) of perpetuating what Alison Donnell has identified as a tendency to marginalize pre-1945 works or to canonize only those that fit a nationalist entelechy. See Donnell, *Twentieth-Century Caribbean Literature: Critical Moments in Anglophone Literary History* (London: Routledge, 2006).

9. Adriana Méndez Rodenas, "Literature and Politics in the Cuban Revolution: The Historical Image," in *A History of Literature in the Caribbean*, vol. 1, *Hispanic and Francophone Regions*, ed. A. James Arnold (Philadelphia: John Benjamins, 1992), 283.

10. Frantz Fanon, *The Wretched of the Earth*, trans. Constance Farrington (London: Penguin, 2001), 193.

11. Trouillot, *Haiti: State against Nation*, 25. Trouillot's definition shares something with Benedict Anderson's now famous description of nations as imagined political communities, although Trouillot is keen to emphasize the distinction that the "nation is not a political fiction; it is a fiction *in politics*" (26). I follow Trouillot here because his approach—particularly his interrogation of the relationship between state and nation—underscores the material relations that determine the context in which such imagining takes place, something that has been obscured in certain strands of postcolonial studies where, as Neil Larsen observes, the idea of nation as narration has led to the reduction of the nation to nothing but text, nothing but "a formal construct, a quasi-absolute contingency of form, subject to perpetual reformulation by the 'national' subjects themselves." See Larsen, *Determinations: Essays on Theory, Narrative, and Nation in the Americas* (New York: Verso, 2001), 86.

12. On these points, see Neil Lazarus, *Nationalism and Cultural Practice in the Postcolonial World* (Cambridge: Cambridge University Press, 1999), 108; and "The Politics of Postcolonial Modernism," *European Legacy* 27, no. 6 (2002): 771–82. Since the mid-1990s, various materialist critiques have been leveled at the field of postcolonial studies on similar grounds, of which see especially Aijaz Ahmad, *In Theory* (New York: Verso, 1992); Timothy Brennan, *At Home in the World: Cosmopolitanism Now* (Cambridge: Harvard University Press, 1997); Arif Dirlik, *The Postcolonial Aura: Third World Criticism in the Age of Global Capitalism* (Boulder, Colo.: Westview Press, 1997); Larsen, *Determinations*; Benita Parry, *Postcolonial Studies: A Materialist Critique* (Oxford: Routledge, 2004); E. San Juan Jr., *Beyond Postcolonial Theory* (New York: St. Martin's Press, 1998).

13. "Notre écriture doit accepter sans partage nos croyances populaires, nos critiques magico-religieuses, notre réalisme merveilleux, les rituels liés aux «milan», aux phénomènes du «majò», aux joutes de «ladja», aux «koudmen»." Jean Bernabé, Patrick Chamoiseau, and Raphaël Confiant, *Éloge de la créolité* (1989; Paris: Gallimard, 1993), 40.

14. Wilson Harris, "History, Fable, and Myth in the Caribbean and Guianas," in *Selected Essays of Wilson Harris*, ed. Andrew Bundy (London: Routledge, 1999), 156.

15. Harris, "Continuity and Discontinuity," in *Selected Essays*, 182.

16. Ibid., 180.

17. These indigenous traditions, specifies Lovelace, "arose or had their meanings in direct response" to the Caribbean reality, even if they drew initially on customs from elsewhere.

18. Earl Lovelace, "The Ongoing Value of Our Indigenous Traditions," in *Growing in the Dark: Selected Essays*, ed. Funso Aiyejina (San Juan, Trinidad: Lexicon Trinidad, 2003), 34, 36.

19. Lovelace, "Artists as Agents of Unity," in *Growing in the Dark*, 99.

20. Raphaël Confiant, "La bête-à-sept-têtes," in *Contes créoles des Amériques* (Paris: Éditions Stock, 1995), 65.

21. The motif of being forced to eat excrement, moreover, is not merely symbolic: it was one of the physical tortures inflicted on the enslaved. See C. L. R. James, *The Black Jacobins* (London: Penguin, 2001), 10.

22. Karl Marx, *Capital*, vol. 1, trans. Ben Fowkes (London: Penguin, 1990), 925.

23. Fredric Jameson, *The Political Unconscious: Narrative as a Socially Symbolic Act* (New York: Routledge, 2002), 48.

24. Marx, *Capital*, vol. 1, 899. See also John O'Neil, "The Disciplinary Society: From Weber to Foucault," *British Journal of Sociology* 37, no. 1 (March 1986): 42–60.

25. Silvia Federici, *Caliban and the Witch: Women, the Body, and Primitive Accumulation* (Brooklyn, N.Y.: Autonomedia, 2004), 12.

26. Ibid., 14.

27. Karl Marx, *Grundrisse*, trans. Martin Nicolaus (London: Penguin and New Left Review, 1973), 489.

28. Theodor W. Adorno and Max Horkheimer, *The Dialectic of Enlightenment* (New York: Verso, 1997), 4, 10.

29. Federici, *Caliban and the Witch*, 15.

30. For a more wide-ranging discussion of the regulation of the body in western Europe and the production of the "rational" subject, see especially Francis Barker, *The Tremulous Private Body* (London: Methuen, 1984); Michel Foucault, *Madness and Civilisation: A History of Insanity in the Age of Reason*, trans. Richard Howard (Oxford: Routledge, 2001), and *Discipline and Punish: The Birth of the Prison*, trans. Alan Sheridan (New York: Vintage Books, 1979).

31. Barker, *The Tremulous Private Body*, 36.

32. Pierre Bourdieu, *The Logic of Practice*, trans. Richard Nice (Stanford, Calif.: Stanford University Press, 1990), 53.

33. Ibid., 55.

34. Ibid., 56.

35. On this point, see Bourdieu, *The Logic of Practice*, 123. See also Karl Marx, *Grundrisse*, trans. Martin Nicolaus (London: Penguin and New Left Review, 1973), 157–58.

36. Russell McDougall, "Music in the Body of the Book of Carnival," *Journal of West Indian Literature* 4, no. 2 (1990): 11.

37. See Rex Nettleford, *Inward Stretch, Outward Reach: A Voice from the Caribbean* (London: Macmillan Caribbean, 1993), 96. The quoted comments are from the writings of two nineteenth-century colonists in Jamaica, James Kelly and William James Gardener, respectively.

38. Lovelace, "The Ongoing Value of Our Indigenous Traditions," in *Growing in the Dark*, 31.

39. Monica Schuler, "Afro-American Slave Culture," in *Roots and Branches: Current Directions in Slave Studies*, ed. Michael Craton (Toronto: Pergamon Press, 1979), 129. See also Jean Besson, "Religion as Resistance in Jamaican Peasant Life," in *Rastafari and Other African-Caribbean Worldviews*, ed. Barry Chevannes (London: Macmillan, 1998), 43–76.

40. Patrick Taylor, "Dancing the Nation: An Introduction," in *Nation Dance: Religion, Identity, and Cultural Difference in the Caribbean*, ed. Patrick Taylor (Bloomington: Indiana University Press, 2001), 4.

41. Nicholls, *From Dessalines to Duvalier*, 36.

42. See Trouillot, *Haiti: State against Nation*, 45–46.

43. Quoted in J. Michael Dash, *The Other America: Caribbean Literature in a New World Context* (Charlottesville: University Press of Virginia, 1998), 45–46.

44. According to C. L. R. James, for example, Toussaint L'Ouverture sought "absolute local independence, on the one hand, but on the other French capital and French administrators, helping to develop and educate the country, and a high official from France as a link between both Governments. The local power was too well safeguarded for us to call the scheme a protectorate in the political content of that dishonest word. All the evidence shows that Toussaint, working alone, had reached forward to that form of political allegiance which we know today as Dominion Status." James, *The Black Jacobins* (London: Penguin, 2001), 214–15. In the late nineteenth century and the early twentieth, the writer and intellectual Anténor Firmin offered some of the strongest arguments for the world-historical significance of events in Haiti, and of the need for the country to pursue an internationalist politics. See his *De l'égalité des races humaines* (1885) and *Lettres de St Thomas* (1910). On this point see also J. Michael Dash, "*Haïti Chimère*: Revolutionary Universalism and Its Caribbean Context," in *Reinterpreting the Haitian Revolution and Its Cultural Aftershocks*, ed. Martin Munro and Elizabeth Walcott-Hackshaw (Jamaica: University of the West Indies Press, 2006), 12–13.

45. Dash, *The Other America*, 15.

46. James, *The Black Jacobins*, 306.

47. Larsen, *Determinations*, 18.

48. Theodor Adorno, "Adorno on Brecht," in *Aesthetics and Politics* (London: New Left Books, 1977), 190.

49. For an excellent discussion of this point, see Lazarus, *Nationalism and Cultural Practice*, 68–143. See also Neil Larsen, who observes that postcolonialist-poststructuralist theory's emphasis on "ambivalence" and the "primitive disunity of identity relations" reflects both "the generalized, historical crisis of the cultural nationalism of the 'Bandung era' . . . *and* the desire to move beyond it." The governing desire of postcolonialism, to this extent, is clearly one of hostility toward nationalism, in "implicit recognition of its betrayal of those who once saw in it the emancipatory alternative to colonialism and imperialism" (*Determinations*, 39).

50. On modernity as inextricable from worldwide capitalism, and for a discussion of its singular yet everywhere heterogeneous expression, see Jameson, *A Singular Modernity: Essay on the Ontology of the Present* (New York: Verso, 2002), 12, 182–83.

51. Samir Amin, *Capitalism in the Age of Globalization: The Management of Contemporary Society* (London: Zed Books, 1997), 95.

52. Homi K. Bhabha, *The Location of Culture* (New York: Routledge, 1994), 159.

53. Critical works that could be said to reflect—to a greater or lesser degree—this tendency to deploy hybridity against nationalism, itself viewed as increasingly outmoded in a postnational world, include Gloria Anzaldúa, *Borderlands/La Frontera: The New Mestiza* (San Francisco: Spinsters/Aunt Lute, 1987); Paul Gilroy, *The Black Atlantic: Modernity and Double Consciousness* (Cambridge: Harvard University Press, 1993); Néstor García Canclini, *Hybrid Cultures: Strategies for Entering and Leaving Modernity*, trans. Christopher Chiappari and Silvia López (Minneapolis: University of Minnesota Press, 1995); Jan Nederveen Pieterse, "Globalization as Hybridization," in *Global Modernities*, ed. Mike Featherstone, Scott Lash, and Roland Robertson (London: Sage, 1995), 45–68; Ramón Grosfoguel and Frances Negrón-Muntaner, eds., *Puerto Rican Jam: Rethinking Colonialism and Nationalism* (Minneapolis: University of Minnesota Press, 1997).

54. Shalini Puri, *The Caribbean Postcolonial: Social Equality, Post-nationalism, and Cultural Hybridity* (New York: Palgrave Macmillan, 2004), 19–20.

55. James Clifford, *The Predicament of Culture* (Cambridge: Harvard University Press, 1988), 173. On the use of the Caribbean as an emblem for global hybridity, see the insightful discussions in Puri, *Caribbean Postcolonial*, 1–15; Donnell, *Twentieth-Century Caribbean Literature*, 77–129; and Mimi Sheller, *Consuming the Caribbean: From Arawaks to Zombies* (London: Routledge, 2003), 188–201.

56. See Puri's excellent discussion of this point in *Caribbean Postcolonial*, 43–79.

57. Sheller, *Consuming the Caribbean*, 188.

58. Ibid., 191.

59. Antonio Benítez-Rojo, *The Repeating Island: The Caribbean and the Postmodern Perspective*, trans. James E. Maraniss (Durham, N.C.: Duke University Press, 1996), 4.

60. Ibid., 81.

61. Ibid., 176.

62. Ibid., 167.

63. Fernando Coronil, "Transculturation and the Politics of Theory: Countering the Center, Cuban Counterpoint," introduction to *Cuban Counterpoint: Tobacco and Sugar*, trans. Harriet de Onís (Durham, N.C.: Duke University Press, 1995), xli.

64. Jonathan Friedman, "Global Systems, Globalization, and the Parameters of Modernity," in *Global Modernities*, ed. Mike Featherstone, Scott Lash, and Roland Robertson (London: Sage, 1995), 82.

65. Friedman, "Global Systems," 82.

66. Fernando Ortiz, *Cuban Counterpoint: Tobacco and Sugar*, trans. Harriet de Onís (Durham, N.C.: Duke University Press, 1995), 98.

67. Ibid., 100–101.

68. Ibid., 4, 98.

69. Coronil, "Transculturation and the Politics of Theory," xxvii.

70. Ibid., xxviii.

71. Ibid., xxx.

72. George Lamming, "Caribbean Labor, Culture, and Identity," in *The Birth of Caribbean Civilisation: A Century of Ideas about Culture and Identity, Nation, and Society*, ed. O. Nigel Bolland (Kingston, Jamaica: Ian Randle, 2004), 621.

73. Walter Rodney, *A History of the Guyanese Working People, 1891–1905* (London: Heinemann Educational Books, 1981), 179.

74. However, Rodney emphasizes that in the nineteenth century, "the existing aspects of cultural convergence were insufficiently developed to contribute decisively to solidarity among the working people of the two major race groups" (179).

75. On this point, see Rex Nettleford, "National Identity and Attitudes towards Race in Jamaica," in *The Birth of Caribbean Civilisation: A Century of Ideas about Culture and Identity, Nation, and Society*, ed. O. Nigel Bolland (Kingston, Jamaica: Ian Randle, 2004), 465–66.

76. E. K. Brathwaite, *The Development of Creole Society in Jamaica, 1770–1820* (Oxford: Clarendon Press, 1971), 311.

77. James Millette, "Decolonization, Populist Movements, and the Formation of New Nations, 1945–70," in *General History of the Caribbean*, vol. 5, *The Caribbean in the Twentieth Century*, ed. Bridget Brereton (London: UNESCO and Macmillan, 2004), 215.

78. Brathwaite, *The Development of Creole Society*, 311.

79. See especially the "Un discours éclaté" section and the essay "Théâtre, conscience du people," in *Le discours antillais* (Paris: Éditions Gallimard, 1997), 465–721.

80. Chris Harman, "The State and Capitalism Today," *International Socialism* 51 (1991): 34.

81. Puri, *Caribbean Postcolonial*, 7.

82. On this point, see Friedman, "Global Systems," 73.

83. On these points, see David Hesmondhalgh, *The Cultural Industries*, 2nd ed. (London: Sage, 2007), 214–19.

84. Leslie Sklair, *Sociology of the Global System*, 2nd ed. (London: Prentice Hall/Harvester Wheatsheaf, 1995). See especially the chapter "The Culture-Ideology of Consumerism in the Third World," 147–90.

85. Lovelace, "In the Dance," in *Growing in the Dark*, 192.

86. Ibid., 187–88.

87. Ibid., 188.

88. Lazarus, *Nationalism and Cultural Practice*, 138.

89. Ibid.

90. On this point, see Ahmad: "To the extent that contemporary imperialism's political system takes the form of a hierarchically structured system of nation-states, it is only by organizing their struggles within the political space of their own nation-state, with the revolutionary transformation of that particular nation-state as the immediate practical objective, that the revolutionary forces of any given country can effectively struggle against the imperialism they face concretely in their own lives" (*In Theory*, 317).

1. The Promise of National Independence

1. Jacques Roumain, *Masters of the Dew*, trans. Langston Hughes and Mercer Cook (London: Heinemann, 1978), 75.

2. Selwyn R. Cudjoe, *Resistance and Caribbean Literature* (Athens: Ohio University Press, 1980), 128.

3. J. Michael Dash, "*Haïti Chimère*: Revolutionary Universalism and Its Caribbean Context," in *Reinterpreting the Haitian Revolution and Its Cultural Aftershocks*, ed. Martin Munro and Elizabeth Walcott-Hackshaw (Jamaica: University of the West Indies Press, 2006), 14.

4. Ibid., 14, 15.

5. Terry Eagleton, *Sweet Violence: The Idea of the Tragic* (Oxford: Blackwell, 2003), 290.

6. J. Michael Dash, *Literature and Ideology in Haiti, 1915–1961* (London: Macmillan, 1981), 148.

7. Roumain, *Masters of the Dew*, 140.

8. M. Jacqui Alexander, "Not Just (Any)*body* Can Be a Citizen: The Politics of Law, Sexuality, and Post-coloniality in Trinidad and Tobago and the Bahamas," *Feminist Review* 48 (Autumn 1994): 13.

9. Jean Besson, "Land, Kinship, and Community in the Post-emancipation Caribbean: A Regional View of the Leewards," in *Small Islands, Large Questions: Society, Culture, and Resistance in the Post-emancipation Caribbean*, ed. Karen Fog Olwig (London: Frank Cass, 1995), 75.

10. Clive Y. Thomas, *The Poor and the Powerless: Economic Policy and Change in the Caribbean* (London: Latin America Bureau, 1988), 120.

11. Mimi Sheller, *Democracy after Slavery: Black Publics and Peasant Radicalism in Haiti and Jamaica* (London: Macmillan, 2000), 44.

12. Thomas, *The Poor and the Powerless*, 121.

13. On Dessalines's attempts at land and property reform, see David Nicholls, *From Dessalines to Duvalier: Race, Colour, and National Independence in Haiti* (London: Macmillan Caribbean, 1996), 37–39; and Joan Dayan, *Haiti, History, and the Gods* (Berkeley: University of California Press, 1995), 27.

14. Sheller, *Democracy after Slavery*, 139.

15. Dash, "*Haïti Chimère*," 14.

16. On this point, see Sidney W. Mintz, *Caribbean Transformations* (New York: Columbia University Press, 1974). Mintz highlights how the "plantation has always battened upon the favouritism of governments, both local and metropolitan, while the peasantries have always been regarded as the 'backward,' 'conservative,' or 'ignorant' sectors of Caribbean rural life" (144). This attitude toward the peasantry was of a piece with the more general suppression of the relationship between rural exploitation and the city, between the plantation—or, more accurately, the work of the black and Indian masses who labored on it—and the wealth of the urban areas, which was built on that labor. This occulted connection can be compared to the relationship between the countryside and the city described in Raymond Williams's *The Country and the City* (London: Hogarth Press, 1985).

17. Fredric Jameson, *The Political Unconscious* (New York: Routledge, 2002).

18. Dash, *Literature and Ideology in Haiti*, 152.

19. Roumain, *Masters of the Dew*, 142–43.

20. Fredric Jameson, "On Magic Realism in Film," *Critical Inquiry* 12, no. 2 (Winter 1986): 301.

21. Ibid., 311.

22. Ibid.

23. Neil Larsen, *Determinations: Essays on Theory, Narrative, and Nation in the Americas* (New York: Verso, 2001), 130.

24. Ibid., 134.

25. Mintz, *Caribbean Transformations*, 220. Mintz points out that some peasant adaptations did

exhibit a high degree of autonomy, especially vis-à-vis the plantation, with the peasantry of Haiti being perhaps the best example (133). However, he goes on to emphasize that even this autonomy was eroded in the twentieth century, not least through external determinations, including U.S. imperialism: "[In Haiti] rural life became stabilised on a peasant base during the middle decades of the nineteenth century, and began to change drastically again only after the United States invasion beginning in 1915. In Puerto Rico and, even more, in Santo Domingo, it was the North Americans again, beginning soon after the start of the twentieth century, who created vast new pressures for change. Another way of saying this is to stress the importance of external forces, both in establishing new style plantations and in changing the tempo and character of peasant life" (144). Roumain, of course, was writing in the aftermath of the U.S. occupation of Haiti and its impact on society.

26. Sylvia Wynter, "Novel and History, Plot and Plantation," *Savacou* 5 (June 1971): 99.

27. On this point, see Gerald Martin, *Journeys through the Labyrinth: Latin American Fiction in the Twentieth Century* (New York: Verso, 1989), 171–79. Martin avers that *Men of Maize* "was the first unmistakable Magical Realist . . . novel" (174).

28. Michael Denning, *Culture in the Age of Three Worlds* (New York: Verso, 2004), 69.

29. Alejo Carpentier, *The Kingdom of This World*, trans. Harriet de Onís (New York: Farrar, Straus and Giroux, 1957), 51–52.

30. See Ernst Bloch, *Erbshaft dieser Zeit* (Frankfurt am Main: Bibliothek Suhrkamp, 1973), and "Nonsynchronism and the Obligation to Its Dialectics," *New German Critique* 11 (Spring 1977): 22–38.

31. Quoted in Michael Richardson, ed., *Refusal of the Shadow: Surrealism and the Caribbean* (New York: Verso, 1996), 13.

32. Larsen, *Determinations*, 134.

33. Sidney W. Mintz, "Enduring Substances, Trying Theories: The Caribbean Region as Oikoumene," *Journal of the Royal Anthropological Institute* 2, no. 2 (June 1996): 298.

34. Ibid., 295.

35. On these points, Mintz echoes C. L. R. James's argument in *The Black Jacobins* concerning the modern character of the plantation system: "When three centuries ago the slaves came to the West Indies, they entered directly into the large-scale agriculture of the sugar plantation, which was a modern system. It further required that the slaves live together in a social relation far closer than any proletariat of the time. The cane when reaped had to be rapidly transported to what was factory production. The product was shipped abroad for sale. Even the cloth the slaves wore and the food they ate was imported. The Negroes, therefore, from the start lived a life that was in its essence a modern life. That is their history—as far as I have been able to discover, a unique history" (305–6).

36. For a critical analysis of perspectives that assume that the history of capitalist modernity in the West corresponds to the telos of modernity as such, see Neil Lazarus's excellent discussion in *Nationalism and Cultural Practice in the Postcolonial World* (Cambridge: Cambridge University Press, 1999), 16–29.

37. Indeed, Mintz has discussed the economic and social development of the Caribbean in explicitly world-systems terms: see his "The So-Called World System: Local Initiative and Local Response," *Dialectical Anthropology* 2 (1977): 253–70.

38. Lazarus, *Nationalism and Cultural Practice*, 25.

39. Édouard Glissant, *Caribbean Discourse: Selected Essays*, trans. J. Michael Dash (Charlottesville: University Press of Virginia, 1989), 100.

40. Ibid., 148.

41. On the issue of the apparently contradictory situation of slave-labor systems existing within a capitalist mode of production, see Mintz, "The So-Called World System." From a global perspective, this contradiction is precisely one in appearance only, since the coerced systems of labor found in the periphery were not self-contained entities but rather underwritten by the capitalist mode of production that structured the world economy.

42. Mintz, *Caribbean Transformations*, 132.

43. Pierre Bourdieu, *The Field of Cultural Production: Essays on Art and Literature* (New York: Columbia University Press, 1993), 164.

44. Roberto Schwarz, "National Adequation and Critical Originality," trans. R. Kelly Washbourne and Neil Larsen, *Cultural Critique* 49 (2001): 31.

45. Roberto Schwarz, *Misplaced Ideas: Essays on Brazilian Culture*, trans. John Gledson (New York: Verso, 1992), 44.

46. Ibid., 53.

47. Ibid., 68.

48. Glissant, *Caribbean Discourse*, 99.

49. Ibid., 100.

50. The term "western European literary field" and the characteristics ascribed to it, while sufficient for the present purposes, should be treated as an imperfect shorthand for, more than anything else, received or consecrated conceptions of this field. In actuality it too has been the site of contestation over the value of various literary products, and its hierarchical classifications are not as clear-cut as they are commonly made out to be. Moreover, to say "European" is to risk homogenizing what is, of course, a highly differentiated set of traditions.

51. On the ideology of the autonomy of the aesthetic, see Raymond Williams, *Marxism and Literature* (Oxford: Oxford University Press, 1977), 147. I have explored this issue further in "Modernity, Cultural Practice, and the Caribbean Literary Field: Crossing Boundaries in Erna Brodber's *Jane and Louisa Will Soon Come Home*," *Caribbean Review of Gender Studies*, no. 2 (2008).

52. Carpentier, *The Kingdom of This World*, 62.

53. Jacques-Stéphen Alexis, "Of the Marvellous Realism of the Haitians," *Présence Africaine* 8–10 (June–November 1956): 267.

54. Ibid., 267.

55. Ibid., 262.

56. Ibid., 268.

57. Ibid., 269.

58. Ibid.

59. The distinction drawn in this paragraph between Carpentier and Alexis is one of degree rather than of absolute difference. While I have tried to suggest that Alexis links his conception of the marvelous real more firmly to particular historical and socioeconomic conditions, his position is an ambivalent one. In *The Other America*, J. Michael Dash points to the influence of Oswald Spengler's

theories on Carpentier's formulation of the marvelous, the German philosopher's view of the cyclical nature of history providing the framework for Carpentier's view of the Americas as representing a youthful repository of myth and magic that had been exhausted in Europe. "In a Spenglerian scheme of things," summarizes Dash, "the Caribbean corresponded to the Mediterranean at the time when Europe still had access to the magical and marvellous" (90). Alexis, he goes on to say, borrows from Carpentier this Spenglerian view of history (94). It is certainly the case that a number of Alexis's pronouncements in "Of the Marvellous Realism of the Haitians" bear out this influence, which would again point to a problematic essentialization of the marvelous real. However, his simultaneous emphasis on the historical situation of "the under-developed populations of the world" allows for an alternative reading of it as the mediation of the socioeconomic conditions of uneven development.

60. Thomas, *The Poor and the Powerless*, 62.

61. Ibid., 66.

62. With respect to Trinidad, for instance, Joy Simpson observes that "between 1946 and 1960, a great exodus began. There was a dramatic movement from both rural and urban areas to urban and suburban areas; a movement so large as to overshadow all other aspects of the re-distribution of the population." Quoted in Malcolm Cross, *Urbanization and Urban Growth in the Caribbean: An Essay on Social Change in Dependent Societies* (Cambridge: Cambridge University Press, 1979), 76. Regarding Martinique, Serge Letchimy notes how "around the 1950s . . . the rural exodus accelerated, resulting in the rapid population expansion in Fort-de-France. Inhabited by 60,000 people in 1954, the city, 15 years later, had nearly 100,000 inhabitants (an increase of 67 per cent)." Letchimy, *De l'habitat précaire a la ville: L'exemple Martiniquais* (Paris: L'Harmattan, 1992), 17.

63. Denning, *Culture in the Age of Three Worlds*, 70.

64. Martin Munro, *Exile and Post-1946 Haitian Literature* (Liverpool: Liverpool University Press, 2007), 61.

65. Ibid., 47.

66. Jacques-Stéphen Alexis, *In the Flicker of an Eyelid*, trans. Carrol F. Coates and Edwidge Danticat (Charlottesville: University of Virginia Press, 2002), 162. Hereafter cited in the text.

67. Carrol F. Coates and Edwidge Danticat, "Afterword," in *In the Flicker of an Eyelid*, by Jacques-Stéphen Alexis, trans. Carrol F. Coates and Edwidge Danticat (Charlottesville: University of Virginia Press, 2002), 259.

68. Fredric Jameson, "Third-World Literature in the Era of Multinational Capitalism," in *The Jameson Reader*, ed. Michael Hardt and Kathi Weeks (Oxford: Blackwell, 2000), 319. The essay was originally published in *Social Text* 15 (1986): 65–88.

69. Ahmad's response, "Jameson's Rhetoric of Otherness and the 'National Allegory,'" was published in *Social Text* 17 (1987): 3–26. It was later reprinted in Ahmad's *In Theory: Classes, Nations, Literatures* (New York: Verso, 1992), 95–122. Ahmad's original article preceded a raft of denunciations of Jameson, although in the process, as Ahmad himself notes, what had begun in his work as a Marxist critique of what he regarded as Jameson's "third-worldism" became a "third-worldist" critique of Jameson's Marxism. See *In Theory*, 10–11. For a discussion of the controversy, see Neil Lazarus, "Fredric Jameson on 'Third-World Literature': A Qualified Defence," in *Fredric Jameson: A Critical Reader*, ed. Sean Homer and Douglas Kellner (New York: Palgrave Macmillan, 2004), 42–61.

70. Larsen, *Determinations*, 19.

71. On these points, see Lazarus, *Nationalism and Cultural Practice*, 138–43; and Ahmad, *In Theory*, 11.

72. Lazarus, "Fredric Jameson on 'Third-World Literature,'" 58.

73. Imre Szeman, "Who's Afraid of National Allegory? Jameson, Literary Criticism, Globalization," *South Atlantic Quarterly* 100, no. 3 (Summer 2001): 810.

74. Sam Selvon, *A Brighter Sun* (Harlow: Longman, 1985), 121. Hereafter cited in the text.

75. Gordon Rohlehr, "The Folk in Caribbean Literature," in *Critics on Caribbean Literature*, ed. Edward Baugh (London: George Allen and Unwin), 28. The essay was originally published in *Tapia* (December 1971–January 1972). A revised and expanded version was published as "Literature and the Folk," in *My Strangled City and Other Essays* (Port of Spain: Longman Trinidad, 1992).

76. Rohlehr, "The Folk in Caribbean Literature," 28.

77. Rohlehr, "Literature and the Folk," 59.

78. Denning draws attention to this connection in his own discussion of magical realism, which (as noted earlier) he characterizes as a second stage of the proletarian avant-garde. Indeed, he argues that although "magical realism is often considered as a successor and antagonist to social realism, its roots lay in left-wing writers' movements." *Culture in the Age of Three Worlds*, 69.

79. Frantz Fanon, *The Wretched of the Earth*, trans. Constance Farrington (London: Penguin, 2001), 162.

80. James, *The Black Jacobins*, xix.

81. George Lamming, *In the Castle of My Skin* (Harlow: Longman, 1987), 20.

82. Ibid., 278.

83. V. S. Naipaul, *Miguel Street* (Oxford: Heinemann, 2000), 48.

84. Édouard Glissant, *The Ripening*, trans. J. Michael Dash (London: Heinemann, 1985), 23.

85. Eagleton, *Sweet Violence*, 276. That the desired idyll is destroyed by the dogs, whose ferocity evokes the role of dogs on the plantation, where they were used to hunt down runaways, would seem to suggest that at least part of the reason for the failure to realize the potential for transformation is the continuing influence of the legacy of colonialism.

86. On this point, see Glissant, *Caribbean Discourse*, 86–87; and Eagleton, *Sweet Violence*, 277.

87. Rohlehr, "Literature and the Folk," 56.

88. Roger Mais, *The Hills Were Joyful Together* (London: Heinemann, 1981), 288.

89. Cudjoe, *Resistance and Caribbean Literature*, 160, 177.

90. Roger Mais, *Brother Man* (London: Heinemann, 1974), 121. On the role of the scapegoat, and in particular its connection to the expulsion of guilt, sin, pollution, and other forms of degradation from the community, see René Girard, *La violence et le sacré* (Paris: Bernard Grasset, 1972).

91. Mais, *Brother Man*, 191.

2. "The people living a life every man for himself"

1. Clive Y. Thomas, *The Poor and the Powerless: Economic Policy and Change in the Caribbean* (London: Latin America Bureau, 1988), 72.

2. See especially Fanon's famous chapter "The Pitfalls of National Consciousness," in *The Wretched*

of the Earth, trans. Constance Farrington (London: Penguin, 2001), 119–165; and Amilcar Cabral, "The Weapon of Theory," in *Revolution in Guinea: Selected Texts*, trans. and ed. Richard Handyside (New York: Monthly Review Press, 1969), 90–111.

3. The phrase "constitutionalist decolonization" is used by Anthony Bogues to describe Norman Manley's approach to nationalist politics, for instance. See Bogues, "Politics, Nation, and PostColony: Caribbean Inflections," *Small Axe* 6, no. 1 (2002): 6.

4. James Millette, "Decolonization, Populist Movements, and the Formation of New Nations, 1945–70," in *General History of the Caribbean*, vol. 5, *The Caribbean in the Twentieth Century*, ed. Bridget Brereton (Oxford: UNESCO and Macmillan, 2004), 183.

5. Andrew Bundy, introduction to *Selected Essays of Wilson Harris: The Unfinished Genesis of the Imagination*, ed. Andrew Bundy (New York: Routledge, 1999), 6–7.

6. On this point, see Anne Walmsley, *The Caribbean Artists Movement, 1966–72: A Literary and Cultural History* (London: New Beacon Books, 1992).

7. Gregory Shaw, "The Novelist as Shaman: Art and Dialectic in the Work of Wilson Harris," in *The Literate Imagination: Essays on the Novels of Wilson Harris*, ed. Michael Gilkes (London: Macmillan Caribbean, 1989), 141.

8. Ibid., 142.

9. Millette, "Decolonization," 209.

10. Ibid., 214.

11. Jeremy Poynting, "Half-Dialectical, Half-Metaphysical: A Discussion of Wilson Harris's Novel *The Far Journey of Oudin*," in Gilkes, *The Literate Imagination*, 109.

12. See Perry Mars, "Ethnic Politics, Mediation, and Conflict Resolution: The Guyana Experience," *Journal of Peace Research* 38, no. 3 (2001): 359–61; and Thomas J. Spinner Jr., *A Political and Social History of Guyana, 1945–1983* (Boulder, Colo.: Westview Press, 1984), 56–58, 89–112.

13. Mars, "Ethnic Politics," 360.

14. Wilson Harris, *Palace of the Peacock*, in *The Guyana Quartet* (London: Faber and Faber, 1985), 116–17. Hereafter cited in the text.

15. Wilson Harris, *Tradition, the Writer, and Society: Critical Essays* (London: New Beacon Publications, 1967), 28.

16. Ibid., 31.

17. Édouard Glissant, *Caribbean Discourse: Selected Essays*, trans. J. Michael Dash (Charlottesville: University Press of Virginia, 1989), 26.

18. Ibid., 25.

19. See Wilson Harris, *Explorations: A Selection of Talks and Articles, 1966–1981* (Mundelstrup, Denmark: Dangaroo Press, 1981), 45.

20. See, e.g., Sandra Drake, *Wilson Harris and the Modern Tradition: A New Architecture of the World* (Westport, Conn.: Greenwood Press, 1986); Michael Gilkes, *Wilson Harris and the Caribbean Novel* (London: Longman Caribbean, 1975); Gilkes, *The Literate Imagination*; Hena Maes-Jelinek, *The Naked Design: A Reading of "Palace of the Peacock"* (Aarhus: Dangaroo Press, 1976; and Maes-Jelinek, *Wilson Harris* (Boston: Twayne, 1982).

21. On these tendencies in the field of postcolonial studies, see my introduction in the pres-

ent work. See also Neil Lazarus, "The Politics of Postcolonial Modernism," *European Legacy* 27, no. 6 (2002): 771–82; and Neil Larsen, *Determinations: Essays on Theory, Narrative, and Nation in the Americas* (New York: Verso, 2001), 83–96. For a discussion of how Harris's work has been read and appropriated in postcolonial studies, and of how elements of his conceptual and textual approach lend themselves to such appropriations, see Kerstin D. Oloff, "Wilson Harris, Regionalism, and Postcolonial Studies," in *Perspectives on the "Other America": Comparative Approaches to Caribbean and Latin American Culture*, ed. Michael Niblett and Kerstin Oloff (New York: Rodopi, 2009), 233–56.

22. Incidentally, in the case of Glissant (and again contra certain appropriations of his work within postcolonial studies), such a move would be fairly straightforward—after all, he makes it clear that the point of entanglement is not a terminus in itself but rather the site at which the forces of creolization must be "put to work" to construct a new future.

23. Pierre Bourdieu, *Practical Reason: On the Theory of Action* (Cambridge: Polity Press, 1998), 40.

24. Ibid., 121.

25. Bogues, "Politics, Nation, Postcolony," 18.

26. Ibid., 23.

27. Keya Ganguly, "Temporality and Postcolonial Critique," in *The Cambridge Companion to Postcolonial Studies*, ed. Neil Lazarus (Cambridge: Cambridge University Press, 2004), 171.

28. Bogues, "Politics, Nation, Postcolony," 25–26.

29. Ibid., 15.

30. M. Jacqui Alexander, "Not Just (Any)*body* Can Be a Citizen: The Politics of Law, Sexuality, and Post-coloniality in Trinidad and Tobago and the Bahamas," *Feminist Review* 48 (Autumn 1994): 13.

31. Oloff, "Wilson Harris, Regionalism, and Postcolonial Studies," 247.

32. Robert Carr, "The New Man in the Jungle: Chaos, Community, and the Margins of the Nation-State," *Callaloo* 18, no. 1 (1995): 135.

33. Wilson Harris, *The Secret Ladder*, in *The Guyana Quartet* (London: Faber and Faber, 1985), 357. Hereafter cited in the text.

34. Karl Marx, *Grundrisse*, trans. Martin Nicolaus (London: Penguin and New Left Review, 1973), 497.

35. Theodor W. Adorno and Max Horkheimer, *The Dialectic of Enlightenment* (New York: Verso, 1997), 10.

36. Ibid., 10.

37. Ibid., 26–27.

38. Mikhail M. Bakhtin, *Rabelais and His World*, trans. Hélène Iswolsky (Cambridge: MIT Press, 1968), 29.

39. Wilson Harris, "Literacy and the Imagination: A Talk," in Bundy, *Selected Essays*, 77–78.

40. On this point, see Walter Rodney, *A History of the Guyanese Working People, 1891–1905* (London: Heinemann Educational Books, 1981). Rodney notes how after emancipation the colonists exerted control over Afro- and Indo-Guyanese laborers through a policy of land distribution designed to accentuate differences between the ethnic groups. White-dominated plantation society, he argues, "found it advisable to accommodate some Indian demands for land. This was done at the expense of Creole Africans—sometimes quite literally by replacing one group by the other." In this

way, the planter class succeeded not only in "interposing another set of landowners between itself and its traditional villagized African antagonists" but also in cultivating racial tensions to its own advantage (182).

41. Bakhtin, *Rabelais and His World*, 26–27.

42. Pierre Bourdieu, *The Logic of Practice*, trans. Richard Nice (Stanford, Calif.: Stanford University Press, 1990), 62.

43. Thomas, *The Poor and the Powerless*, 181.

44. Ibid., 192.

45. Clive Y. Thomas, *The Rise of the Authoritarian State in Peripheral Societies* (New York: Monthly Review Press, 1984), 123–24.

46. Ibid., 119.

47. Shona N. Jackson, "Subjection and Resistance in the Transformation of Guyana's Mytho-colonial Landscape," in *Caribbean Literature and the Environment*, ed. Elizabeth M. DeLoughrey, Renée K. Gosson, and George B. Handley (Charlottesville: University of Virginia Press, 2005), 97n12.

48. Ibid., 90.

49. On this point, see Brackette F. Williams, *Stains on My Name, War in My Veins: Guyana and the Politics of Cultural Struggle* (Durham, N.C.: Duke University Press, 1991). Commenting on the legacy of the colonial Anglo-European hegemony in Guyana, Williams notes that we have "ample evidence to suggest that . . . subordinated ethnic segments accepted European cultural domination in practice and . . . utilized racial stereotypes derived from this elite stratum to compete for and to justify their rights to certain economic and political benefits. At the same time, in more general terms, whether intended by the European elite, subordinates also viewed the sociocultural order as a hierarchy of ethnically differentiated groups. This image was reinforced by formal and informal administrative policies that encouraged group competition and a notion that political representation along ethnic lines was essential to protect the interests of the different groups" (159).

50. Poynting, "Half-Dialectical, Half-Metaphysical," 107.

51. Bakhtin, *Rabelais and His World*, 19.

52. Such ambivalence might thus also suggest Harris's own recognition of the need to revise certain of the philosophical precepts underpinning the visionary climax of *Palace of the Peacock*.

53. Franco Moretti, *Graphs, Maps, Trees: Abstract Models for Literary History* (New York: Verso, 2007), 89.

54. Enrique A. Laguerre, *The Labyrinth*, trans. William Rose (Maplewood, N.J.: Waterfront Press, 1984), 183–84.

55. Bakhtin, *Rabelais and His World*, 11.

56. Laguerre, *The Labyrinth*, 186.

57. "Le people en délire, les yeux fermés, hurlait de plus en plus, possédé par les sons du tambour . . . réfugié dans d'ancestrales coutumes qui, pour l'instant, lui apportaient la trompeuse sensation de la liberté." Marie Chauvet, *Amour, colère, et folie* (Paris: Gallimard, 1968), 268.

58. "Toute communauté vit un espace-temps qui est *plus ou moins* médiatisé, et . . . cette proportion singularise le comportement de chaque membre de la communauté, «à travers» les episodes de l'histoire individuelle et les détmerinations physiologiques." Édouard Glissant, *Le discours antillais* (Paris: Éditions Gallimard, 1997), 145.

59. Ibid., 146.

60. Glissant, *Caribbean Discourse*, 105.

61. On these issues, see Thomas, *Rise of the Authoritarian State*, 94–98.

62. See Louis James, "Earl Lovelace," in *West Indian Literature*, 2nd edition, ed. Bruce King (London: Macmillan Education, 1995), 226.

63. On these events, see Millette, "Decolonization," 215–17.

64. Earl Lovelace, *The Wine of Astonishment* (Oxford: Heinemann Educational Publishers, 1986), 21–22. Hereafter cited in the text.

65. Rene Juneja, *Caribbean Transactions: West Indian Culture in Literature* (London: Macmillan Caribbean, 1996), 90.

66. Ibid., 90.

67. V. S. Naipaul, *The Mimic Men* (London: Picador, 2002), 229–30.

68. Fanon, *The Wretched of the Earth*, 159.

69. In addition to the works featuring a sacrificial victim referenced in the previous chapter, one might also cite, from the Anglophone Caribbean, George Lamming's *Of Age and Innocence* (1958), Orlando Patterson's *The Children of Sisyphus* (1964), and Sylvia Wynter's *The Hills of Hebron* (1966).

70. Shiva Naipaul, *Black and White* (London: Abacus, 1985), 15.

71. "Á une vision critique mais tumours personnalisée de l'ensemble du système. Cet aspect fortement individualisé (non global) de la résistance dans la «classe» moyenne . . . renforcera la tendance en l'adoption charismatique de leaders populaires issues du cette classe." Glissant, *Le discour antillais*, 120.

72. Gordon K. Lewis, *The Growth of the Modern West Indies* (London: Modern Reader Paperbacks, 1968), 208–10.

73. John Brannigan, "'The Regions Caesar Never Knew': Cultural Nationalism and the Caribbean Literary Renaissance in England," *Jouvert* 5, no. 1 (2000): 10.

74. René Girard, *Violence and the Sacred*, trans. Patrick Gregory (Baltimore, Md.: Johns Hopkins University Press, 1977), 10.

75. Ibid., 79.

76. Ibid., 78.

77. Ibid., 68–72.

78. See, e.g., James, "Earl Lovelace," 228; and M. Keith Booker and Dubravka Jarages, *The Caribbean Novel in English: An Introduction* (Kingston, Jamaica: Ian Randle, 2001), 114.

79. Glissant, *Caribbean Discourse*, 25.

3. Literary Deliriums

1. Patrick Chamoiseau, *Chronicle of the Seven Sorrows*, trans. Linda Coverdale (Lincoln: University of Nebraska Press, 1999), 99, 100.

2. Édouard Glissant, *Caribbean Discourse: Selected Essays*, trans. J. Michael Dash (Charlottesville: University Press of Virginia, 1989), 61.

3. "Une recherché négative, inconsciente, traumatique, de la sécurisation dans l'espace-temps vécu." Édouard Glissant, *Le discours antillais* (Paris: Éditions Gallimard, 1997), 148.

4. Patrick Chamoiseau, *Solibo Magnificent*, trans. Rose-Myriam Réjouis and Val Vinokurov (London: Granta Books, 2000), 20. Hereafter cited in the text.

5. Richard D. E. Burton, "The French West Indies *à l'heure de l'Europe*," in *French and West Indian: Martinique, Guadeloupe, and French Guiana Today*, ed. Richard D. E. Burton and Fred Reno (London: Macmillan, 1995), 3–4.

6. Beverly Ormerod, "French West Indian Writing since 1970," in Burton and Reno, *French and West Indian*, 170–71. In addition to the work of Glissant and Placoly, Ormerod cites Jeanne Hyvrard's three novels of 1975–77 (*Les prunes de Cythère, Mère la mort, La meurtritude*) as typical of this trend.

7. "La saccade du corps soudain cambré dans l'impossibilité de dire quoi que ce soit." Édouard Glissant, *Malemort* (Paris: Éditions du Seuil, 1975), 124.

8. Gordon Rohlehr, "Literature and the Folk," in *My Strangled City and Other Essays* (Port of Spain: Longman Trinidad, 1992), 56–57.

9. John Stewart, *Last Cool Days* (Toronto: TSAR Publications, 1996), 53.

10. Ibid., 120. In addition to Heath's and Stewart's works, one might also cite here Orlando Patterson's *An Absence of Ruins* (1967), with its alienated protagonist Alexander Blackman, and Andrew Salkey's *The Late Emancipation of Jerry Stover* (1968). In Salkey's novel, the title character's feelings of disillusionment and apathy see him join a Rastafarian community, which seems to hold out the prospect of a different form of social life to that institutionalized under the Jamaican national bourgeoisie. The abrupt way in which a group of Jerry's friends are killed in a catastrophic landslide at the end of the novel, the natural disaster short-circuiting narrative closure on the social and political threads of the text, would seem to register formally the deadlock and sense of frustration over the contemporary political situation.

11. Luis Rafael Sánchez, *Macho Camacho's Beat*, trans. Gregory Rabassa (Dalkey Archive Press, 2001), 17. Hereafter cited in the text.

12. Luis Rafael Sánchez, *La guaracha del Macho Camacho* (Buenos Aires: Ediciones de la Flor, 1976), 27.

13. Lizabeth Paravisini-Gebert, "Writers Playin' Mas': Carnival and the Grotesque in the Contemporary Caribbean Novel," in *A History of Literature in the Caribbean*, vol. 3, *Cross-Cultural Studies*, ed. A. James Arnold (Philadelphia: John Benjamins, 1997), 231.

14. Walter Benjamin, *Illuminations*, trans. Harry Zohn (London: Pimlico, 1999), 91.

15. Glissant, *Le discours antillais*, 173.

16. Richard Price, *The Convict and the Colonel: A Story of Colonialism and Resistance in the Caribbean* (Boston: Beacon Press, 1998), 173.

17. Glissant, *Caribbean Discourse*, 102.

18. "Avec la standarisation des entreprises . . . , avec l'importation de tous les produits naturels ou fabriqués . . . , le créole en fait, dans la logique du système, *n'a plus de raison d'être*. Une langue *dans laquelle* on ne fabrique plus rien (si on peut ainsi dire) est une langue menacée. Une langue folklorique." Glissant, *Le discours antillais*, 298–99.

19. Glissant, *Caribbean Discourse*, 198.

20. Ibid., 207.

21. Frantz Fanon, *The Wretched of the Earth*, trans. Constance Farrington (London: Penguin, 2001), 195.

22. Glissant, *Caribbean Discourse*, 208–9.

23. Karl Marx, *Capital*, vol. 1, trans. Ben Fowkes (London: Penguin, 1990), 165–66.

24. On the issue of the emergence of what feels like a perpetual present under late capitalism, see Fredric Jameson, "Marx's Purloined Letter," *New Left Review* 4 (July–August 2000): 103, 108.

25. Fredric Jameson, *Postmodernism, or, The Cultural Logic of Late Capitalism* (New York: Verso, 1991), 25.

26. Ibid., 27–28.

27. Karl Marx, *Economic and Philosophic Manuscripts of 1844*, trans. Martin Milligan (Mineola, N.Y.: Dover, 2007), 106.

28. Ibid.

29. Ibid., 107.

30. Ibid., 118.

31. Terry Eagleton, *The Ideology of the Aesthetic* (Oxford: Blackwell, 1990), 200.

32. Ibid.

33. Ibid.

34. E. San Juan Jr., "Art against Imperialism, for the National Struggle of Third World Peoples," in *Ruptures, Schisms, Interventions: Cultural Revolution in the Third World* (Manila, Philippines: De La Salle University Press, 1988), 130.

35. Amilcar Cabral, "The Weapon of Theory," in *Revolution in Guinea: Selected Texts*, trans. and ed. Richard Handyside (New York: Monthly Review Press, 1969), 102.

36. "Quand, dans une société, les rapports de production et d'échange (qui «déterminent» des rapports de classes) sont *dominés* par un facteur extérieur, les rapports de classes à leur tour en sont obscurcis, deviennent factices *quant au lien social*, c'est-à-dire que la société donnée devient incapable de trouver en elle-même les «motifs» de son évolution." Glissant, *Le discours antillais*, 633.

37. Ibid., 627.

38. See Glissant, *Le discours antillais*, 486–502. See also Celia Britton's excellent exegesis of Glissant's theory of verbal delirium in *Édouard Glissant and Postcolonial Theory: Strategies of Language and Resistance* (Charlottesville: University Press of Virginia, 1999), 83–93.

39. Glissant, *Le discours antillais*, 363.

40. Ibid., 627–28.

41. Ibid., 635.

42. See Gerald Guinness, "Images in Contemporary Puerto Rican Literature," in *Images and Identities: The Puerto Rican in Two World Contexts*, ed. Asela Rodríguez de Laguna (New Brunswick, N.J.: Transaction Books, 1987), 40. The translated version of the quotation from Sánchez's novel reads: "Papi Papikins said: set a date and organize a get-together of teachers in your Mama's molto bello gardeno: a get-together with uniformed waiters, cold cuts from La Rotisserie, barrels of Beujolais and sparkling Lambrusco: a get-together that I'll pay for through my expense account for senatorial representation" (104–5). The sense of linguistic pileup is somewhat lost in translation; on this issue, see Guinness, "Is *Macho Camacho's Beat* a Good Translation of *La guaracha del Macho Camacho*," in Rodríguez de Laguna, *Images and Identities*, 187–95.

43. See Arcadio Díaz Quiñones, *Conversación con José Luis González* (Río Piedras: Huracán, 1976), 14. Quoted in Guinness, "Images in Contemporary Puerto Rican Literature," 40.

44. Glissant, *Caribbean Discourse*, 103.

45. Glissant, *Le discours antillais*, 651.

46. Ibid., 647.

47. Ibid., 655.

48. Ibid.

49. Ibid.

50. For example: "I had often seen my master and Dick employed in reading; and I had a great curiosity to talk to the books, as I thought they did. . . . I have often taken up a book, and have talked to it, and then put my ears to it, when alone, in hopes it would answer me." Olaudah Equiano, *The Interesting Narrative of the Life of Olaudah Equiano*, ed. Angelo Costanzo (Ontario: Broadview Press, 2001), 83. Other examples of this motif can be found in James Gronniosaw, *A Narrative of the Most Remarkable Particulars in the Life of James Albert Ukawsaw Gronniosaw, an African Prince, as Related by Himself*; Ottobah Cugoano, *Thoughts and Sentiments*; and John Jea, *The Life, History, and Unparalleled Sufferings of John Jea*. On the meaning and significance of the trope, see Henry Louis Gates Jr., *The Signifying Monkey: A Theory of African-American Criticism* (Oxford: Oxford University Press, 1998), 127–69.

51. Quoted in Delphine Perret, *La créolité: Espace de création* (Martinique: IBIS Rouge Edition, 2001), 253.

52. Wilson Harris, *Palace of the Peacock*, in *The Guyana Quartet* (London: Faber and Faber, 1985), 95–96.

53. Ibid., 96.

54. Wilson Harris, *Tradition, the Writer, and Society: Critical Essays* (London: New Beacon Publications, 1967), 28. Regarding critical commentary on Harris's fictional and theoretical writing, see chap. 2, n. 20, in this volume.

55. Ibid., 29.

56. Ibid.

57. Ibid., 28.

58. Ibid., 31.

59. Ibid., 55.

60. Cf. Glissant: "Genesis, which is the fundamental explanation, and ordering, which is the ritualised narrative, anticipates what the West would ascribe to Literature" (*Caribbean Discourse*, 72).

61. Wilson Harris, "Literacy and the Imagination: A Talk," in *Selected Essays of Wilson Harris: The Unfinished Genesis of the Imagination*, ed. Andrew Bundy (New York: Routledge, 1999), 82.

62. Wilson Harris, *The Far Journey of Oudin*, in *The Guyana Quartet* (London: Faber and Faber, 1985), 218. That it is Beti, moreover, who performs this task as part of the emergence of a new form of cross-cultural consciousness, presaging the potential creation of a new social order, again suggests that Harris is questioning and attempting to revise the masculinist nationalist narrative associated with the trope of the tragic male sacrifice.

63. Harris, "Literacy and the Imagination," 82.

64. Ibid., 83.

65. Édouard Glissant, *Mahogany* (Paris: Gallimard, 1997), 28.

66. Glissant, *Caribbean Discourse*, 149.

67. Ibid.

68. Earl Lovelace, *The Dragon Can't Dance* (London: Faber and Faber, 1998), 112. Hereafter cited in the text.

69. Aaron Love, "The Crisis of Caribbean History: Society and Self in C. L. R. James and Earl Lovelace," in *Caribbean Literature after Independence: The Case of Earl Lovelace*, ed. Bill Schwarz (London: Institute for the Study of the Americas, 2008), 86.

70. On this point, see M. Jacqui Alexander's arguments cited in the previous chapter.

71. Stefano Harney, *Nationalism and Identity: Culture and the Imagination in a Caribbean Diaspora* (London: Zed Books, 1996), 54.

72. Earl Lovelace, "Abu Bakr: Speaking for the People?" in *Growing in the Dark: Selected Essays*, ed. Funso Aiyejina (San Juan, Trinidad: Lexicon Trinidad, 2003), 144. Cf. Basil Davidson, who makes a similar point with regard to postindependence states in Africa: "The 'national conflict,' embodied in the rivalries for executive power between contending groups or individuals among the 'elites,' [has taken] priority over a 'social conflict' concerned with the interests of most of the inhabitants of these new nation-states." Davidson, *The Blackman's Burden: Africa and the Curse of the Nation-State* (London: James Currey, 1992), 114.

73. Neil Larsen, *Determinations: Essays on Theory, Narrative, and Nation in the Americas* (New York: Verso, 2001), 39.

74. Ibid., 40.

75. Neil Lazarus, *Nationalism and Cultural Practice in the Postcolonial World* (Cambridge: Cambridge University Press, 1999), 108.

76. Ibid., 109.

77. Ibid., 117.

78. Lovelace, "In the Voice of the People," in *Growing in the Dark*, 103. "By ordinary people," writes Lovelace, "I mean those who are not the elite by property, education or privilege and status as has been developed from a colonial society in which race and colour were the basis of privilege. By ordinary people, I mean, in fact, those who might be said to have struggled against colonialism, affirming themselves through maintaining and establishing religion, cultural practices and by warring against attempts to dehumanise them or place them as a lower order of human beings" (102).

79. Lovelace, "In the Dance," in *Growing in the Dark*, 185.

80. Lovelace, "Abu Bakr," in *Growing in the Dark*, 145.

81. Lovelace, "Involvement Is the People's Only Guarantee," in *Growing in the Dark*, 130.

82. David Williams, "The Artist as Revolutionary: Political Commitment in *The Dragon Can't Dance* and *Interim*," in *West Indian Literature and Its Social Context: Proceedings of the Fourth Annual Conference on West Indian Literature*, ed. Mark McWatt (Barbados: University of the West Indies Press, 1985), 145.

83. Harney, *Nationalism and Identity*, 44.

84. Marx, *Economic and Philosophic Manuscripts*, 107.

85. Ibid.

4. From Breakdown to Rebirth

1. Fredric Jameson, *A Singular Modernity: Essay on the Ontology of the Present* (New York: Verso, 2002), 214.

2. Ibid., 215.

3. "Archaeologies of the Future" is also the title Jameson gives to his collection of essays on utopian and science fictions. Here he elaborates on the construction of such archaeologies and makes clear how they can serve a diagnostic function in relation to the present. Discussing the utopian fantasy of the demand for full employment on a global scale, for instance, which of necessity would "at once usher in a society structurally distinct from this one in every conceivable way," he writes that "about such a future, imaginary or not, I would also wish to note that it returns upon our present to play a diagnostic and a critical-substantive role: to foreground full employment in this way, as the fundamental Utopian requirement, then allows us to return to concrete circumstances and situations and to read their dark spots and pathological dimensions as so many symptoms and effects of unemployment." See *Archaeologies of the Future: The Desire Called Utopia and Other Science Fictions* (New York: Verso, 2007), 147.

4. As noted in chapter 1, the separation of the aesthetic sphere from other fields of cultural and social life has been less marked in the Caribbean than in a western European tradition shaped by the ideology of the autonomy of the aesthetic.

5. Theodor Adorno, *Aesthetic Theory*, trans. Robert Hullot-Kentor (London: Continuum, 2004), 5–6.

6. Ibid., 7.

7. Ibid., 14.

8. Jameson, *Archaeologies of the Future*, xv.

9. Ernst Bloch, *Erbshaft dieser Zeit* (Frankfurt am Main: Bibliothek Suhrkamp, 1973).

10. Ernst Bloch, "Nonsynchronism and the Obligation to Its Dialectics," *New German Critique* 11 (Spring 1977): 31.

11. On this point, see Keya Ganguly, "Temporality and Postcolonial Critique," in *The Cambridge Companion to Postcolonial Studies*, ed. Neil Lazarus (Cambridge: Cambridge University Press, 2004), 174. Emphasizing that for Bloch nonsynchronicity represented a barrier to social mobilization, Ganguly compares this with Homi Bhabha's (mis)reading of nonsynchronicity as an argument about agency, and as an inherently oppositional force. This is of a piece with the tendency in poststructuralist-postcolonialist criticism to view the sociocultural disparities and multiple temporalities present in the postcolonial setting strictly in terms of hybridity (itself understood as subversive), rather than as a symptom of uneven development and exploitation.

12. Bloch, "Nonsynchronism," 34.

13. Ibid.

14. Ibid., 36.

15. Ibid., 33.

16. Wilson Harris, *Tradition, the Writer, and Society: Critical Essays* (London: New Beacon Publications, 1967), 31.

17. Ibid., 32.

18. Ibid., 35–36.

19. Wilson Harris, *The Infinite Rehearsal*, in *The Carnival Trilogy* (London: Faber and Faber, 1993). Elsewhere I have argued for the significance of totalization and the process of "cognitive mapping" to the political and utopian dimensions of this novel. See "The Unfinished Body: Narrative, Politics, and Global Community in Wilson Harris's *The Infinite Rehearsal*," *Journal of Postcolonial Writing* 43, no. 1 (April 2007): 18–31.

20. Carolyn Cooper, "Afro-Jamaican Folk Elements in Brodber's *Jane and Louisa Will Soon Come Home*," in *Out of the Kumbla: Caribbean Women and Literature*, ed. Carole Boyce Davies and Elaine Savory Fido (Trenton, N.J.: Africa World Press, 1990), 279.

21. Evelyn O'Callaghan, "Re-discovering the Natives of My Person: A Review of Erna Brodber, *Jane and Louisa Will Soon Come Home*," *Jamaica Journal* 16, no. 3 (1983): 61.

22. Édouard Glissant, *Caribbean Discourse: Selected Essays*, trans. J. Michael Dash (Charlottesville: University Press of Virginia, 1989), 65.

23. Ibid., 64.

24. See Erna Brodber, "Oral Sources and the Creation of a Social History of the Caribbean," *Jamaica Journal* 16, no. 4 (1983): 2–11.

25. O'Callaghan, "Re-discovering the Natives of My Person," 61.

26. Hilary Beckles, "Sex and Gender in the Historiography of Caribbean Slavery," in *Engendering History: Caribbean Women in Historical Perspective*, ed. Verene Shepherd, Bridget Brereton, and Barbara Bailey (Kingston, Jamaica: Ian Randle, 1995), 125.

27. Alison Donnell, *Twentieth-Century Caribbean Literature: Critical Moments in Anglophone Literary History* (New York: Routledge, 2006), 147.

28. Erna Brodber, *Jane and Louisa Will Soon Come Home* (London: New Beacon Books, 1980), 123. Hereafter cited in the text.

29. Rhonda Cobham, "Revisioning Our Kumblas: Transforming Feminist and Nationalist Agendas in Three Caribbean Women's Texts," *Callaloo* 16, no. 1 (Winter 1993): 52.

30. Carolyn Cooper, *Noises in the Blood: Orality, Gender, and the "Vulgar" Body of Jamaican Popular Culture* (London: Macmillan, 1993), 8.

31. On this point, see Cooper, *Noises in the Blood*, 1–36.

32. Cobham, "Revisioning Our Kumblas," 53.

33. Ibid.

34. Ibid.

35. Ibid., 59.

36. Margarite Fernández Olmos and Lizabeth Paravisini-Gebert, *Creole Religions of the Caribbean: An Introduction from Vodou and Santería to Obeah and Espiritismo* (New York: New York University Press, 2003), 144.

37. Hortense Spillers, quoted in Renu Juneja, *Caribbean Transactions: West Indian Culture in Literature* (London: Macmillan Caribbean, 1996), 59.

38. Maya Deren, *Divine Horseman: The Living Gods of Haiti* (New York: McPherson, 1983), 249–50.

39. Fredric Jameson, *The Political Unconscious* (New York: Routledge, 2002), 138.

40. Frantz Fanon, *Black Skin, White Masks*, trans. Charles Lam Markmann (London: Pluto Press, 1986), 109.

41. Paget Henry, *Caliban's Reason: Introducing Afro-Caribbean Philosophy* (London: Routledge, 2000), 79, 80. The relevant passages from Fanon are in *Black Skin, White Masks*, 10, 140.

42. Henry, *Caliban's Reason*, 80.

43. Ibid., 62.

44. Ibid., 63.

45. Ibid., 63, 53.

46. Ibid., 82–87.

47. Frantz Fanon, *The Wretched of the Earth*, trans. Constance Farrington (London: Penguin, 2001), 182–82.

48. Although the emphasis at present (following Henry) is on the influence of certain Afro-Caribbean religious forms within literature, this is not to deny the impact of religious and philosophical practices and worldviews associated with other cultural traditions present in the region. In the next chapter, I revisit some of the ideas considered here in light of Indo-Caribbean belief systems and ritual practices. Many of the writers discussed in the present chapter, moreover, use a whole range of cultural forms and traditions (see Harris, for example, who draws extensively on Amerindian arts and practices, Hinduism, Chinese philosophical traditions, and so on); the attention given here to the Afro-Caribbean element is, more than anything, an imperfect response to a lack of space to consider these diverse influences in a systematic way. It is also worth stressing that to speak of "Afro-Caribbean" religious forms and practices is to speak of creolized phenomena that reflect contact with, and borrowings from, not only Christian rituals and beliefs but also those of other traditions, such as Hindu and Tamil (on this point, see, e.g., Fernández Olmos and Paravisini-Gebert, *Creole Religions of the Caribbean*, 140, 142, 152).

49. Harris, *Tradition, the Writer, and Society*, 51.

50. "La Créolité est *l'agrégat interactionnel ou transactionnel*, des éléments culturels caraïbes, européens, africains, asiatiques, et levantins, que le joug de l'Histoire a réunis sur le même sol." Jean Bernabé, Patrick Chamoiseau, and Raphaël Confiant, *Éloge de la créolité* (1989; Paris: Gallimard, 1993), 26.

51. "La Créolité c'est *«le monde diffracté mais recomposé»*, un maelstrm de signifiés dans un seul signifiant: une Totalité." Ibid., 27.

52. Shalini Puri, *The Caribbean Postcolonial: Social Equality, Post-nationalism, and Cultural Hybridity* (New York: Palgrave Macmillan, 2004), 32.

53. See, e.g., the critiques by Richard Price and Sally Price, "Shadowboxing in the Mangrove," *Cultural Anthropology* 12, no. 1 (1997): 3–36; and Sylvia Wynter, "'A Different Kind of Creature': Caribbean Literature, the Cyclops Factor, and the Second Poetics of the Propter Nos," in *Sisyphus and Eldorado: Magical and Other Realisms in Caribbean Literature*, ed. Timothy J. Reiss (Asmara, Eritrea: African World Press, 2002), 143–67.

54. Bernabé, Chamoiseau, and Confiant, *Éloge de la créolité*, 22.

55. Mary Gallagher, *Soundings in French Caribbean Writing since 1950: The Shock of Space and Time* (Oxford: Oxford University Press, 2002), 26.

56. See Deren, *Divine Horsemen*. "The cross-roads is the most important of all ritual figures. Where other cultures might conceive of the physical and metaphysical as, at best, a parallelism, a necessarily irreconcilable dualism, the Haitian peasant resolves the relationship in the figure of right angles. . . . The foot of this vertical plane rests in the waters of the abyss, the source of all life. Here

is *Guinée*, Africa, the legendary place of racial origin. Here, on the Island Below the Sea, the loa have their permanent residence, their primal location. To it the souls of the dead return, taking marine or insect forms until their reclamation into the world, their rebirth" (35–36).

57. Ibid., 44.

58. In *Black Skin, White Masks* Fanon suggests that the black Antillean who is bent on demonstrating his or her "whiteness" always has a sense that something is "lacking" while he or she remains in the Caribbean; he or she can achieve fulfillment only by journeying to the "mother-country" and receiving affirmation that one is in fact French (19). Thus for Gros-Joseph the failure of his trip bespeaks the lack of such affirmation and confronts him with the lived reality of his blackness.

59. Patrick Chamoiseau, *Texaco*, trans. Rose-Myriam Rejouis and Val Vinokurov (London: Granta Books, 1998), 219. Hereafter cited in the text.

60. Mireille Rosello, *Littérature et identité créole aux Antilles* (Paris: Karthala, 1992), 114, 128.

61. *Mentôs* are recurring figures in Chamoiseau's fiction. They are powerful healers with an expansive knowledge of local history, the landscape, sacred customs, and cultural rituals.

62. In his *Aesthetics*, Hegel characterizes epic works as "nothing less than the proper foundations of a national consciousness. . . . In epic proper, the childlike consciousness of a people is expressed for the first time in poetic form." See *Aesthetics: Lectures on Fine Art*, vol. 2, trans. T. M. Knox (Oxford: Clarendon Press, 1988), 1045.

63. "Du principe d'une Genèse et du principe d'une filiation, dans le but de rechercher une légitimité sur une terre qui à partir de ce moment devient territoire." Édouard Glissant, *Introduction à une poétique du divers* (Paris: Gallimard, 1996), 59–60.

64. Mikhail M. Bakhtin, *The Dialogic Imagination: Four Essays*, ed. Michael Holquist, trans. Caryl Emerson and Michael Holquist (Austin: University of Texas Press, 1981), 16–17.

65. Georg Lukács, *The Theory of the Novel*, trans. Anna Bostock (London: Merlin Press, 1971), 66.

66. Derek Walcott, "A Letter to Chamoiseau," in *What the Twilight Says: Essays* (London: Faber and Faber, 1998), 218–19.

67. Bakhtin, *The Dialogic Imagination*, 23.

68. Bakhtin, *Rabelais and His World*, trans. Hélène Iswolsky (Bloomington: Indiana University Press, 1984), 19, 27.

69. Bakhtin, *The Dialogic Imagination*, 170.

70. Ibid.

71. In addition to vodun, one might also cite the Spiritual Baptists' ceremony of initiation and baptism, in which candidates are subjected to sensory deprivation before their immersion in the waters, during which time they "travel" spiritually as a prelude to rebirth. See George Eaton Simpson, *Religious Cults of the Caribbean: Trinidad, Jamaica, and Haiti* (Puerto Rico: University of Puerto Rico, Rio Piedras, 1980), 145. In the Martinican context, it is worth highlighting the Quimbois practice of the *bain démarré*, a special bath used for healing purposes (see Fernández Olmos and Paravisini-Gebert, *Creole Religions of the Caribbean*, 152).

72. Deren, *Divine Horsemen*, 27.

73. Ibid., 27–28.

74. Ibid., 33.

75. Walcott, "Letter to Chamoiseau," 218. On Chamoiseau's engagement with Perse, see also Mary

Gallagher, "Re-membering Caribbean Childhoods: Saint-John Perse's 'Eloges' and Patrick Chamoiseau's *Antan d'enfance*," in *The Francophone Caribbean Today: Literature, Language, Culture*, ed. Gertrud Aalo-Buscher and Beverly Ormerod-Noakes (Barbados: University of the West Indies Press, 2003), 45–59.

76. "Palmes! Et la douceur / D'une vieillesse des racines . . . ! Les souffles alizés, les ramiers et la chatte marronne / trouaient l'amer feuillage oú, dans la crudité d'un soir au parfum de Déluge, / Les lunes roses et vertes pendaient comme des mangues." Saint-John Perse, *Pour fêter une enfance*, in *Éloges, suivi de La Gloire des Rois, Anabase, Exil* (Paris: Gallimard, 1960), 39.

77. "C'etait le mois de fouilles pour la plantée des cannes, et cependant les fouilles l'on sarclait l'herbe folle. La pluie fine-fine se mit à s'obstiner, hypnotisant le travail, forçant les homes à guetter ses humeurs, à tracquer le temps perdu dans des veilles prolongées. Puis, elle se prit les mauvaises façons d'une cascade pérenne jusqu'à se compliquer d'un orchestre de vents, trompettes en patience pleine des neuf tonnerres du sort." Patrick Chamoiseau, *Texaco* (Paris: Gallimard, 1992), 74.

78. Graham Huggan, "Ghost Stories, Bone Flutes, Cannibal Counter Memory," in *Cannibalism and the Colonial World*, ed. Francis Barker, Peter Hulme, and Margaret Iversen (Cambridge: Cambridge University Press, 1998), 139.

79. Charles Baudelaire, "Dawn," in *The Flowers of Evil*, trans. James McGowan (Oxford: Oxford University Press, 1993), 211.

80. Fanon, *The Wretched of the Earth*, 30.

81. On the importance of the plan, and of the geometric organization of space, to the enforcement of a particular social order within the colonial context, see Timothy Mitchell, *Colonising Egypt* (Berkeley: University of California Press, 1991); and Angel Rama, *The Lettered City*, ed. and trans. John Charles Chasten (Durham, N.C.: Duke University Press, 1996).

82. Fanon, *Black Skin, White Masks*, 24.

83. Nathaniel Mackey, "Wringing the Word," in *The Art of Kamau Brathwaite*, ed. Stewart Brown (Bridgend, Wales: Seren, 1995), 137.

84. Fanon, *The Wretched of the Earth*, 40.

85. On this topic, see, e.g., Richard D. E. Burton, "Trois statues: Le conquistador, l'impératrice, et le libérateur: Pour une sémiotique de l'histoire coloniale de la Martinique," *Carbet* 11 (1991): 147–64; Burton, *La famille coloniale: La Martinique et la mère patrie, 1789–1992* (Paris: L'Harmattan, 1994); and Renée K. Gosson, "What Lies Beneath? Cultural Excavation in Neocolonial Martinique," http://www .facstaff.bucknell.edu/rgosson/beneath.

86. Aimé Césaire, *Cahier d'un retour au pays natal / Notebook of a Return to My Native Land*, trans. Mireille Rosello and Annie Pritchard (Newcastle upon Tyne: Bloodaxe Books, 1995), 75.

87. "Se mit donc au garde-à-vous pendant trois semaines devant le monument aux morts . . . la main droite figée dans un salut militaire impeccable." Raphaël Confiant, *L'allée des soupirs* (Paris: Grasset, 1994), 131.

88. "Des feuillets couverts de gribouillis de la sacoche bourrée de dictionaries. . . . J'ai souffert de la présence du Blanc dans ma plus stricte intimité. . . . J'avais le sentiment d'être habité par quelque espion intérieur, quelque cheval de Troie qui me dérobait ce que j'avait de plus mien." Ibid., 132.

89. "Rétabli l'esclavage pour que les Nègres restent à travailler dans les champs de canne son

beau-père . . . un Nègre l'a barbouillée de caca. C'était la seule chose qu'il avait pu trouver à faire."
Alfred Parépou, *Atipa*, trans. Marguerite Fauquenoy (Paris: Éditions L'Harmattan, 1987), 181.

90. Césaire, *Cahier d'un retour*, 77.

91. Cf. Rimbaud's "Le bateau ivre," for example: "I know the skies splitting with lightnings, and the waterspouts / And the backwashes and currents; I know the evening, / The Dawn rising like a flock of doves / . . . I have seen the low sun, stained with mystic horrors." See Arthur Rimbaud, "Le bateau ivre," in *Poésies, Une saison en enfer, Illuminations*, ed. Louis Forestier (Paris: Gallimard, 1999), 123. "Je sais les cieux crevant en éclairs, et les trombes / Et les ressacs et les courants: je sais le soir, / L'Aube exaltée ainsi qu'un peuple de colombes, / . . . J'ai vu le soleil bas, taché d'horreurs mystiques."

92. Karl Marx, *Economic and Philosophic Manuscripts of 1844*, trans. Martin Milligan (Mineola, N.Y.: Dover, 2007), 107.

93. In *De l'habitat précaire a la ville: L'exemple Martiniquais* (Paris: L'Harmattan, 1992), a geographic study of Martinique's popular quarters that informs many of the details of Chamoiseau's portrayal of Texaco, Serge Letchimy explains how, during the first postwar wave of rural-to-urban migration, the struggle to survive in Fort-de-France meant that in "the first years of settlement, the families rediscovered the countryside (or almost). . . . Consequently, life in the quarter, between 1958 and 1968, was organized on the model provided by the country peasant, on spaces that made reference to the material world" (60). Letchimy's characterization of these spaces provides the basis for the understanding of the quarters in *Texaco*: they are "free . . . non-private space[s], associated dynamically with construction"; their "designation and mode of utilisation . . . depend on how they are appropriated and the function attributed them. . . . They represent the principal supports of the social and economic life of the community" (32).

94. However, we should note that a certain amount of ambivalence clings to this image of independence. Insofar as Texaco concretizes a radically different form of spatial and social organization to that instantiated in the city center, and given the degree of self-sufficiency its inhabitants exhibit, it is justifiable to view the squatter settlement as a figure for the prospective transformation of the island into an independent nation-state. However, it is also possible to view the city center and the quarters as representative of France and Martinique respectively. This in turn allows one to read the dependence that is said to exist between City and Texaco, as well as the transformation they are both set to undergo as a result of the alliance between Marie-Sophie and the urban planner—described as "City taking us [Texaco] under its wing" (381)—as suggestive of a demand to recalibrate the departmental relationship, rather than to break with it altogether. This ambivalence and the different readings it generates testify, I think, to the difficulty of even articulating the possibility of separation and independence in the context of Martinique's assimilation by France, which, as I noted in chapter 3, Glissant characterizes as the "only extreme (or successful?) colonization in modern history."

95. Fanon, *The Wretched of the Earth*, 179.

96. Earl Lovelace, *Salt* (Boston: Faber and Faber, 1996), 3. Hereafter cited in the text.

97. Bakhtin, *The Dialogic Imagination*, 297.

98. Earl Lovelace, "Rhythm and Meaning," in *Growing in the Dark: Selected Essays*, ed. Funso Aiyejina (San Juan, Trinidad: Lexicon Trinidad, 2003), 94.

99. Lukács, *The Theory of the Novel*, 53.

100. Jameson, *Archaeologies of the Future*, 174.

101. In this regard we might draw a distinction between the position of Bango and Myrtle and that of Brother Man and Minette in Roger Mais's novel, analyzed in chapter 1. There I argued that although Brother Man and Minette do establish a relationship based on equality and reciprocity that might serve as a figure for a different kind of politics beyond the one mediated by the trope of tragic sacrifice, the resonance of such a figure is limited. In the public sphere, it is still the act of the tragic sacrifice, as performed by Brother Man, that dominates. By contrast, the change in Bango and Myrtle's relationship is the forerunner to Bango breaking with his position of isolated martyrdom publically, in the prime minister's office, as part of an explicit attempt, alongside Myrtle, to change the political landscape.

102. Lovelace, "A Caribbean Place for the Caribbean Artist," in *Growing in the Dark*, 162.

103. Funso Aiyejina, introduction to *Growing in the Dark: Selected Essays*, ed. Funso Aiyejina (San Juan, Trinidad: Lexicon Trinidad, 2003), xvi–xvii.

104. Lovelace, "In the Dance," in *Growing in the Dark*, 185.

105. Raphaël Confiant, *Le Nègre et l'Amiral* (Paris: Grasset, 1988), 153–71.

106. A number of critics have construed such returns to the past in not only Confiant's work but also Chamoiseau's as a wallowing in nostalgia for an era that has either already been eroded by modernization or did not exist in the first place. For Richard D. E. Burton, it represents a "falling back, in a last desperate recourse against decreolization, into a real or imagined plenitude of *an tan lontan* (olden times)." "*Ki Moun Nou Ye?* The Idea of Difference in Contemporary French West Indian Thought," *New West Indian Guide* 67 (1993): 23. Similarly, Richard and Sally Price contend that "there is a tendency for the literary works of the créolistes to be complicitous with the celebration of a museumified Martinique, a diorama'd Martinique, a picturesque and 'pastified' Martinique that promotes a 'feel-good' nostalgia for people who are otherwise busy adjusting to the complexities of a rapidly modernizing lifestyle." "Shadowboxing in the Mangrove," 15. While this criticism is justified in some respects, I would suggest it is also possible to view the Créolistes' evocations of the past as working in a way similar to how Bloch argues nonsynchronous pasts can be recuperated, refitted, and made to stand as a critique of the present, providing a sense of a different form of social organization that can be used to invigorate projections for the future. In this context, the "imagined plenitude" criticized by Burton would in a sense be precisely the point: this plenitude, whether real or not, represents an antipathy toward the dissolution of social bonds and the destruction of the lifeworld wrought by capitalist modernization; it provides a utopian resource for envisaging the possibility of a radically other world beyond the present one. Of course, the issue remains whether the memory of the future summoned up by the Créolistes is effectively refitted in this way, or whether it does ultimately regress into benign nostalgia. In this regard, Confiant's work is probably more vulnerable to the criticisms leveled at it by Burton and the Prices, since there are certainly times when his depiction of Martinican cultural forms, sexual mores, and social practices appears merely folkloric and picturesque. Chamoiseau, I would argue, is less open to this charge, his novels being careful always to emphasize the destructuring and restructuring impact of modernization, not only marking clearly the loss of a past that cannot now be returned to "as it was" (as Solibo's decline underscored, for example), but also elaborating on what was lost in terms of how this might help in conceiving a way

out of the paralysis of the present. The use of folklore and myth in *Biblique des derniers gestes* exemplifies this approach; see my "The Body Grotesque: The Ecology of Identity in Patrick Chamoiseau's *Biblique des derniers gestes*," in *What Is the Earthly Paradise? Ecocritical Responses to the Caribbean*, ed. Erin Somerville and Chris Campbell (Cambridge: Cambridge Scholars Press, 2007).

5. "No Pain like This Body"

1. The chapter title "No Pain like This Body" alludes to Sonny Ladoo's 1972 novel of that name, which itself takes its title from a passage in the Buddhist scripture the Dhammapada.

2. Earl Lovelace, *Salt* (Boston: Faber and Faber, 1996), 234. Hereafter cited in the text.

3. On the emergence of the NAR, its electoral defeat in 1991, and the struggle between the PNM and UNC, see Kirk Meighoo, *Politics in a "Half-Made Society": Trinidad and Tobago, 1925–2001* (Kingston, Jamaica: Ian Randle, 2003). Between 1991 and 2010, government office continued to be held either by the PNM or the UNC. In May 2010, however, the People's Partnership coalition won the general election. Although headed by the UNC's Kamla Persad-Bissessar, the coalition also comprised the Congress of the People, the Tobago Organization of the People, and two labor and nongovernmental organizations: the National Joint Action Committee and the Movement for Social Justice.

4. "Ils voulaient transformer chaque commune en hôtel. Installer des agences de voyages à l'entrée des églises. Poser des gîtes sous les grands arbres. Dresser des papillons pour qu'ils dansent à l'entour des guinguettes. . . . Les touristiqueurs se proposaient de peindre les merles en bleu, de parfumer les manicous, et de récompenser les jeunes capables de sourire aux couvées de touristes. . . . Les terres agricoles du pays, plus ou moins dévitalisées, subirent un assaut sans précédent. Plus besoin de cultiver ou de produire quoi que ce soit. Seuls devaient pousser hôtels, piscines et marinas, touring-clubs et auberges de jeunesse, villages-vacances et casinos." Patrick Chamoiseau, *Biblique des derniers gestes* (Paris: Éditions Gallimard, 2002), 771–72.

5. Evelyn O'Callaghan, "Form, Genre, and the Thematics of Community in Caribbean Women's Writing," *Shibboleths: A Journal of Comparative Theory* 2, no. 2 (2008): 107.

6. Anthony Bogues, "Politics, Nation, and PostColony: Caribbean Inflections," *Small Axe* 6, no. 1 (2002): 6.

7. Samir Amin, *Capitalism in the Age of Globalization: The Management of Contemporary Society* (London: Zed Books, 1997), 96. That this long-term structural crisis in capitalism continues to this day is evidenced by the recent convulsions in the world economy following the global "credit crunch" that began in 2007. With the breakdown of the financialization strategies designed to compensate for declining rates of return on capital investment, the underlying contradictions of the world system were made violently manifest. On these points see David Harvey, *The Enigma of Capital and the Crises of Capitalism* (London: Profile Books, 2010); and John Bellamy Foster and Fred Magdoff, *The Great Financial Crisis: Causes and Consequences* (New York: Monthly Review Press, 2009).

8. Amin, *Capitalism in the Age of Globalization*, 96.

9. Ibid.

10. On the issue of the shrinking bases of accumulation within the capitalist world system and

the collapse of modernization projects, see Neil Larsen's discussions of the work of the economist Robert Kurz in *Determinations: Essays on Theory, Narrative, and Nation in the Americas* (New York: Verso, 2001), 23–24, 55–57.

11. Andrés Serbin, *Sunset over the Islands: The Caribbean in an Age of Global and Regional Challenges* (London: Macmillan Education, 1998), 66–67. Serbin offers a succinct account of the impact on the Caribbean region of neoliberal globalization: "Evidently the pressure for the transformation of the international system and concerns about marginalisation from the international economic system have stimulated the processes of economic adjustment, trade liberalisation and opening, and subregional integration. These pressures have led to a series of political reforms that affect the role of the state and political society, with significant social and political costs, generally under the banner of the neoliberal logic of the predominance of the market. . . . In this process the privatisation of state enterprises, deregulation, decentralisation and the reform of the state, dictated by the intellectual atmosphere imposed by neoclassical economic concepts, have gone hand in hand with the restructuring and cutting back of distributive mechanisms including employment and social policies which have affected different sectors of the population" (54–55).

12. I mean to suggest by this only that women writers became more prominent in this period, not that they suddenly emerged as if from out of a literary vacuum. As Alison Donnell notes (with regard specifically to the Anglophone Caribbean), critical studies of Caribbean literature have tended to present women's writing as having a kind of spontaneous genesis in a second boom during the 1970s and 1980s (following the male-dominated boom of the 1950s and 1960s). Against this, she points to the often overlooked history of earlier female authors including Phyllis Allfrey, Elma Napier, Vera Bell, Una Marson, and Raj Kumari Singh. See Donnell, *Twentieth-Century Caribbean Literature: Critical Moments in Anglophone Literary History* (London: Routledge, 2006), 137–42. For a brief explanation of the increase in women writers after 1980, see Helen Scott, "Reading the Text in Its Worldly Situation: Marxism, Imperialism, and Contemporary Caribbean Women's Literature," *Postcolonial Text* 2, no. 1 (2006): 11.

13. Scott, "Reading the Text," 11–12.

14. Peoples of East Indian descent comprise approximately 2–3 percent and 7–15 percent of the populations of Martinique and Guadeloupe respectively. See Singaravelou, "La diaspora indienne dans la Caraïbe: Essai de bilan," in *Présences de l'Inde dans le monde*, ed. Gerry L'Etang (Paris: Éditions L'Harmattan, 1994), 87.

15. Patrick Chamoiseau and Raphaël Confiant, *Lettres créoles: Tracées antillaises et continentales de la littérature, 1635–1975* (Paris: Hatier, 1991), 47.

16. "Quand aujourd'hui les jeunes parlent de pélerinage aux sources, il n'est point question d'opérer un retour au pays des aieux, mais d'aller puiser là-bas, les éléments indispensables à la compréhension et à la consolidation de l'indianité antillaise. . . . Il s'agit de ressusciter le passé, d'alimenter la mémoire collective, de faciliter l'appropriation des valeurs esthétiques afin d'authentifier l'identité antillaise." Ernest Moutoussamy, "L'Indianité dans les Antilles 'Françaises,'" in "L'Inde en nous: Des Caraïbes aux Mascareignes," special issue, *Revue Carbet* 9 (1989): 72.

17. "Avec leur tamoul de la nuit pour le bannissement duquel les tyrans avaient coupé jadis bien des langues refusant la capitulation et la trahison, ils ressuscitaient l'Inde, luttaient contre l'oubli,

gonflaient la jeunesse en la tournant resolument vers la Guadeloupe. . . . Ils fécondaient aussi le avenir, cherchaient des solutions à leur intégration à ce monde hostile." Ernest Moutoussamy, *Aurore* (Paris: Éditions L'Harmattan, 1987), 118–19. Hereafter cited in the text.

18. It is worth noting here that the form of Hinduism present in the French Antilles has a number of distinguishing features. The majority of indentured Indians brought to the islands were Tamils of lower caste from the south of India. Consequently "Antillean Hinduism is a popular religion that makes little mention of the most revered gods in the Hindu pantheon. Brahma, Vishnu, and Shiva are rarely represented in temples in the French Antilles, even if they might be evoked in symbolic form." Instead the most commonly found deities are incarnations of village divinities or of the mother goddess, with Mariaman, Madouraiviren, and Kali held in especially high regard. See Lucien René Abenon, "Les origines de l'hindouisme aux Antilles françaises," in *Présences de l'Inde dans le monde*, ed. Gerry L'Etang (Paris: Éditions L'Harmattan, 1994), 230.

19. "Pour briser maille après maille la chaîne du servage de ses congénères, Râma proposa à Vitalien un système de troc. Il lui livra du riz . . . en échange de sel, de graisse et de poisson. . . . Tout se fit dans la confiance, l'on respecta de part et d'autre les quantitiés. Ce nouveau type de relation modifia profondément les comportements. L'habitation secouée par un vent d'indépendance vit naître dans cette ravine de la fraternité une autre espèce d'homme. . . . Le troc défia les lois de la servitude. Les mains croisées dans l'obscurité menacèrent l'abondance et la puissance des Pauvert."

20. "Guadeloupe deviendrait véritablement sa patrie. Cette union mettrait fin définitivement aux tentations de retour, transformerait l'exil en asile et dégagerait encore plus nettement les perspectives d'intégration dans la société local."

21. Indeed, one can understand the relationship between the political and romantic plotlines in terms of Fredric Jameson's suggestion that we read a given literary style as "a projected solution, on the aesthetic or imaginary level, to a genuinely contradictory situation in the concrete world of everyday life." Jameson, *The Political Unconscious* (New York: Routledge, 2002), 214.

22. "Soudain gagné par un malaise, une lassitude qui s'étendait à toutes les parties du corps et le faisait bâiller. Il vacilla. L'air se chargeait de bruits de paille piétinée, de feuilles qui glissaient dans un chuintement de cocotier et d'éclats de voix. Josaphat rouvrit les yeux. Son rythme cardiaque s'était accéléré. Sa poitrine en vibrait." Michel Ponnamah, *Dérive de Josaphat* (Paris: Éditions L'Harmattan, 1991), 10–11. Hereafter cited in the text.

23. Gerry L'Etang, "Du Tamoul de la Martinique: Portée symbolique d'une langue cérémonielle," in "L'Inde en nous: Des Caraïbes aux Mascareignes," special issue, *Revue Carbet* 9 (1989): 85–87.

24. Oonya Kempadoo, *Buxton Spice* (London: Phoenix House, 1998), 43. Hereafter cited in the text.

25. Donnell, *Twentieth-Century Caribbean Literature*, 199.

26. Ibid.

27. See the discussion in chapter 2 on the way Burnham's regime promulgated a model of national citizenship and collectivity in which discrete communities and ethnic groups were to be held together by the state as an all-encompassing force operating above society.

28. Donnell, *Twentieth-Century Caribbean Literature*, 194.

29. Scott, "Reading the Text," 4.

30. See Doris Sommer, *Foundational Fictions: The National Romances of Latin America* (Berkeley: University of California Press, 1991), for a discussion of the multiple uses of images of the family as a means to allegorize the nation in nineteenth-century Latin American and Caribbean literature.

31. Kempadoo, *Buxton Spice*, 81.

32. O'Callaghan, "Form, Genre," 114.

33. Narmala Shewcharan, *Tomorrow Is Another Day* (Leeds: Peepal Tree Press, 1994), 197.

34. Ibid., 72.

35. Donnell, *Twentieth-Century Caribbean Literature*, 204.

36. M. Jacqui Alexander, "Not Just (Any)*body* Can Be a Citizen: The Politics of Law, Sexuality, and Post-coloniality in Trinidad and Tobago and the Bahamas," *Feminist Review* 48 (Autumn 1994): 6.

37. See Brian Meeks, *Narratives of Resistance: Jamaica, Trinidad, the Caribbean* (Barbados: University of the West Indies Press, 2000), 122–23.

38. Ibid., 125.

39. Ibid., 124.

40. Margaret Cezair-Thompson, *The True History of Paradise* (New York: Dutton, 1999), 245.

41. Scott, "Reading the Text," 12.

42. Michelle Cliff, *No Telephone to Heaven* (New York: Plume, 1996), 12. Hereafter cited in the text.

43. Neil Lazarus, "The Politics of Postcolonial Modernism," *European Legacy* 27, no. 6 (2002): 771.

44. On this point, see Scott, "Reading the Text," 2–7. She quotes the critic Kathleen Renk as illustrative of an approach that construes nationalist and feminist concerns as incompatible. Renk writes: "Anglophone Caribbean women writers reject a narrow nationalism as they seek to redefine the term nation by reimagining what constitutes national community. . . . Given the diversity of the Caribbean and the cross-cultural process in the Caribbean as a whole, it is easy to see why the national ideal, based on one truth, is rejected by these writers." An interesting slippage occurs here, which we will see again when examining some of the critical work on Mootoo's *Cereus Blooms at Night*, from targeting a certain kind of "narrow" nationalism to condemning the "national ideal" as such.

45. Oonya Kempadoo, *Tide Running* (London: Picador, 2002), 62. Hereafter cited in the text.

46. The phrase is Leslie Sklair's. See her *Sociology of the Global System*, 2nd ed. (London: Prentice Hall–Harvester Wheatsheaf, 1995).

47. Jennifer Rahim, "Electronic Fictions and Tourist Currents: Constructing the Island-Body in Kempadoo's *Tide Running*," *Anthurium: A Caribbean Studies Journal* 2, no. 2 (Autumn 2004): 2.

48. Clive Y. Thomas, *The Poor and the Powerless: Economic Policy and Change in the Caribbean* (London: Latin America Bureau, 1988), 94.

49. Rahim, "Electronic Fictions and Tourist Currents," 11.

50. Ibid., 13.

51. Meeks, *Narratives of Resistance*, 157. Meeks's point here is that in the 1970s, Cuba came to stand as a beacon of hope and possibility for many other Caribbean countries. The full quotation runs: "Until the early seventies, Cuba had remained a pariah, particularly in the Anglophone Caribbean, but on the basis of booming sugar prices, windfalls from the resale of Soviet oil and visionary social policies, it had emerged, despite the continued question marks concerning democratic procedure, as, at minimum, a rough facsimile of what Utopia might look like" (156–57). On the impact

of the Cuban revolution on the wider Caribbean, see also James Millette, "Decolonization, Populist Movements, and the Formation of New Nations, 1945–70," and Marifeli Pérez-Stable, "The Cuban Revolution and Its Impact on the Caribbean," in *General History of the Caribbean*, vol. 5, *The Caribbean in the Twentieth Century*, ed. Bridget Brereton (London: UNESCO and Macmillan, 2004), 174–223, 282–311.

52. Ernesto Che Guevara, "Socialism and Man in Cuba," in *Che Guevara Reader*, ed. David Deutschmann (New York: Ocean Press, 2003), 220.

53. See Pérez-Stable, "The Cuban Revolution," 298–301.

54. Pedro Juan Gutiérrez, *Dirty Havana Trilogy*, trans. Natasha Wimmer (London: Faber and Faber, 2001), 259. Hereafter cited in the text.

55. On the aesthetics of shit and dirt in the novel, see Guillermina De Ferrari, "Aesthetics under Siege: Dirty Realism and Pedro Juan Gutiérrez's *Trilogía de sucia de la Habana*," *Arizona Journal of Hispanic Cultural Studies* 7 (2003): 23–43.

56. Edmundo Desnoes, *Memories of Underdevelopment*, trans. Edmundo Desnoes (Middlesex: Penguin, 1971), 22. Hereafter cited in the text.

57. De Ferrari, "Aesthetics under Siege," 40.

58. Homi K. Bhabha, *The Location of Culture* (New York: Routledge, 1994), 159.

59. Grace Kyungwon Hong, "'A Shared Queerness': Colonialism, Transnationalism, and Sexuality in Shani Mootoo's *Cereus Blooms at Night*," *Meridians: Feminism, Race, Transnationalism* 7, no. 1 (2006): 75.

60. Ibid., 76.

61. Ibid.

62. Neil Lazarus, *Nationalism and Cultural Practice in the Postcolonial World* (Cambridge: Cambridge University Press, 1999), 121.

63. Hong, "A Shared Queerness," 98.

64. Ibid.

65. As Timothy Brennan observes with regard to the importance of nation-states to the working poor: "Such states continue to represent, as they have always done, jurisdictional acts of enclosure designed to perpetuate class privileges over specified regions. Today, however, they are also the terrains on which new constituencies can work along varied axes of power. They are, in fact, the only effective structures for doing so. National states impose labour discipline on the working poor and adjudicate disputes among local elites. These have always been among their primary functions. But in the current phase of worldwide neo-liberal hegemony, they also offer a manageable (albeit top-heavy) site within which the working poor can make limited claims on power, and have at least some opportunity to affect the way they are ruled." Brennan, "Cosmopolitanism and Internationalism," *New Left Review* 7 (January–February 2001): 75.

66. Lazarus, *Nationalism and Cultural Practice*, 139.

67. Shani Mootoo, *Cereus Blooms at Night* (London: Granta, 1999), 186.

68. Shalini Puri, *The Caribbean Postcolonial: Social Equality, Post-nationalism, and Cultural Hybridity* (New York: Palgrave Macmillan, 2004), 167.

69. Chamoiseau, *Biblique des derniers gestes*, 808. On the issues of gender, sexuality, and power in this novel, see my "'Not woman enough everywhere': Gender, Nation, and Narration in the Work of

Patrick Chamoiseau," in *The Cross-Dressed Caribbean: Sexual Politics after Binarism*, ed. Benedicte Ledent, Maria Cristina Fumagalli, and Roberto del Valle Alcalá (Charlottesville: University of Virginia Press, forthcoming).

70. Lawrence Scott, *Witchbroom* (Oxford: Heinemann, 1992), 12.

71. On the relative neglect of Brodber and Lovelace in postcolonial studies, see Donnell, *Twentieth-Century Caribbean Literature*, 86–87, 104–13.

72. Junot Díaz, *The Brief Wondrous Life of Oscar Wao* (New York: Faber and Faber, 2008), 1. Hereafter cited in the text.

73. See Thomas, *The Poor and the Powerless*, 335–38.

74. Quoted in Gordon K. Lewis, *Main Currents in Caribbean Thought: The Historical Evolution of Caribbean Society in Its Ideological Aspects, 1492–1900* (Baltimore, Md.: Johns Hopkins University Press, 1983), 93.

75. Quoted in Silvio Torres-Saillant, *An Intellectual History of the Caribbean* (New York: Palgrave Macmillan, 2006), 144.

76. Norman Girvan, "Globalisation and Caribbean Cooperation," public lecture to launch Caribbean Studies Institute, London Metropolitan University, December 4, 2002, p. 11.

77. C. L. R. James, "Parties, Politics, and Economics in the Caribbean," in *Spheres of Existence: Selected Writings* (London: Allison and Busby, 1980), 155.

78. Édouard Glissant, *Malemort* (Paris: Éditions du Seuil, 1975), 183.

79. "Marie Celat courait aux endroits des bords de mer d'où par temps découvert on reconnaissait la Dominique au nord, . . . ou Sainte-Lucie au sud . . . ; elle apostrophait les îles. Répondez, la Dominique. Je vous appelle à conférence. . . . Ho répondez Jamaïque. Venez à la naissance et appelez dans la danse, Haïti ho Haïti." Édouard Glissant, *La case du commandeur* (Paris: Gallimard, 1997), 181.

80. Sam Selvon, "Three into One Can't Go: East Indian, Trinidadian, Westindian," in *India in the Caribbean*, ed. David Dabydeen and Brinsley Samaroo (Hertford: Hansib, 1987), 22.

81. Serbin, *Sunset over the Islands*, 115.

82. Meeks, *Narratives of Resistance*, 171.

83. Margarite Fernández Olmos, "Trans-Caribbean Identity and the Fictional World of Mayra Montero," in *Sacred Possessions: Vodou, Santería, Obeah, and the Caribbean*, ed. Margarite Fernández Olmos and Lizabeth Paravisini-Gebert (New Brunswick, N.J.: Rutgers University Press, 1997), 267.

84. Frank Martinus Arion, "The Great Currasow, or The Road to Caribbeanness," *Callaloo* 21, no. 3 (1998): 448; Fabian A. Badejo, "Introduction to Literature in English in the Dutch Windward Islands," *Callaloo* 21, no. 3 (1998): 679.

85. "En dehors de l'effort et de la solidarité des autres pays de la Caraïbe ou des voisins continentaux de la Guyane. Cet espace devenu solidaire devrait se constituer en une des zones bleues du monde." Patrick Chamoiseau, Gérard Delver, Édouard Glissant, and Bertène Juminer, "Manifeste pour un projet global," published as "Manifeste pour refonder les DOM," in *Le Monde*, January 21, 2000. For a discussion of the manifesto, see Eric Prieto, "The Uses of Landscape: Ecocriticism and Martinican Cultural Theory," in *Caribbean Literature and the Environment*, ed. Elizabeth M. DeLoughrey, Renée K. Gosson, and George B. Handley (Charlottesville: University of Virginia Press, 2005), 244–46.

86. Brennan, "Cosmopolitanism and Internationalism," 77.

87. Frantz Fanon, *The Wretched of the Earth*, trans. Constance Farrington (London: Penguin, 2001), 199.

88. Fanon's "On National Culture" was originally delivered at the Second Congress of Black Artists and Writers in Rome in 1959.

89. Sam Selvon, *An Island Is a World* (London: Allan Wingate, 1993), 107.

90. Brennan, "Cosmopolitanism and Internationalism," 84.BMT

Bibliography

Abenon, Lucien René. "Les origines de l'hindouisme aux Antilles françaises." In *Présences de l'Inde dans le monde*, ed. Gerry L'Etang, 225–33. Paris: Éditions L'Harmattan, 1994.

Adorno, Theodor. "Adorno on Brecht." In *Aesthetics and Politics*, 177–95. London: New Left Books, 1977.

———. *Aesthetic Theory*. Trans. Robert Hullot-Kentor. London: Continuum, 2004.

Adorno, Theodor W., and Max Horkheimer. *The Dialectic of Enlightenment*. New York: Verso, 1997.

Ahmad, Aijaz. *In Theory*. New York: Verso, 1992.

———. "Jameson's Rhetoric of Otherness and the 'National Allegory.'" *Social Text* 17 (1987): 3–26.

Aiyejina, Funso. Introduction to *Growing in the Dark: Selected Essays*, ed. Funso Aiyejina, v–xx. San Juan, Trinidad: Lexicon Trinidad, 2003.

Alexander, M. Jacqui. "Not Just (Any)*body* Can Be a Citizen: The Politics of Law, Sexuality, and Postcoloniality in Trinidad and Tobago and the Bahamas." *Feminist Review* 48 (Autumn 1994): 5–23.

Alexis, Jacques-Stéphen. *In the Flicker of an Eyelid*. Trans. Carrol F. Coates and Edwidge Danticat. Charlottesville: University of Virginia Press, 2002.

———. "Of the Marvellous Realism of the Haitians." *Présence Africaine* 8–10 (June–November 1956): 249–75.

Amin, Samir. *Capitalism in the Age of Globalization: The Management of Contemporary Society*. London: Zed Books, 1997.

Anzaldúa, Gloria. *Borderlands/La Frontera: The New Mestiza*. San Francisco: Spinsters/Aunt Lute, 1987.

Arion, Frank Martinus. "The Great Currasow, or The Road to Caribbeanness." *Callaloo* 21, no. 3 (1998): 447–52.

Badejo, Fabian A. "Introduction to Literature in English in the Dutch Windward Islands." *Callaloo* 21, no. 3 (1998): 676–79.

Bakhtin, Mikhail M. *The Dialogic Imagination: Four Essays*. Ed. Michael Holquist. Trans. Caryl Emerson and Michael Holquist. Austin: University of Texas Press, 1981.

———. *Rabelais and His World*. Trans. Hélène Iswolsky. Cambridge: MIT Press, 1968.

Barker, Francis. *The Tremulous Private Body*. London: Methuen, 1984.

Baudelaire, Charles. *The Flowers of Evil*. Trans. James McGowan. Oxford: Oxford University Press, 1993.

Beckles, Hilary. "Sex and Gender in the Historiography of Caribbean Slavery." In *Engendering History: Caribbean Women in Historical Perspective*, ed. Verene Shepherd, Bridget Brereton, and Barbara Bailey. Kingston, Jamaica: Ian Randle, 1995.

Benítez-Rojo, Antonio. *The Repeating Island: The Caribbean and the Postmodern Perspective*. Trans. James E. Maraniss. Durham, N.C.: Duke University Press, 1996.

Benjamin, Walter. *Illuminations*. Trans. Harry Zohn. London: Pimlico, 1999.

Bernabé, Jean, Patrick Chamoiseau, and Raphaël Confiant. *Éloge de la créolité*. 1989; Paris: Gallimard, 1993.

Besson, Jean. "Land, Kinship, and Community in the Post-emancipation Caribbean: A Regional View of the Leewards." In *Small Islands, Large Questions: Society, Culture, and Resistance in the Post-emancipation Caribbean*, ed. Karen Fog Olwig, 73–99. London: Frank Cass, 1995.

———. "Religion as Resistance in Jamaican Peasant Life." In *Rastafari and Other African-Caribbean Worldviews*, ed. Barry Chevannes, 43–76. London: Macmillan, 1998.

Bhabha, Homi K. *The Location of Culture*. New York: Routledge, 1994.

Bloch, Ernst. *Erbshaft dieser Zeit*. Frankfurt am Main: Bibliothek Suhrkamp, 1973.

———. "Nonsynchronism and the Obligation to Its Dialectics." *New German Critique* 11 (Spring 1977): 22–38.

Bogues, Anthony. "Politics, Nation, and PostColony: Caribbean Inflections." *Small Axe* 6, no. 1 (2002): 1–30.

Booker, M. Keith, and Dubravka Jarages. *The Caribbean Novel in English: An Introduction*. Kingston, Jamaica: Ian Randle, 2001.

Bourdieu, Pierre. *The Field of Cultural Production: Essays on Art and Literature*. Columbia: Columbia University Press, 1993.

———. *The Logic of Practice*. Trans. Richard Nice. Stanford: Stanford University Press, 1990.

———. *Practical Reason: On the Theory of Action*. Cambridge: Polity Press, 1998.

Brannigan, John. "'The Regions Caesar Never Knew': Cultural Nationalism and the Caribbean Literary Renaissance in England." *Jouvert* 5, no. 1 (2000): 1–16.

Brathwaite, E. K. *The Development of Creole Society in Jamaica, 1770–1820*. Oxford: Clarendon Press, 1971.

Brennan, Timothy. *At Home in the World: Cosmopolitanism Now*. Cambridge: Harvard University Press, 1997.

———. "Cosmopolitanism and Internationalism." *New Left Review* 7 (January–February 2001): 75–84.

Britton, Celia. *Édouard Glissant and Postcolonial Theory: Strategies of Language and Resistance*. Charlottesville: University Press of Virginia, 1999.

Brodber, Erna. *Jane and Louisa Will Soon Come Home*. London: New Beacon Books, 1980.

———. *Myal*. London: New Beacon Books, 1988.

———. "Oral Sources and the Creation of a Social History of the Caribbean." *Jamaica Journal* 16, no. 4 (1983): 2–11.

Bundy, Andrew. Introduction to *Selected Essays of Wilson Harris: The Unfinished Genesis of the Imagination*, ed. Andrew Bundy, 1–34. New York: Routledge, 1999.

Burton, Richard D. E. "The French West Indies à l'heure de l'Europe." In *French and West Indian: Martinique, Guadeloupe, and French Guiana Today*, ed. Richard D. E. Burton and Fred Reno, 1–19. London: Macmillan, 1995.

———. "*Ki Moun Nou Ye?* The Idea of Difference in Contemporary French West Indian Thought." *New West Indian Guide* 67 (1993): 5–32.

———. *La famille coloniale: La Martinique et la mère patrie, 1789–1992*. Paris: L'Harmattan, 1994.

———. "Trois statues: Le conquistador, l'impératrice, et le libérateur: Pour une sémiotique de l'histoire coloniale de la Martinique." *Carbet* 11 (1991): 147–64.

Cabral, Amilcar. "National Liberation and Culture." In *Return to the Source: Selected Essays of Amilcar Cabral*, 39–56. New York: Monthly Review Press, 1973.

———. "The Weapon of Theory." In *Revolution in Guinea: Selected Texts*, trans. and ed. Richard Handyside, 90–111. New York: Monthly Review Press, 1969.

Canclini, Néstor García. *Hybrid Cultures: Strategies for Entering and Leaving Modernity*. Trans. Christopher Chiappari and Silvia López. Minneapolis: University of Minnesota Press, 1995.

Carpentier, Alejo. *The Kingdom of This World*. Trans. Harriet de Onís. New York: Farrar, Straus and Giroux, 1957.

Carr, Robert. "The New Man in the Jungle: Chaos, Community, and the Margins of the Nation-State." *Callaloo* 18, no. 1 (1995): 133–56.

Césaire, Aimé. *Cahier d'un retour au pays natal / Notebook of a Return to My Native Land*. Trans. Mireille Rosello and Annie Pritchard. Newcastle upon Tyne: Bloodaxe Books, 1995.

Cezair-Thompson, Margaret. *The True History of Paradise*. New York: Dutton, 1999.

Chamoiseau, Patrick. *Biblique des derniers gestes*. Paris: Éditions Gallimard, 2002.

———. *Chronicle of the Seven Sorrows*. Trans. Linda Coverdale. Lincoln: University of Nebraska Press, 1999.

———. *Solibo Magnificent*. Trans. Rose-Myriam Réjouis and Val Vinokurov. London: Granta Books, 2000.

———. *Texaco*. Trans. Rose-Myriam Réjouis and Val Vinokurov. London: Granta Books, 1998.

———. *Texaco*. Paris: Gallimard, 1992.

Chamoiseau, Patrick, and Raphaël Confiant. *Lettres créoles: Tracées antillaises et continentales de la littérature, 1635–1975*. Paris: Hatier, 1991.

Chamoiseau, Patrick, Gérard Delver, Édouard Glissant, and Bertène Juminer. "Manifeste pour un projet global." Published as "Manifeste pour refonder les DOM," *Le Monde*, January 21, 2000.

Chauvet, Marie. *Amour, colère, et folie*. Paris: Gallimard, 1968.

Cliff, Michelle. *No Telephone to Heaven*. New York: Plume, 1996.

Clifford, James. *The Predicament of Culture*. Cambridge: Harvard University Press, 1988.

Coates, Carrol F., and Edwidge Danticat. Afterword to *In the Flicker of an Eyelid*, by Jacques-Stéphen Alexis, trans. Carrol F. Coates and Edwidge Danticat, 255–71. Charlottesville: University of Virginia Press, 2002.

Cobham, Rhonda. "Revisioning Our Kumblas: Transforming Feminist and Nationalist Agendas in Three Caribbean Women's Texts." *Callaloo* 16, no. 1 (Winter 1993): 44–64.

Confiant, Raphaël. *Contes créoles des Amériques*. Paris: Éditions Stock, 1995.

———. *L'allée des soupirs*. Paris: Grasset, 1994.

———. *Le nègre et l'amiral*. Paris: Grasset, 1988.

Cooper, Carolyn. "Afro-Jamaican Folk Elements in Brodber's *Jane and Louisa Will Soon Come Home*." In *Out of the Kumbla: Caribbean Women and Literature*, ed. Carole Boyce Davies and Elaine Savory Fido. Trenton, N.J.: Africa World Press, 1990.

———. *Noises in the Blood: Orality, Gender, and the "Vulgar" Body of Jamaican Popular Culture*. London: Macmillan, 1993.

Coronil, Fernando. "Transculturation and the Politics of Theory: Countering the Center, Cuban Counterpoint." Introduction to *Cuban Counterpoint: Tobacco and Sugar*, trans. Harriet de Onís, ix–lvi. Durham, N.C.: Duke University Press, 1995.

Cross, Malcolm. *Urbanization and Urban Growth in the Caribbean: An Essay on Social Change in Dependent Societies*. Cambridge: Cambridge University Press, 1979.

Cudjoe, Selwyn R. *Resistance and Caribbean Literature*. Athens: Ohio University Press, 1980.

Dash, J. Michael. "*Haïti Chimère*: Revolutionary Universalism and Its Caribbean Context." In *Reinterpreting the Haitian Revolution and Its Cultural Aftershocks*, ed. Martin Munro and Elizabeth Walcott-Hackshaw, 9–19. Jamaica: University of the West Indies Press, 2006.

———. *Literature and Ideology in Haiti, 1915–1961*. London: Macmillan, 1981.

———. *The Other America: Caribbean Literature in a New World Context*. Charlottesville: University Press of Virginia, 1998.

Davidson, Basil. *The Blackman's Burden: Africa and the Curse of the Nation-State*. London: James Currey, 1992.

Dayan, Joan. *Haiti, History, and the Gods*. Berkeley: University of California Press, 1995.

De Ferrari, Guillermina. "Aesthetics under Siege: Dirty Realism and Pedro Juan Gutiérrez's *Trilogía de sucia de la Habana*." *Arizona Journal of Hispanic Cultural Studies* 7 (2003): 23–43.

Denning, Michael. *Culture in the Age of Three Worlds*. New York: Verso, 2004.

Dépestre, René. *Le métier à metisser*. Paris: Éditions Stock, 1998.

Deren, Maya. *Divine Horseman: The Living Gods of Haiti*. New York: McPherson, 1983.

Desnoes, Edmundo. *Memories of Underdevelopment*. Trans. Edmundo Desnoes. Middlesex: Penguin, 1971.

Díaz, Junot. *The Brief Wondrous Life of Oscar Wao*. New York: Faber and Faber, 2008.

Díaz Quiñones, Arcadio. *Conversación con José Luis González*. Río Piedras: Huracán, 1976.

Dirlik, Arif. *The Postcolonial Aura: Third World Criticism in the Age of Global Capitalism*. Boulder, Colo.: Westview Press, 1997.

Donnell, Alison. *Twentieth-Century Caribbean Literature: Critical Moments in Anglophone Literary History*. London: Routledge, 2006.

Drake, Sandra. *Wilson Harris and the Modern Tradition: A New Architecture of the World*. Westport, Conn.: Greenwood Press, 1986.

Eagleton, Terry. *The Ideology of the Aesthetic*. Oxford: Blackwell, 1990.

———. *Sweet Violence: The Idea of the Tragic*. Oxford: Blackwell, 2003.

Equiano, Olaudah. *The Interesting Narrative of the Life of Olaudah Equiano*. Ed. Angelo Costanzo. Ontario: Broadview Press, 2001.

Fanon, Frantz. *Black Skin, White Masks*. Trans. Charles Lam Markmann. London: Pluto Press, 1986.

———. *The Wretched of the Earth*. Trans. Constance Farrington. London: Penguin, 2001.

Federici, Silvia. *Caliban and the Witch: Women, the Body, and Primitive Accumulation*. Brooklyn, N.Y.: Autonomedia, 2004.

Fernández Olmos, Margarite. "Trans-Caribbean Identity and the Fictional World of Mayra Montero." In *Sacred Possessions: Vodou, Santería, Obeah, and the Caribbean*, ed. Margarite Fernández Olmos and Lizabeth Paravisini-Gebert, 267–82. New Brunswick, N.J.: Rutgers University Press, 1997.

Fernández Olmos, Margarite, and Lizabeth Paravisini-Gebert. *Creole Religions of the Caribbean: An Introduction from Vodou and Santería to Obeah and Espiritismo*. New York: New York University Press, 2003.

Foster, John Bellamy, and Fred Magdoff. *The Great Financial Crisis: Causes and Consequences*. New York: Monthly Review Press, 2009.

Foucault, Michel. *Discipline and Punish: The Birth of the Prison*. Trans. Alan Sheridan. New York: Vintage Books, 1979.

———. *Madness and Civilisation: A History of Insanity in the Age of Reason*. Trans. Richard Howard. Oxford: Routledge, 2001.

Friedman, Jonathan. "Global Systems, Globalization, and the Parameters of Modernity." In *Global Modernities*, ed. Mike Featherstone, Scott Lash, and Roland Robertson, 69–90. London: Sage, 1995.

Gallagher, Mary. "Re-membering Caribbean Childhoods: Saint-John Perse's 'Eloges' and Patrick Chamoiseau's *Antan d'enfance*." In *The Francophone Caribbean Today: Literature, Language, Culture*, ed. Gertrud Aalo-Buscher and Beverly Ormerod-Noakes, 45–59. Barbados: University of the West Indies Press, 2003.

———. "Seminal Praise: The Poetry of Saint-John Perse." In *An Introduction to Caribbean Francophone Writing*, ed. Sam Haigh, 17–34. London: Berg, 1999.

———. *Soundings in French Caribbean Writing since 1950: The Shock of Space and Time*. Oxford: Oxford University Press, 2002.

Ganguly, Keya. "Temporality and Postcolonial Critique." In *The Cambridge Companion to Postcolonial Studies*, ed. Neil Lazarus, 162–79. Cambridge: Cambridge University Press, 2004.

Gates, Henry Louis, Jr. *The Signifying Monkey: A Theory of African-American Criticism*. Oxford: Oxford University Press, 1998.

Gilkes, Michael. *Wilson Harris and the Caribbean Novel*. London: Longman Caribbean, 1975.

Gilroy, Paul. *The Black Atlantic: Modernity and Double Consciousness*. Cambridge: Harvard University Press, 1993.

Girard, René. *Violence and the Sacred*. Trans. Patrick Gregory. Baltimore, Md.: Johns Hopkins University Press, 1977.

Girvan, Norman. "Globalisation and Caribbean Cooperation." Public lecture to launch Caribbean Studies Institute, London Metropolitan University, December 4, 2002.

Glissant, Édouard. *Caribbean Discourse: Selected Essays*. Trans. J. Michael Dash. Charlottesville: University Press of Virginia, 1989.

———. *Introduction à une poétique du divers*. Paris: Gallimard, 1996.

———. *La case du commandeur*. Paris: Gallimard, 1997.

———. *Le discours antillais*. Paris: Éditions Gallimard, 1997.

———. *Mahogany*. Paris: Gallimard, 1997.

———. *Malemort*. Paris: Éditions du Seuil, 1975.

———. *The Ripening*. Trans. J. Michael Dash. London: Heinemann, 1985.

Gosson, Renée K. "What Lies Beneath? Cultural Excavation in Neocolonial Martinique." http://www.facstaff.bucknell.edu/rgosson/beneath.

Grosfoguel, Ramón, and Frances Negrón-Muntaner, eds. *Puerto Rican Jam: Rethinking Colonialism and Nationalism*. Minneapolis: University of Minnesota Press, 1997.

Guevara, Ernesto Che. "Socialism and Man in Cuba." In *Che Guevara Reader*, ed. David Deutschmann, 212–28. New York: Ocean Press, 2003.

Guinness, Gerald. "Images in Contemporary Puerto Rican Literature." In *Images and Identities: The Puerto Rican in Two World Contexts*, ed. Asela Rodríguez de Laguna, 36–46. New Brunswick, N.J.: Transaction Books, 1987.

———. "Is *Macho Camacho's Beat* a Good Translation of *La guaracha del Macho Camacho*?" In *Images and Identities: The Puerto Rican in Two World Contexts*, ed. Asela Rodríguez de Laguna, 187–95. New Brunswick, N.J.: Transaction Books, 1987.

Gutiérrez, Pedro Juan. *Dirty Havana Trilogy*. Trans. Natasha Wimmer. London: Faber and Faber, 2001.

Harman, Chris. "The State and Capitalism Today." *International Socialism* 51 (1991): 3–54.

Harney, Stefano. *Nationalism and Identity: Culture and the Imagination in a Caribbean Diaspora*. London: Zed Books, 1996.

Harris, Wilson. "Continuity and Discontinuity." In *Selected Essays of Wilson Harris*, ed. Andrew Bundy, 176–83. London: Routledge, 1999.

———. *Explorations: A Selection of Talks and Articles, 1966–1981*. Mundelstrup, Denmark: Dangaroo Press, 1981.

———. *The Far Journey of Oudin*. In *The Guyana Quartet*. London: Faber and Faber, 1985.

———. "History, Fable, and Myth in the Caribbean and Guianas." In *Selected Essays of Wilson Harris*, ed. Andrew Bundy, 152–66. London: Routledge, 1999.

———. *The Infinite Rehearsal*. In *The Carnival Trilogy*. London: Faber and Faber, 1993.

———. "Literacy and the Imagination: A Talk." In *Selected Essays of Wilson Harris*, ed. Andrew Bundy, 75–89. London: Routledge, 1999.

———. *Palace of the Peacock*. In *The Guyana Quartet*. London: Faber and Faber, 1985.

———. *The Secret Ladder*. In *The Guyana Quartet*. London: Faber and Faber, 1985.

———. *Tradition, the Writer, and Society: Critical Essays*. London: New Beacon Publications, 1967.

Harvey, David. *The Enigma of Capital and the Crises of Capitalism*. London: Profile Books, 2010.

Hegel, G. W. F. *Aesthetics: Lectures on Fine Art*. Vol. 2. Trans. T. M. Knox. Oxford: Clarendon Press, 1988.

Henry, Paget. *Caliban's Reason: Introducing Afro-Caribbean Philosophy*. London: Routledge, 2000.

Hesmondhalgh, David. *The Cultural Industries*. 2nd ed. London: Sage, 2007.

Hong, Grace Kyungwon. "'A Shared Queerness': Colonialism, Transnationalism, and Sexuality in Shani Mootoo's *Cereus Blooms at Night*." *Meridians: Feminism, Race, Transnationalism* 7, no. 1 (2006): 73–103.

Huggan, Graham. "Ghost Stories, Bone Flutes, Cannibal Counter Memory." In *Cannibalism and the Colonial World*, ed. Francis Barker, Peter Hulme, and Margaret Iversen, 126–41. Cambridge: Cambridge University Press, 1998.

Jackson, Shona N. "Subjection and Resistance in the Transformation of Guyana's Mytho-colonial Landscape." In *Caribbean Literature and the Environment*, ed. Elizabeth M. DeLoughrey, Renée K. Gosson, and George B. Handley, 85–98. Charlottesville: University of Virginia Press, 2005.

James, C. L. R. *The Black Jacobins*. London: Penguin, 2001.

———. "Parties, Politics, and Economics in the Caribbean." In *Spheres of Existence: Selected Writings*, 151–56. London: Allison and Busby, 1980.

James, Louis. "Earl Lovelace." In *West Indian Literature*, 2nd ed., ed. Bruce King, 222–32. London: Macmillan Education, 1995.

Jameson, Fredric. *Archaeologies of the Future: The Desire Called Utopia and Other Science Fictions*. New York: Verso, 2007.

———. "Marx's Purloined Letter." *New Left Review* 4 (July–August 2000): 75–109.

———. "Notes on Globalization as a Philosophical Issue." In *The Cultures of Globalization*, ed. Fredric Jameson and Masao Miyoshi, 54–77. Durham, N.C.: Duke University Press, 1998.

———. "On Magic Realism in Film." *Critical Inquiry* 12, no. 2 (Winter 1986): 301–25.

———. *The Political Unconscious: Narrative as a Socially Symbolic Act*. New York: Routledge, 2002.

———. *Postmodernism, or, The Cultural Logic of Late Capitalism*. New York: Verso, 1991.

———. *A Singular Modernity: Essay on the Ontology of the Present*. New York: Verso, 2002.

———. "Third-World Literature in the Era of Multinational Capitalism." In *The Jameson Reader*, ed. Michael Hardt and Kathi Weeks, 319–93. Oxford: Blackwell, 2000.

Juneja, Rene. *Caribbean Transactions: West Indian Culture in Literature*. London: Macmillan Caribbean, 1996.

Kempadoo, Oonya. *Buxton Spice*. London: Phoenix House, 1998.

———. *Tide Running*. London: Picador, 2002.

Laguerre, Enrique A. *The Labyrinth*. Trans. William Rose. Maplewood, N.J.: Waterfront Press, 1984.

Lamming, George. "Caribbean Labor, Culture, and Identity." In *The Birth of Caribbean Civilisation: A Century of Ideas about Culture and Identity, Nation and Society*, ed. O. Nigel Bolland, 617–31. Kingston, Jamaica: Ian Randle, 2004.

———. *In the Castle of My Skin*. Harlow: Longman, 1987.

Larsen, Neil. *Determinations: Essays on Theory, Narrative, and Nation in the Americas*. New York: Verso, 2001.

Lazarus, Neil. "Fredric Jameson on 'Third-World Literature': A Qualified Defence." In *Fredric Jameson: A Critical Reader*, ed. Sean Homer and Douglas Kellner, 42–61. New York: Palgrave Macmillan, 2004.

———. *Nationalism and Cultural Practice in the Postcolonial World*. Cambridge: Cambridge University Press, 1999.

———. "The Politics of Postcolonial Modernism." *European Legacy* 27, no. 6 (2002): 771–82.

L'Etang, Gerry. "Du Tamoul de la Martinique: Portée symbolique d'une langue cérémonielle." In "L'Inde en nous: Des Caraïbes aux Mascareignes," special issue, *Revue Carbet* 9 (1989): 81–100.

Letchimy, Serge. *De l'habitat précaire a la ville: L'exemple Martiniquais*. Paris: L'Harmattan, 1992.

Lewis, Gordon K. *The Growth of the Modern West Indies*. London: Modern Reader Paperbacks, 1968.

———. *Main Currents in Caribbean Thought: The Historical Evolution of Caribbean Society in Its Ideological Aspects, 1492–1900*. Baltimore, Md.: Johns Hopkins University Press, 1983.

Love, Aaron. "The Crisis of Caribbean History: Society and Self in C. L. R. James and Earl Lovelace." In *Caribbean Literature after Independence: The Case of Earl Lovelace*, ed. Bill Schwarz, 76–93. London: Institute for the Study of the Americas, 2008.

Lovelace, Earl. "Abu Bakr: Speaking for the People?" In *Growing in the Dark: Selected Essays*, ed. Funso
Aiyejina, 142–46. San Juan, Trinidad: Lexicon Trinidad, 2003.

———. "A Caribbean Place for the Caribbean Artist." In *Growing in the Dark: Selected Essays*, ed.
Funso Aiyejina, 158–62. San Juan, Trinidad: Lexicon Trinidad, 2003.

———. *The Dragon Can't Dance*. London: Faber and Faber, 1998.

———. *Growing in the Dark: Selected Essays*. Ed. Funso Aiyejina. San Juan, Trinidad: Lexicon Trinidad, 2003.

———. "In the Dance." In *Growing in the Dark: Selected Essays*, ed. Funso Aiyejina, 184–96. San Juan,
Trinidad: Lexicon Trinidad, 2003.

———. "In the Voice of the People." In *Growing in the Dark: Selected Essays*, ed. Funso Aiyejina, 102–6.
San Juan, Trinidad: Lexicon Trinidad, 2003.

———. "Involvement Is the People's Only Guarantee." In *Growing in the Dark: Selected Essays*, ed.
Funso Aiyejina, 129–30. San Juan, Trinidad: Lexicon Trinidad, 2003.

———. "Rhythm and Meaning." In *Growing in the Dark: Selected Essays*, ed. Funso Aiyejina, 93–97.
San Juan, Trinidad: Lexicon Trinidad, 2003.

———. *Salt*. Boston: Faber and Faber, 1996.

———. *The Wine of Astonishment*. Oxford: Heinemann Educational Publishers, 1986.

Lukács, Georg. *History and Class Consciousness*. Trans. Rodney Livingstone. London: Merlin Press,
1990.

———. *The Theory of the Novel*. Trans. Anna Bostock. London: Merlin Press, 1971.

Mackey, Nathaniel. "Wringing the Word." In *The Art of Kamau Brathwaite*, ed. Stewart Brown, 132–51.
Bridgend, Wales: Seren, 1995.

Maes-Jelinek, Hena. *The Naked Design: A Reading of "Palace of the Peacock."* Aarhus: Dangaroo Press,
1976.

———. *Wilson Harris*. Boston: Twayne, 1982.

Mais, Roger. *Brother Man*. London: Heinemann, 1974.

———. *The Hills Were Joyful Together*. London: Heinemann, 1981.

Mars, Perry. "Ethnic Politics, Mediation, and Conflict Resolution: The Guyana Experience." *Journal of
Peace Research* 38, no. 3 (2001): 353–72.

Martin, Gerald. *Journeys through the Labyrinth: Latin American Fiction in the Twentieth Century*. New
York: Verso, 1989.

Marx, Karl. *Capital*. Vol. 1. Trans. Ben Fowkes. London: Penguin, 1990.

———. *Economic and Philosophic Manuscripts of 1844*. Trans. Martin Milligan. Mineola, N.Y.: Dover,
2007.

———. *Grundrisse*. Trans. Martin Nicolaus. London: Penguin and New Left Review, 1973.

McDougall, Russell. "Music in the Body of the Book of Carnival." *Journal of West Indian Literature* 4,
no. 2 (1990): 1–24.

Meeks, Brian. *Narratives of Resistance: Jamaica, Trinidad, the Caribbean*. Barbados: University of the
West Indies Press, 2000.

Meighoo, Kirk. *Politics in a "Half-Made Society": Trinidad and Tobago, 1925–2001*. Kingston, Jamaica:
Ian Randle, 2003.

Millette, James. "Decolonization, Populist Movements, and the Formation of New Nations, 1945–70." In *General History of the Caribbean*, vol. 5, *The Caribbean in the Twentieth Century*, ed. Bridget Brereton, 174–223. London: UNESCO and Macmillan, 2004.

Mintz, Sidney W. *Caribbean Transformations*. New York: Columbia University Press, 1974.

———. "Enduring Substances, Trying Theories: The Caribbean Region as Oikoumene." *Journal of the Royal Anthropological Institute* 2, no. 2 (June 1996): 289–311.

———. "The So-Called World System: Local Initiative and Local Response." *Dialectical Anthropology* 2 (1977): 253–70.

Mitchell, Timothy. *Colonising Egypt*. Berkeley: University of California Press, 1991.

Mootoo, Shani. *Cereus Blooms at Night*. London: Granta, 1999.

Moretti, Franco. *Graphs, Maps, Trees: Abstract Models for Literary History*. New York: Verso, 2007.

Moutoussamy, Ernest. *Aurore*. Paris: Éditions L'Harmattan, 1987.

———. "L'Indianité dans les Antilles 'Françaises.'" In "L'Inde en nous: Des Caraïbes aux Mascareignes," special issue, *Revue Carbet* 9 (1989): 69–76.

Munro, Martin. *Exile and Post-1946 Haitian Literature*. Liverpool: Liverpool University Press, 2007.

Naipaul, Shiva. *Black and White*. London: Abacus, 1985.

Naipaul, V. S. *Miguel Street*. Oxford: Heinemann, 2000.

———. *The Mimic Men*. London: Picador, 2002.

Nettleford, Rex. *Caribbean Cultural Identity*. Kingston, Jamaica: Ian Randle, 2003.

———. *Inward Stretch, Outward Reach: A Voice from the Caribbean*. London: Macmillan Caribbean, 1993.

———. "National Identity and Attitudes towards Race in Jamaica." In *The Birth of Caribbean Civilisation: A Century of Ideas about Culture and Identity, Nation and Society*, ed. O. Nigel Bolland, 461–73. Kingston, Jamaica: Ian Randle, 2004.

Niblett, Michael. "The Body Grotesque: The Ecology of Identity in Patrick Chamoiseau's *Biblique des derniers gestes*." In *What Is the Earthly Paradise? Ecocritical Responses to the Caribbean*, ed. Erin Somerville and Chris Campbell. Cambridge: Cambridge Scholars Press, 2007.

———. "Modernity, Cultural Practice, and the Caribbean Literary Field: Crossing Boundaries in Erna Brodber's *Jane and Louisa Will Soon Come Home*." *Caribbean Review of Gender Studies*, no. 2 (2008).

———. "'Not woman enough everywhere': Gender, Nation, and Narration in the Work of Patrick Chamoiseau." In *The Cross-Dressed Caribbean: Sexual Politics after Binarism*, ed. Benedicte Ledent, Maria Cristina Fumagalli, and Roberto del Valle Alcalá. Charlottesville: University of Virginia Press, forthcoming.

———. "The Unfinished Body: Narrative, Politics, and Global Community in Wilson Harris's *The Infinite Rehearsal*." *Journal of Postcolonial Writing* 43, no. 1 (April 2007): 18–31.

Nicholls, David. *From Dessalines to Duvalier: Race, Colour, and National Independence in Haiti*. London: Macmillan Caribbean, 1996.

O'Callaghan, Evelyn. "Form, Genre, and the Thematics of Community in Caribbean Women's Writing." *Shibboleths: A Journal of Comparative Theory* 2, no. 2 (2008): 107–17.

———. "Re-discovering the Natives of My Person: A Review of Erna Brodber, *Jane and Louisa Will Soon Come Home*." *Jamaica Journal* 16, no. 3 (1983): 61–64.

Oloff, Kerstin D. "Wilson Harris, Regionalism, and Postcolonial Studies." In *Perspectives on the "Other America": Comparative Approaches to Caribbean and Latin American Culture*, ed. Michael Niblett and Kerstin D. Oloff. New York: Rodopi, 2009.

O'Neil, John. "The Disciplinary Society: From Weber to Foucault." *British Journal of Sociology* 37, no. 1 (March 1986): 42–60.

Ormerod, Beverly. "French West Indian Writing since 1970." In *French and West Indian: Martinique, Guadeloupe, and French Guiana Today*, ed. Richard D. E. Burton and Fred Reno, 167–87. London: Macmillan, 1995.

Ortiz, Fernando. *Cuban Counterpoint: Tobacco and Sugar*. Trans. Harriet de Onís. Durham, N.C.: Duke University Press, 1995.

Paravisini-Gebert, Lizabeth. "Writers Playin' Mas': Carnival and the Grotesque in the Contemporary Caribbean Novel." In *A History of Literature in the Caribbean*, vol. 3, *Cross-Cultural Studies*, ed. A. James Arnold, 215–36. Philadelphia: John Benjamins, 1997.

Parépou, Alfred. *Atipa*. Trans. Marguerite Fauquenoy. Paris: Éditions L'Harmattan, 1987.

Parry, Benita. *Postcolonial Studies: A Materialist Critique*. Oxford: Routledge, 2004.

Patterson, Orlando. *An Absence of Ruins*. London: Hutchinson, 1967.

Pérez-Stable, Marifeli. "The Cuban Revolution and Its Impact on the Caribbean." In *General History of the Caribbean*, vol. 5, *The Caribbean in the Twentieth Century*, ed. Bridget Brereton, 282–311. London: UNESCO and Macmillan, 2004.

Perret, Delphine. *La créolité: Espace de création*. Martinique: IBIS Rouge Edition, 2001.

Perse, Saint-John. *Pour fêter une enfance*. In *Éloges, suivi de La Gloire des Rois, Anabase, Exil*, 27–39. Paris: Gallimard, 1960.

Pieterse, Jan Nederveen. "Globalization as Hybridization." In *Global Modernities*, ed. Mike Featherstone, Scott Lash, and Roland Robertson, 45–68. London: Sage, 1995.

Ponnamah, Michel. *Dérive de Josaphat*. Paris: Éditions L'Harmattan, 1991.

Powell, Patricia. *A Small Gathering of Bones*. Oxford: Heinemann, 1994.

Poynting, Jeremy. "Half-Dialectical, Half-Metaphysical: A Discussion of Wilson Harris's Novel *The Far Journey of Oudin*." In *The Literate Imagination: Essays on the Novels of Wilson Harris*, ed. Michael Gilkes, 103–27. London: Macmillan Caribbean, 1989.

Price, Richard. *The Convict and the Colonel: A Story of Colonialism and Resistance in the Caribbean*. Boston: Beacon Press, 1998.

Price, Richard, and Sally Price. "Shadowboxing in the Mangrove." *Cultural Anthropology* 12, no. 1 (1997): 3–36.

Prieto, Eric. "The Uses of Landscape: Ecocriticism and Martinican Cultural Theory." In *Caribbean Literature and the Environment*, ed. Elizabeth M. DeLoughrey, Renée K. Gosson, and George B. Handley, 236–46. Charlottesville: University of Virginia Press, 2005.

Puri, Shalini. *The Caribbean Postcolonial: Social Equality, Post-nationalism, and Cultural Hybridity*. New York: Palgrave Macmillan, 2004.

Rahim, Jennifer. "Electronic Fictions and Tourist Currents: Constructing the Island-Body in Kempadoo's *Tide Running*." *Anthurium: A Caribbean Studies Journal* 2, no. 2 (Autumn 2004): 1–17.

Rama, Angel. *The Lettered City*. Ed. and trans. John Charles Chasten. Durham, N.C.: Duke University Press, 1996.

Richardson, Michael, ed. *Refusal of the Shadow: Surrealism and the Caribbean*. New York: Verso, 1996.

Rimbaud, Arthur. *Poésies, Une saison en enfer, Illuminations*. Ed. Louis Forestier. Paris: Gallimard, 1999.

Robertson, Roland. "Glocalization: Time-Space and Homogeneity-Heterogeneity." In *Global Modernities*, ed. Mike Featherstone, Scott Lash, and Roland Robertson, 25–44. London: Sage, 1995.

Rodenas, Adriana Méndez. "Literature and Politics in the Cuban Revolution: The Historical Image." In *A History of Literature in the Caribbean*, vol. 1, *Hispanic and Francophone Regions*, ed. A. James Arnold, 283–94. Philadelphia: John Benjamins, 1992.

Rodney, Walter. *A History of the Guyanese Working People, 1891–1905*. London: Heinemann Educational Books, 1981.

Rohlehr, Gordon. "Literature and the Folk." In *My Strangled City and Other Essays*, 52–85. Port of Spain: Longman Trinidad, 1992.

———. "The Folk in Caribbean Literature." In *Critics on Caribbean Literature*, ed. Edward Baugh, 27–30. London: George Allen and Unwin.

Rosello, Mireille. *Littérature et identité créole aux Antilles*. Paris: Karthala, 1992.

Roumain, Jacques. *Masters of the Dew*. Trans. Langston Hughes and Mercer Cook. London: Heinemann, 1978.

Salkey, Andrew. *The Late Emancipation of Jerry Stover*. Harlow, Essex: Longman, 1968.

San Juan, E., Jr. "Art against Imperialism, for the National Struggle of Third World Peoples." In *Ruptures, Schisms, Interventions: Cultural Revolution in the Third World*, 129–42. Manila, Philippines: De La Salle University Press, 1988.

———. *Beyond Postcolonial Theory*. New York: St. Martin's, 1998.

Sánchez, Luis Rafael. *La guaracha del Macho Camacho*. Buenos Aires: Ediciones de la Flor, 1976.

———. *Macho Camacho's Beat*. Trans. Gregory Rabassa. London: Dalkey Archive Press, 2001.

Schuler, Monica. "Afro-American Slave Culture." In *Roots and Branches: Current Directions in Slave Studies*, ed. Michael Craton, 121–55. Toronto: Pergamon Press, 1979.

Schwarz, Roberto. *Misplaced Ideas: Essays on Brazilian Culture*. Trans. John Gledson. New York: Verso, 1992.

———. "National Adequation and Critical Originality." Trans. R. Kelly Washbourne and Neil Larsen. *Cultural Critique* 49 (2001): 18–42.

Scott, Helen. "Reading the Text in Its Worldly Situation: Marxism, Imperialism, and Contemporary Caribbean Women's Literature." *Postcolonial Text* 2, no. 1 (2006): 1–20.

Scott, Lawrence. *Witchbroom*. Oxford: Heinemann, 1992.

Selvon, Sam. *A Brighter Sun*. Harlow: Longman, 1985.

———. *An Island Is a World*. London: Allan Wingate, 1993.

———. "Three into One Can't Go: East Indian, Trinidadian, Westindian." In *India in the Caribbean*, ed. David Dabydeen and Brinsley Samaroo, 13–24. Hertford: Hansib, 1987.

Serbin, Andrés. *Sunset over the Islands: The Caribbean in an Age of Global and Regional Challenges*. London: Macmillan Education, 1998.

Shaw, Gregory. "The Novelist as Shaman: Art and Dialectic in the Work of Wilson Harris." In *The Literate Imagination: Essays on the Novels of Wilson Harris*, ed. Michael Gilkes, 141–51. London: Macmillan Caribbean, 1989.

Sheller, Mimi. *Consuming the Caribbean: From Arawaks to Zombies*. New York: Routledge, 2003.

———. *Democracy after Slavery: Black Publics and Peasant Radicalism in Haiti and Jamaica*. London: Macmillan, 2000.

Shewcharan, Narmala. *Tomorrow Is Another Day*. Leeds: Peepal Tree Press, 1994.

Simpson, George Eaton. *Religious Cults of the Caribbean: Trinidad, Jamaica, and Haiti*. Puerto Rico: University of Puerto Rico, Rio Piedras, 1980.

Sklair, Leslie. *Sociology of the Global System*. 2nd ed. London: Prentice Hall/Harvester Wheatsheaf, 1995.

Sommer, Doris. *Foundational Fictions: The National Romances of Latin America*. Berkeley: University of California Press, 1991.

Spinner, Thomas J., Jr. *A Political and Social History of Guyana, 1945–1983*. Boulder, Colo.: Westview Press, 1984.

Stewart, John. *Last Cool Days*. Toronto: TSAR Publications, 1996.

Szeman, Imre. "Who's Afraid of National Allegory? Jameson, Literary Criticism, Globalization." *South Atlantic Quarterly* 100, no. 3 (Summer 2001): 803–27.

Taylor, Patrick. "Dancing the Nation: An Introduction." In *Nation Dance: Religion, Identity, and Cultural Difference in the Caribbean*, ed. Patrick Taylor, 1–13. Bloomington: Indiana University Press, 2001.

Thomas, Clive Y. *The Poor and the Powerless: Economic Policy and Change in the Caribbean*. London: Latin America Bureau, 1988.

———. *The Rise of the Authoritarian State in Peripheral Societies*. New York: Monthly Review Press, 1984.

Torres-Saillant, Silvio. *An Intellectual History of the Caribbean*. New York: Palgrave Macmillan, 2006.

Trouillot, Michel-Rolph. *Haiti: State against Nation: The Origins and Legacy of Duvalier*. New York: Monthly Review Press, 1990.

Walcott, Derek. "A Letter to Chamoiseau." In *What the Twilight Says: Essays*, 213–32. London: Faber and Faber, 1998.

Williams, Brackette F. *Stains on My Name, War in My Veins: Guyana and the Politics of Cultural Struggle*. Durham, N.C.: Duke University Press, 1991.

Williams, David. "The Artist as Revolutionary: Political Commitment in *The Dragon Can't Dance* and *Interim*." In *West Indian Literature and Its Social Context: Proceedings of the Fourth Annual Conference on West Indian Literature*, ed. Mark McWatt, 141–47. Barbados: University of the West Indies Press, 1985.

Williams, Raymond. *The Country and the City*. London: Hogarth Press, 1985.

———. *Marxism and Literature*. Oxford: Oxford University Press, 1977.

Wynter, Sylvia. "'A Different Kind of Creature': Caribbean Literature, the Cyclops Factor, and the Second Poetics of the Propter Nos." In *Sisyphus and Eldorado: Magical and Other Realisms in Caribbean Literature*, ed. Timothy J. Reiss, 143–67. Asmara, Eritrea: African World Press, 2002.

———. "Novel and History, Plot and Plantation." *Savacou* 5 (June 1971): 95–102.

Index

CPSIA information can be obtained at www.ICGtesting.com
Printed in the USA
BVOW011606070212

282161BV00002B/6/P